HER MAJESTY'S NAVY

VOL. II.

H R H PRINCE GEORGE OF WALES.

Her Majesty's Navy.

COASTGUARDSMAN

VOL. II.

HER MAJESTY'S NAVY

INCLUDING

ITS DEEDS AND BATTLES

BY

LIEUT. CHAS. RATHBONE LOW, F.R.G.S.

(Late Indian Navy)

AUTHOR OF "HISTORY OF THE INDIAN NAVY," "LIFE OF LORD WOLSELEY," ETC., ETC.

With Coloured Illustrations

BY W. CHRISTIAN SYMONS AND W. FRED. MITCHELL

VOL. II.

The Naval & Military Press Ltd

Published by

The Naval & Military Press Ltd
Unit 5 Riverside, Brambleside
Bellbrook Industrial Estate
Uckfield, East Sussex
TN22 1QQ England

Tel: +44 (0)1825 749494

www.naval-military-press.com
www.nmarchive.com

In reprinting in facsimile from the original, any imperfections are inevitably reproduced and the quality may fall short of modern type and cartographic standards.

CONTENTS.

VOL. II.

CHAPTER I.
PAGE

The American War—Services of the Navy at Charlestown and New York—The Fighting on Lake Champlain and on the North River—Declaration of War with France—Admiral Keppel's Indecisive Action with Count D'Orvilliers—Court-Martials on Admirals Keppel and Palliser—The French and Spanish fleets in the Channel—Admiral Byron's Engagement with Count D'Estaing off the Island of Grenada—Capture of the *Serapis* and *Scarborough* by Paul Jones—Loss of the *Quebec*—Admiral Rodney's Defeat of a Spanish Squadron and First Relief of Gibraltar—Naval Events on the American Coast and in the West Indies—Action of the 17th April, 1780, between Sir George Rodney and Admiral De Guichen—Partial Action between the same—Losses in the Great Hurricane in the West Indies—Declaration of War with Holland—Vice-Admiral Hyde Parker's Action with the Dutch Fleet on the 7th August, 1781—Capture of the Dutch Islands in the West Indies 1

CHAPTER II.

Sir Samuel Hood's Partial Engagements with the French Fleet off Martinique on the 29th and 30th April, 1781—Arbuthnot's Action off the Virginian Coast with a French Squadron—Repulse of De Suffren's Attack on Commodore Johnstone's Squadron in the Cape de Verde Islands—Frigate Actions in the year 1781—Foundering of the *Royal George*—Loss of Minorca—Relief of Gibraltar by Sir George Rodney—Sir Samuel Hood's Partial Action with the Count de Grasse—Loss of St. Kitts and other West India Islands—Sir George Rodney's Great Victory over the Count de Grasse on the 12th April, 1782—Frigate Actions in 1782—The Naval War in the East Indies—Five Desperate but Indecisive Engagements between Sir Edward Hughes and Admiral De Suffren—Conclusion of Peace 29

CHAPTER III.

Biographical Notices of Distinguished Admirals between 1763 and 1793—Viscount Keppel—Early Service in the *Centurion*—The Expedition to the Barbary Coast and Goree—Keppel's Services under Sir Edward Hawke, and at the Capture of Belleisle and Havanna—His Battle with the French Fleet in July, 1778—Sir John Moore—His Services in the East Indies, under Admiral Hawke, and at the Capture of Guadaloupe—Services of Captain Suckling, Lord Nelson's Uncle—Sir Charles Hardy—His Career in American Waters and under Sir Edward Hawke—Also in command of the Channel Fleet—Admiral Kempenfeldt in the East Indies and in the Channel—His Death in the *Royal George*—The Services of Sir Piercy Brett—Admiral the Honourable John Byron—Loss of the *Wager*—His Career and Engagement in the West Indies with Admiral D'Estaing, on the 6th July, 1778—Some Account of Sir Hyde Parker and Sir John Lockhart-Ross—The Career of Sir Edward Hughes—Capture of Negapatam and Trincomalee and his Five Indecisive Engagements with the French Fleet—Lord Rodney—His Services under Admiral Knowles, Commodore Fox, Sir Edward Hawke, and Admiral Boscawen—He Relieves Gibraltar—His Action with De Guichen on the 14th April, 1780—Rodney's Great Victory over the Count de Grasse 53

CHAPTER IV.

Outbreak of the Revolutionary War in January, 1793—The Unsuccessful Operations at Toulon—Destruction of the Arsenal and Ships by Sir Sydney Smith—Repulse at Corsica—Frigate Actions—The *Nymphe* and *Cléopatre*—*Boston* and *Embuscade*—*Crescent* and *Réunion*—Captain Horatio Nelson in the Mediterranean—

vi   *CONTENTS.*

                                                                                                   PAGE

The *Thames* and *Uranie*—The *Antelope* and *Atalante*—Attack on the French Possessions in the West Indies—Capture of the Islands of St. Pierre and Miquelon—Reduction of Pondicherry and the French Settlements in the East Indies—Losses and Gains during the Year 1793—Lord Howe's Great Victory over the French Fleet on the "Glorious 1st of June" 80

CHAPTER V.

Admiral Montagu's Escape from the French Fleet—Lord Howe's Last Cruise—Capture of the *Alexander*—Mutiny on Board the *Culloden*—Operations in Corsica—Capture of San Fiorenzo—Captain Horatio Nelson at Bastia—He is Wounded at Calvi—Engagement between Sir John Borlase Warren's Squadron and some French Frigates—Action between the East India Company's Ships and French Privateers—Capture of the *Duguay-Trouin* and Action off Mauritius—The *Swiftsure* and *Atalante*—Actions between the *Carysfort* and *Castor*, *Romney* and *Sibylle*—Destruction of the *Volontaire* by Sir John Warren's Squadron—Expedition to the West Indies—Capture of Martinique, St. Lucia, and Guadaloupe—Loss of St. Lucia, St. Vincent, Guadaloupe and Grenada—Operations at St. Domingo—Daring Reconnaissance of Brest made by Sir Sydney Smith—Admiral Cornwallis's masterly Retreat before a Superior French Fleet—Lord Bridport's Action of the 23rd June, 1795—The Expedition to Quiberon Bay—Disastrous Gale in the Channel—Loss of the *Berwick* off Corsica 119

CHAPTER VI.

Vice-Admiral Hotham's Action off Genoa with the French Fleet and Capture of the *Ça Ira* and *Censeur*—His engagement off Hyères and Capture of the *Alcide*—Loss of a British Convoy and the *Censeur*—Rupture with Holland and Seizure of Dutch Ships—Action between the *Blanche* and *Pique*, and Death of Captain Faulknor—The *Lively* and *Tourterelle*—*Astræa* and *Gloire*—The *Thetis* and *Hussar* with Five French Storeships—The *Dido* and *Lowestoft* with the *Minerve* and *Artemise*—The *Southampton* and *Vestale*—The *Rose* and Three Privateers—The *Mermaid* and Two Corvettes—Loss of the *Boyne*—Capture of the Cape of Good Hope and of a Dutch Squadron sent to its Relief—Also of the Dutch Possessions in Ceylon and India . 144

CHAPTER VII.

Commodore Nelson's Services in the Mediterranean—War with Spain—Evacuation of Corsica—Retreat of the British Fleet to Gibraltar before the United Navies of France and Spain—Loss of the *Courageux* and *Bombay Castle*—Services of Sir Sydney Smith in the *Diamond*—Capture of the *Etoile* and *Unité*—Sir Sydney Smith is made Prisoner—His Escape from Paris—Capture of the *Virginie*—Cutting Out of a Lugger at the Penmarcks—Capture of the *Argo*—Action between the *Santa Margarita* and *Tamise*—The *Unicorn* and *Tribune*—*Dryad* and *Proserpine*—*Southampton* and *Utile*—The *Glatton* and a French Squadron—The *Aimable* and *Pensée*—The *Mermaid* and *Vengeance*—Admiral Sercey's Cruise in the East Indies—Action between his Squadron and the Seventy-fours *Arrogant* and *Victorious*—The *Pelican* and *Medée*—The *Lapwing* at Anguilla—*Terpsichore* and *Mahonessa*—*Terpsichore* and *Vestale*—The *Minerve* and *Sabina*, and the *Blanche* and *Ceres*—Capture of the Dutch Settlements in the West Indies, and of the Islands of St. Lucia, St. Vincent, and Grenada—Attack on St. Domingo—Capture of the Dutch Possessions in the Moluccas, and of a Squadron in Simon's Bay 164

CHAPTER VIII.

The Invasion of Ireland—Dispersion of the French Fleet—Action between the *Droits de l'Homme* and the *Indefatigable* and *Amazon* Frigates—Shipwreck of the French Seventy-four and *Amazon*—The Mutiny at Spithead and the Nore—Disaffections on other Stations—Sir John Jervis's Victory over the Spanish Fleet off Cape St. Vincent—Sir Horatio Nelson at Cadiz—Repulse of his Attack on Santa Cruz—Admiral Duncan's Victory over the Dutch Fleet off Camperdown—Frigate Actions during the Year 1797—Loss of the *Tribune*—Capture of Trinidad—Cutting-out Affairs in the West Indies—Action between the *Mars* and *Hercule*—Repulse of the French Channel Flotilla 186

CONTENTS.

CHAPTER IX.

French Expeditions to Ireland—Capture of the *Hoche* and Consorts—*Mermaid* and *Loire*—*Anson* and *Loire*—*Fisgard* and *Immortalité*—Buonaparte's Expedition to Egypt—Nelson's Victory over the French Fleet at Aboukir Bay—Capture of the *Leander* by the *Généreux*—Results of the Battle of the Nile . . . 225

CHAPTER X.

Events in the Mediterranean—Capture of Minorca—Actions between Single Ships in 1798—The *St. George* and Spanish Privateers—*Melampus* and *Volage*—*Speedy* and *Papillon*—*Coburg* and *Revanche*—*Seahorse* and *Sensible*—The *Sibylle* and *Fox* at Manilla—Loss of the *Resistance*—Capture of the *Seine*—*Lion* and four Spanish Frigates—Boats of the *Melpomene*—*Espoir* and *Liguria*—Capture of the *Flore* and *Furie*—Loss of the *Ambuscade*—Lord Nelson at Naples—The British Navy at Capua, Gaeta, and Rome—Defence of Acre by Sir Sydney Smith—Operations on the Coast of Egypt and in Holland—Loss of the *Proserpine* Frigate and Boat Actions in 1799—The *Sibylle* and *Forte*—The *Dædalus* and *Prudente*—Destruction of the *Preneuse*—The *Espoir* and *Africa*—*Clyde* and *Vestale*—Capture of Spanish Frigates with Specie—Cutting-out of the *Hermione*—Actions in the Channel and at Gibraltar—Acquisition of Surinam—Loss of the *Queen Charlotte* by Fire—Wreck of the *Repulse* and *Marlborough*—Siege of Genoa—Cutting-out of the *Prima* Galley—Capture of the *Généreux* and *Guillaume Tell*—Surrender of Malta and Curaçoa—Capture of the *Pallas* and *Heureux*—Boat Expeditions on the French and Spanish Coasts—Cutting-out of the *Désirée* and *Cerbère*—Capture of the *Concorde* and *Médée*—The *Seine* and *Vengeance*—The *Millbrook* and *Bellone* . . 248

CHAPTER XI.

The Battle of Copenhagen—Results of Lord Nelson's Victory—Submission of Sweden and Russia—The Boulogne Flotilla of Invasion—Repulse of the British Boat Attacks—Admiral Ganteaume's Attempts to reach Egypt—Loss of the *Swiftsure*—Capture of the *Success* and *Bravoure*—The Defence of Porto Ferrajo—Services of the Navy in the Expedition to Egypt—Sir James Saumarez at Algeciras—His Second Action in the Straits of Gibraltar—Cutting-out of the *Sénégal*—Lieutenant Fitton's Exploit—Capture of the *Chiffonne*—The *Phœbe* and *Africaine*—Lord Cochrane's Early Career—Naval Officers and their Rating—The *Speedy* and *Gamo*—Cutting-out of the *Chevrette*—Other Boat Actions—Services of the *Sylph*—The Peace of Amiens . 286

CHAPTER XII.

Rupture with France—Attacks on the French Flotilla and Towns in the Channel—Lord Nelson in the Mediterranean—Boat and Frigate actions—Loss of the *Minerve*—Services of the *Racoon*—Loss and Recapture of the *Lord Nelson*—Boats of the *Blanche* at St. Domingo—Recapture of the French and Dutch Colonies in the West Indies—Events in the East Indies—Commodore Dance and Admiral Linois—The *Marengo* and Consorts with the *Centurion*—French Preparations for the Invasion of England—Actions with the Invasion Flotilla—Lord Nelson's pursuit of the French Fleet, under Admiral Villeneuve, to the West Indies—Defence of the Diamond Rock—Return of Nelson to England—Cutting-out of the *Curieux*—Exploits in the West Indies—Cutting out of the *Atalante*—The *Wilhelmina* and *Psyche*—Loss of the *Lily* and Repulse of the Boats of the *Galatea*—Repulse at Curaçoa and Capture of Surinam 318

CHAPTER XIII.

Capture of four Spanish Frigates and Declaration of War by Spain—Movements of Admirals Cornwallis and Ganteaume—Sir Robert Calder's Action off Cape Finisterre—Admiral Cornwallis' Partial Action off Brest—Nelson proceeds to sea to encounter the combined French and Spanish Fleets 342

LIST OF ILLUSTRATIONS.

VOL. II.

		PAGE
H.R.H. Prince George of Wales	*Frontispiece.*	
Coastguardsman	*Vignette.*	
A 38-Gun Frigate about 1770	*To face*	28
H.M.S. "Bramble"		60
A 28-Gun Frigate about 1794		96
H.M.S. "Undaunted"		112
H.M.S. "Latona"		128
A 74-Gun Ship of the Line about 1794		148
H.M.S. "Colossus"		176
H.M.S. "Hero"		192
H.M.S. "Rodney"		224
Boatswain about 1829		260
H.M.S. "Victoria" (The Last of the Three-Deckers)		286
H.M.S. "Victoria"		318

HER MAJESTY'S NAVY.

CHAPTER I.

The American War—Services of the Navy at Charlestown and New York—The Fighting on Lake Champlain and on the North River—Declaration of War with France—Admiral Keppel's Indecisive Action with Count D'Orvilliers—Court-Martials on Admirals Keppel and Palliser—The French and Spanish Fleets in the Channel—Admiral Byron's Engagement with Count D'Estaing off the Island of Grenada—Capture of the *Serapis* and *Scarborough* by Paul Jones—Loss of the *Quebec*—Admiral Rodney's Defeat of a Spanish Squadron, and First Relief of Gibraltar—Naval Events on the American Coast and in the West Indies—Action of the 17th April, 1780, between Sir George Rodney and Admiral De Guichen—Partial Actions between the same—Losses in the Great Hurricane in the West Indies—Declaration of War with Holland—Vice-Admiral Hyde Parker's Action with the Dutch Fleet on the 5th August, 1781—Capture of the Dutch Islands in the West Indies.

THE naval history of England during the ten years succeeding the peace of 1763 was an uneventful one, but in 1773 occurred the first incident in the series of events which launched us into a war with our American Colonies, which lost half a continent for us, and left the renown and resources of this country at a very low ebb.

On the 18th December in that year, when the three annual tea-ships arrived at Boston, some armed men, disguised as Indians, boarded them, and in a few hours threw into the sea the contents of 600 chests from each ship. At Charlestown 200 chests from a tea-ship were discharged overboard, but at New York the tea was landed under the guns of a ship-of-war. This violent course of conduct was due to the enforcement, by Act of Parliament, of the ill-judged tax on tea imported into America.

The protracted and eventful war which ensued with the "Thirteen United Colonies," began in 1775 with the battles of Lexington and Bunker's Hill, near Boston, a hardly-won victory for the royal troops, in which the ships-of-war *Glasgow* and *Lively* participated by their fire. But the operations were chiefly conducted between the land forces of the Colonies and the Mother Country, and the navy played a subordinate part. The colonists displayed great daring and achieved many successes. They seized Ticonderoga and Crown Point, situated on the lakes, the gates of Canada, and captured Montreal, but suffered a disastrous repulse at Quebec, where the American General Montgomery was slain, and Colonel Arnold wounded. The Virginians compelled the governor, Lord Dunmore, to seek safety on board the British war-ship, *Fowey*, and the navy retaliated on the town of Norfolk, which was cannonaded and burned to the ground by the *Liverpool* and three ships-of-war, for refusing to supply provisions to the King's ships. In the early part of the war the fleet served as an asylum to the expelled functionaries, while the army was ingloriously cooped up in Quebec and Boston. The colonists issued letters of marque, and one of the privateers captured the ordnance ship *Woolwich*, which placed them in possession of guns, arms, and military stores.

Washington now undertook the siege of Boston, but mutual jealousies, prevailed between the army and navy, and General Howe, brother of the admiral, who had received no advices or succour from England since the preceding October, abandoned the place in March, 1776, and removed his troops to Halifax, and General Washington marched into the town, with drums beating and colours flying.

In Canada the royalists were more successful. Here General Carleton defended Quebec, before which the *Isis* and two frigates arrived, having forced their way through the ice. The unexpected appearance of these ships threw the besiegers into the greatest alarm, of which General Carleton took advantage by sallying out, on the 6th May, on the Provincials, who fled on all sides, abandoning the guns and stores. This repulse resulted in the abandonment of Canada by the insurgents. Early in June the combined army and fleet, the latter under Sir Peter Parker, arrived before Charlestown, in South Carolina. The admiral arranged the plan of attack with General Clinton, who, with Lord Cornwallis, commanded the troops, which were landed on Long Island, with which General Lee, commanding the Provincials, held communication by means of a bridge of boats. On the 28th June, the *Thunder*, bomb-vessel, shelled the fort on Sullivan's Island, to the westward of Long Island, supported by the *Bristol*, *Solebay*, *Experiment*, and *Active*, while the *Sphinx*, *Syren* and *Actæon* enfiladed the fort from the westward, between the end of the island and Charlestown. This latter part of the operations ended in failure, owing to the unskilfulness of the pilots, and all three frigates stuck fast in the sand, where the *Actæon* had to be abandoned and burnt on the following morning to prevent her guns and stores falling into the hands of the enemy. The fort on Sullivan's Island was too strong to be silenced, and so terrible was the fire experienced by the British, that the quarter-deck of the *Bristol* was at one time cleared of every person but Captain Morris, who received several wounds, but disdained to leave his station until darkness put an end to the conflict, which had lasted over ten hours. Sir Peter Parker then withdrew his shattered ships, the *Bristol* having lost 111 men killed and wounded, and the *Experiment* 79.

All prospect of a termination of the fratricidal struggle disappeared, when, on the 4th July, 1776, the "Thirteen United States" promulgated the Act of Independence, and a long and sanguinary struggle ensued. A few weeks after the issue of this memorable Declaration, Admiral Lord Howe arrived at Halifax with a powerful squadron and strong military reinforcements, which raised the royal army to 35,000 men. A fortnight before the arrival of his brother, General Howe had left Halifax, with his troops on board Admiral Shuldane's squadron, for New York, the conquest of which was one of the most important objects of the war. It was found that the insurgents, or patriots, as they ought rather to be called, had erected defensive works on Long, New York, and Staten Islands; but as those on the last named were the least powerful, General Howe effected a landing here, and was joined by the Royalist Governor, Tryon, who, like his colleagues, had taken refuge on shipboard. Lord Howe arrived off Staten Island on the 14th July, and, on being joined by Sir Peter Parker with his squadron, an attack was projected against Long Island. A landing was effected, and the enemy were driven from their works, the ships distracting their attention by attacking a battery at Red Hook.

General Washington came here from New York, and witnessed the discomfiture of his troops; but with singular promptitude and ability, effected a retreat from the island to New York on the night of the 29th July, bringing away his artillery and stores. Had the British general pushed his success, a surrender must have been the result; and not less blameworthy was the conduct of the admiral, who had failed to station ships in the East River, and thus cut off the retreat of the colonists. When daylight broke, the British commanders found the enemy's lines abandoned, and the last of their rear-guard in the boats out of danger.

Batteries were now thrown up opposite New York, and everything being ready, General Clinton's division, covered by five ships-of-war, proceeded to Kepp's Bay, the works of which were abandoned after a cannonade from the ships, when the troops were landed. The enemy thereupon evacuated the city, and retired towards the north at King's Bridge, by which the connection with the mainland was kept open. General

Washington displayed great skill in his dispositions for defence, while he avoided risking any engagement; but Lord Cornwallis took Fort Lee and advanced into the Jerseys, and later extended his winter cantonments from New Brunswick to the Delaware. In December, a squadron, under Sir Peter Parker, co-operated with General Clinton's division in an attack on Rhode Island, which was successful.

Meanwhile, fighting was in progress on Lake Champlain, from which General Carleton sought to drive the enemy, and carry the war into the colonists' own country. On the 11th October, a squadron, consisting of the *Inflexible*, which had been reconstructed at St. John's, carrying eighteen 12-pounders, and two schooners, mounting fourteen and twelve 6-pounders, and twenty small gun-boats, armed with field-pieces and howitzers, the whole manned by 700 seamen, commanded by Captain Pringle, proceeded to encounter the hostile fleet, consisting of fifteen vessels, under the command of the famous Colonel Benedict Arnold. The enemy's squadron was found drawn up to defend the passage between the island of Valicour and the western mainland, and a severe engagement ensued. Owing to the wind being unfavourable, the *Inflexible* could not take part in the action, the brunt of which fell on the schooner *Carleton* and the gun-boats. During the night the enemy fled, but after a long chase they were brought to action at noon on the 13th, a few leagues from Crown Point. Arnold fought with determined valour, and succeeded in running ashore the *Congress*, galley, in which he himself was, with other gun-boats, and they were blown up; but the *Washington*, galley, with Brigadier-General Waterburg, second-in-command, was captured, though a galley and three gun-boats passing Crown Point escaped to Ticonderoga. Thus Lake Champlain was recovered, and the hostile squadron entirely defeated. The Provincials abandoned Crown Point, but the season was too far advanced for the army to attempt an attack on the strong fort of Ticonderoga with any prospect of success.

The American privateers continued to prey on British commerce, and so successful were they that the loss incurred by our merchants was more than one million sterling. The Ministry retaliated by issuing letters of marque, but with small results, and meanwhile the great armaments which were being raised in the French and Spanish ports demanded great sacrifices on the part of the English people to meet the apprehended coalition against us, while General Washington displayed his genius for war by his Fabian tactics, and not only saved Philadelphia, but recovered the greater part of the Jerseys, and obliged an army greatly his superior in numbers and discipline to act upon the defensive.

As the summer of 1777 drew on, the British commander determined to strike a blow at Philadelphia, and on the 23rd July a force of 36 battalions proceeded from Sandy Hook in nearly 300 sail, and made for the Capes of the Delaware, but the information received induced them to change their design and undertake the enterprise by Chesapeake Bay to Maryland. The middle of August was past before the great armament entered the Bay, and proceeding up the Elk River, landed without opposition at Elk Ferry on the 25th August. On the 3rd September, General Howe began his march for Pennsylvania, in defence of which Washington had concentrated 13,000 men, but after some severe fighting, the city was evacuated by the Provincials, and occupied by the British army on the 26th September. Meanwhile, Lord Howe removed the fleet and transports round to the Delaware, in order to supply the army with the necessary stores and provisions, but the passage to the capital of Pennsylvania was impracticable, owing to the strong fortifications and batteries constructed by the enemy, until a combined movement was made against them.

While Lord Howe ordered the heavy sloops and frigates to approach Mud Island, which was the main object of the assault, the general erected batteries on the Pennsylvania shore to assist in dislodging the enemy, and a strong body of Hessians attacked the redoubt at Red Bank. The operations by land and water were equally unsuccessful. The Hessians were repulsed with slaughter on the 22nd October, and the ships could not bring their fire to bear with effect. The *Augusta*, 64, and *Merlin*, sloop, grounded, when the former took fire and blew up and the latter was also destroyed.

A second attempt was made on the 15th November, when the *Isis* and *Somerset* attacked the enemy's works in front, and several frigates engaged a newly-erected fort near Manto Creek. Their efforts were crowned with success, and the forts were silenced and abandoned. The American shipping in the river being without protection, sought to escape past Pennsylvania to places of security higher up the stream, but the *Delaware*, frigate, now lying off that city, went in pursuit of them, and some seventeen vessels were burnt after the crews had abandoned them.

The army went into winter quarters at Pennsylvania, and the loyalists congratulated themselves on this important victory, but its advantages were more than negatived by the disaster that befell the force of 7,000 men under General Burgoyne, the successor of General Carleton in the command in the North. At first all went well, Ticonderoga was taken, and the remainder of the enemy's squadron on Lake Champlain defeated, and it seemed as though the combined movement, arranged with Sir Henry Clinton and

Commodore Hotham, who were to advance northwards from New York on both sides of the river, would end in the break-up of resistance in the North. But the disgraceful policy of letting loose hordes of armed savages on the Provincials roused to arms the whole population of the country and frontier, and General Gates, a West Point officer, and the gallant Arnold, cooped up the unfortunate Burgoyne in Saratoga, and, after a brief and desperate struggle to extricate himself, he was compelled, on the 17th October, to enter into a convention for the surrender of his troops, which dealt a blow on the Royal cause from which it never recovered.

Meantime the army and navy conducted to a successful issue the combined operations on the North River. Having embarked three thousand men, with a squadron of frigates, armed galleys, and smaller vessels, General Clinton attacked the forts at Montgomery and Clinton, which were carried by storm by the troops, while the seamen co-operated by a heavy fire from the ships and galleys. Another fort, called Constitution, was set on fire and abandoned. The artillery taken in these works numbered sixty-seven pieces, and a large boom, constructed at an extraordinary expenditure of time and money, was sunk or carried away, and barracks for one thousand five hundred troops were destroyed. Sir James Wallace, in command of the flying squadron, and General Vaughan, with some troops, made four expeditions up the river, and caused much loss to the patriots, who, however, continued the struggle with undiminished fervour.

On the 13th March, 1778, the Marquis de Noailles, French Ambassador to England, announced that his Government had concluded a treaty of friendship and commerce with the United States, upon which the British Ambassador was recalled from Paris, and an embargo was laid on the French shipping in the English ports, to which King Louis replied by similar acts of hostility. The nation made extraordinary efforts to meet the ancient foe who had thus taken advantage of their country's need to deprive her of the empire in America which she had wrested from her in the "Seven Years' War." In a short time the Navy was raised to a strength of two hundred and twenty-eight ships-of-the-line, frigates and sloops, in commission, of which fifty sail-of-the-line were retained for the defence of the shores of Great Britain, one hundred and thirty ships were stationed in American waters, besides the squadron in the Leeward Islands and Jamaica, under Admirals Barrington and Sir Peter Parker, and the remainder formed the fleet in the Mediterranean under Admiral Duff.

The greater part of the fleet in America remained at Rhode Island, whence squadrons were sent to cruise before the principal ports. Early in May, Captain Henry and Major Maitland succeeded in destroying the American ships lying in the river between Pennsylvania and Trenton, and Captain Clayton and Colonel Campbell did the same in neighbouring waters. In June, Sir Henry Clinton, who had succeeded Sir William Howe in command of the army, evacuated Pennsylvania, which had been acquired with such great effort, and the British troops returned to Gloucester Point, whence they crossed the Delaware, under the protection of the Navy, and arrived in safety at New York. The passage, on the 5th July, to Sandy Hook Island, was made on a bridge of flat-bottomed boats, constructed by the Navy, and they were afterwards conveyed to New York, while the fleet anchored off Staten Island.

Meanwhile, Admiral D'Estaing, on the 13th April, escaped from Toulon with twelve sail-of-the-line, besides three frigates and some store ships, and arrived off the coast of Virginia on the 5th July, and a week later anchored about four miles from Sandy Hook. The British Ministry wasted much time in sending out reinforcements to Lord Howe, but at length Admiral Byron sailed on the 5th June with fourteen ships. A gale of wind, however, scattered the squadron on the 3rd July, and on the 18th August the *Princess Royal*, flying the admiral's flag, arrived in sight of Sandy Hook, where the French fleet of twelve sail was discovered at anchor. As the British admiral could neither get into the roads of Sandy Hook nor of New York without passing through the midst of the enemy, he bore away for Halifax, where, on his arrival on the 26th August, he found the *Culloden;* and the rest of the squadron dropped in there or reached New York.

But Lord Howe was not the officer to remain idle in presence of a French fleet even of greatly superior force. His seamen desired nothing better than to be led against the enemy, and to make up his crews one thousand volunteers joined from the transports, while the soldiers in New York displayed equal enthusiasm in offering their services to man the fleet, which consisted of six ships carrying 64 guns, three of 50, and two of 40, with some frigates and sloops. He prolonged his line, consisting of the *Isis, Eagle, Somerset, Trident, Nonsuch,* and *Ardent,* by adding the *Leviathan,* storeship, manned with volunteers, and erected batteries, mounting two howitzers and three 18-pounders, on the point of land which the enemy must pass to enter the channel within the Hook. D'Estaing, who had been engaged in sounding the bar, weighed on the 22nd July, with the apparent intention of attacking the British line, but instead of doing so, he bore off to the southward, to the disappointment of the sailors who had anticipated an opportunity of adding to the laurels of their noble service.

During the next few days, Lord Howe was joined by the *Renown*, 50, from the West Indies, and the *Raisonable*, *Centurion*, and *Cornwall*, and as his advice-boats had brought intelligence that the French fleet had sailed for Rhode Island, he put to sea in order to save the British garrison, and on the 9th August arrived off Narragansett Harbour. On the following morning the wind blew directly out of the harbour, and D'Estaing, though still in superior force, made sail to stand out to sea, closely followed by the English admiral, who was at the disadvantage of being to leeward, and therefore unable to force on an action, which his adversary seemed bent on avoiding. Night put an end to the manœuvres of the rival commanders, and morning found them in the same relative positions. Lord Howe, in order the better to conduct the battle, which he hoped to bring on during the day, shifted his flag from the *Eagle*, in the centre of the line, to the *Apollo*, frigate, and having observed that D'Estaing had placed his strongest ships in the van, strengthened his rear in order to receive their attack.

About five o'clock, the French admiral altered his bearing, and then formed his line to engage to leeward. Lord Howe covered the intervals of the English line with the frigates and fire-ships, and made a signal for his ships to shorten sail, and close to the centre. The engagement seemed now to be decided on by the commanders of both squadrons; but D'Estaing again changed his mind, and bearing to the southward, his ships were soon, from the state of the weather, entirely out of sight.

The gale increased to such violence that, notwithstanding Lord Howe ordered his ships to lay to all night, one division was totally separated from the rest, the centre and van with most of the frigates still keeping together.

The *Apollo* having lost her fore-mast in the night, the admiral shifted his flag next day to the *Phœnix*, Captain Hammond, then in company with the *Centurion*, *Ardent*, *Richmond*, *Vigilant*, and *Roebuck*. The whole fleet was greatly disabled by the storm, their sails shattered, their masts sprung, and the fire-ships rendered by the wet totally unfit for service. But though the elements warred against them they did their best to give a good account of the enemy. On the evening of the 13th, Captain Dawson, in the *Renown*, 50, fell in with the *Languedoc*, having in company D'Estaing's flagship totally dismasted. Having run close under her lee, he gave her a broadside from his upper-deck guns, then standing off to windward, opened his lower ports, and at half a cable's length, poured in three broadsides. The darkness obliged him to lie to for the night, in the resolution of renewing the attack next morning, but at the first dawn, six French ships hove in sight, three of which remained with the wreck, and the other three gave him chase. The same evening Commodore Hotham would have taken the *Tonnant*, had it not been for the intervention of other French ships.

The *Cæsar*, 74, nearly became a prize to the *Isis*, 64, after an action which displayed the brilliant courage of British seamen. Captain Rayner, of the *Isis*, discovering the superior force of his opponent, at first endeavoured to escape her, but she proved to be the faster sailer. In a short time they were close on board each other, and engaged for an hour and a half within pistol shot. Notwithstanding the disproportion of force, the Frenchman was obliged to put before the wind, the *Isis* being incapable of pursuing him owing to the shattered condition of her masts and rigging. Monsieur Bougainville, the French captain, lost his arm, the first lieutenant, his leg, and they acknowledged 70 men killed and wounded, whereas the *Isis* had but one man killed and 14 wounded. After thus upholding the honour of the flag, the British ships sailed for the general rendezvous, which the admiral had appointed at the Hook, where they found their consorts almost as much shattered by the storm, as they had been by the storm and the French fleet together.

While his ships were repairing damages, Lord Howe sent the *Experiment* to reconnoitre, when she brought intelligence that D'Estaing had returned to Rhode Island, and, on the following day, Lieutenant Stanhope, who had passed through the French fleet in a whale boat, brought more complete information. D'Estaing still lay at the harbour's mouth, but Sir Robert Pigot, who commanded the English garrison, stated he hoped to be able to meet the attack of the patriot army, under General Sullivan, numbering 20,000 men, though if the French fleet came in he could not guarantee the security of the place committed to his charge. Lord Howe at once put to sea, but was met by the *Galatea* with the information that D'Estaing had steered in the direction of Boston. Thereupon, detaching three ships to Rhode Island, the admiral proceeded to Boston Bay, where he discovered the enemy at anchor. Finding that he could not attack them with any prospect of success, his lordship sailed for Newport, where he learned that General Sullivan had retired from before Rhode Island on being abandoned by the French fleet. Lord Howe afterwards returned to Sandy Hook, and his health being infirm, surrendered the command to Admiral Gambier and proceeded to England.

In Europe the war with France was equally barren of results. In May the French Ministry had mustered at Brest a fleet of three 80-gun ships, seventeen 74's and fourteen frigates, under the command of the Count D'Orvilliers. To blockade or engage this fleet, Admiral Keppel sailed from Spithead on the 8th June, with 27 ships. On the 17th, when 25 miles distant from the Lizard, they sighted two frigates watching the fleet, to which they gave chase, and in the evening the *Licorne*, frigate, struck to the *America*, 64, commanded by Lord Longford. The second ship was the *Belle Poule*, which was engaged the same night by the *Arethusa*, 32, but after a severely contested engagement lasting over two hours, the French frigate, being of superior weight of metal, managed to make her escape, leaving her plucky antagonist, " the saucy *Arethusa*," of the old naval song, with her spars and rigging much shattered. In this action the *Arethusa* lost eight killed and 36 wounded, and the *Belle Poule* acknowledged to having 40 killed and 47 wounded. On the following day, the *Pallas*, a 32-gun French frigate, was captured by three ships-of-the-line, and from papers found on board her, it was discovered that the French fleet at Brest and in the neighbouring waters numbered no less than 32 sail-of-the-line. As his own fleet was so vastly inferior, Admiral Keppel thought it desirable not to risk a defeat, which would place the dockyards and shipping in the Channel at the mercy of the enemy, and returned for reinforcements to Spithead, where he anchored on the 27th June.

On the arrival of ships from the West Indies and Levant, Admiral Keppel was enabled to increase his fleet and crews, and on the 9th July sailed again with 24 ships-of-the-line, which was increased in the Channel to 30 sail,* which brought him nearly to a condition of equality with Count D'Orvilliers, who had sailed on the previous day from Brest.

The two fleets came within sight of each other on the afternoon of the 23rd July, in the Bay of Biscay, about 35 leagues to the westward of Brest. At first the French admiral seemed desirous to bring on an engagement, but on coming nearer, and discovering the British fleet was in about equal strength, he evidently determined to avoid an action. This plan he adhered to for the three following days, notwithstanding every effort used by the British admiral to bring him to action. All the advantage Admiral Keppel could obtain in four days was to separate two of the enemy's line-of-battle-ships, which

---

* The following were the ships of Admiral Keppel's fleet ; *Victory*, 100 guns, Admiral Honourable Augustus Keppel, commander-in-chief ; *Queen*, 90, Vice-Admiral Sir Robert Harland ; *Formidable*, 90, Vice-Admiral Sir Hugh Palliser ; *Duke, Sandwich, Prince George*, and *Ocean*, 90-gun ships ; *Foudroyant*, 80 ; *Monarch, Shrewsbury, Hector, Centaur, Cumberland, Berwick, Thunderer, Courageux, Valiant, Vengeance, Elizabeth, Robuste, Egmont, Terrible*, and *Ramillies*, 74's ; *Exeter, Stirling Castle, Bienfaisant, Vigilant, Worcester, Defiance*, and *America*, 64's. Also the frigates, *Proserpine* and *Fox*, 28, *Andromeda, Arethusa, Milford* and *Media*, 32 ; and two fire-ships. The *Defiance* and *Resolution*, 74's, joined afterwards, making 32 ships-of-the-line, mounting 2,428 guns, and carrying 19,788 men, exclusive of the six frigates and two fire-ships.

returned to Brest, and could not afterwards rejoin their flag, thus placing both fleets upon an equality as to line-of-battle-ships. On the 24th the admiral threw out the signal to chase to windward, which was continued the two following days, keeping at the same time his ships as much together as possible, in order to seize the first opportunity of bringing the enemy to a close engagement; but this proved ineffectual, the French cautiously avoiding coming to an action, and in their manœuvres showing great skill. About four o'clock on the morning of the 27th July, the enemy were discovered to windward about five miles distant.

Admiral Keppel, finding some of his fleet too much scattered, made signals to collect them together, still continuing to follow the enemy. About ten o'clock a heavy squall came on, and when it cleared up, the two fleets, by a shift of wind, had neared each other, but on different tacks. An hour later Admiral Keppel made the signal for a general engagement, and the ships as they came up began firing. The French attacked at some distance the headmost of Sir Robert Harland's division, which formed the van. Their fire was warmly returned by almost every ship in the fleet as they ranged along the line, and all were soon engaged, as the two fleets passed each other. The cannonade was very heavy, and did considerable execution on both sides. The enemy, as usual, fired chiefly at the rigging, while the British sailors continued the old way of fighting, by firing principally at the hulls of the enemy's ships. The action lasted about three hours. The loss on the side of the British was 133 killed and 373 wounded, while the French acknowledged having 150 killed and about 600 wounded.

After the ships had repaired their damages, the commander-in-chief, about three o'clock in the afternoon, made the signal to form the line of battle ahead. Sir Robert Harland's division immediately obeyed; but Sir Hugh Palliser's never came into the line during the rest of the day, the admiral alleging that his ship, the *Formidable*, was so much disabled that he could not obey the signal.

Expectation in England had been raised by an announcement made a few days before the engagement, by Admiral Keppel in a letter to the Admiralty, that he had been in chase of the enemy; so the disappointment was proportionate when his brief despatch announced an indecisive action, not a ship of the enemy being captured or sunk. Both sides claimed a victory to which neither was entitled. "The French," says Campbell, "soon after the engagement, drew up in a line of battle to leeward, and continued during the afternoon in that position, with an intention, they asserted, to renew the engagement. According to the French *Gazette* the English stole away during the night without showing any lights, and in the morning the French, having no expectation of being able to renew the action, and finding themselves unexpectedly off Ushant by the efforts of wind and currents, while they supposed themselves near thirty leagues from the land, they took that opportunity of putting into Brest in order to land their wounded men.

"This account is false, for it appeared by the evidence of witnesses upon oath, in the subsequent trials of Admirals Keppel and Palliser, that the French, in order to deceive, stationed, soon after it was dark, three of their best sailing ships in a line, at considerable distances from each other, with lights, in order to have the appearance of their whole fleet. This *finesse* had the intended effect; their fleet stole away in the night, and the three ships followed them at daylight in the morning. The British fleet were nearly in line of battle all night, excepting the *Formidable* and some other ships of Sir Hugh Palliser's division. Both Admiral Keppel and Sir Robert Harland had lights out, but Sir Hugh Palliser, not being in his station, had no lights. The men were on deck all night in every ship of the fleet, stationed at their guns ready to renew the action in the morning, but in this they found themselves disappointed, the enemy's fleet being out of sight, excepting the three ships above mentioned, which were at too great a distance to be overtaken."

Whatever may have been the cause of this failure to strike a decisive blow at the French fleet, the result was to be deplored. Admiral Keppel arrived off Plymouth on the 31st July, and on the 22nd of the following month sailed with the same ships, to look for the French commander. But Count D'Orvilliers had no stomach for again trying conclusions with his antagonist, and leaving the Bay of Biscay free to the depredations of our fleet and privateers, bore away for Cape Finisterre, and ultimately returned to Brest, a few days after Admiral Keppel cast anchor at Spithead.

Now a storm of invectives and recriminations arose in the press between the adherents of Admirals Keppel and Palliser, and the latter having written a letter in justification of his action on the 27th July, the commander-in-chief replied to the demand addressed to him by the House of Commons, vindicating his conduct in the battle.* This drew from

* In this document Admiral Keppel says:—"If he was to go over the business of the 27th July again, he would conduct himself in the same manner. Everything that could be done had been done, and he was happy to say, the British flag had not been tarnished in his hands. He felt himself perfectly easy on that head, and should never be ashamed of his conduct on the day alluded to. The oldest and most experienced officers in his Majesty's Navy, in every engagement, saw something which they were before unacquainted with, and that they presented something new. He impeached no man of neglect of duty, because he was satisfied that the officer alluded to had manifested no want of courage, the quality most essential in a British seaman." He added, "he was much surprised when an officer under his command had made an appeal to the public in a common newspaper, signed with his name, before any accusation had been made against him, and which tended to render him odious and despicable in the eyes of his countrymen."

Sir Hugh Palliser a specific " charge of misconduct and neglect of duty " against his superior officer. The officers and seamen of the Navy, with whom Admiral Keppel was most popular, resented this stigma cast on an officer in whose gallantry and professional skill they had confidence, while they regarded him as a victim to the dislike of the Ministry, and the result was the presentation of a memorial to the king, signed by the principal admirals of the Navy, conveying a severe censure on Sir Hugh Palliser and the Admiralty. The latter, however, issued orders for the convening of a court-martial on Admiral Keppel, which sat between the 7th January and 11th February.

In the course of the evidence submitted by the prosecution, no facts were proved that could support the charge of misconduct; on the other hand, the admiral's witnesses testified that if he had waited for forming the line of battle, and had not immediately taken advantage of a change of wind to close with the enemy, there could have been no engagement on the 27th July. It was proved that, having passed the French fleet, he wore ship in order to renew the engagement, and he could not have done it sooner without throwing the ships astern into the greatest confusion. The English fleet at no time exhibited any signs of flying from the enemy; and when the French, after the engagement, edged away, and made for some of our disabled ships, it was necessary to wear again, in order to prevent them from falling into their hands. The three French ships which were seen on the morning of the 28th July could not have been pursued with the smallest prospect of success. These facts entirely destroyed the charge against Admiral Keppel, whose evidence and that of Admiral Campbell, acting as flag-captain, and of Sir John Lindsay and Captain Jervis, proved that the reason why the British fleet did not again attack the French was the disobedience of Sir Hugh Palliser, who disregarded the admiral's signal for forming the line, which continued flying from three o'clock in the afternoon till the evening. The unanimous decision of the court-martial was as follows :—

" That it is their opinion the charge against Admiral Keppel is malicious and ill-founded; it having appeared that the said admiral, so far from having, by misconduct and neglect of duty on the day therein alluded to, lost an opportunity of rendering essential service to the state and thereby tarnished the honour of the British Navy, behaved as became a judicious, brave, and experienced officer."

As a necessary result of this acquittal, Sir Hugh Palliser was brought to a court-martial on the 12th April, which sat till the 5th May, when he was acquitted; the opinion of the court being, " that his conduct and behaviour on those days were in many respects highly exemplary and meritorious, at the same time the court cannot help thinking it was incumbent upon him to make known the disabled state of the *Formidable*, which he might have done by the *Fox* at the same time she joined him, or by other means. Notwithstanding his omission in this particular, the court are of opinion he is not, in any other respect, chargeable with misconduct or misbehaviour on the days above mentioned, and therefore they acquit him, and he is hereby acquitted accordingly."

A historian has well observed:—" Perhaps on no occasion was party spirit more alive and virulent than on the trials of Admiral Keppel and Sir Hugh Palliser. The former was a known partisan of the Opposition; of course he was defended by them; while he heaped all the blame of misconduct on Sir Hugh Palliser. This circumstance, independently of the latter's connections with Ministers, was sufficient to make them and that part of the nation which approved of their measures, attach themselves strongly to his cause and defence. The issue of party spirit thus working, where a regard for the public good alone should have existed and been brought into action, was such as might naturally have been expected; each party served the man in whose defence they stood forth, while the sober and dispassionate portion of the nation, after having witnessed gross misconduct in the management of the battles of the 27th and 28th July, 1778, had the additional mortification to find that no person was to be punished, or even severely blamed for it."

During the year 1778, no decisive engagement took place in America, and the loss of Dominica in the West Indies was balanced by the capture of the islands of St. Pierre and Miquelon, the only remaining settlements of the French in North American waters. As though she had not enough on her hands already, this country found herself embroiled with Spain, and on the 16th July war was declared against the Court of Madrid, which had long been intriguing with that of France, and thought the present a favourable opportunity for renewing the attempts to wrest Gibraltar from us. The addition of the Spanish navy to that of France was a serious aggravation of the already difficult position of this country.

On the 15th August the combined fleets, numbering sixty-six sail-of-the-line, appeared in the Channel off Plymouth, and captured the *Ardent*, 64. But they did not dare to avail themselves of their great numerical superiority, and when Sir Charles Hardy, commanding the Channel fleet, taking advantage of a change of wind, entered the Channel, the combined fleet followed him nearly to Falmouth, and then gave up the pursuit.

In America Sir George Collier, who took command of the fleet on the return home of Admiral Gambier, sailed from New York for the Chesapeake, and destroyed the towns of Norfolk, Suffolk, Portsmouth, and Gosport, on the coast of Virginia, and captured one hundred and thirty vessels, and a second expedition up the North River was equally successful, and thirty-seven vessels were destroyed. Soon after, this active officer was superseded by Vice-Admiral Arbuthnot, who arrived from England with some ships-of-the-line. In the West Indies, Admiral Byron joined Admiral Barrington, thus attaining a superiority over Count D'Estaing, who lay inactive at Port Royal. Soon afterwards he eluded the vigilance of the British admirals, and effected a junction with Count de Grasse, who had arrived in the West Indies with a strong squadron, but again the superiority reverted to the British, who were reinforced by Admiral Rowley's squadron from England.

Taking advantage of Admiral Byron's absence to escort a large and valuable convoy from St. Kitts to England, the French admiral seized on the island of St. Vincent, and then proceeded with his fleet of 26 sail-of-the-line and ten frigates, on board which were embarked 10,000 troops, to Grenada, which was also compelled to surrender, after a brief but spirited resistance. Byron, not knowing of D'Estaing's superiority, sailed from St. Lucia with 21 sail-of-the-line to encounter the French admiral, who, satisfied with his success, used his utmost endeavours to avoid an engagement.

The British admiral threw out the signal for the chase, and then for close action, and at half past seven in the morning, Admiral Barrington, in the *Princess of Wales*, with his two seconds, the *Boyne* and *Sultan*, having reached the van of the enemy, commenced an attack upon them with great vigour and spirit. These ships, however, having greatly outsailed the rest of the division, were obliged to sustain for a considerable time the fire of the whole French van, when Admiral Barrington was wounded. Still the Count D'Estaing maintained his resolution of not coming to a close and general engagement, which, owing to his ships being better sailers, he was enabled to effect. The French ships, accordingly, either bore down in superior numbers on such of our fleet as reached them, or stood away under a press of sail when they perceived more ships coming up to join in the engagement. At length Admiral Byron, finding that it was impossible to bring the enemy to a close battle, left off firing a little after noon, as did likewise Count D'Estaing, who had obtained the only object he had in view, that of preventing the British from compelling him to fight, and at the same time injuring and disabling their ships as much as possible.

The British loss in this action was 183 killed and 346 wounded, and that of the French was said to be no less than 1,200 slain and 1,500 wounded. Count D'Estaing retired to Grenada, and Admiral Byron to Antigua, whence he soon after proceeded to England, leaving Sir Hyde Parker in command of the fleet.

An incident characteristic of the chivalrous valour of the British sailor is told on the occasion of an attack made by Captain Luttrell, commanding a small squadron, on the Spanish fort of Ornoa on the night of the 16th October, when the place was captured together with stores and some vessels in port. "A sailor scrambled over the wall of the fort with a cutlass in each hand, when he fell in with a Spanish officer just roused from sleep, who, in the hurry and confusion, had forgotten his sword; the tar, disdaining to take advantage of an unarmed foe, and willing to display his courage in single combat, presented the officer with one of the cutlasses, saying, 'You are now on a footing with me!' The astonishment of the officer at such an act of generosity, and the facility with which a friendly parley took place, when he expected nothing else than to be cut to pieces, could only be rivalled by the admiration which the story excited in his countrymen." Upon the circumstance being mentioned to Admiral Parker on the return of the squadron, he appointed this intrepid fellow to be boatswain of a sloop-of-war; a few years afterwards, in a fit of drunkenness he forgot himself so far as to strike the lieutenant of the *Ferret*, sloop-of-war, for which he was tried by a court-martial, condemned to suffer death, and executed.

A spirited, though unfortunately unsuccessful, action was fought between two British ships and a squadron commanded by the famous Paul Jones, a man half buccaneer and half naval officer, but gifted with great professional attainments. On the 23rd September, 1779, the *Serapis*, 40, Captain Richard Pearson, and *Countess of Scarborough*, 20, Captain Piercy, escorting a large convoy of merchant ships, were off the Yorkshire coast when they received information that an enemy's squadron had been seen there a few days before. Captain Pearson took measures to secure the convoy, and prepared for action with the enemy's squadron, consisting of a ship of 40 guns on two decks, and two frigates. Soon after seven o'clock the engagement commenced, the largest ship attacking the *Serapis*, Captain Pearson, assisted occasionally by one of the frigates, which engaged the *Countess of Scarborough*. The object of the largest vessel, called the *Bon Homme Richard*, which was commanded by Paul Jones, was from the commencement of the engagement to board the *Serapis*. For this purpose she manœuvred in various ways. At first, after firing two or three broadsides, she dropped within pistol-shot of the British frigate's quarters, but being repulsed in this attempt to board, she sheered off. Afterwards, when Captain Pearson manœuvred his ship in order to lay her alongside of the enemy, the latter laid the *Serapis* athwart hawse, where she lay for some time, till at last, having got clear, the two ships brought up close alongside of each other, the muzzles of their guns actually touching. For two hours the battle raged in this situation with fury, the enemy making several attempts to set fire to the *Serapis* by means of combustibles which they threw on board her; their attempts, fortunately, were unsuccessful. About half-past nine, all the guns of the *Serapis*, abaft the main-mast, were rendered useless by an explosion, which also destroyed all the officers and men who were in that part of the ship. Her loss was further increased by the fire of one of the enemy's frigates, which kept sailing round and raking her.

Paul Jones now had recourse to a stratagem. Some of his men called for quarter, and on Captain Pearson hailing to inquire if they had struck, no answer was returned; supposing that, though unwilling to yield, they were not in a state to make further resistance, he ordered his men to board the enemy; but they had scarcely succeeded in this, before a greatly superior number of men, armed with pikes, who had lain concealed, attacked them, and compelled them to retreat to the *Serapis*. At this critical juncture, before the men could regain their guns, the French frigate poured in a broadside with terrible effect, so that Captain Pearson, unable to bring even a single gun to bear, was under the painful necessity of striking his colours. The *Bon Homme Richard* had a crew of three hundred and seventy-five men, and the frigate which had been employed raking the Serapis was the *Alliance*, of 40 guns and three hundred men. The former, which had lost no less than 306 men killed and wounded, was so disabled that soon after the action the crew were obliged to quit her. The loss of the *Serapis* was forty-nine killed and sixty-eight wounded.

The battle between the *Countess of Scarborough* and her opponent, the *Pallas*, a French frigate of 32 guns and 275 men, was fought with great obstinacy, but after a contest of two hours, Captain Piercy, perceiving the second frigate bearing down on him, was compelled to strike his flag, with the loss of forty-seven killed and twenty wounded. Captain Pearson was rewarded for his gallantry by knighthood, and received the post of Lieutenant-Governor of Greenwich Hospital.

On the 6th October following, the *Quebec*, 32 guns, Captain Farmer, and the *Rambler*, cutter, Lieutenant George, fell in with a large French frigate and a cutter to the south-west of Ushant. The frigate, which proved to be the *Surveillante*, of 40 guns opened fire on the *Quebec* long before she could do any execution, while the latter reserved her fire till she was within point-blank range of the enemy. In the meantime the *Rambler*, cutter, stood in between the frigate and the French cutter, in order, if possible, to cut the latter off; the action between these continued for nearly three hours, when the enemy, taking advantage of the damage she had done to the masts and rigging of the *Rambler*, made sail and bore away. The engagement between the two frigates lasted three hours and a half, and was fought with such obstinacy on both sides that, at the end of that time, both ships were dismasted, and lay like complete wrecks on the water. The sails of the *Quebec*, which came down with her masts, not having been cleared away, took fire, and the ship was soon in flames, which spread in every direction till, about six in the evening, she blew up, with her colours flying, when her captain and most of her crew perished with her.

As soon as Lieutenant George saw the condition of the *Quebec* he endeavoured to make sail towards her, in order that he might assist in extinguishing the flames, or, if that were impracticable, save the crew; but his little vessel, having suffered severely, and being considerably to leeward, with little wind and a great swell, he was in a great measure unable to accomplish his object. He despatched, indeed, the boat of the cutter, but the guns of the *Quebec* going off as the flames reached them, the boat's crew were afraid to approach her as often as they could have wished. Several of the men of the *Quebec* were also saved by the French frigate, and they bore testimony to the kindness with which they were treated. When it is considered that the enemy's ship, at the time she received on board such of the crew of the *Quebec* as could be saved, was a complete wreck, and that the majority of her men were either killed or wounded, great credit is due to them for their humanity, and it is worthy of mention that the French captain, though dying, expressed with his last breath his satisfaction in having had such an opportunity for the exercise of humanity.

The year 1780 was entered upon by this country with small prospects of success, as regarded the war with our refractory colonists, while the English people were smarting under the disgrace of seeing the combined fleets of France and Spain actually sail up the Channel and threaten Plymouth. The time was one of unexampled anxiety to the nation, as France, in order to ingratiate herself with Spain, had agreed to assist her in an attack on Gibraltar. The Spaniards, from the very commencement of their war with this country, had sat down before this important fortress, and though no immediate apprehension for its safety was entertained, yet common prudence required that early and effectual efforts should be made for its relief. For this purpose Sir George Rodney, who was going out to take command of the Leeward Islands station, was directed on the way to relieve Gibraltar. He was accompanied by a squadron, under the command of Rear-Admiral Digby, which, when the relief had been accomplished, was to return to England.

On the 27th December, 1779, this great seaman put to sea, with twenty sail-of-the-line and nine frigates, convoying the merchant vessels bound to Portugal and the West Indies, along with the store-ships and victuallers destined for Gibraltar.

Soon after the fleet sailed, it fell in with a convoy bound from St. Sebastian to Cadiz, consisting of fifteen sail of merchantmen, under the protection of a 64-gun ship and four frigates. The whole fleet was taken, and proved to be a rich prize, as several of the merchant vessels belonged to the Royal Company of the Caraccas, and were laden with wheat and other supplies and naval stores. Those with provisions Admiral Rodney took along with him to Gibraltar, while he sent such as were laden with naval stores to England, where they were very much wanted.

Off Cape St. Vincent, on the 16th January, Admiral Rodney fell in with a Spanish squadron of eleven sail-of-the-line, under the command of Don Juan Langara. The enemy used every endeavour to avoid an engagement, and were assisted by their vicinity to the coast, the roughness of the weather, and the time of the year, but Sir George Rodney evinced great skill and adroitness in counteracting their determination. He at first had thrown out a signal for a line of battle abreast, but fearing the enemy might escape, made a signal for a general chase, and that the ships, each as they came up with the enemy, should commence the engagement.

It was very late in the short days of January, and had it not been that the British ships, especially those that were copper-bottomed, sailed remarkably well, the enemy would have got away. But the Spaniards, being more anxious to escape than to fight, fell into considerable confusion, and when they perceived a battle was inevitable, had neither the time nor opportunity to arrange their ships in order of battle. They fought, however, with great spirit, and returned the English fire with considerable effect. The night that succeeded was dark and tempestuous, and the horrors of battle and storm were greatly augmented by the blowing up of the Spanish ship, *San Domingo*, which happened early in the action. Of her crew of 600 men not a soul was saved. The *Bienfaisant*, which was alongside of her at the time of the explosion, very narrowly escaped a similar fate. The Spaniards sought safety in flight, and were pursued during the whole night, and it was cited as a proof of the skill with which the British ships were worked, and the good management of the admiral, that though the action and pursuit continued for upwards of nine hours, the vessels did no damage to each other nor even mistake their own for the ships of the enemy in the darkness. The Spanish flag-ship, of 80 guns, and three of 70 guns were captured, but the former was afterwards retaken; another 70-gun ship that was taken, ran on the breakers and was completely lost, and four of the Spanish fleet escaped into Cadiz more or less damaged.

When day broke, the skill of the British admiral and sailors was put to a severe test, and stood the trial. The victorious fleet was lying near the coast of the enemy, in very stormy weather, many of their own ships considerably damaged, and the prizes requiring attention. A circumstance occurred which must not pass unnoticed, as it was not less honourable to the humanity of the British than to the good faith of the Spaniards. Small-pox of a malignant kind prevailed on board Captain Macbride's ship, and as he had taken the Spanish flag-ship, the *Phœnix*, it was his duty to send men on board to take charge of her, as well as to bring the prisoners into his own ship. Afraid, however, of communicating the infection to the Spaniards, he informed Don Langara of the state in which his crew were, and proposed to place on the *Phœnix* a prize crew of only 100 British sailors who were free from the disorder, under the command and management of the Spaniards, provided that in case of separation, the Spanish admiral would give his word of honour still to consider himself as the prisoner, and his ship as the prize, of the British. This proposal was willingly accepted by Don Langara, and he faithfully adhered to the conditions.

Admiral Rodney continued his course to Gibraltar, whence, having effectually executed the commission on which he was sent, he sailed to the West Indies, while Admiral Digby, with the greater part of the fleet and the Spanish prizes, returned to England. On the 23rd February, this officer discovered and gave chase to a French convoy, consisting of thirteen sail from Brest, bound to the Mauritius, laden chiefly with military and naval stores, and succeeded in capturing three of the convoy and one ship-of-the-line, the remainder owing their escape to the boisterous weather.

In American waters, Savannah held out against every effort of Count D'Estaing to effect its capture, and Vice-Admiral Arbuthnot, in conjunction with Sir Henry Clinton, undertook the reduction of Charlestown. After making, for a fortnight, repeated attempts to pass the bar of the harbour, the fleet ran the gauntlet of the heavy batteries of Fort Moultrie, on Sullivan's Island, and gained possession of the harbour. Siege operations were commenced on the 1st April, 1780, and pushed with vigour, the utmost harmony prevailing between the military and naval commanders. The seamen obtained possession of the works on Sullivan's Island and Fort Moultrie without opposition, and as the investment of the town was complete and there was no chance of relief, General Lincoln capitulated, and Charlestown became one of the few important conquests effected by the British during the war.

In the month of April, Commodore Cornwallis engaged successfully a superior French squadron. While cruising off the Jamaica station in the *Lion*, 64, in company with the *Bristol*, 50, and *James*, 44, he was observed and chased by De la Motte Piquet with four 74-gun ships and two frigates, and after a running fight, which lasted all night, the *James* was so much disabled that her two consorts bore up to her assistance. This brought on a general engagement, in which, though greatly superior in force, the enemy suffered so much, that they were compelled to lie to and refit. On renewing the pursuit, the *Ruby*, 64, and two frigates hove in sight, when the French squadron sought safety in flight.

About this time Admiral George Rodney succeeded in engaging the French fleet under De Guichen. Rodney had arrived at St. Lucia on the 27th March, and hearing that the French admiral had appeared off the island, determined to bring matters to an issue between them. On the 15th April, De Guichen slipped out of Fort Royal Bay, in Martinique, with 23 sail-of-the-line and four frigates, which were sighted on the following day by the British admiral, who threw out the signal for a general chase. At sunset he came up with the enemy, and formed his fleet in a line of battle ahead, with two frigates between him and his adversary, to watch his movements. At daylight on the 17th, De Guichen, seeing no prospect of eluding his persistent foe, also formed in line of battle on the same tack, as Rodney by his skilful manœuvres had gained the weather-gage, and was thus enabled to choose his own mode and time of attack. Just as the fleets were about to engage, the French admiral, perceiving that his rear was to be the object of attack, wore his fleet to the port tack, which compelled Rodney to place his ships in the position they had before occupied, line of battle ahead on the starboard tack with two cables length (480 yards) between each ship.

When the fleets bore down to commence the engagement, they were parallel to each other, and shortly before one o'clock some of the headmost ships of the British fleet brought the enemy to action, and nearly at the same time Admiral Rodney, in the *Sandwich*, 90, began the battle in the centre. This ship was fought with so much skill and gallantry that she soon drove three of the enemy's fleet out of the line, when Admiral

De Guichen, in the *Couronne*, a ship of the same force as the *Sandwich*, supported by the *Fendant* and *Triomphant*, bore up against her; notwithstanding the great inequality of force, the *Sandwich* not only kept her station, but compelled the three ships of the enemy to retire, thus leaving the centre completely broken. The defeat of the French would have been more complete had not Captain Bateman, of the *Yarmouth*, and Carkit, of the *Stirling Castle*, and other ships of the van division, mistaking the signals of the admiral, bore away so far that the British van was at a great distance from the centre. Admiral Rodney, when he perceived that his fleet was separating, signalled them to keep closer, but not being able to effect this, was obliged to suffer a victory, apparently within his reach, to pass from him. The action continued till about four o'clock, when the French fleet bore away before the wind, and the British not being in a condition to chase, the firing ceased.

Admiral Rodney was by no means pleased with the conduct of some of his captains in this engagement, and in his public despatches complained that his signals had not been obeyed. The *Sandwich*, and the flagship of Admiral Rowley, commanding the rear division, who well supported the commander-in-chief, suffered most, and the *Cornwall* and *Trident* also lost many men, the total British loss being 120 killed and 362 wounded, and that of the enemy, 158 and 820 respectively. Captain Corbett, who, as first lieutenant of the *Monument*, had fought that ship in her memorable action with the *Foudroyant*, after Captain Gardiner's death, and Captain Bateman were brought to a court-martial, and the latter was dismissed the service.

After refitting, the rival fleets were soon again at sea, and on the 20th April Rodney, sighting the enemy, made the signal for a general chase, which continued for three days, but the French ships sailed so much better than ours that they were enabled to reach the shelter of the forts and batteries of Basseterre, in the island of Guadaloupe. Admiral Rodney, suspecting that their ulterior object was to regain Martinique, directed his course thither; but, after waiting some time, the condition of his ships obliged him to retire to St. Lucia. Here he heard that the enemy were at sea, and having put his fleet into good condition, again set sail, and on the 10th May perceived them a few leagues to windward. The French, as before, seemed determined to avoid coming to an engagement, and from their ships being so much cleaner than the British, they were enabled for several days to bear down nearly close on them, then haul their wind and retire beyond the reach of our squadron.

Rodney, however, by a shift of wind was on one occasion enabled to bring on a partial engagement. The van of the British fleet, led on by Captain Bowyer, about seven in the evening reached their centre, and for a considerable time he sustained the fire of several of their ships, till he was supported by the *Conqueror*, Captain Rowley.

The two fleets still continued in sight of each other, but nothing material happened till the 19th, when the British admiral made another skilful effort to gain the wind; although this was not completely successful, yet it brought the two fleets so close together, that the French, in order to preserve their rear, were obliged to hazard a partial engagement. Accordingly they bore across the British line, keeping up a heavy cannonade, but at too great a distance to be effective, or to bring on a general battle. As soon as they had effected the escape of their rear, the whole fleet bore away, with all the sail they could carry. In these two actions the British loss amounted to 68 slain and 293 wounded, of which number the *Albion*, Captain Bowyer's ship, had 20 killed and 123 wounded.

On the 22nd, Admiral Rodney arrived with his fleet in Carlisle Bay, in the island of Barbados, where he first heard of the declaration of war against Spain, and that a fleet of that nation had already sailed from Cadiz for the West Indies. In consequence of this intelligence, he despatched frigates to give him the earliest notice of their approach, but they succeeded in effecting a junction with the French fleet under De Guichen. On hearing of this, he sailed with his whole force to St. Lucia, where he placed his squadron so as most effectually to resist any attempt they might make. The allied fleet did not, however, venture to attack him, but in the beginning of July, having left Martinique, separated, the French proceeding to Cape François, and the Spaniards to the Havannah.

Admiral Rodney, soon after this, having been reinforced with several ships from England, under Commodore Walsingham, despatched him and Rear-Admiral Rowley with ten sail-of-the-line to Jamaica, and proceeded himself with ten ships and a frigate to New York, whence he returned to St. Kitts on the 18th December.

The West Indies this year suffered most severely from a hurricane, which especially desolated Barbados, Martinique, and Jamaica. On the Leeward Islands station, the *Vengeance*, 74, sustained great damage in the harbour of St. Lucia, the *Ajax* and *Montague* were forced out to sea from the same harbour, and were exposed to great danger, and the *Egmont* and *Endymion* were dismasted and took refuge in Jamaica. Two ships foundered at sea with all hands, two were wrecked on Martinique, and one on St. Lucia, and only a few men were saved from each ship; besides other ships of war were considerably damaged.

On the Jamaica station, the loss sustained by the British fleet was unprecedented. Sir Peter Parker in command had detached a considerable part of his squadron, under Admiral Rowley and Commodore Walsingham, to convoy a fleet of merchantmen through the Gulf of Mexico. Walsingham proceeded on to Europe with the fleet, but Rowley, with the *Thunderer, Hector, Berwick, Ruby, Trident, Stirling Castle,* and *Bristol,* having seen them safe through the Gulf, steered, according to orders, for Cape François. About midnight on the 5th October, the wind blew a perfect hurricane. The *Thunderer* foundered, the *Grafton* was dismasted, her tiller snapped in two, and five of her guns broke loose; and in this dreadful situation she survived the storm only by the exertions of her crew. The *Trident, Ruby,* and *Bristol* suffered nearly in an equal degree. Scarcely had the crews refitted their ships before they encountered another gale on the 16th, but after suffering great hardships, reached Port Royal on the 26th October. The *Berwick* was so much damaged that the captain bore up for England; and the *Stirling Castle* struck on some rocks off the coast of Hispaniola, and went to pieces during the night. The *Phœnix* frigate was also wrecked off the island of Cuba, the *Scarborough* frigate and the *Victor* and *Barbadoes,* sloops-of-war, foundered, and all their crews perished, and the *Ulysses* and *Pomona* reached Jamaica with the loss of their masts, and several of their guns thrown overboard to lighten the ships.

Since the commencement of hostilities with the combined powers, England had captured as many merchant vessels as she had lost, but in 1780 the balance was decidedly against this country. Early in the year a French squadron of eleven sail, under De Bousset, joined a Spanish fleet at Cadiz, and fell in off Cape Finisterre with the outward bound East and West India fleets, consisting of five large ships belonging to the East India Company, eighteen vessels laden with provisions and stores of all descriptions for the use of the fleet and garrisons in the West Indies, and carrying a regiment of foot for Jamaica, and 40 merchant ships for different parts of the West Indies. This numerous and valuable fleet was under the convoy of the *Ramillies,* 74, Captain Moutray, and the *Thetis* and *Southampton,* frigates. When the combined squadron was first discovered, Captain Moutray, supposing them to be neutral merchant vessels, stood on, but on discovering his mistake, made the signal for the merchantmen to haul their wind, the *Ramillies* taking the lead. This signal, however, which might have saved a great part of the convoy, was imperfectly obeyed, and many of the merchant ships bore away, endeavouring to escape the danger by that means. The consequence of this disobedience of orders was that, on the morning of the 9th August, the convoy found themselves in the middle of the enemy's squadron, to which they became an easy prey. Out of the 63 vessels of which the convoy was composed, only two store-ships and six merchantmen escaped by obeying the signals, and following the track of the men-of-war; the value of those which were captured being estimated at a million and a half sterling, and the number of prisoners taken amounting to 2,865.

A great outcry arose against Captain Moutray, though he had done all in his power to save his convoy after he discovered the nationality of the strange fleet. He was brought to a court-martial at Jamaica, and sentenced to be suspended from the command of his ship, but a few months later he was appointed to the *Edgar*, 74.

Notwithstanding the disastrous character of this war, the prowess of British seamen was displayed in many actions between single ships or small squadrons. On the 15th June the *Apollo*, frigate, Captain Powell, engaged near Ostend the *Stanislas*, mounting 26 guns, and after a two hours' engagement—during which Captain Powell was killed, when the command was assumed by Lieutenant Pellew, a famous name in the annals of the Revolutionary War—the enemy sought safety by running into shoal water. A few miles from Ostend she got aground and would have been a prize to the *Apollo*, but her commander claimed the protection of a neutral power.

On the 10th August the *Flora*, 36, Captain Williams, sighted near Ushant a large ship and cutter, and soon after five brought the former to action. At the end of an hour, the wheel of the *Flora* being shot away, and nearly the whole of her rigging cut to pieces, she fell on board of the enemy, and continued the battle for fifteen minutes, causing great havoc on her decks. The Frenchmen were unable to bear this mode of fighting, and deserting their guns, made a desperate attempt to board the *Flora*, in which, however, they were repulsed, and the *Flora's* men, having boarded in their turn, drove the enemy from their quarters, and struck her colours. The French frigate proved to be *La Nymphe*, commanded by the Chevalier De Romain, pierced for 40 guns, but mounting only 32, and carrying 291 men, of whom 63 were killed and 73 wounded. The *Flora* had only nine killed and 27 wounded.

A gallant action performed by a letter-of-marque deserves to be recorded. The *Ellen*, of Bristol, Captain Borrowdale, mounting eighteen 6-pounders, had a crew of 64 people, one half of whom were either boys or landsmen, 16 being trained to serve as marines by an officer who was going as passenger to join his regiment at Jamaica. The *Ellen* sailed on the 14th March, and on the 16th April sighted a vessel, which hoisted Spanish colours, and fired a gun. Captain Borrowdale determined to fight, in which resolve he was seconded by his crew. In order to come quickly to close action, the captain at first showed American colours, and besides the usual charge for the guns, he ordered that a bag of grape-shot should be added. On the enemy bearing down alongside, Captain Borrowdale ordered the American flag to be lowered, and the British ensign to be run up in its place, and poured a broadside into the enemy, accompanied with a well-directed fire from the marines. The effect was instantaneous in clearing the quarter-deck of the enemy, and throwing them into complete confusion. She fell to leeward, and the *Ellen* was thus enabled to bring her lee guns to bear upon her. The enemy now sought to escape, but was pursued by the *Ellen*, which, again coming up with her, poured in another broadside. A running fight was thus maintained for upwards of an hour and a half, when the Spanish vessel, completely disabled, struck her colours. She proved to be a sloop-of-war, mounting 16 six-pounders, and carrying 104 men, of whom seven were killed in the action. The *Ellen* had one man killed and three wounded.

Towards the close of the year 1780, this country added to her enemies by declaring war against Holland, which had been intriguing with our revolted colonies, and Parliament granted supplies for the maintenance of 90,000 seamen and marines, the total amount voted being nearly nine millions sterling.*

Admiral Hyde Parker, commanding in the North Sea, was stationed in the Downs to watch a Dutch fleet with four ships-of-the-line, one of 50 guns, one of 44, and some frigates. Early in July, 1781, Admiral Zoutman, commanding the Dutch squadron of seven ships-of-the-line, ten frigates, and five sloops, sailed from the Texel with a convoy of merchantmen, and Admiral Parker, who was reinforced by Commodore Stewart, with the *Berwick*, 74, and *Tartar* and *Belle Poule*, frigates, encountered the enemy at daybreak on the 5th August, near the Dogger Bank. The British admiral, who had the weather-gage, after signalling the merchantmen under his protection to make the best of their way under the protection of the *Tartar*, made a signal for a line of battle

* The squadrons at sea were commanded by the following admirals:—In the Channel Fleet, Vice-Admiral Darby in the *Britannia*, 100, Rear-Admiral Digby in the *Prince George*, 98, Rear-Admiral Sir J. Ross in the *Royal George*, 100, and Rear-Admiral Kempenfeldt in the *Victory*, 100, from which ship he later shifted his flag to the *Royal George*. In the North Sea, Vice-Admiral Hyde Parker, in the *Fortitude*, 74, was the flag-officer. In North America, there were Vice-Admiral Arbuthnot in the *Royal Oak*, 74, and Rear-Admiral Graves in the *London*, 98. Off the coast of Newfoundland, Rear-Admiral Edwards commanded in the *Portland*, of 50 guns. In the Leeward Islands there were Admiral Sir George Rodney in the *Formidable*, of 98 guns, Rear-Admiral Sir Samuel Hood in the *Barfleur*, 98, Rear-Admiral Drake in the *Princessa*, 76, and Commodore Affleck in the *Bedford*, 74. On the Jamaica Station was Vice-Admiral Sir Peter Parker; and Commodore Johnstone hoisted his flag in the *Romney*, of 50 guns, to sail on an expedition to the Cape, while Vice-Admiral Sir Edward Hughes was dispatched to the East Indies in the *Superb*, 74.

abreast in order to engage Admiral Zoutman, who seemed nothing loth to come to close quarters, but directing his convoy to "lie to" a little to leeward of his ships-of-war, formed the latter on the port tack. The British fleet bore down on the enemy, and about eight o'clock arrived within range, without having received a shot from the Dutch ships, which might have raked them with effect.

The first ship on our side to engage was the *Berwick*, but she was soon obliged to quit the line in consequence of the loss of her mizen top-mast; though in a short time she once more got into action with the van ship of the enemy. The *Dolphin* also was compelled to make sail and quit the line, in order to weather the van of the Dutch squadron, and the *Buffalo* was incapable, from the damage she received early in the engagement, to bear down and close with her opponent. This mishap considerably deranged the van of the British line, while the van of the enemy having suffered very little, Admiral Parker did not find himself in a condition to prevent them from bearing away unmolested. The cannonade continued without intermission for three hours and forty minutes, and both sides displayed great obstinacy and spirit.

The Dutch had greater weight of metal, and several frigates of a large size, particularly the American frigate, *Charlestown*, of 32 guns, mostly 32-pounders, which took an effective part in the engagement. At 12 o'clock, when Admiral Parker hauled down the signal for battle, the ships on both sides were so completely unmanageable that the utmost efforts of their respective crews could not keep them within the necessary distance to continue the battle. It was observed that the English ships were principally damaged in their masts and rigging, while the Dutch suffered chiefly in their hulls. The *Hollandia*, 64, went down during the night after the battle so suddenly that her crew were obliged to abandon her without bringing off their wounded shipmates. As she sunk in shallow water her pennant was discovered and taken off the next morning as a trophy by one of the English frigates.

The British loss in the action was 104 killed and 339 wounded, of which the *Fortitude* contributed 20 and 67 respectively. The Dutch casualties were said to number 1,100, but another account placed it at 142 killed and 403 wounded. Both sides claimed the victory, which can be awarded to neither of the combatants, but the Dutch dimmed the laurels they undoubtedly gained by their gasconading account of the action. Admiral Parker was much dissatisfied with the condition of the ships with which he was expected to do battle with so doughty a foe as the Dutch, and when the king, as a special mark of distinction, paid him a visit on board his flagship at the Nore, the veteran admiral is said to have remarked to his Majesty that "he wished him younger officers, and better ships. He was grown too old for the service."

Soon after Admiral Rodney returned from the West Indies, he determined, in conjunction with General Vaughan, to attempt the capture of St. Vincent. But it was found that the enemy was well prepared to receive them, and the troops which had already been landed, were re-embarked, and the combined expedition proceeded to the Dutch island of St. Eustatius, which fell into their hands without resistance, and afforded booty of no less value than three millions sterling, besides a 38-gun frigate, five smaller vessels, and one hundred and fifty merchantmen, many with cargoes of great value.

Admiral Rodney, hearing that a richly-laden fleet had sailed a few days before his arrival from Europe, under convoy of a single ship-of-war, despatched Captain Reynolds with the *Monarch*, *Panther*, and *Sybil* in pursuit, which overtook the Dutch ships and captured the whole of them. The island of St. Eustatius was suffered to be surprised later on in the year by a body of French troops, but the Dutch colonies of Demerara and Essequibo were captured without opposition, only, however, to relapse to their former possessors a little later.

A 38-GUN FRIGATE, ABOUT 1770

CHAPTER II.

Sir Samuel Hood's Partial Engagements with the French Fleet off Martinique on the 29th and 30th April, 1781—Arbuthnot's Action off the Virginian Coast with a French Squadron—Repulse of De Suffren's Attack on Commodore Johnstone's Squadron in the Cape de Verde Islands—Frigate Actions in the year 1781—Foundering of the *Royal George*—Loss of Minorca—Relief of Gibraltar by Sir George Rodney—Sir Samuel Hood's Partial Action with the Count de Grasse—Loss of St. Kitts and other West India Islands—Sir George Rodney's Great Victory over the Count de Grasse on the 12th April, 1782—Frigate Actions in 1782—The Naval War in the East Indies—Five Desperate but Indecisive Engagements between Sir Edward Hughes and Admiral De Suffren—Conclusion of Peace.

THE French Ministry, having determined to carry on an aggressive war in the East and West Indies, and assist the American colonists, despatched Count de Grasse on the 22nd March, 1781, from Brest, with a fleet of twenty-five sail-of-the-line, of which twenty proceeded direct to Martinique with a convoy of over three hundred sail, merchantmen and transports, carrying 6,000 troops, the remaining five, under De Suffren, sailing to the East Indies.

Sir George Rodney, anxious to prevent a junction between De Grasse's fleet and the squadron of eight ships already in the West Indies, despatched Sir Samuel Hood with seventeen sail-of-the-line to cruise off Fort Royal Bay, in Martinique, retaining only at St. Eustatius his flagship, the *Sandwich*, 90, and the *Triumph*, 74. On the 29th April, Admiral Hood sighted the French fleet drawn up in line of battle ahead, to protect the convoy while entering Fort Royal, and made an attempt to bring them to action, which, however, he was unable to effect, owing to their having the advantage of the weather-gage. Count de Grasse declined the challenge, and a partial engagement at long range took place, though without result. The loss of the British fleet in this affair was only 36 killed and 161 wounded. On the following day, Rodney attempted to bring the enemy to close action, and nearly succeeded by his skilful measures in doing so, but some of his ships had been disabled by the long-range firing of the preceding day, and ultimately he bore up for Antigua, when the *Torbay*, having fallen astern, received considerable damage before she could be relieved.

The French military and naval commanders, taking advantage of their numerical superiority, inflicted great injury on British interests in the West India Islands. Though beaten off at St. Lucia, they were able to subjugate Tobago, after which De Grasse, having escorted a convoy on its return to Europe, sailed to the Chesapeake to assist the American colonists, whither he was followed by Sir Samuel Hood, who had assumed command of the fleet on the return of Sir George Rodney to England on sick leave.

Meanwhile Admiral Arbuthnot, commanding on the American station, had quitted Long Island to reconnoitre the French squadron in Newport Harbour, Rhode Island, but encountering very heavy weather, in which one of his ships was lost and another quite crippled, he returned to his old station off the west coast of Long Island. Having refitted his ships, Arbuthnot sailed in pursuit of Admiral De Barras, who had left Newport on the 10th April, and on the 16th one of his look-out frigates reported that she had sighted the French squadron, consisting of eight ships-of-the-line and three frigates, steering for the Capes of Virginia.

That afternoon the rival fleets had neared one another, and by 2.30 the British van and centre were engaged, and succeeded in breaking the French line, which, however, wore ship and formed line again on the other tack. Owing to a thick haze, Admiral Arbuthnot was unable to continue the action, but he had gained his point, and the French admiral returned to his former anchorage at Newport, in Rhode Island. In this action the British ships which chiefly suffered were those in the van, the *Robust, Europe,* and *President*. Early in July, Admiral Arbuthnot resigned the command and returned to England, leaving Admiral Graves in charge of the fleet on the American coast.

Sir Samuel Hood arrived off the Chesapeake on the 25th August, with fourteen line-of-battle ships and some frigates, and three days later anchored at New York. On the same day Admiral Graves, who assumed command of the united British fleet, learned that De Barras had sailed to the southward to effect a junction with Count de Grasse, and as it was of cardinal importance to prevent this, he sailed in pursuit of him. On the 5th September, the French fleet, consisting of twenty-four ships-of-the-line, were sighted at anchor near Cape Henry, but slipping their cables, they stood out to sea. Though inferior in strength by five ships, Graves and Hood made ready to accept battle, but the French commander-in-chief declined the challenge, as his main object was to assist the American cause by retaining possession of the mouths of the Chesapeake.

A partial engagement, however, ensued, and the rear division, under Admiral Drake, severely handled some ships of De Grasse's command. Several of the English ships were damaged in the rigging, but the loss in killed and wounded was only 236, while the enemy owned to having 700 casualties. But the engagement was indecisive and only partial, as Sir Samuel Hood's division was unable to participate. De Grasse, nevertheless, achieved his purpose and enabled the French troops from Rhode Island, under the Count of Rochambeau and Lafayette, to be landed to assist in the investment of the British lines at Yorktown, the capitulation of which by Lord Cornwallis dealt the death blow to the cause of England.

In March of the following year, Lord North's Ministry, of which Lord Hawke and the Earl of Sandwich had been the successive heads of the Admiralty, resigned, and the Marquis of Rockingham assumed power, with Mr. Fox (who had been the energetic promoter of peace with the revolted Colonies), as Secretary of State, and Admiral Keppel as First Lord of the Admiralty; and the latter remained in office in Lord Shelburne's Administration, which came into power in the following July, when Mr. William Pitt, son of the Great Commoner, and not less great than his father, became Chancellor of the Exchequer. The "pilot who weathered the storm" of the French Revolution, was at the time only twenty-three years of age, and remained in office until his death in 1806, after the glorious victory of Trafalgar and the disastrous Austrian defeat at Austerlitz.

We have mentioned that Admiral de Suffren, certainly one of the best and most successful officers the French Navy has produced, sailed from Brest, in company with Count de Grasse, in command of four sail-of-the-line, a 64-gun ship, and some frigates. His destination was the Cape of Good Hope, then in possession of the Dutch, against which, as the French Ministry learned from a spy, the British Government had despatched Commodore Johnstone with a squadron consisting of one 74-gun ship, one 64, three ships of 50 guns, three frigates, and several armed transports, having troops on board, under General Meadows, intended for India. Commodore Johnstone sailed from Spithead on the 13th March, 1781, and nine days later De Suffren quitted Brest in pursuit. The British squadron arrived at Port Praya, in the Cape de Verde Islands, belonging to the Portuguese Government, and Commodore Johnstone, being unsuspicious of danger, was ashore with 1,500 men from his ships, when suddenly, on the 16th April, the French admiral, regardless of the immunities of a neutral port, made his appearance off the island, and proceeded to attack the British squadron. Separating from his convoy, De Suffren soon reached the centre of the British line, his ships firing broadsides on each ship as they passed, and successively dropping anchor and taking up their stations. The engagement continued for an hour and a half, and, though taken at a disadvantage, the British ships more than held their own, and at length De Suffren, followed by the rest of his squadron, cut his cable and stood out to sea, pursued by the enemy he had made certain of beating. The armed ships of the East India Company took part in the action, and materially contributed to the success achieved.

Commodore Johnstone was unable to overtake the enemy, and pursued his course for the Cape. On arriving at Table Bay he found that De Suffren had preceded him, and decided that it would be hopeless to attack the settlement with the considerable reinforcements that had been landed. Having, however, received information that some Dutch ships were lying at anchor in Saldanha Bay, to the northward of Cape Town, Commodore Johnstone made his way thither with great promptitude, and surprised the enemy before they had time either to escape or destroy the ships. The crews, cutting their cables, ran them ashore, and tried to set them on fire, but only succeeded in destroying one, which they blew up. The British sailors managed, by dint of great exertions, to float the remaining ships, which carried between twenty and twenty-four guns each, and were of 1,000 and 1,100 tons burden. Commodore Johnstone now returned to England with a portion of his squadron, and despatched three ships to reinforce Sir Edward Hughes in Indian waters.

Of actions between single ships worthy of chronicle in the year 1781, two are of special merit. The *Nonsuch*, 64, Captain Sir James Wallace, the look-out ship of Admiral Darby's squadron, on her return from revictualling Gibraltar, sighted, on the 14th May, and gave chase to, a large ship which proved to be the *Actif*, 74. On getting alongside of the enemy at 10.30 P.M., the latter fired a broadside. The *Nonsuch* returned the fire, wore, and raked her; and the action continued with great vigour and without interruption on both sides for an hour and a half, during part of which time the ships were aboard each other. The *Actif*, though much superior to the *Nonsuch* in weight of metal, was so greatly cut up that she took the opportunity, when the heads of the two ships were different ways, to make sail with intent to escape. The *Nonsuch* pursued, but owing to the damage she had sustained in her rigging, only got alongside of her at five on the following morning, when Sir James Wallace discovered that his opponent was a ship-of-the-line. Nothing daunted, he renewed the action, which continued till half-past six, when the *Nonsuch* was so much disabled that it was impossible for her to continue the battle; Captain Wallace, therefore, thought proper to haul his wind in order to refit his ship, and the enemy, taking advantage of this, steered for Brest. In this action the *Nonsuch* had 26 killed and 64 wounded.

On the 29th May, the *Flora* and *Crescent*, frigates, being on a cruise off the coast of Barbary, discovered two Dutch frigates, and on the following morning, as soon as each ship had ranged close alongside of her antagonist, a furious action commenced. The *Flora*, Captain Peare Williams, engaged the *Castor*, mounting 32 guns, with 230 men on board, while the *Crescent*, commanded by the Hon. Thomas Pakenham, was opposed to the *Brill*, a frigate of the same force as the *Castor*. After the firing between the two first had continued for two hours and a quarter, the *Castor* struck her colours, having had 22 men killed and 41 wounded, while the loss of the *Flora* was nine killed and 32 wounded.

The *Crescent* was not so fortunate. Her opponent's fire carried away her main and mizen-masts, which, along with the rigging, falling on board the vessel, rendered her unmanageable. In this situation, Captain Pakenham was compelled to strike his colours. This happened a very short time after the other Dutch frigate had yielded, and Captain Williams, relieved from his opponent and perceiving the fate of the *Crescent*, placed his frigate in such a position, that the *Brill* could not take advantage of the capture she had made by boarding the *Crescent*, but judged it prudent to make off with as much sail as she could set. In this severely contested action, the *Crescent* had 26 men killed and 67 wounded. Before Captain Williams was able to reach the Channel with his disabled vessels, he was chased by two large frigates, and, finding it impossible to do more than save his own vessel, was compelled to abandon his prize and the *Crescent* to their fate. A court-martial, according to custom, sat upon Captain Pakenham, who was honourably acquitted, and the court expressed their approval of his conduct on this occasion.

The year 1782, the last of this prolonged and, for England, unfortunate war, was rendered memorable by many important naval events; chief among them being the relief of Gibraltar, Rodney's great victory over the French fleet in the West Indies, and the sanguinary and indecisive actions in the East Indies between Sir Edward Hughes and De Suffren. The year is also rendered memorable by the saddest fatality that had occurred in the Navy since the loss of the *Victory*, Sir John Balchen's flagship.

On the 29th August, the *Royal George*, 100 guns, flag-ship of Rear-Admiral Kempenfeldt, went down at her moorings at Spithead. In order to repair some damage to her copper sheathing, the ship was careened over, and while lying in this position, a sudden squall struck the noble three-decker, and the lower deck ports being open, she rapidly filled and went down. The crew, with many visitors from the shore, were at dinner, and the greater number were lost. Every effort was made by the ships of the fleet to pick up the drowning men, but only Captain Waghorn, two lieutenants, and about 300 people were saved. Admiral Kempenfeldt, most of his officers, and about 900 men perished, and the service experienced a serious catastrophe, not only in the loss of one of the finest ships on the Navy list, but in the death of the admiral, who was regarded as perhaps the most experienced in the art of manœuvring a fleet of any officer then living. Captain Waghorn was tried by court-martial, but honourably acquitted. This great national disaster was the medium of giving to the literature of our country one of the noblest lyrics in our language, and nearly every school-boy knows by heart Cowper's stately verses, commencing.—

> "Toll, toll for the brave,
> For the brave that are no more."

From the time Spain participated in the war against this country, she had been directing her chief efforts for the recovery of Gibraltar and Minorca. An army of 16,000 men, with 109 battering guns and 36 mortars, under the Duke de Crillon, laid siege to the Fort of St. Philip, in the latter island, and General Murray, who held the place with a weak garrison, was at length compelled to surrender, the effectives numbering only 660 out of 2,692 men, originally under his command.

The undivided efforts of Spain were now directed to reduce Gibraltar, the acquisition of which, even more than of Minorca, as forming part of the soil of the country, was the heart-felt desire of every patriotic Spaniard. The siege of this great fortress was commenced by the Spanish army in the summer of 1779, and by the spring of the following year they had constructed numerous batteries, which wrought great destruction in the town, but did little damage to the fortifications. The English Government was alive to the necessity of relieving the garrison, and, on the 13th March, Admiral Darby sailed with the Channel fleet to effect this object, which he achieved with success.

But the Spanish king and nation recognised that now, if ever, was the time to reconquer the historic fortress, when England was struggling with a combination of powerful foes. They redoubled their efforts to capture Gibraltar, and the Duke de Crillon arrived from France with 12,000 choice troops to assist the Spanish army of 30,000 men, and was accompanied by many of the best officers and most distinguished military engineers of both countries, chief among whom was the Chevalier D'Arcon, an officer of original and acknowledged skill in his profession. Assisting the army, which was equipped with all the resources at the disposal of the military art, was a fleet of no less than 47 ships-of-the-line, besides frigates and floating batteries, which were specially fitted to assist in the operations.

But the English garrison, led and inspired by General Elliot, were equally determined to hold the great fortress to the last extremity, and the success with which they carried out this resolve, forms one of the proudest memories of the British army.

The French and Spanish engineers exhausted their ingenuity in their plans and devices for capturing Gibraltar. Ten great ships were cut down and turned into floating bomb-proof batteries, their sides being rendered invulnerable, while 154 brass guns of large calibre were mounted in them, and a novel kind of match was invented by the Chevalier D'Arcon, who claimed for his discovery that it "emulated lightning in the quickness of its consumption and the rapidity of its action." No less than 1,200 pieces of ordnance and 83,000 barrels of powder were collected for the bombardment, and as success was assured, in the belief of the besiegers, the Count D'Artois and the Duke de Bourbon, brother and cousin of the French king, arrived in camp about the middle of August to witness the triumph of the united arms of France and Spain.

General Elliot, meanwhile, did his utmost to thwart the plans and prevent the completion of the works, and on the morning of the 9th September opened a heavy fire, by which the Mahon and another battery were set on fire and destroyed.

But this had no effect in delaying the grand attack, which was opened by the Duke de Crillon on the following day. The Spanish batteries fired daily at the rate of 6,500 shot and 1,080 shells, while the ships co-operated by attacking Europa Point. On the 13th September the floating batteries joined in the attack, taking up a station about 900 yards from the works, and the gun and mortar-boats and bomb-ketches played their part in the terrible bombardment. The gallant defenders were not a whit daunted by the unexampled fire brought to bear on the works, but replied with a spirit and telling accuracy which were rewarded with success. During the afternoon the boasted floating batteries, notwithstanding all that had been done to make them fire and bomb-proof, began to collapse, and the red-hot shot set them ablaze. The squadron of gun-boats, lying under the New Mole, commanded by Commodore Curtis, now commenced a raking fire on the Spanish floating batteries, thus preventing the ships of the enemy's fleet from removing the unfortunate crews, and it was only by the humane exertions of the seamen of the British gun-boats that a great sacrifice of life was averted.

An historian describes the terrible scenes in vivid terms:—"It was not till the morning of the 14th that the whole compass and extent of the defeat of the Spaniards was discovered, or that the efforts of Commodore Curtis in the cause of humanity could be successfully exerted; when daylight appeared the scene was most dreadful. In the midst of the flames great numbers of the enemy were discovered crying out for assistance, while others were seen floating on pieces of timber, liable every moment either to be washed off, or to be destroyed by the shot from the garrison. As soon as the effects of the fire from Gibraltar were clearly seen, and it was put beyond a doubt that the enemy were completely conquered, the firing ceased entirely, every thought, which but a few minutes before had been directed to the destruction of the Spaniards, being now turned to their relief and succour. In a moment it was forgotten that they were enemies, and only remembered by the British that they were suffering fellow-creatures. In a moment, those vessels which had been employed to deal destruction among them were used for the purpose of saving them; and it would be impossible to determine whether the British displayed more intrepidity in their endeavours to save or to destroy. In this sacred and honourable employment, Commodore Curtis and his marine brigade were almost exclusively engaged. It is impossible to describe the exertions they made, the dangers to which they exposed themselves, or the skill which they displayed on this occasion. One instance may, however, be given; they succeeded in dragging out from the holds of the burning ships an officer and 79 men, most dreadfully scorched. It may indeed be said that none but Britons could have defended Gibraltar as it was defended, and none but Britons could have served their enemies in such a dreadful situation.

"At one time apprehension was entertained that Commodore Curtis had fallen a victim to his noble and generous humanity; the boat in which he was employed in saving the unfortunate Spaniards lay close to one of the largest of the battering-ships at the very moment she exploded; for a short period everything was involved in the utmost darkness. General Elliot and all the garrison kept their eyes fixed on the spot, and soon had the happiness to perceive the Commodore's pinnace safe when the smoke was dispelled. The escape, however, was almost miraculous; a large piece of timber struck the boat and made a hole in her bottom, and she was only preserved from instantly sinking by the seamen stuffing their jackets into the hole. Nearly 400 of the enemy were saved from instant and inevitable destruction by means of Commodore Curtis and his brigade of marines; while their loss in the battering vessels alone was estimated at 1,500."

Relief was now at hand. Lord Howe, flying his flag in the *Victory*, Nelson's renowned flagship, which exists to this day in Portsmouth harbour, had been despatched from England in September, with 32 sail-of-the-line and a vast convoy of transports and store-ships. Among his captains were some of the most famous seamen of that or any other age. There were Sir John Jervis, commanding the *Foudroyant*, 74, afterwards Earl St. Vincent; Duncan, the hero of Camperdown, commanding the *Blenheim*; Hotham, the victor of Lissa; Hyde Parker, who held the command at Copenhagen, of which another, the greatest of all, reaped the honours; and Rear-Admiral Alexander Hood, brother of Sir Samuel Hood, who was raised to the peerage as Lord Bridport.

On the afternoon of the 11th October, the *Latona*, frigate, arrived at Gibraltar with the news of succour, and the same evening, the British fleet cast anchor in the Bay. It was fortunate, indeed, they had not arrived on the preceding day, as a gale of wind had thrown the hostile fleet into great disorder, and one ship, the *St. Michael*, 74, was driven ashore under the walls of the town, and her crew of 650 men were made prisoners.

Owing to bad handling by the masters of the transports, twenty-seven out of thirty-one ships missed the anchorage and drove into the Mediterranean, where they were followed by the enemy's fleet, of which forty-two were ships-of-the-line, with the object of capturing them. On observing this, Lord Howe, signalling the convoy to take shelter on the African coast, stood out with his fleet, numbering thirty-two sail-of-the-line, to encounter the enemy, who, however, displayed no disposition to engage. On the 18th, the British admiral succeeded in landing two regiments from the transports, with 1,500 barrels of powder from the fleet, and then, re-passing the Straits, formed in line of battle to engage the enemy. But though to windward, they disregarded the challenge, only maintaining a distant and ineffective cannonade.

During the manœuvres on this occasion, three ships of the British fleet, the *Union*, *Buffalo*, and *Vengeance*, being considerably astern of the rest, Don Louis de Cordova, in the *Santissima Trinadada*, of 120 guns, and a French admiral, supported by ten large ships, bore down with the intention of cutting them off. These vessels reserved their fire till the enemy came within musket shot, when they engaged them with such effect, that their opponents were thrown into confusion. The ship of the Spanish admiral, unwieldy from her great size, was taken completely aback, and obliged to haul her wind and withdraw from the action. As night came on they seemed disposed to renew the attack, but were again so well received, that after a distant cannonade, which lasted about an hour, they sheered off.

Lord Howe is entitled to great credit for achieving the paramount object of relieving Gibraltar, though there were not wanting those who censured him for not using more zealous exertions in bringing the united French and Spanish fleets to action after that event. But his lordship is scarcely justly amenable to this blame, as no object was to be gained by a general action, and he had besides received orders to detach ships to the coast of Ireland and the West Indies. Accordingly, before returning home, he sent six to the former station and eight to the latter.

In the West Indies the Dutch settlements of Demerara and Essequibo were retaken by the French Marquis de Bouilli, who now resolved to make an attempt on St. Kitts. Sir Samuel Hood sailed for Antigua, where he took on board some troops, under General Prescott, and appeared before Basseterre roads, in St. Kitts, whence Count de Grasse issued with his superior fleet to give battle. But he was out-manœuvred by his antagonist, who, drawing him away from his anchorage, possessed himself of it. Incensed at being thus outwitted, De Grasse attacked the rear of the British squadron as they were going into the bay, and on the following day made an onslaught with his whole force, but on both occasions was repulsed with the loss, it is said, of 1,000 killed and wounded, that of the English fleet being 72 killed and 244 wounded. But the Marquis de Bouilli, notwithstanding, pressed the siege of Basseterre, and on the 13th February Governor Shirley was compelled to surrender St. Kitts. The islands of Nevis and Montserrat were also soon captured by the French general, when only Jamaica, Barbados, and Antigua remained of all our West India possessions.

Reversing the order that hitherto obtained in our history, the French Navy was dominant in the West Indies, and Count de Grasse and the Marquis de Bouilli made preparations to wrest from us the island of Jamaica, to effect which the Spanish commander in Cuba offered the co-operation of his troops, while the addition of the ships of the Spanish marine raised the available naval force to a strength of no less than sixty sail-of-the-line.

Admirals Rodney and Hood effected a junction in order to thwart this expedition, and, being strengthened by the arrival of three more ships-of-the-line from England, resolved to take the initiative, and prevent the French commander-in-chief, who was refitting his ships in Martinique, from joining the Spanish squadron at Cuba, when the fate of the British West India Islands would have been sealed. Without this reinforcement the rival fleets were well-matched, the French admiral having under his command thirty-six sail-of-the-line, and his antagonist two less. The former had, however, according to French custom, considerably stronger crews, and carried nearly 6,000 troops on board, while, on the other hand, the British fleet was in better condition.

On a comparison, therefore, the fleets were not unequally matched, when, at daybreak on the 8th April, Count de Grasse, bearing his flag on board the *Ville de Paris*, of 110 guns and 1,300 men, including soldiers, quitted Fort Royal Bay, with a numerous convoy under his protection, in order to reach the Spanish ports in Cuba. Sir George Rodney, who was ready for sea in St. Lucia, had posted a chain of frigates, of which he had fourteen under his command, to give him notice of the departure of the French fleet, and on hearing that De Grasse had weighed, he signalled his ships to put to sea, and by noon his whole fleet was clear of Gross Islet Bay, thus affording by their smartness and efficiency a good augury for the approaching battle which was to decide the fate of the empire in this part of the world.

Before sunset the fleets came in sight of each other, and De Grasse, perceiving that an action was inevitable, sent away his convoy, and formed his ships in line of battle, as did also Rodney, who continued the pursuit all night. The British van division, commanded by Sir Samuel Hood, favoured by a breeze, neared the enemy on the following morning, while the centre, under the commander-in-chief, and the rear division, under Admiral Drake, were becalmed under the high land of Dominica. It still lay within the power of the French admiral to avoid a conflict, but, doubtless, he was influenced by the unsupported position of Hood's division to attempt its destruction before assistance could be afforded.

At nine in the morning of the 9th April, the engagement began, and soon the British van was hotly engaged with the French fleet. Admiral Hood, in the *Barfleur*, at one time had seven ships firing upon him, and his other ships were also attacked by superior numbers, but animated by the resolve to detain the enemy until the centre and rear could arrive to their assistance, these eight ships maintained the conflict with the greatest gallantry. At length the former felt the influence of the freshening breeze, and the leading ships of the centre arrived on the scene, and were soon followed by Rodney, in the *Formidable*, supported by the *Namur* and *Duke*, all of 90 guns. The French commander-in-chief, now perceiving that it was out of his power to destroy the British van, as the remainder of the fleet were fast approaching, relinquished the attempt and made sail, despatching two of his ships that had suffered most to Guadaloupe. Two of Rodney's ships had also been severely handled, but they were repaired at sea, so that the rival fleets were now equalised as regards numbers. While the damaged ships were refitting, on the night of the 9th April and the following day, the British fleet lay to, and when this was completed, the pursuit was continued, Drake's division being now in the van.

Both fleets were engaged working up the narrow channel between Dominica and Guadaloupe, but on the 11th, when De Grasse had turned the point of the latter island, a fair wind enabled him to gain considerably on his persistent enemy, who was almost out of sight astern. Rodney continued the chase in the hope of being able to overtake the enemy on a change of wind, which is very variable in these latitudes, or, by cutting off two of their ships which were lagging behind, owing to the injuries they had received, to induce De Grasse to return to their succour and thus bring on a general engagement. In this expectation he was successful, for the French admiral, finding that the damaged ships would fall a prey to the fastest sailers of the British van, bore down with his whole fleet to protect them.

So passed the day and night of the 11th April, and at daybreak on the following morning—the British fleet being then on the starboard tack, about five leagues off Prince Rupert's Bay, and the French on the port tack, to windward of the Saintes—Sir George Rodney made the signal for close action, and the van of the British line, led by the *Marlborough*, 74, flag-ship (formed at one cable's length between each ship, instead of two, the usual formation), became closely engaged with the enemy about eight o'clock. As each ship successively came up, she ranged close alongside her opponent, and about eleven, Rodney's and Hood's divisions had closed up with the van, the fleets sailing on parallel lines, but in opposite directions.

About noon the British commander-in-chief resolved to carry into execution a manoeuvre of a novel nature, which has conferred special interest on this battle. Perceiving a break in the enemy's line within three ships of the centre, he directed his flag-captain, Sir Charles Douglas, to keep a close "luff" and steer straight for the opening. Supported by the *Namur*, the *Duke*, and the *Canada*, the *Formidable* bore down under all sail, and passed through the enemy's line; the other ships of his division followed the flagship, and then all wore round, doubling upon the enemy, and thus placing the French van between two fires. As soon as he had "wore ship,"* Rodney signalled his van to tack, by which they gained the weather-gage of the enemy, and thus completed the dis-

---

* In these days of steam, when seamanship is a lost art, it may, perhaps, be necessary to explain to the non-nautical reader that to "wear" ship, the head of the vessel is put away from the wind, and turned round twenty points. This is mostly done in very heavy weather, when there is plenty of sea-room. The opposite of this is "tacking," when the ship's course is changed from one board to the other by bringing her up suddenly into the wind, and thus causing her to fall off on the other tack, turning round twelve points of the compass.

order into which they had been thrown by the breaking of their line. De Grasse made an attempt to reform his line by his van bearing away to leeward, but it was ineffectual, and Hood, whose division had been becalmed all this time, and unable to take part in the action, opportunely came on the scene with his foremost ships, and thus served to render the victory more decisive on the one side, and the ruin greater on the other.

The fighting before the arrival of this welcome reinforcement, had been desperate and close as anything recorded since the Dutch wars of Blake and Van Tromp. Says an old writer:—" The *Canada*, of 74 guns, Captain Cornwallis, took the French *Hector*, of the same force, single handed. Captain Inglefield, in the *Centaur*, of 74 guns, came up from the rear to the attack of the *Cæsar*, of 74 also. Both ships were yet fresh and unhurt, and a most gallant action took place, but though the French captain had evidently much the worse of the combat, he still disdained to yield. Three other ships came up successively, and he bore to be torn almost to pieces by their fire. His courage was inflexible; he is said to have nailed his colours to the mast, and his death could only put an end to the contest. When she struck, her masts went overboard, and she had not a foot of canvas without a shot hole. The *Glorieux* likewise fought nobly, and did not strike till her masts, bowsprit, and ensign were shot away. The English *Ardent*, of 64 guns, which had been taken by the enemy in the beginning of the war, near Plymouth, was now retaken, either by the *Belliqueux*, or the *Bedford*. The *Diadem*, a French 74-gun ship, went down by a single broadside, which some accounts attribute to the *Formidable*, though it has also been said that she was lost in a generous exertion to save her admiral. De Grasse was nobly supported, even after the line was broken, and till the disorder and confusion became irremediable towards evening, by the ships that were near him. His two seconds, the *Languedoc* and *Couronne*, were particularly distinguished, and the former narrowly escaped being taken in her last efforts to extricate the admiral. The *Ville de Paris*, after being already much battered, was closely laid alongside by the *Canada*, and in a desperate action lasting nearly two hours, was reduced almost to a wreck. Captain Cornwallis was so intent on his design upon the French admiral, that, without taking possession of the *Hector*, he left her to be picked up by a frigate, while he pushed on to the *Ville de Paris*. It seems as if De Grasse was determined to sink rather than strike to anyone under an admiral; but he likewise undoubtedly considered the fatal effects which the striking of his flag might produce on the rest of his fleet. Other British ships came up in the heat of the action with the *Canada*, but he still held out. At length Sir Samuel Hood came up in the *Barfleur*, almost at sunset, and poured in a tremendous and destructive fire, which is said to have killed 60 men outright, but Admiral de Grasse, wishing to signalize as much as possible the loss of so fine and favourite a ship, endured the repetition of this fire for about a quarter of an hour longer. He then struck his flag to the *Barfleur*, and surrendered himself to Sir Samuel Hood. It was said that at the time the *Ville de Paris* struck there were but three men left alive and unhurt on the upper deck, and that the Count de Grasse was one of the three."

Long before the French admiral had struck his flag, his fleet had sought refuge in flight, and that they might more easily accomplish their object, they went off before the wind in small squadrons and single ships. They were at first closely pursued, but on the approach of night, Admiral Rodney made the signal of recall.

The British fleet lay under Guadaloupe for three days to repair damages, but on the 17th, Admiral Rodney detached Sir Samuel Hood with those vessels of his division which had suffered the least. On the 19th, five sail of the enemy were perceived endeavouring to effect their escape through the Mona Passage, when the signal for chase was given, and before the French could enter the passage, they were becalmed and overtaken. Captain Goodall, of the *Valiant*, was the first who came up with them, and he laid his ship alongside the *Caton*, of 64 guns, which struck at the first broadside. Without, however, stopping to take possession of her, Goodall pushed on, and attacked the *Jason*, a vessel of the same force as the former, which held out about twenty minutes, and then struck. A frigate of 32 guns and a sloop of 16 were also taken.

The whole loss of the enemy amounted to eight ships; one of these had been sunk, one, the *Cæsar*, blew up after her capture, when a lieutenant and 50 English seamen perished, with about 400 prisoners, and six ships remained in the possession of the conquerors. On board the *Ville de Paris* were found thirty-six chests of money, for the pay of the troops intended for the invasion of Jamaica; and the train of artillery, with the battering cannon that were to have been employed on the same enterprise, was captured in the prizes. The *Ville de Paris*, the only first-rate man-of-war that ever was taken and carried into port by any commander of any nation, had been a present to Louis XIV. from the city of Paris, and was said to have cost £176,000 sterling in her building and equipment, an unheard-of price in those days, when £1,000 a gun was the ordinary charge for a ship-of-the-line.

The exact loss of the French was never known, but they are said to have lost 3,000 killed and about double that number wounded. On board the *Ville de Paris* alone 400 men perished. In the British fleet the loss was also great. Including both actions, on the 9th and 12th, the number of the killed amounted to 267, and of wounded to 766. Among the former was Captain Blair, of the *Anson*, who had distinguished himself the preceding year in the action off the Dogger Bank with the Dutch; and Lord Robert Manners, son of the great Marquis of Granby, was so dangerously wounded that he died on his passage to England. The French commander-in-chief himself acknowledged the superiority of his fleet, according to Rodney, who says, in a letter to his wife, which is published in Mundy's "Life" of the admiral:—"Count de Grasse, who is at this moment sitting in my stern gallery, tells me that he thought his fleet superior to mine, and does so still, though I had two more in number. And I am of his opinion, as his was composed of all large ships, and ten of mine were sixty-fours."

The nation was overjoyed at this great victory, which, moreover, came very seasonably in other respects. On land and even at sea, says Campbell, except where Admiral Rodney was engaged, we had not been able to meet the enemy on any occasion with great and decisive advantage; and in too many instances we had retired from the contest not in the most honourable manner. As the means also of procuring more favourable terms of peace, this victory was hailed with joy and exultation, and the gratitude of the nation towards Admiral Rodney was deeply felt and expressed in warm and glowing language. Within a little more than two years he had given a severe blow to each of our three powerful enemies, the French, Spaniards, and Dutch. He had taken an admiral of each nation, a circumstance perhaps unique; and he had in that time added twelve line-of-battle ships, all taken from the enemy, to the British Navy, and destroyed five more.

The successful admiral was created a peer of Great Britain, Sir Samuel Hood a peer of Ireland, and Rear-Admiral Drake and Commodore Affleck were made baronets. The thanks of both Houses of Parliament were unanimously voted to these and the other officers and the seamen and marines of the fleet, and on the 23rd May a vote of Parliament was passed, by which a monument was ordered to be erected to the memory of Captains Mayne, Blair, and Lord Robert Manners, who had so bravely fallen in defence of their king and country.

Rodney proceeded to Jamaica with the prizes and the ships of the British fleet that were most disabled, leaving Sir Samuel Hood to watch the movements of the enemy, and about the beginning of August, Admiral Pigot, having arrived to take the command on the West India station, Lord Rodney returned to England.

Before, however, surrendering the command, he sent directions to Admiral Graves to proceed home with the prizes, and such of the British fleet as stood most in need of repair. Accordingly that officer sailed from Jamaica about the end of July, but the ships under his command were by no means fit for the voyage they were about to undertake, and were besides incompletely manned. The ships with which Admiral Graves sailed for England were the *Ramillies, Canada,* and *Centaur,* of 74 guns each, and the *Pallas,* a 36-gun frigate; also the French prizes, *Ville de Paris, Glorieux, Hector, Ardent, Jason,* and *Caton.* On the 17th September, he was overtaken by a terrible hurricane, which proved fatal to most of the squadron of nine ships-of-the-line. Only the *Canada* and *Jason* reached England, the *Ardent* was compelled to put back, and the *Caton* to bear away for Halifax; the *Ville de Paris, Ramillies, Centaur, Glorieux,* and *Hector* foundered, and the *Pallas,* frigate, was run ashore at Fayal. It is computed that no fewer than 3,500 men perished on this occasion, and the sufferings of many that were saved were most dreadful, particularly of Captain Inglefield, of the *Centaur,* and ten of his men, who for sixteen days were exposed to fatigue and famine in the midst of the Atlantic, in a small leaky boat, without compass, quadrant or sail, and with provisions sufficient only for a very few days' consumption, and two quarts of water.

Thus not a single trophy, except the *Ardent,* remained of that victory which had been won with so much glory and honour.* The success of the 12th April came too

---

* Admiral Rodney, before he left England to resume his command of the fleet on the West India station, had expressed his determination to put his famous manœuvre of breaking the enemy's line into execution, on the first opportunity that presented itself. There is some difference of opinion whether the perusal of Mr. Clark's celebrated work on Naval Tactics first suggested the idea to Admiral Rodney, or whether the admiral had, previously to his having read that work, entertained the same idea himself; but all authorities agree on this point, that the admiral had determined long before the 12th April so to manœuvre the first time he met the fleet of the enemy as, if possible, to break their line. After the battle he always represented his evolutions to have been directed to that object, and ascribed the victory to their successful execution, and, says Campbell, "he had the magnanimity afterwards to acknowledge that the victory gained over the French fleet on the 12th April, 1782, was fought upon Clark's system."

Mr. Clark, who was a Scotch gentleman of independent fortune, was first led to the consideration of naval tactics in consequence of the investigation which took place respecting Admiral Keppel's engagement in 1778. On this battle he drew up some strictures containing his general ideas on the subject of naval tactics; these he afterwards enlarged and published in the beginning of the year 1782. His essay in the same form was republished in 1790; and the second, third, and fourth parts were added in 1797. The whole was republished entire, with a preface explaining the origin of his discoveries in naval tactics, in the year 1804.

In the first part of his work, Mr. Clark gives a series of demonstrations on the mode of attack from windward. He then proceeds to give the details of the principal naval engagements from that of Admiral Byng in the Mediterranean, in 1756, to Admiral Graves off the Chesapeake on the 5th September, 1781. In Byng's engagement our fleet, having gained the wind of the French, bore down in a slanting line to bring them to battle from van to rear. In Byron's engagement off Grenada on the 6th July, 1779, the British fleet followed nearly the same mode of attack, and the French received and defeated our assault in the same manner, the principal difference being that the enemy did not wait till our ships came close up, but edged away to leeward before we could either bring

late to affect the course of events in America, but it saved the West India Islands and soothed the pride of the nation, which had been grievously wounded by the humiliating disasters suffered on land, and the indecisive character of recent engagements afloat.

Two frigate actions fought in this, the last year of the war, are worthy of mention. On the 29th July, the *Santa Margaritta*, carrying 36 guns and 255 men, commanded by Captain Salter, was cruising near Cape Henry when she descried and gave chase to a strange sail, which proved to be the *Amazone*, French frigate of 36 guns and 301 men. About five o'clock the British frigate was within a cable's length of the enemy, which fired a broadside and wore, but was followed by the *Santa Margaritta*, which, reserving her fire until she was in a position to rake her, poured in a broadside with great effect at pistol-shot range. The action raged with fury on both sides for an hour and a quarter, when the *Amazone* hauled down her flag, her loss in the engagement being seventy killed, including her captain, the Viscount de Montquiote, and nearly eighty wounded, that of the British frigate being only five and seventeen respectively. The *Amazone* was taken in tow, but early on the following morning a hostile squadron of eight ships was sighted, and the prize had to be abandoned.

Another action deserving of notice was that fought off Cape Ferrol, between the *Mediator*, 44, Captain Hon. James Luttrell, and a French squadron of five sail,—the *Eugene*, 36 guns, 130 men; the *Menagere*, 30 guns, and a crew of 212; the *Alexandre*,

their rear into action, or force a close engagement in the van. The consequence of the system thus pursued by the French was, in the action with Admiral Byng, the loss of Fort St. Philip in Minorca; and in the action with Admiral Byron, the capture of the island of Grenada.

Mr. Clark then proves that the French, when, in opposition to their usual practice, they had kept to windward, as in Admiral Arbuthnot's action off the Chesapeake, were careful never to make the attack themselves: this, indeed, is abundantly evident from their manœuvre to gain the leeward in the engagement off the Chesapeake. In the two engagements, also, which they had with Admiral Rodney on the 15th and 19th May, 1780, to the windward of Martinique, in Sir Samuel Hood's engagement on the 17th April, 1781, off the same island, and in Admiral Keppel's, in 1778, off Ushant, the two adverse fleets passed each other on opposite tacks, the French being as desirous to get to leeward as the British were to obtain the weather-gage; the former even passed the fire of the British to obtain this position.

Mr. Clark, having pointed out the great error of our old system of naval tactics, which, when fleet was opposed to fleet, rendered the superior bravery and skill of our seamen of little or no avail, proposed two modes of attack, from windward and from leeward, both founded upon one plain and simple principle, that of directing the attack against the weakest and most vulnerable part of the opposing line, whereas the old system endeavoured to carry the whole fleet by a general attack.

Of the great merit of Mr. Clark's system, says Campbell, in conclusion, this circumstance alone is a sufficient proof, that no naval battle since the year 1782 has ever proved indecisive, and no commander has hesitated to act upon it whenever circumstances would permit. During three successive wars before the time of Rodney, all our naval engagements were indecisive, except, as in the defeat of Conflans by Hawke, when we possessed a superiority of numbers. Perhaps, however, this very instance proves that, under a really great commander like Hawke, genius will carry the day. His victory near Quiberon remains the most crushing and admirable, from a professional point of view, of any achieved by our Navy for more than a century.

24 guns and 102 men; the *Dauphin Royal*, 28 guns and 120 men; and an American brig of 14 guns and 70 men. Captain Luttrell determined to take the offensive so as to cut off and capture part of the squadron, and bore down upon the *Menagere*, stationed near the centre of the enemy's line. Going ahead till she got beyond the *Dauphin Royal*, the *Mediator* tacked and poured a broadside into her and the sternmost ship, which drew out of the line, while the rest stood away under easy sail.

There remained the three still in line, and Captain Luttrell bore down on the *Alexandre*, which he succeeded in cutting off from her consorts. The *Alexandre* struck at the first broadside, when the *Eugene* and *Menagere* made off before the wind under all the canvas they could carry. Having taken the crew out of his prize, Captain Luttrell stood after the *Menagere*, and coming up with her about seven in the evening, renewed the action, when she also struck her colours. The *Eugene* escaped, and as the *Mediator* had drawn very near the Spanish coast in the ardour of pursuit, she stood off, and the *Dauphin Royal* and American brig got away. During the succeeding night, the captain of the *Alexandre*, an American holding the French king's commission, made a plot with his fellow-prisoners to seize the *Mediator*, the signal for which was to be the firing of a gun, but Captain Luttrell, on hearing the explosion, promptly turned his crew out and secured the prisoners.

In the East Indies no less than five actions were fought between the English and French fleets, and unhappily the bloodshed was without result, neither side attaining a decided advantage. The commanders were Sir Edward Hughes and Admiral de Suffren, who had made a bold and almost successful attempt to inflict a defeat on Commodore Johnstone, and was an officer of commanding talent and resources.

On hearing of the rupture with Holland, Admiral Hughes and the officer in command of the British land forces attacked and possessed themselves of Negapatam, and thence sailed for the Dutch settlement of Trincomalee, in the island of Ceylon, which was taken by assault on the 11th January, 1782. Leaving troops in Trincomalee, which from its excellent harbour was an important acquisition, Admiral Hughes sailed for Madras, off which De Suffren appeared on the 15th February with twelve sail-of-the-line. But though having only nine two-decked ships, one of which carried but 50 guns, the British admiral prepared for battle, and placed his ships with springs on their cables, so that their broadsides were brought to bear on an advancing enemy. The French admiral declined to attack under such circumstances, and stood out to sea, upon which Hughes weighed and followed in pursuit with the object of bringing him to action, or at least, capturing some of the numerous transports under his protection. In this he succeeded, upon which the French admiral bore down to protect his convoy, and about four in the afternoon of the 17th February, the hostile fleets came into collision. At that hour De Suffren, favoured by a squall, was enabled to attack with his whole force the five ships of the English centre and rear, their van being at the time becalmed. The former maintained the unequal conflict for about two hours, when the remainder of the British fleet came to their assistance. Soon after this De Suffren hauled his wind and stood to the northward.

It was said that he had suffered considerably, but there can be no doubt he inflicted great loss on two of the English ships, the *Superb* and the *Exeter*. The latter, flying the broad pennant of Commodore King, for a considerable time sustained the concentrated fire of five French ships, and at the close of the action, when she was quite disabled, two more ships attacked her. At this critical time the master asked him for instructions, on which Commodore King replied, "There is nothing to be done but to fight her till she sinks." Fortunately aid came to her before the necessity arose for this alternative, but Captain Reynolds, of this ship, and Captain Stephens, of the *Superb*, together with 32 men were killed, and 95 were wounded.

Sir Edward Hughes repaired damages at Trincomalee, and being reinforced by the *Sultan*, 74, and the *Magnanime*, 64, put to sea to protect a valuable convoy from England, which De Suffren made a determined effort to capture before it had effected a junction with his antagonist.

On the 8th April, the rival fleets came in sight of each other, that of the French having still the advantage in strength, and being cleaner and therefore better able to manœuvre. At the end of the third day, Admiral Hughes changed his course for Trincomalee, distant about 45 miles, which gave De Suffren the advantage of the weather-gage, and on the 12th April, a day rendered memorable by Rodney's great victory over De Grasse, a second action was fought. De Suffren bore down on the British squadron in two divisions, one of five ships on the van, and the other of seven, with his flagship, the *Heros*, 74, leading, on the *Superb*, Hughes' flagship, which was in the centre, and on the *Monmouth* and *Monarch*, astern of her. The *Heros* and another 74-gun ship, the *Orient*, attacked the *Superb* with great determination at pistol-shot range, but were received with such warmth by the latter, that De Suffren shot ahead, leaving others of his ships to take his place, while he engaged the *Monmouth*. This ship, attacked simultaneously by three sail-of-the-line, suffered so severely that she was at length compelled to quit the line, with the loss of her main and mizen-masts, when Sir Edward Hughes, apprehensive that she would drift into shoal water, made the signal for the squadron, which was dangerously near the land, to wear, and, soon after, to anchor. It was now nearly dark and the action came to an end, both sides having suffered severely, the French ships not less than the British, and De Suffren had been compelled to shift his flag to the *Hannibal*.

As soon as the *Monmouth* was fitted with jury-masts, Sir Edward Hughes weighed anchor and proceeded to Trincomalee, and the French admiral made for Batacolo, a Dutch fort in Ceylon, about 20 leagues to the southward. In this indecisive action the *Superb* and *Monmouth* were the greatest sufferers, the latter having no less than 45 killed and 102 wounded, nearly one-third of her crew, while the flagship had two lieutenants, her master, and 62 men killed, and 96 wounded, a greater loss than the *Victory* experienced at Trafalgar. The total casualties were 137 slain and 343 wounded, and that of the French 139 and 364 respectively.

Having refitted his fleet, the British admiral again proceeded in quest of his enemy, whose avowed object was to assist Hyder Ali, the ruler of Mysore, in the deadly conflict in which he was engaged with this country.

On the 24th June he anchored in Negapatam Roads, and on the 5th July the French fleet brought to about eight miles distant. Admiral Hughes, in order that he might not again engage the enemy in a situation where he had not sufficient sea room to manœuvre, got under way, and on the following day gained the wind of the enemy, who were formed in line of battle. De Suffren also weighed, when the British admiral made the signal for his ships to bear down and engage at close quarters. The French, according to their custom, opened fire with the object of disabling their opponents, who, however, reserved their fire until they had nearly taken up their respective positions, when they began a heavy and well-directed cannonade, and soon after noon the action became general all along the line. Everything denoted a decided success for the British fleet, one French ship having quitted the line and another lost her mainmast, when a change of wind threw the English van and rear into confusion, some of the ships being taken aback, and as they had suffered greatly aloft, it was difficult to manœuvre so as to regain their positions. Sir Edward Hughes signalled his fleet to wear in order to chase the enemy, who took advantage of the confusion into which they had been thrown by the change of wind to escape, but the damaged condition of the masts and rigging of most of the British ships obliged him to abandon the design, and at 5.30 he anchored to repair damages, as did also De Suffren, about nine miles to the northward. On the following morning the latter returned to Cuddalore Roads, but the British fleet was in too damaged a condition to pursue.

During the engagement, the *Sévere*, 64, one of the French squadron, had fallen on board the *Sultan* at the time when the sudden change of wind took place, and struck her colours. The captain of the *Sultan* was prevented taking possession of her by reason of his anxiety to obey the signal, just then thrown out, of wearing and joining the admiral. The *Sévere* took advantage of this circumstance, and being separated from the *Sultan*, hoisted her colours again and poured a broadside into the British ship. In consequence of this conduct, so contrary to the rules of naval war, Sir Edward Hughes sent a flag of truce to Monsieur De Suffren demanding the *Sévere* as a lawful prize; to which the French admiral sent an evasive answer, denying that the colours had been actually struck, but maintaining that they had been shot away by accident. In this action which, like the preceding one, was obstinate but indecisive, the British had 77 killed and 233 wounded, and the enemy, 178 killed and 601 wounded.

Sir Edward Hughes, having refitted his fleet, sailed for Trincomalee, but on arriving in the roads, on the night of the 2nd September, was mortified to find the French fleet lying at anchor there, the officer placed in command of the fort having surrendered three days before. De Suffren, though he had gained one of the objects he had in view, displayed no desire to decline a fresh encounter, but gallantly weighed anchor and stood out to sea towards his adversary, who was not less ready to meet him. The relative strength of the fleets was about the same, Admiral Hughes, who had been reinforced by the *Sceptre*, 64, having twelve sail-of-the-line, including one of 50 guns, and four frigates, and the French admiral having under his command fourteen sail-of-the-line, three frigates, and a fireship.

The British admiral drew the enemy as far from Trincomalee as possible, De Suffren following, and about noon the *Worcester*, rear ship of the British fleet, having fallen considerably astern, the action was commenced by two of the enemy's ships falling upon her with great fury. She resisted the attack with equal firmness until the *Monmouth* had time to bear down to her assistance. Meanwhile, five of the French ships, crowding sail, attacked the *Exeter* and *Isis*, the two headmost of the British ships, which maintained the unequal conflict for some time, until the former was compelled to draw out of the line, when the enemy tacked and fired upon the whole of the van as they passed them in succession. The fiercest fighting took place between the centres of the hostile fleets, where the admirals were stationed. The *Superb* and *Heros* engaged in a desperate duel, but about five o'clock the French were again saved from defeat by a sudden shift of wind, when Sir Edward Hughes was compelled to signal his fleet to wear, the enemy performing a similar manœuvre. The engagement was renewed, but about seven o'clock De Suffren steered to the southward, and owing to the disabled condition of the *Superb, Burford, Eagle* and *Monmouth*, the British admiral was unable to follow him.

In this action the French suffered greatly, their loss being 412 killed and 672 wounded, the *Heros* alone having had 140 slain and 240 wounded out of 1,200 men embarked on board her. The British fleet, on the other hand, had only 51 killed and 283 wounded, but among the former were the captains of the *Worcester, Sultan,* and *Isis*.

Sir Edward Hughes sailed for Madras, and thence to Bombay, and De Suffren, who was so displeased with the conduct of some of his captains that he cashiered six of them, made his way to Trincomalee, where, owing to unskilful handling, one of his ships, the *Orient*, 74, went on shore and was lost.

At Bombay Admiral Hughes was joined by Sir Richard Bickerton, with five ships from England, and on his return to the Coromandel Coast encountered for the fifth and last time his gallant antagonist, De Suffren. The British admiral in order to assist the army in the attack on Cuddalore, where the French army, under De Bussy, had taken post, sent five sail thither, and early in June himself proceeded from Madras in search of De Suffren. The fleet was in a condition that rendered it almost incapable of undertaking warlike operations, no less than 1,125 men being ill with scurvy, of whom 605 were in the last stage of that disorder, so that none of the ships under his command could muster more than 80 or 90 seamen fit for duty.

On the 13th June, the French fleet, consisting of fifteen sail-of-the-line and three frigates, was descried to windward, but several days were passed in elaborate manœuvres, and it was not until the 20th of the month that the British admiral could bring his antagonist to action. On perceiving that at length De Suffren had determined to fight, Admiral Hughes signalled to the fleet to form the line of battle ahead, "lying to" to receive the enemy, who bore down upon him before the wind. As usual, the French ships opened fire as soon as they got within range, but appeared disinclined to come to close quarters. Thus the cannonade raged between the fleets for about three hours, when the French hauled their wind and made off, pursued by the British admiral, who on the 22nd found them at anchor off Pondicherry. He did all in his power to induce them to come out, but they declined to leave the protection of the batteries, and ultimately Sir Edward Hughes sailed for Madras, his sick and wounded being greatly in need of relief.

In this engagement the British loss was 99 killed and 431 wounded, but that of the French was never accurately ascertained. Soon after the return of the British fleet to Madras, news was received of the signature of peace, and hostile operations between the rival squadrons and armies ceased.

Seldom, if ever, has a series of five battles been fought between contending fleets with results so indecisive, while the losses incurred were unusually severe. This was due to the seamanlike skill in handling ships displayed by the rival admirals, who were equally well matched in gallantry and knowledge of their profession.

The total loss incurred by the British fleet in these battles was 1,866, of whom the *Superb* had 324 killed and wounded; the *Hero*, 120; the *Sultan*, 117; the *Monmouth*, 183; the *Monarch*, 143; the *Burford*, 155; the *Exeter*, 262; the *Worcester*, 106; the *Magnanime*, 63; the *Eagle*, 69; the *Sceptre*, which only took part in the last two actions, 89; and the *Isis* (a 50-gun ship), 148. The balance of loss was incurred by the ships that joined from England under Sir Richard Bickerton.

The provisional articles of peace between England and her American colonies, whose independence was acknowledged, were signed on the 30th November, 1782, but the ratification was deferred until the conditions of a treaty were agreed upon between France and England, which was done on the 20th January in the succeeding year at Versailles, Spain and Holland being also parties to the treaty.

By the terms of this compact, the limits of the French fishing * off Newfoundland,

---

* By the Treaty of Utrecht and others since concluded, the sovereignty of Great Britain over Newfoundland was fully recognised, and in none of them was mention made of any territorial rights upon the part of France. On that basis the thirteenth article of the treaty of Utrecht was drawn up. It ran thus :—" The Island called Newfoundland, with the adjacent islands, shall from this time forward belong of right wholly to Great Britain, and to that end the town and fortress of Placentia and whatever other places in the said islands are in possession of the French, shall be yielded and given up within seven months from the exchange of the ratifications of this treaty, or sooner if possible, by the Most Christian King to those who have a commission from the Queen of Great Britain for that purpose. Nor shall the most Christian King, his heirs and successors, or any of their subjects, at any time hereafter, lay claim to any right to the said island or islands, or of any part of it or them. Moreover it shall not be lawful for the subjects of France to fortify any place in the said island of Newfoundland, or to erect any building there, besides stages made of boards, and huts necessary and useful for the drying of fish. But it shall be allowed to the subjects of France to catch fish and dry them on land, in that part only, and on no other besides that, of the said island of Newfoundland which stretches from the place called Cape Bona Vista to the northern part of the said island, and from thence, running down by the western side, reaches as far as the point called Point Reche."

This article was affirmed by the Treaty of Paris in 1762, by the Treaty of Versailles in 1783, and by the declaration of George III. (on which the French base their claims of a prohibition to Newfoundland fisherman to settle on a which has been a source of irritation ever since it was sanctioned by the Treaty of Utrecht in 1713, were extended and defined, and the islands of St. Pierre and Miquelon were restored. In the West Indies the island of Tobago was ceded, and St. Lucia given back to the same power, as also Goree and Senegal in West Africa. In Asia, this country restored to France her possessions in Bengal and Orissa, and the seaports of Pondicherry and Mahé were guaranteed to her. In return for these great concessions, France restored to England the West India islands of Grenada, St. Vincent, Dominica, St. Kitts, Nevis, and Montserrat, and acknowledged her settlements on the Gambia. To Spain England ceded Minorca and Florida, while, on the other hand, the Bahamas were restored to her and the right of cutting logwood in Honduras restricted to her subjects. Holland received back Trincomalee and the other places in Ceylon wrested from her, and ceded Negapatam on the Coromandel coast.

These terms placed England in a humiliating position, such as she had long been unaccustomed to fill, but they were perhaps as favourable as she could have expected from the course of the long and disastrous war on which her unwise King and Ministers had embarked with a light heart. Lord Keppel, First Lord of the Admiralty, alone of the Ministry now in power, refused to be a consenting party to an instrument which he considered placed his country in the position of a conquered power, and he resigned his post, and was succeeded by Lord Howe.

The relief to the impoverished taxpayers of the United Kingdom was, however, immediate and great. Whereas, during the last few years of the war, no less than 110,000 seamen and marines were annually voted for the naval service, and of the total supplies, amounting to nineteen millions sterling, granted for the land and sea forces, the latter swallowed up over $6\frac{1}{4}$ millions, we find that for the year 1784, only 26,000 men and £3,154,000 were voted for the Navy, and in 1792, the year before the outbreak of the great Revolutionary War with France, the numbers had sunk to 16,000 men, and the supplies to some £15,000 below two millions; and yet, so excellent were the discipline and *morale* of the service, that within two years the veteran Lord Howe crowned his great career by winning the victory known in our annals as "The Glorious First of June."

certain portion of the land), the only difference being that the limits of French rights named in the last treaty were Cape St. John and Cape Ray; and the French rights were thus confined to that part of the east coast of Newfoundland which lies to the north of Cape St. John, and to the west coast of the island.

CHAPTER III.

Biographical Notices of Distinguished Admirals between 1763 and 1793—Viscount Keppel—Early Service in the *Centurion*—The Expedition to the Barbary Coast and Goree—Keppel's Services under Sir Edward Hawke, and at the Capture of Belleisle and Havannah—His Battle with the French Fleet in July, 1778—Sir John Moore—His Services in the East Indies, under Admiral Hawke, and at the Capture of Guadaloupe—Services of Captain Suckling, Lord Nelson's Uncle—Sir Charles Hardy—His Career in American Waters and under Sir Edward Hawke—Also in Command of the Channel Fleet—Admiral Kempenfeldt in the East Indies and in the Channel—His Death in the *Royal George*—The Services of Sir Piercy Brett—Admiral the Honourable John Byron—Loss of the *Wager*—His Career and Engagement in the West Indies with Admiral D'Estaing, on the 6th July, 1778—Some Account of Sir Hyde Parker and Sir John Lockhart-Ross—The Career of Sir Edward Hughes—Capture of Negapatam and Trincomalee and his Five Indecisive Engagements with the French Fleet—Lord Rodney—His Services under Admiral Knowles, Commodore Fox, Sir Edward Hawke, and Admiral Boscawen—He Relieves Gibraltar—His Action with De Guichen on the 14th April, 1780—Rodney's Great Victory over the Count de Grasse.

ADMIRAL VISCOUNT KEPPEL was a remarkable member of a family that has supplied many scions to the British Navy. One of the most eminent officers of our own day is Admiral of the Fleet the Hon. Sir Harry Keppel, a man whose name in the early years of the reign of Queen Victoria was a household word in the East, as the coadjutor of another famous Englishman, Sir James Brooke, Rajah of Sarawak, in the suppression of the Dyak pirates of Borneo.

Lord Keppel, the subject of this notice, was a son of the second Earl of Albemarle, a nobleman of Dutch extraction, his family having come over, like that of the Duke of Portland, with William III. He was born on the 2nd April, 1725, and entered the navy at the age of thirteen. Young Keppel served under Commodore Anson in the *Centurion*, in his famous voyage round the world, and became a great favourite with his commander, who gave him every opportunity of learning his profession and distinguishing himself, of which the youngster, even then remarkable for his smartness and love of his profession, never failed to avail himself. At the attack on Paita, under Lieutenant (afterwards Sir Piercy) Brett, he was one of the storming party, and had a narrow escape, a musket-ball carrying off the peak of his cap. On the capture of the Spanish galleon, young Keppel behaved with such gallantry that Commodore Anson promoted him to the rank of lieutenant.

On the return of the *Centurion* to England in 1744, Mr. Keppel, when only nineteen years of age, was appointed to the command of a ship-of-war, and in December of the same year he was promoted to the rank of captain, and appointed to the *Sapphire*, frigate. Captain Keppel displayed great activity, and in April, 1745, captured a large French West Indiaman, bound from Martinique to Rochefort, with a valuable cargo. Again in the following May, he captured, off the Irish coast after a long chase, a Spanish privateer. In 1746 we find Captain Keppel in command of the *Maidstone*, 50, which was lost in July of the following year on the French coast, when in chase of a privateer. All the officers and crew of the *Maidstone* were saved, and were well treated by the people of Nantz, when the ship was wrecked. Captain Keppel was acquitted of all blame for his misfortune by a court-martial, and appointed by the Admiralty to the command of the *Anson*, a new ship of 64 guns.

The peace of Aix-la-Chapelle, in 1748, put an end temporarily to his active career, but in 1750, he was despatched with a squadron to the Dey of Algiers, to demand reparation for an outrage perpetrated by a corsair on a British packet-boat, which was plundered of some treasure it was conveying. In this mission he was completely successful, and extracted a treaty of amity from the Dey. In April of the following year, Captain Keppel returned to Algiers with the ratified treaty, and to demand satisfaction for a second act of piracy, which the Algerine ruler promptly accorded. In the ensuing summer he concluded identical treaties with the States of Tunis and Tripoli, and returned to England in August, 1753.

In the following year, Commodore Keppel convoyed a body of troops sent to America, under General Braddock, to check the encroachments of the Indians, made at the instigation of the French, on the Virginian Settlements, and after the defeat of that officer, returned to England. On the declaration of war with France, on account of their unfriendly conduct, Commodore Keppel sailed for the Mediterranean in command of a squadron, but returned in consequence of an epidemic that had broken out in his ships, and took command of another squadron with which he cruised in the Channel.

Captain Keppel was now returned to Parliament as Member for Chichester, but at the general election was brought in for Windsor, which borough he continued to represent till 1780, when he was chosen Member of Parliament for the county of Surrey. The gallant officer served on the court-martial which tried Admiral Byng, and remonstrated from his place in the House of Commons against the conduct of the Admiralty, in suppressing the recommendation to mercy with which the verdict of guilty was accompanied. The Ministry, upon this, brought in a bill to release the members of the court from the oath of secrecy, which the Commons passed, but the Lords, after examining all the members, rejected the measure.

In 1757, Keppel served under Sir Edward Hawke in the successful expedition to Rochefort, and in the following year commanded a squadron in the Channel, and the expedition which captured the French settlement of Goree on the African coast. On the 29th November, the *Litchfield*, 60, and *Somerset*, transport, were driven by stormy weather on the coast of Barbary, when the crews unhappily either perished or were detained in captivity by the Moors. Prosecuting the object of his voyage, with the remainder of his squadron, Commodore Keppel captured the island of Goree, on the 29th December, and soon after returned to England. He was now placed in command of the *Torbay*, and was present at Sir Edward Hawke's victory off Belleisle, where he greatly distinguished himself. At a critical period of the action, after having silenced a line-of-battle ship, Captain Keppel suddenly wore and engaged the *Thesée*, 74, yard-arm to yard-arm, and poured so destructive a fire into her, that she sank within half an hour, carrying down with her most of her crew. After the battle he took command of a squadron to watch the movements of the French fleet, and in January, 1760, removed into the *Valiant*, 74, a new ship, in which he again served under Admiral Hawke in Quiberon Bay.

On the 29th March in the following year, Commodore Keppel sailed from Spithead with ten sail-of-the-line and several frigates and transports, conveying troops under General Hodgson, to make a descent on the French coast. An attempt to land troops at Lamoria Bay, in the island of Belleisle, on the 8th April, resulted in a repulse, but the troops were ultimately disembarked, and the lines that covered the town being captured, the Chevalier De St. Croix surrendered the citadel on the 7th June. Keppel remained at Belleisle for six months and blockaded a French squadron, but encountering a violent storm on the 12th January, his ship was driven off the station, and arrived at Plymouth with five feet of water in her hold, the remainder of his squadron being scattered.

His next service was as second-in-command of the fleet, under Sir George Pocock, at the reduction of Havannah, when his elder brother, the Earl of Albemarle, commanded the troops. Commodore Keppel, with six ships-of-the-line, covered the disembarkation of the army, about six miles to the eastward of Moro, and after a brave and obstinate defence, the castle was surrendered by the Spanish governor on the 14th August, and the commodore received the warmest commendations from the commander-in-chief for his "spirit, activity, and intelligence." In September, while on his way to Jamaica, Keppel captured a fleet of twenty-five merchantmen, together with its convoy, and carried them into Port Royal. On the 21st October, 1762, when in his thirty-sixth year, he was advanced to flag-rank, and in the following year, after the peace, was appointed one of the Commissioners of the Admiralty, an office he occupied for three years.

In 1778 took place the most memorable event in his life, his battle with the French fleet, which gave rise to much recrimination, not only in the Navy, but throughout the country and in Parliament, where he was in Opposition. His enemies called for a judicial investigation, the result of which was a complete justification of the gallant admiral from the aspersions thrown on his professional character by party spite.

Admiral Keppel sailed from Spithead on the 13th June, 1778, with twenty sail-of-the-line and several frigates, to engage the French fleet at Brest, and protect British commerce on the high seas. But when at sea, Keppel learned from the commander of a French schooner, captured by the *Alert*, cutter, Lieutenant Fairfax in command, that the French fleet outnumbered his by several line-of-battle ships, and he felt himself constrained, in view of the great national interests committed to his charge, to avoid an engagement with so superior a force. He says, "That he never in his life felt so deep a melancholy as when he found himself obliged to turn his back on France, and that his country was never put to such a trial as in that retreat, but that it was his firm persuasion that his country was saved by it." He accordingly returned to Portsmouth, and on the 9th July sailed again with twenty-four sail-of-the-line, and a few days later was reinforced by six more ships.

In July took place his action with Count D'Orvilliers, off Ushant, of which we have given an account in a preceding chapter. The engagement was only partial, owing to the conduct of Sir Hugh Palliser, commanding the rear division, who disobeyed the commander-in-chief's signal, and took no part in the action. Then took place the court-martial on charges of "misconduct and neglect of duty," brought against him by Admiral Palliser, which resulted in his acquittal, the court expressing an opinion that he had "behaved as became a judicious, brave, and experienced officer." So great was the enthusiasm aroused in the fleet by this verdict that the ships at Spithead "saluted and cheered," and the East Indiamen at the Motherbank "fired nineteen volleys," while the populace cheered the admiral as he walked from the courthouse to his apartments, preceded by a band and accompanied by the admirals and captains of the fleet. The House of Commons passed a motion of thanks to Admiral

Keppel with only one dissentient voice, and his acquittal was received with enthusiastic demonstrations of approval in the metropolis and throughout the kingdom.

In March, 1782, when Lord Rockingham came into power, Admiral Keppel became First Lord of the Admiralty, and was made a privy councillor, and in the following month he was raised to the peerage. On the death of the Prime Minister in January, 1783, and the formation of Lord Shelburne's short-lived administration, he resigned office, but in April resumed his post on a change of government. But it was for no long period, as early in the following year the younger Pitt came into power, and Lord Keppel finally retired from public life.

His death took place on the 2nd October, 1786, and we cannot better conclude this review of his services and character than by an extract from an eloquent tribute to his worth from the pen of his friend, the great Edmund Burke: "The other day, in looking over some fine portraits, I met with the picture of Lord Keppel. It was painted by an artist worthy of the subject; the excellent friend of that excellent man from their earliest youth, and a common friend of us both, with whom we lived for many years without a moment of coldness, of peevishness, of jealousy, or of jar, to the day of our final separation. I ever looked on Lord Keppel as one of the greatest and best men of his age; and I loved him and cultivated him accordingly. He was much in my heart, and, I believe, I was in his to the very last beat. It was after his trial at Portsmouth, that he gave me this picture. With what zeal and anxious affection, I attended him through that his agony of glory, what part my son,* in the early flush and enthusiasm of his virtue, and the pious passion with which he attached himself to all my connections; with what prodigality we both squandered ourselves, in courting almost every sort of enmity for his sake! I believe he felt, just as I should have felt, such friendship on such an occasion. I partook indeed of this honour, with several of the first, and best, and ablest men in the kingdom, but I was behindhand with none of them; and I am sure, that if, to the eternal disgrace of this nation, and to the total annihilation of every trace of honour and virtue in it, things had taken a different turn from what they did, I should have attended him to the quarter-deck, with no less good-will and more pride, though with far other feelings, than I partook of the general flow of national joy that attended the justice that was done to his virtue."

Admiral Sir John Moore was son of the Earl of Drogheda, his mother being widow

* The untimely death of this young man was a crushing blow to Mr. Burke, and determined him to decline the peerage with the title of Lord Beaconsfield, on which he had fixed.

of the famous seaman, Sir George Rooke, the perusal of whose memoirs had created an enthusiasm for the sea in the mind of the boy, which his mother tried to curb. Young Moore had his wish, and at the early age of ten went to sea, and rapidly passed through the usual grades. He served as lieutenant in the *Namur* under Admiral Matthews, and in May, 1744, when only twenty-six, proceeded to the East Indies in Commodore Barnet's squadron as captain of the *Diamond*. In accordance with a plan formed by Commodore Barnet for intercepting the French ships in their passage from China, the *Diamond* and *Medway*, disguised as Dutchmen, took up their stations in the Straits of Malacca. On their way they captured at Atcheen a large French privateer, and in the Straits a ship from Manilla with gold and silver coins to the value of £73,000. The privateer was afterwards purchased into the service, and commissioned as a 40-gun ship, under the name of the *Medway's Prize*. In March, 1745, on the death of the captain of the *Deptford*, Captain Moore was removed to the command of that ship by Commodore Barnet, who entertained a high opinion of his capacity, and had asked him to accompany the expedition to India. The death of the commodore on the 29th April, 1746, deprived him of a friend, and placed the command in the hands of Captain Peyton, the incompetent commander of the *Medway*, who disgraced the service by his pusillanimity. Captain Moore returned to England in the *Deptford*, which, as well as the *Diamond*, was ordered home.

As captain of the *Devonshire*, 66, he served under Admiral Hawke in the brilliant victory achieved by that officer over the French fleet in October, 1747, when only the *Tonnant* and *Intrepide* escaped capture. Admiral Hawke said of Captain Moore in his official letter that he had "signalized himself greatly," and he was sent home in the *Hector* with the despatches. On his arrival in England, Captain Moore received the usual gratuity of £500 for bringing home the first intelligence of a victory. All the ships captured by Admiral Hawke, except the *Neptune*, were purchased into the Navy.

In 1757 Commodore Moore, flying his broad pennant in the *Cambridge*, commanded a squadron in the West Indies, and, in conjunction with a strong military force, assisted at the attack on the island of Martinique, and the capture of Guadaloupe on the 1st May, 1759, the richest and most important of the French colonies in those seas. After these events, Commodore Moore returned to England in the *Berwick*, 64, and arrived in the Downs in June, 1760. He became a rear-admiral in October of the following year, and was made a baronet for his services, and received the Order of the Bath. But he went no more to sea, and died on the 24th March, 1778, and was buried in the churchyard of St. Martin's in the Fields.

Captain Maurice Suckling merits some notice here, if for no other reason than his relationship to the immortal Nelson, though his own merits deserve recognition. Being without interest, he had no advancement, but remained ten years a lieutenant. On the resumption of hostilities with France, he was appointed, on the 2nd December, 1755, captain of the *Dreadnought*, 60, and sailed for the West Indies, where he found an opportunity for displaying his gallantry. The *Dreadnought* was one of a squadron of three ships, the others being the *Augusta*, 64, Commodore Forrest, and the *Edinburgh*, 60, Captain Langdon, which, on 21st October, 1751, fell in with four French sail-of-the-line and three frigates off Cape François. The squadron put to sea with the object of annihilating the three British ships, but the latter, nothing daunted by the disparity of force, accepted battle. The circumstances of the council of war, convened by Commodore Forrest, which only lasted half a minute, are sufficiently remarkable to be worth mention.

As soon as the enemy's squadron was discovered to be in motion, and the circumstance was communicated by signal to Commodore Forrest, he signalled Captains Suckling and Langdon to come on board him. The boats of both ships reached the *Augusta* together, on opposite sides, so that the two gentlemen arrived on the gangway at the same instant. Commodore Forrest was standing in the centre of the quarter-deck near the barricade. "There are those fellows," said he, "pretending to come out and drive us off the coast; what do you say, shall we meet them or not?" Captain Langdon replied, "Yes"; Captain Suckling, "By all means." "Then go back to your ships," rejoined the commodore, "and clear for action." They did so, and actually returned without either of them having stepped from the gangway on to the quarter-deck of the *Augusta*.

In respect to the part taken in the action by Captain Suckling himself, the *Dreadnought*, getting on the *Intrepide*'s bows, kept her helm hard-a-starboard to rake her, or if she stood on, to fall on board her in the most advantageous manner, but she chose to bear up,* and continued to do so during the action till she became disabled. By this manœuvre those astern were thrown into disorder, from which they never recovered, and when the *Intrepide* was relieved by the *Opiniatre*, the *Greenwich* fell on board her,

---

* To bear up is to put the the helm up, and keep off the course to leeward, and is the same as to bear away, which is applied to the ship.

in confusion, and the *Sceptre* pressing on, the whole of the enemy's ships were furiously cannonaded by the *Edinburgh* and *Augusta*, especially the *Intrepide*, which lay in a very shattered condition, flying a signal for relief.

Captain Suckling returned to England in 1761, and was appointed to the *Lancaster*, 60, employed cruising in the Channel, under Sir Edward Hawke and Sir Thomas Hardy, but the enemy were too cowed and feeble to be brought to action. In 1770, he hoisted his pennant on board the *Raisonable*, 64, and in May of the following year, in the *Triumph*, 74, where his youthful nephew, Horatio Nelson, imbibed the rudiments of the profession of which he became the brightest ornament. This command he held for three years, and was then appointed Comptroller of the Navy, in succession to Sir Hugh Palliser, and was returned to Parliament for the borough of Portsmouth, but died in July, 1778.

Sir Charles Hardy came of a naval family, and his father and grandfather were knighted for their services afloat. After a varied career, we find him in 1745, in command of the *Jersey*, 60, when he had a spirited encounter with the French 74-gun ship, *St. Esprit*, which bore up for Cadiz. In 1755 he was knighted, and in the following year, promoted to flag rank, and had command of the fleet which sailed from New York, of which he was governor, for the reduction of Louisbourg, until the arrival of his superior officer, Vice-Admiral Holbourne. But nothing was done, and Sir Charles Hardy returned with his ships, which had been disabled by a storm. In 1758, he served as second-in-command, under Admiral Boscawen, at the capture of Louisbourg, and displayed great vigilance in blockading the port and preventing the enemy from receiving any supplies. He also destroyed all the ships in the harbour, numbering five sail-of-the-line and seven other men-of-war, except two frigates, which escaped, and commanded the squadron which accompanied General Wolfe in the expedition for destroying the French settlements in the Gulf of St. Lawrence.

In 1759 Sir Charles Hardy served in the Channel under Sir Edward Hawke, but was prevented by the retreat of Conflans' ships, while bearing down to the assistance of the commander-in-chief, from taking part in the encounter with the French fleet. In 1762 he alternated with Hawke in the command of the squadrons stationed off Brest, and in March, 1779, on the resignation of Admiral Keppel, was appointed to the command of the Channel fleet, when the combined Spanish and French squadrons, having eluded his notice, appeared off Plymouth, but returned to their own shores without effecting anything, though in greatly superior force to the British admiral, who thought it expedient to act merely on the defensive.

H. M. S. BRAMBLE.
1st class gunboat.

In May, 1780, Sir Charles Hardy died suddenly at Portsmouth, and the country lost in him an experienced and trusted commander, whose character the historian Charnock sums up as "brave, prudent, gallant and enterprising."

Admiral Richard Kempenfeldt, whose name conjures up memories of a sad national disaster, was the son of a native of Sweden, who served as colonel in the British army, in Queen Anne's reign, and died as Governor of Jersey in that of her successor. Young Kempenfeldt entered the Navy at the age of ten. He first made his mark in 1758, when captain of the *Elizabeth*, 64, forming a portion of the squadron serving in the East Indies, under Commodore Stevens. In the engagement with Count D'Aché, he greatly distinguished himself, and a few weeks after was removed to the *Queensborough*, frigate, for the purpose of convoying to Madras, then besieged by the French, the *Revenge*, Indiaman, having on board a detachment of Colonel Draper's regiment, under the command of Major Monson, a timely reinforcement, which induced Count Lally to raise the siege and retire to Pondicherry.

When Commodore Stevens, on promotion to the rank of rear-admiral, shifted his flag to the *Grafton*, 64, Kempenfeldt accompanied him as his captain, and served in the last action of the war. On Admiral Pocock's return to England, Stevens hoisted his flag in the *Norfolk*, 74, when Kempenfeldt served as his flag-captain, and, on his lamented death, continued in the same capacity with his successor, Admiral Cornish. At the reduction of Manilla, he displayed skill, resolution and despatch, and on taking possession of Cavite, was appointed by Sir William Draper governor of the place, "as a small acknowledgment of the great services which the whole army had received from him, being assured that no one can discharge that trust with more conduct and abilities." Admiral Cornish sent him to England with the despatches, but, in 1762, Captain Kempenfeldt again sailed for India, as captain of the *Norfolk*, and on the conclusion of peace in the following year returned to England with the fleet.

Captain Kempenfeldt commanded the *Buckingham*, 70, in 1770, and on the declaration of war with France, eight years later, was appointed to the *Alexander*, 74, and in the following year to the *Victory*, bearing the flag of Sir Charles Hardy. In 1779, he was promoted to the rank of rear-admiral, but continued, notwithstanding, to serve as captain of the fleet, his skill in naval tactics being only equalled by that of Lord Hawke, while his code of numerical signals made him prominent in that branch of the naval art. He continued to serve as captain of the fleet under Admirals Gray and Darby, until 1781, when he was appointed to an independent command, and, hoisting his flag on board the

Victory, put to sea with twelve sail-of-the-line and five frigates, in search of the Count de Guichen, who had sailed from Brest for the West Indies to join De Grasse.

Kempenfeldt fell in with the enemy, escorting a large convoy, on the 12th December, but found them much stronger than he had been led to expect; the disparity of nineteen sail to twelve being too great to risk an engagement. Having the weather-gage he accompanied the French fleet for some distance, and a favourable opportunity presenting itself, his van bore down on their rear, and he succeeded in capturing the whole of the convoy, numbering fifteen sail, carrying military stores and over 900 troops, and sank four frigates escorting them. The admiral, forming his fleet in two divisions, one towing the captured vessels and the other keeping up a running fight with the enemy, bore up for the English coast under a press of sail, and brought all his prizes in safety into Plymouth. Kempenfeldt proceeded thence to Spithead, and in the spring shifted his flag into the *Royal George*, as second-in-command to Admiral Barrington, and put to sea in order to intercept a French squadron about to sail from Brest for the West Indies. In this the admirals succeeded, and captured two ships-of-the-line and eleven transports.

On returning from this cruise, Admiral Kempenfeldt sailed to join Lord Howe off Ushant, where they fell in with the French fleet, but were unable to accept battle, as the latter were in greatly superior force. Here Kempenfeldt had an opportunity of displaying his skill in naval tactics, when covering the retreat of some ships, which were in danger of being cut off by the enemy's van. The *Royal George* being leaky, the admiral returned to Spithead, and, with the view of having the repairs expeditiously effected, the ship was careened at her moorings on the 29th August, with the fatal results that have become historical.

The weather was favourable, with a light breeze, and by ten o'clock, the *Royal George* was heeled sufficiently to enable the workmen to get to the leaky part, but, in order to repair it effectually, she was heeled another streak, or about two feet more. After this was done, the ship's crew were allowed to go to dinner, but the carpenters and caulkers continued at their work, and had almost finished, when a sudden squall took the ship on the raised side, and the lower deck ports to leeward having been unaccountably left open, the water rushed in. In less than eight minutes the ship filled and sank, carrying down with her, it was said, upwards of 1,200 persons, including 300 women and others who had come off to see their friends.

The watch on deck to the number of over 200, were saved by laying out on the topsail yards, which remained above water after the ship settled on the bottom. About 70 more were picked up by the boats from other ships at Spithead. Among these were four lieutenants and eleven women. Admiral Kempenfeldt, the rest of the officers, and 900 people were drowned.*

The masts of the *Royal George* remained standing for a considerable time afterwards, and, until she was covered with sand, parts of the hull were visible at low water. Repeated attempts were made to weigh her, but in vain, and ultimately, about fifty years after her loss, she was blown up.

Cowper has commemorated in noble verse the loss the country experienced in the death of this tried and able officer.

> "Toll for the brave!
> Brave Kempenfeldt is gone,
> His last sea-fight is fought,
> His work of glory done.
>
> "His sword was in its sheath,
> His fingers held the pen,
> When Kempenfeldt went down
> With twice four hundred men.
>
> "Brave Kempenfeldt is gone,
> His victories are o'er,
> And he and his eight hundred
> Shall plough the wave no more."

The character of Admiral Kempenfeldt greatly resembled that of his father, Colonel Kempenfeldt, as drawn by Addison in the *Spectator*, No. 2, under the name of Captain Sentry. "A gentleman of great courage, good understanding, but invincible modesty. He was one of those who deserve very well, but are very awkward at putting their talents within the observation of such as should take notice of them. I have heard him often lament, that in a profession where merit is placed in so conspicuous a view, impudence should get the better of industry; when he has talked to this purpose, I never heard him make a sour expression. The same frankness runs through all his conversation. His life has furnished him with many adventures, in the relation of which he is

---

* In 1783, a monument was erected in the churchyard of Portsea, to the memory of Rear-Admiral Kempenfeldt and his fellow-sufferers, which bears the following inscription :—"On the 29th day of August, 1782, his Majesty's ship, the *Royal George*, being on the heel at Spithead, overset and sank, by which fatal accident about 900 persons were instantly launched into eternity, among whom was that brave and experienced officer, Rear-Admiral Kempenfeldt. Nine days after, many bodies of the unfortunate floated, 35 of whom were buried in one grave near this monument, which is erected by the parish of Portsea as a grateful tribute to the memory of that great commander and his fellow-sufferers."

very agreeable, for he is never overbearing, though accustomed to command men in the utmost degree below him; nor even too obsequious from a habit of obeying men highly above him."

Sir Piercy Brett, like Lord Keppel, first sailed under Commodore Anson's command, in his expedition round the world. He was a midshipman on board the *Gloucester*, 50, and on the promotion of Mr. Cheap to be captain of the *Wager*, storeship, was appointed second lieutenant of the *Centurion*. He executed with success and skill the attack on Paita, and on the arrival of the *Centurion* at Macao, in September, 1743, was appointed her captain by Commodore Anson, who had a high opinion of his merits.

In April, 1745, Captain Brett was nominated to the command of the *Lion*, 58, and on the 29th June captured a notorious privateer, that had long infested the Channel. On the 9th of the ensuing month, he fought a desperate action with a French ship-of-the-line of superior weight of metal. The official account says:—

"His Majesty's ship the *Lion*, of 58 guns, being in the latitude of 47 deg. 57 min. north, and west from the meridian of the *Lizard* 39 leagues, Captain Brett, her commander, saw two sail to leeward, to which he immediately bore down, and by three in the afternoon found them to be two of the enemy's ships. By four o'clock he was within two miles of them, when they hoisted French colours and shortened sail. One of them was a man-of-war of 64 guns, and the other a ship of 16 guns. At five the *Lion* run alongside the large ship, and began to engage within pistol-shot. The ships continued in that situation till ten, during which time they kept a continual fire at each other, when the *Lion's* rigging being cut to pieces, her mizen-mast, mizen-top-mast, main-yard, fore-topsail-yard, and main-topsail-yard shot away, all her lower masts and top-masts shot through in many places, so that she lay muzzled on the sea, and could do nothing with her sails, the French ship sheered off and in less than an hour was out of sight, the *Lion* not being able to follow her. The small ship in the beginning of the engagement made two attempts to rake the *Lion*, but was soon beat off by her stern chase, and after that lay off at a great distance. Forty-five of the *Lion's* men were killed outright, and 107 wounded, 7 of whom died of their wounds soon after. Captain Brett was wounded and much bruised in the arm, his master lost his right arm, and his lieutenants were all wounded; nevertheless they would not leave the deck, excepting the first lieutenant, who was so much hurt that he was obliged to be carried off."

The ship engaged by Captain Brett convoyed the frigate in which the son of the

Pretender, then on his passage to Scotland, had embarked. A private letter from the Hague, dated the 30th, makes the following mention of the loss she experienced:— "The frigate, on board of which the eldest son of the Pretender had embarked, was joined off Belleisle by the *Elizabeth*, of 66 guns. They intended to go round Ireland and land in Scotland, but were met on the 20th by some English merchant ships, convoyed by three ships of war, one of which, the *Lion*, bore down on the *Elizabeth* and attacked her, upon which the Pretender sailed away in the frigate. The fight lasted nine hours, but night coming on the *Elizabeth*, quite disabled, got away to Brest, the captain and 64 men were killed, 136 dangerously wounded, and a great number slightly. She had on board £400,000 sterling and arms for several thousand men." The devotion of Captain Brett was thus the means of effecting incalculable service to the State, as it frustrated the rising by cutting off the supplies of money and arms, and prevented the sacrifice of thousands of lives.

In Anson's action with De la Jonquiere in 1747, Captain Brett commanded the *Yarmouth*, 64, and in 1753 he was knighted by the king, and subsequently, up to the year 1763, when he was promoted to the rank of rear-admiral, was constantly employed afloat in the Channel or the Mediterranean, where he served as second in command to Sir Charles Saunders. After his promotion he served no more afloat, but between 1766 and 1770 held office as Lord of the Admiralty, and died in May, 1781.

Admiral the Hon. John Byron, whose strange adventures have been recorded in his narrative of the loss of the *Wager*, and are referred to by his immortal grandson, the great poet, who speaks in "Don Juan" of his "grand-dad," was a son of the fourth Lord Byron, and entered upon a nautical career in 1731, when only eight years of age.

In September, 1740, Mr. Byron sailed in the *Wager*, storeship, commanded by Captain Cheap, one of Commodore Anson's squadron, and the hardships and adventures he encountered in the loss of that ship on the 14th May, 1741, on the Chili coast, form the groundwork of one of the most interesting tales of adventure in the language. Captain Cheap succeeded in landing from the wreck a considerable amount of stores, but his men displayed a rebellious spirit, and unfortunately they were incited to mutiny by a midshipman of the name of Cozens. On the 10th June, a seaman having had his allowance of grog stopped, this officer, who had repeatedly displayed insubordination, demanded of the purser his reasons for this measure. The latter, apprehending a mutiny, fired a pistol at Cozens, which only failed of taking effect by a bystander knocking up the purser's arm. Captain Cheap, hearing the shot, ran out of his tent with a cocked pistol, and hearing from Lieutenant Hamilton, of the Marines, that Cozens was endeavouring to incite the men to acts of mutiny, he discharged the weapon. The ball took effect in the cheek, and Cozens died of the wound on the fourteenth day. This increased the ill feeling between the officers and crew, numbering over 100 men, who, on the completion of the long-boat (which had been lengthened to accommodate all hands), refused to permit the captain to proceed in her to the rendezvous at the Island of Juan Fernandez, but announced their intention of returning through the Straits of Magellan. The long-boat, which received the name of the *Speedwell*, was launched on the 12th October, but the malcontents, headed by Captain Pemberton, of the Marines, and Lieutenant Beans, placed the captain under arrest, together with Lieutenant Hamilton and the two midshipmen, Mr. Byron and Mr. Campbell. The mutineers sailed a few days later, leaving behind these officers, together with the surgeon and some men, the whole party numbering 20 souls. For their support were left 28 pieces of beef and pork and 120 pounds of flour, with the pinnace and barge.

Captain Cheap did not set out for Chiloe, the nearest Spanish settlement on that coast, till the 15th December, but after vainly battling for two months with the tempestuous weather, and losing the pinnace, he was compelled to return to the desolate spot, called Wager Island, whence he had set out. A fortnight later a party of Indians arrived in two canoes, and were prevailed upon to conduct the party, now reduced to 13, to the northward. One day Captain Cheap and three other officers, having gone on shore to procure provisions, and the Indians being absent in search of seals, the men left in the barge abandoned their officers to their fate. The native chief, nevertheless, was induced by the offer of a reward to guide the officers to Chiloe, with the exception of Mr. Hamilton, who, being too ill to proceed, was left under the care of some Indians. The three other officers, after encountering great hardships, reached Chiloe in June, thirteen months from the date of the loss of their ship, and were taken in a Spanish ship to a settlement, whence the governor sent a party to fetch Hamilton, who here rejoined his companions.

On the 2nd January, 1743, the party sailed for Valparaiso, where they were thrown into prison, but were eventually conducted to Santiago, the capital of the province. Here they remained for two years, and were hospitably treated by the inhabitants. On the 20th December, 1744, Captain Cheap, Mr. Hamilton, and Mr. Byron embarked in the *Lys*, a French ship, for Europe, and on the 27th October following came to an anchor in Brest Roads. Here they were treated with great harshness, but at length received permission to proceed to England, and left for Dover in a Dutch ship. Even now their troubles were not at an end, as the master of the vessel betrayed an inclination to reland them on French soil, but the *Squirrel*, frigate, coming up with the Dutchman, took out the three officers, who were landed at Dover in March, 1746, after an absence of five and a half years.

Mr. Byron was promoted on his arrival in England to the command of a sloop-of-war, and in the following December was advanced to the rank of captain, and posted to the *Syren*, frigate. After much service afloat of an uneventful character, we find him, in 1757, commanding the *America*, 60, in Hawke's expedition to Rochefort. In the same year he was commodore of a small squadron, sent to cruise on the coast of France, consisting, besides his own ship, of the *Brilliant* and *Coventry*. The frigates each captured a privateer, and the *America*, in chasing a ship, having on board a valuable cargo of furs, set her on fire, when only 24 out of her crew of 70 men were saved. After the surrender of Louisbourg, Commodore Byron succeeded with the *Fame*, 74, and two other ships, in destroying three of the enemy's frigates, with many store-ships, in Chaleur Bay. After the peace of 1763, he commanded an expedition sent on a voyage of exploration, and discovered many islands in the South Pacific. On his return he was appointed Governor of Newfoundland, and in March, 1775, was advanced to flag-rank.

When it was discovered that Count D'Estaing was about to sail for America with twelve sail-of-the-line, Vice-Admiral Byron was despatched thither to counteract his plans with a squadron of nearly the same force, and hoisted his flag on board the *Princess Royal*, 90. The squadron was dispersed by a storm, and, on the 18th August, the admiral arrived alone off New York, whence he sailed for Halifax. By October he had collected his fleet, and again sailed for New York, to blockade D'Estaing in Boston, but with the ill-fortune that pursued him, his ships were again dispersed by a storm, and most of them steered for Rhode Island in a shattered condition. D'Estaing took advantage of this to sail for the West Indies, whither Byron followed in pursuit and reinforced Admiral Barrington, who had succeeded in making himself master of St. Lucia. Both sides received considerable accessions, and in June, 1779, Byron put to sea with 21 sail-of-the-line, in order to engage the French fleet, which was about to attack Grenada. On arriving, however, off the island, he found that they were in superior strength, numbering twenty-seven line-of-battle ships, mostly carrying heavier metal than his own. The action that ensued was indecisive, and Byron, being encumbered with transports, was unable to prevent the fall of Grenada. He says in his despatch:—"Although it was evident, throughout the whole day, that they resolved to avoid a close engagement, I could not allow myself to think, that with a force so greatly superior, the French admiral would allow us to carry off the transports unmolested."

Soon after this action, Admiral Byron returned to England, leaving Admiral Parker in command, and he died in 1786, leaving behind the reputation of a gallant, but not very fortunate officer. His second son, George Anson, a captain in the Navy, was father of the celebrated poet, who, in 1793, became Lord Byron.

Did space permit, we should give some account of the gallant services of Admirals Sir Francis Geary, Sir Edward Affleck, and Sir Richard Bickerton, who received baronetcies, and also of Sir Hugh Palliser, who was awarded the same honour, which he had well merited, notwithstanding his reprehensible conduct in the action under Lord Keppel on the 27th July, 1778.

Sir Hyde Parker, a family which has produced a succession of fine seamen, was another distinguished officer. He performed exellent service under Admirals Stevens and Cornish in the East Indies, and was second in command under Admiral Byron when he succeeded to the command in the West Indies. He was very successful in protecting the commerce of the country and harassing that of the enemy, and took five of their frigates, and recaptured the *Sphinx*, a British ship-of-war. On the 18th December, one of his look-out frigates, stationed between Martinique and St. Lucia, reported a fleet, when Admiral Parker, who was lying with his squadron in Gros Islet Bay, in the latter island, put to sea and stood over to Fort Royal.

The admiral writes in his despatch:—"No sooner was the signal made on board the *Princess Royal*, than a signal was thrown out for the ships under my command to slip their cables and chase to windward. The captains were then assembled at a court-martial, and as the ships were in a course of fitting, some lay on the heel, others had their sails unbent, and from all of them great numbers were employed on shore in wooding and watering. Under these circumstances the alertness and despatch with which the ships put to sea was surprising even to me who am no stranger to the activity of English officers and seamen. As the squadron stood over from Fort Royal, the enemy's ships were discovered to be a convoy. Before four in the afternoon, nine or ten of them ran themselves on shore near the island of Martinico, and were set on fire by our boats either immediately or the next morning. About the same time I observed the *Boreas* engaged with a French frigate in Fort Royal Bay ; a French rear-admiral with two other

74-gun ships slipped their cables and bore down upon him, which obliged the *Boreas* to sheer off. This dexterous manœuvre saved their frigate and some of their merchant ships. The French admiral hauled his wind in good time, and kept plying for the road."

In February 1780, De Guichen arrived at Martinique with 17 ships-of-the-line, which compelled Parker to remain on the defensive until he was reinforced by Sir George Rodney, on the 27th March, with four ships, when the British fleet proceeded off the island, but the French admiral, though in superior force, did not care to venture out. Eventually, however, he put to sea, and Admiral Parker served in command of the van division of Rodney's fleet in the action of the 17th April. He now returned to England and commanded the squadron in the battle with the Dutch fleet, off the Dogger Bank, but no blame was held to attach to him for the result. In October, 1782, Admiral Parker, who had succeeded his brother in the baronetcy, sailed for the East Indies, as commander-in-chief, in the *Cato*, 58, a new ship, but from the 12th December, when she quitted Rio, no word was ever heard of the unfortunate ship, which disappeared from view with her admiral, officers, and crew.

Sir James Lockhart-Ross was an officer of great professional distinction and saw considerable service. He served under Admiral Knowles in the West Indies, and in the *Devonshire*, flag-ship of Sir Peter Warren, and was present in Lord Anson's action of the 15th May, 1747, and with Lord Hawke in the engagement off Cape Finisterre in the following October.

On the outbreak of hostilities with France in 1755, he was made captain and appointed to the *Tartar*, 24, carrying 24 nine-pounders, and four four-pounders, with a crew of 200 men. On the 20th September, he engaged and drove into Morlaix two French 28-gun frigates, and his activity was so great that the Admiralty dispensed with the usual audit of his accounts, an indulgence which, his biographer declares, was never accorded to any officer before or since. Captain Ross was employed cruising for the protection of the trade between the Isle of Bas and the Lizard between the 20th September, 1756, and the 19th October, 1758, during which period he took nine privateers, carrying an aggregate of 2,500 men and 220 guns; three of them were of superior force and offered a spirited resistance. But his most brilliant feat at this time was the capture of the *Melampe*, frigate, of 36 twelve-pounders and 300 men, fitted out at Bayonne expressly to engage and bring into port the *Tartar*. After an obstinate action, the French captain struck his flag, but, with singular treachery, made a desperate attempt to board the British frigate, when he was repulsed with slaughter, 50 men being either killed or drowned.

Captain Ross's name struck terror into the hearts of the enemy, and it is recorded that, on one occasion, a British privateer having fallen in with an enemy of superior force during the night, the commander, in order to save her from capture, ran his ship alongside of the enemy, and calling upon her to surrender to the *Tartar*, Captain Ross, the Frenchman immediately hauled down his flag. In token of their esteem and gratitude for his many brilliant services, the merchants of London and Bristol presented Captain Ross with some plate, bearing a suitable inscription.

In November, 1758, the gallant officer was appointed to the command of a new ship, the *Chatham*, 50, and served under Rodney and Hawke, when he frequently displayed his daring and skill. On the occasion of Hawke's action with the French fleet on the 19th October, 1759, off Quiberon Bay, Captain Ross narrowly escaped capture; but Sir Edward Hawke appearing in sight with twenty-two sail, the tables were turned, when the *Magnanime* and *Chatham* engaged the *Hero*, 74, and obliged her to strike. On the 22nd, the English fleet stood into Vilaine Bay, but could make no attack on the enemy's ships over the bar, though Captain Ross succeeded in burning the *Soleil Royal*, flag-ship of the French admiral, and the *Hero*. He sailed for Portsmouth in July, 1760, and was appointed to the command of the *Bedford*, 70, when he joined Admiral Boscawen's squadron, at Quiberon Bay, where he distinguished himself by his activity.

In 1761, Captain Ross returned to England, and having estates in Scotland, was elected to Parliament for Lanark, but on the outbreak of war with France, in 1777, he commissioned the *Shrewsbury*, 74, and in March of the following year, joined Admiral Keppel's fleet at Spithead. He participated in the action of the 27th July, his ship being the first to engage the enemy. In the following April he was promoted to flag rank, and hoisted his flag on board the *Royal George*, one of the Channel fleet, under the command of Sir Charles Hardy. The French and Spanish fleets appeared in superior force in the Channel, but appeared disinclined to bring on an engagement, and Sir John Lockhart-Ross sailed with Sir George Rodney's fleet of twenty sail-of-the-line. Gibraltar was relieved and a Spanish 64-gun ship and her convoy of twenty-one sail were captured, when Sir George Rodney parted company, proceeding to the West Indies, while Admirals Digby and Ross returned to Plymouth.

Sir John Ross was soon again at sea, serving under Admirals Geary and Darby, and in March, 1781, he participated in the second relief of Gibraltar by Admiral Darby at the head of twenty-six sail. Shifting his flag into the *Alexander*, 74, he proceeded into the Bay, and superintended the unloading of the stores from sixty transports, when he landed 7,000 tons of provisions and 2,000 barrels of gunpowder, under a heavy fire from the Spanish flotilla of gunboats. On the conclusion of this service, which he accomplished in six days, Admiral Ross again hoisted his flag in the *Royal George*, and returned to England with the fleet. Soon after he proceeded to the North Sea in command of twelve sail-of-the-line, and blockaded the Dutch fleet in the Texel, which was his last service afloat. He died in June, 1790, at the age of 68, much and deservedly regretted. Though not reckoned among England's greatest naval commanders, few officers of his day saw more service, and none attained a higher reputation for coolness and intrepidity in the hour of battle than Sir John Lockhart-Ross.

Another of England's great admirals was Sir Edward Hughes. This officer gained his lieutenantcy for gallantry displayed at the capture of Porto Bello, and seven years later received promotion, owing to the misconduct of the commander of the *Lark*, 40. He was a passenger on board this ship, which, in company with the *Warwick*, 60, was ordered to Louisbourg with a convoy. The squadron sighted a Spanish 74-gun ship, which the *Warwick* engaged singly, and was disabled before her consort arrived to her assistance. For this remissness the captain of the *Lark* was brought to a court-martial at Louisbourg, and Lieutenant Hughes was posted to command her with the rank of captain.

He served in 1758 under Admiral Boscawen in the expedition to Louisbourg, and in the following year, at the capture of Quebec, attracted the notice of Sir Charles Saunders, who appointed him his flag-captain in the *Blenheim*. In 1770 he proceeded to the Falkland Islands, in command of the *Somerset*, and three years later was appointed commodore on the East India station, whither he sailed in the *Salisbury*, 50. In 1777 Commodore Hughes returned to England, and in the following January was promoted to the rank of rear-admiral, received the Order of the Bath, and, hoisting his flag in the *Superb*, 74, sailed for the East Indies as commander-in-chief, in company with the 70-gun ships *Exeter* and *Burford*, and the *Eagle*, *Belleisle*, and *Worcester*, each of 64 guns.

On arriving in India, Sir Edward Hughes sent home the *Belleisle*, *Asia*, and *Ripon*, under the command of Commodore Vernon, and, though the affairs of the East India Company were in a critical condition, owing to the rising power of Hyder Ali, he could afford little assistance to the army. However, he was able to inflict serious loss on the ruler of Mysore, by destroying his fleet at Mangalore, on the Malabar coast, his principal seaport. He writes in a letter from Bombay, dated 2nd January, 1781:—

"On the 8th December I saw two ships, a large snow, three ketches, and many smaller vessels at an anchor in the road, with Hyder Ali's colours flying on board them. Standing with the squadron close into the road, I found them to be vessels of force, and all armed for war, on which I anchored as close to the enemy's vessels as possible with safety to the ships, and ordered the armed boats of the squadron to attack and destroy them, under cover of the fire of the Company's two armed snows, and of the prize ship cut out of Calicut road, which were anchored in shoal water, and close to the enemy's ships. The service was conducted on the part of our boats with a spirit and activity that do much honour to the officers and men employed in them. In two hours they took and burnt two ships, one of 28, the other of 26 guns; one ketch of 12 guns was blown up by the enemy at the instant our boats were boarding her; another ketch of ten guns, which cut her cables and endeavoured to put to sea, was taken, and the third ketch, with the smaller vessels, were all forced on shore, the snow only escaping into the harbour, after having thrown everything overboard to lighten her."

In November, 1781, Sir Edward Hughes, in conjunction with Sir Hector Monro, attacked and captured the Dutch settlement of Negapatam, when the squadron lost 30 seamen and marines killed and 56 wounded.

On the 11th January following, the admiral took by assault the town of Trincomalee, together with two Dutch ships. He says in his despatch, "The necessary dispositions were made for the attack to begin at daylight on the morning of the 11th, and accordingly, the storming party, composed of 450 seamen and marines, and their officers, with each flank covered by a party of pioneers, and twenty seamen, carrying the scaling ladders, and armed with cutlasses, with a reserve of three companies of marines, with two field-pieces to support it, followed by the Company's troops, advanced at daybreak towards the fort, and the sergeant's party in front, getting in at the embrasures unperceived by the enemy, was immediately followed by the whole of the storming party, who soon drove the enemy from their works, and possessed themselves of the fort; and all the ships and vessels in the harbour immediately surrendered. In this assault I had the misfortune to lose Lieutenant George Long, my second lieutenant, a most worthy and deserving officer, who was killed in advancing bravely to the assault at the head of his company, and also twenty non-commissioned officers and private seamen, and marines; Lieutenant Wolseley, who commanded a party of seamen, Lieutenant Samuel Orr, of the Marines, who commanded their grenadier company and did duty as Brigade-Major, and forty non-commissioned officers, private seamen, and marines, were wounded. The enemy lost but few men, as they mostly threw down their arms, and their forfeited lives were spared, by that disposition to mercy which ever distinguishes Britons."

The supremacy of the British fleet had hitherto been undisputed in Indian waters but in the latter part of 1781, Admiral de Suffren arrived with a powerful and well-equipped fleet, in which was embarked a body of troops, to co-operate with Hyder Ali in his desperate attempt to subvert British power. The first action between these equally gallant and experienced admirals took place on the 17th February, 1782, and though indecisive, the result was regarded, by those best qualified to judge, as distinctly favourable to the British cause. The Governor-General and Council of Bengal wrote to him in the following terms:—"We regard your action with the French fleet as the crisis of our fate in the Carnatic, and as the result of it we see that province relieved and preserved, and the permanency of the British power in India firmly established." They add:—"A proof so unequivocal of the superior courage and discipline of the officers and seamen under your command, and of their confidence in their leader, must excite, in the minds of all the powers in India, a confirmed opinion of the unrivalled military character of the British nation." The Governor and Council of Madras addressed the admiral in equally flattering terms:—"The very masterly and spirited manner in which you bore down upon the French fleet at your departure from these roads, claimed at that time our warmest thanks; and we now most sincerely congratulate you on the new honour which the British flag has acquired, by the courage and conduct so eminently displayed by you in the late combat against such superior numbers."

On the 30th March, the admiral was joined at sea by the *Sultan* and *Magnanime* from England, the crews of which were very sickly and much reduced by scurvy. As Sir Edward had on board the squadron a reinforcement of troops for the garrison of Trincomalee, and a quantity of military stores, he decided to proceed directly for Trincomalee, "without," as he says, "either seeking or avoiding the enemy." On the 6th April, the squadron fell in with a French ship, which they chased on shore and burnt, near Tranquebar, but the officers and men escaped.

On the 8th, at noon, the enemy's squadron, consisting of eighteen sail, was discovered in the north-east quarter, and during the three following days kept in sight, without any encounter taking place; but on the 12th, at daylight, Admiral de Suffren having obtained the weather-gage, in consequence of Sir Edward bearing up for Trincomalee, and their copper-bottomed ships coming up fast with the rear of the British squadron, the admiral, notwithstanding their superiority, engaged them. The action has already been described, and was again indecisive. On the departure of the French fleet, Sir Edward steered for Trincomalee, where he arrived on the 22nd, and immediately landed the reinforcements and military stores for the garrison, and the sick and wounded.

Having refitted the *Monmouth* and the rest of his ships, as well as circumstances would permit, Admiral Hughes sailed from Trincomalee on the 24th June, and on the following day anchored in Negapatam Roads. Here he was informed that the French squadron was at anchor off Cuddalore, which had surrendered to the land forces. The admiral continued at anchor off Negapatam till the 5th July, when at noon the French fleet, consisting of eighteen sail, twelve of which were of the line, came in sight. During the afternoon he weighed with the squadron, and stood to the southward all that evening and night, in order to get to windward of the enemy.

Then followed the action which has already been detailed. Admiral Hughes says in his despatch:—"I am extremely happy to inform their lordships, that in this engagement his Majesty's squadron under my command gained a decided superiority over that of the enemy; and had not the wind shifted, and thrown his Majesty's squadron out of the action, at the very time when some of the enemy's ships had broken their line, and were running away, and others of them greatly disabled, I have good reason to believe it would have ended in the capture of several of their line-of-battle ships. I am also happy to inform their lordships, that the officers and men of the squadron behaved to my satisfaction, and have great merit for their bravery and steady conduct. The captains—Gell of the *Monarca*, Rainier of the *Burford*, and Watt of the *Sultan*—eminently distinguished themselves by a strict attention to my signals, and the utmost exertion of courage and conduct against the enemy. I am obliged to Colonel Fullarton, of the 98th regiment, who has been my companion in the *Superb* since I left Madras roads in March last, preferring to serve with his corps on board to living inactive on shore. The officers and men of this regiment have behaved with great regularity on board the ships of the squadron, and done their duty well on all occasions. Major Grattan, an officer late of General Meadow's staff, and a captain in the 100th regiment, has also served with great credit on board the *Superb* on this occasion, in the absence of his corps, now on the Malabar Coast. The death of Captain Maclellan, of the *Superb*, who was shot through the heart with a grape shot early in the engagement, is universally regretted by all who knew him. I had experienced in him an excellent officer in every department of the service."

The British fleet made for Madras to repair damages and procure a fresh supply of provisions and ammunition, and sailed for Trincomalee on the 20th August, but on their arrival off the fort, on the 2nd September, they had the mortification to find the French colours flying there, and the enemy's fleet at anchor in the bay.

On the following day took place another action, the fourth within seven months, between the British and French fleets, the latter having been reinforced by the *Illustré*, 74, *St. Michael*, 64, and *Elizabeth*, 50, formerly belonging to the East India Company. Between the 17th February and the 3rd September, the *Superb* had no less than 81 men killed and 192 wounded, out of her reduced complement.

The admiral repaired to Bombay, where he was joined by a squadron from England, under Sir Richard Bickerton, consisting of the *Gibraltar*, 80, *Cumberland* and *Defence*, 74's, *Africa*, *Inflexible*, and *Sceptre*, 64-gun ships, and *Bristol*, 50. Sir Edward Hughes, though his crews were decimated by the scurvy, returned to the Coromandel Coast in the following year, and on the 13th June, when off Cuddalore, then besieged by a force under General Stuart, the French fleet again hove in sight. At the end of a week, passed in manœuvres, De Suffren, having the weather-gage, bore down upon the British fleet, and after a heavy cannonade, which continued three hours, the action was terminated by the enemy quitting the scene of strife. In this last encounter, the *Superb* had 12 men killed and 41 wounded. The enemy were seen off Pondicherry two days later, but both sides appeared weary of the resultless bloodshed, and on the 25th Admiral Hughes arrived at Madras, where he heard of the conclusion of peace early in the year. The British fleet returned to England in divisions, and Sir Edward Hughes passed the remainder of his days in peace, and died on the 17th February, 1794.

The last of the British admirals of this period, whose glorious career we will briefly record in this chapter, was, perhaps, the most illustrious of all.

George Brydges Rodney was born in December, 1718, and entered the Navy at a very early age, under the patronage of his godfather, the king, after whom he was named. His first command was in the Mediterranean, under Admiral Matthews, by whom he was promoted, in November, 1742, to the rank of captain, and appointed to the *Plymouth*, 60. After commanding various ships, we find him in the *Eagle*, 60, in

1746, when he captured two privateers, one of which, the *Shoreham*, had been a frigate in the British service. In the following year he was with Commodore Fox, when the British squadron intercepted De la Motte, who, with four sail-of-the-line, was convoying a merchant fleet of 170 sail, homeward bound from St. Domingo. The French commander left his convoy to their fate, when forty-eight sail were captured, of which Rodney took six in the *Eagle*. In Hawke's memorable victory, later on in the same year, over Admiral De l'Etendeur, off Cape Finisterre, Rodney was in the thick of the fight. The *Eagle* and the *Edinburgh*, 70, Captain Coles, were almost overpowered by the *Tonnant*, 84, the French admiral's flagship, and the *Intrepide*, 74, when the *Devonshire*, 66, bearing Hawke's flag, ranged up to their assistance. The *Eagle* had her wheel shot away, and, being unmanageable, fell on board the British flagship, thus rendering both ships temporarily unable to continue the action. At a later period Captain Rodney joined the *Yarmouth* and *Nottingham* in the pursuit of the *Tonnant* and *Intrepide*, but was unable to close with them, and they escaped, favoured by the darkness.

The peace of Aix la Chapelle put an end to Rodney's opportunities of earning distinction, but he filled the office of Governor of Newfoundland. then always held by a naval officer, and in May, 1751, was elected to Parliament as member for Saltash, and successively sat for Oakhampton and Northampton. On the outbreak of war Captain Rodney was placed in command of the *Dublin*, 74, and took part in an unsuccessful descent on the French coast, near Rochelle, in September, 1757, under the command of Admirals Hawke and Boscawen. He also accompanied the latter officer in the expedition to Louisbourg in 1758.

In June of the following year Rodney was raised to the rank of rear-admiral, and signalised his promotion by bombarding Havre de Grace, and destroying a magazine of stores for the flotilla of flat-bottomed boats, constructed with much labour for the transport of troops to invade this country. In 1760 he destroyed another fleet of these boats at the mouth of the Seine, and in October of the following year sailed in the *Marlborough* with four ships and three bomb-ketches, and, with Sir James Douglas, assisted at the reduction of the islands of Martinique, Grenada, St. Lucia, and St. Vincent, known as the Caribbees.

In 1764, the year succeeding the peace, Rodney was created a baronet and made Governor of Greenwich Hospital, but he resigned that post on being appointed commander-in-chief on the West India station, with his flag in the *Amelia*, 80.

On his return from Jamaica, Admiral Rodney's fortune was so much impaired by his parliamentary contests, that he lived in France, and the French Government actually made an offer to him to accept the command of the French fleet in the West Indies, with the promise of paying his debts. The gallant sailor could scarcely believe his ears as the French Minister, whose guest he was at his country house, made this singular proposal; but he promptly replied, "My distresses, sir, it is true, have driven me from the bosom of my country, but no temptation whatever can estrange me from her service. Had this offer been a voluntary one of your own, I should have deemed it an insult, but I am glad to learn it proceeds from a source that can do no wrong."

Sir George Rodney returned to England, but hostilities had already commenced between the two countries, and the admiral, who was appointed to the command in the West Indies, sailed thither with twenty-two sail-of-the-line and eight frigates, having his flag in the *Sandwich*, 90, accompanied by Admiral Digby, in the *Prince George*, 98—on board of which Prince William, afterwards William IV., was a midshipman—and Sir John L. Ross, in the *Royal George*, 100. It was a gallant fleet that sailed from these shores, under England's finest seaman, to whom was entrusted the task of seeking to regain the command of the seas which, for the first time for a century, she had temporarily lost, and nobly he acquitted himself of the duty.

On the 29th December, 1779, Rodney sailed from Spithead

> "Full charged with England's thunder
> To plough the distant main."

Having taken a convoy of storeships and relieved Gibraltar, services for which the admiral received the thanks of the House of Commons and the freedom of the City of London, Sir George Rodney sent Admiral Digby home with part of the fleet, and the Spanish prizes he had captured, and in March, 1780, arrived in the West Indies. De Guichen escaped from Martinique, on the 13th April, with twenty-three sail-of-the-line and eight frigates, and on the following day Rodney sailed from St. Lucia in pursuit with twenty ships, and on the 17th, after a display of skilful manœuvring, succeeded in bringing the enemy to action. Setting an example to his ships, some of which, however, failed to obey his signals—though others, notably the *Montague* and *Intrepid*, did their duty, and the *Terrible, Princess Royal, Grafton*, and *Trident* put the enemy's van in disorder—Rodney bore down on the French flagship, and for more than an hour the *Sandwich* sustained the combined attack of the *Couronne*, 90, assisted by her seconds ahead and astern, and when, at length, the *Princess Royal* bore down to her assistance, the French ships drew off, leaving the *Sandwich*, which had fired no less than 3,500 cannon shot, a perfect wreck, with seventeen shot-holes between wind and water. For twenty-four hours she could with difficulty be kept afloat, and yet so great was the activity of her crew that, within a further space of twenty-four hours, she was refitted aloft, and ready for action. Sir George Rodney said in his despatch:—"The action in the centre continued until fifteen minutes after four P.M., when Monsieur Guichen in the *Couronne*, which mounted 90 guns, with the *Triomphant* and *Pendant*, after engaging the *Sandwich* for an hour and a half, bore away. The superiority of the fire from the *Sandwich* and the gallant behaviour of her officers and men enabled her to sustain so unequal a combat, though, before this attack, she had beat three ships out of their line of battle, had entirely broke it, and was to leeward of the wake of the French admiral."

Sir George Rodney, who received for his services the Order of the Bath, was joined, early in 1781, by Sir Samuel Hood with a reinforcement of seven sail-of-the-line. War having been declared with Holland, Rodney attacked the Dutch possessions in the West Indies. St. Eustatius was taken, and a richly-laden convoy, which had left for Europe on the preceding day, was pursued by Commodore Reynolds with three ships, and the whole were captured and brought back, after the Dutch commodore had sacrificed his life in the gallant endeavour to protect his charge with a single 54-gun ship. The Dutch islands of St. Martin and Saba now surrendered, and also the colonies of Demerara and Essequibo, on the mainland.

Sir George Rodney crowned the great services he had rendered to his country by his glorious and decisive victory over the Count de Grasse on the 12th April, 1782, when the French commander-in-chief was himself captured in the *Ville de Paris*, together with four others of his ships, besides one sunk in the action. The entire British fleet performed their duty with zeal, and Rodney expressed his special acknowledgments to Sir Samuel Hood and Admiral Drake, as well as to Commodore Affleck, who led the centre division. The successful admiral was created a peer and received a pension of £2,000 a year, to descend to his heirs in perpetuity. As Beattie says, he had now climbed

"the steep where
Fame's proud temple shines afar."

Lord Rodney served no more afloat, but died in London on the 24th May, 1792, a few months before his country was involved in hostilities with the ancient foe he had so often encountered on the deep. In him England possessed an officer of conspicuous valour and knowledge of his profession, remarkable even among the unsurpassed band of seamen trained under his eye, who rendered such eminent services in the great struggle in which they were about to enter. The name of Rodney is for ever memorable as the conqueror in one of those epoch-making battles, the fame of which will never fade.

CHAPTER IV.

Outbreak of the Revolutionary War in January, 1793—The Unsuccessful Operations at Toulon—Destruction of the Arsenal and Ships by Sir Sydney Smith—Repulse at Corsica—Frigate Actions—The *Nymphe* and *Cléopatre*—*Boston* and *Embuscade*—*Crescent* and *Réunion*—Captain Horatio Nelson in the Mediterranean—The *Thames* and *Uranie*—The *Antelope* and *Atalante*—Attack on the French Possessions in the West Indies—Capture of the Islands of St. Pierre and Miquelon—Reduction of Pondicherry and the French Settlements in the East Indies—Losses and Gains during the Year 1793—Lord Howe's Great Victory over the French Fleet on the "Glorious 1st of June."

AFTER Rodney's great victory over the Count de Grasse, and the humiliating peace with our revolted colonists and the European Powers, France, Spain, and Holland, a profound peace reigned for ten years. But then arose the greatest and most prolonged period of hostilities with which the Continent of Europe has been afflicted in historic times. For twenty-two years, save for a brief intermission, this country was involved in a desperate and sanguinary struggle with France, which at times had for her allies a coalition of the European powers, and peace was only at length assured by the crowning victory of Waterloo, the utter exhaustion of France, and the surrender of the great soldier whose name will for ever resound down the aisles of time, and be the proudest memory of the country whose armies he led in an unparalleled series of triumphs.

On the 24th January, 1793, three days after the execution of Louis XVI., Lord Grenville intimated to the French Minister that he must quit London in eight days, and on the 1st February the National Assembly unanimously agreed to a resolution declaring the Republic of France at war with the King of Great Britain and the Stadtholder of the United Netherlands, and on the 7th March a similar declaration was issued against Spain.* Parliament voted supplies for 40,000 seamen and 5,000 marines, and twenty-one ships-of-the-line and several frigates, besides those already in commission, were ordered to be prepared for sea with all expedition. According to James—to whose excellent "Naval History of Great Britain from 1793 to 1820," we are chiefly indebted in the preparation of the succeeding chapters—the strength of the French Navy, on the 1st October, 1792, was 246 vessels, of which eighty-six,

* France had been at war with Austria, Prussia, and Sardinia for some time, and had defeated the armies of the allies.

including twenty-seven in commission, were of the line, and seventy-eight, frigates. On the declaration of war the French Government ordered seventy-one ships to be laid on the stocks, of which twenty-five were of the line. The British Navy at this time consisted of 158 line-of-battle ships, but James places the number fit for service at 115 as against seventy-six French ships, the number of guns being respectively 8,718 and 6,002, and as the French guns were of superior calibre, the aggregate broadside weight of metal, in pounds, was 88,957 and 73,957.

Lord Howe proceeded to sea with the Channel fleet, consisting of seventeen sail and nine frigates, but all his efforts to bring the French admirals to action ended in failure. Lord Howe's first cruise began on the 14th July, and he reached the latitude of Belleisle, but Admiral Morard de Galles, though commanding an equal force and being in sight of the British fleet, declined an engagement. Again on the 23rd August, the Channel fleet sailed to the westward to afford protection to the outward-bound Newfoundland trade and homeward-bound West India convoy, and returned to Torbay on the 4th September. A third time, on the 27th October, Lord Howe put to sea with twenty-two sail on a cruise in the Bay of Biscay, but Admiral Vanstabel, whose fleet was sighted on the 19th November, avoided an action, and got back in safety to Brest, having captured a convoy of seventeen ships. After cruising until the middle of December, Lord Howe returned to Spithead, without encountering the enemy, which created great dissatisfaction, though his lordship was not in fault.

The French republic having assembled in Toulon seventeen sail-of-the-line and several frigates ready for sea, besides thirteen refitting, the British Ministry determined to make an effort to secure that great arsenal and port, where a strong royalist party existed. With this object Lord Hood, who, as Sir Samuel Hood, was second in command under Lord Rodney in his victory over Count de Grasse, was despatched to the Mediterranean. The world-famous *Victory*, of 100 guns, which had borne the flag of Rodney at the relief of Gibraltar, and was a favourite ship with other commanders, was selected as his flagship by Lord Hood, who was accompanied by Sir Hyde Parker. The *Britannia*, 100, carried the flag of Vice-Admiral William Hotham, the *Windsor Castle*, 100, of Vice-Admiral Philip Cosby; the *Princess Royal*, 98, of Rear-Admiral Charles Goodall; and the *St. George*, 98, of Rear-Admiral John Gell.

In addition to these five flag-ships, there were twelve seventy-fours, and four sixty-fours, among the latter the *Agamemnon*, bearing the pennant of Captain Horatio Nelson, who, though so young an officer, had earned the command of a line-of-battle ship by his exertions during the peace in protecting our trade in the West Indies, where he was known as "the great little man of whom every one was afraid," from the encroachments of the American merchants. So great was his zeal and judicious the manner in which he carried out this duty, that, though he was opposed by the Admiral and Military Governor of the Leeward Islands, yet they ultimately recognised the superior wisdom of his views, and in spite of the misrepresentations of certain officials, whose corruption and malpractices he fearlessly exposed, Nelson received, on his return to England, the approval of Lord Howe, the First Lord of the Admiralty.

On arriving off Toulon, Lord Hood issued proclamations to the Royalists in the town and the south of France, who responded by proclaiming the youthful Dauphin, Louis XVII., King of France, and on the 27th August his lordship landed 1,500 troops and 2,000 seamen and marines, who occupied the forts which commanded the ships in the roads. The same day he was joined by Admiral Langara with seventeen sail. Count de Trogoff, commanding the French fleet, threw in his lot with the Royalists, but the majority of the seamen adhered to Admiral St. Julien, who withdrew with 5,000 men, when the remaining French ships removed into the inner harbour. On the following day 1,000 Spanish soldiers were landed, and on the 31st, Captain Elphinstone, of the *Robust*, marched with 600 men and dislodged a detachment of the enemy, posted with two guns, in the neighbourhood. Lord Hood sent away, in four ships-of-the-line, the 5,000 seamen, who were landed at Brest under a flag of truce. The situation, however, daily became worse, and more difficult for the allies. On the 30th September the Republican troops in the neighbourhood took by surprise the heights of Pharon, whence they were dislodged with heavy loss by a detachment of the Spanish and Neapolitan troops, of whom 5,000 had lately arrived, under General Mulgrave, and also, on the 8th October, from three batteries situated on heights commanding the town and harbour.

On the 15th November, a large force of the enemy made an attack on Fort Mulgrave, one of the principal British posts, but they were beaten back with the loss of 600 men, and from this time forward every day brought disaster to the allies. In no ways discouraged by their early losses the French continued their efforts, and opened a battery, mounting twenty guns, which shelled the town and arsenal. On the 30th November, General O'Hara, commanding the British troops and Governor of

Toulon, sent a body of 2,200 men,* under General Dundas to destroy this work. They succeeded in ascending the heights and captured the battery, but pursuing the flying enemy with too great impetuosity, they encountered their main body, and were in turn attacked and routed, the British alone losing more than two-thirds of their number, among the prisoners being General O'Hara, who had sallied out to rally them.

Reinforcements daily arrived, and General Dugommier assumed the command, among the artillery officers who were most prominent being the young Napoleon Buonaparte, who here entered upon his remarkable career—his first and last military experiences being against the English enemies of his country—and by his gallantry and skill earned the rank of brigadier-general. By this time the Republican troops were gradually raised to between 40,000 and 50,000, the allies being reduced to 11,000 effectives, of whom only the 2,000 British soldiers were reliable.

On the 16th December, on a dark and stormy night, the Republican troops stormed Fort Mulgrave, thus gaining command of the town and harbour, and on the following day, took possession of the whole peninsula, when the ships had to be moved from the inner harbour and placed beyond cannon-shot range. Lord Hood now called a council of war, at which it was resolved to evacuate the town and arsenal and burn the French ships-of-war. On the same evening the stores and artillery, with the troops and some thousands of the Royalists, were embarked, and Sir Sydney Smith, than whom perhaps the British Navy had no more capable and dauntless officer, undertook, with three English and three Spanish gunboats, to make the necessary preparations for burning the ships in the inner harbour and the stores in the arsenal. Having placed the combustibles in the different store-houses and on board the ships, in the face of the opposition of six hundred galley slaves, whom he overawed by his guns, at nightfall the *Vulcan*, fire-ship, under the direction of Lieutenant Gore, was placed across the tier of ships-of-war, and on the signal being given, the arsenal and magazines were set on fire, and the flames spreading, soon enveloped the shipping. The scene at this time was impressive, and its grandeur was increased by the fire of the enemy's guns, directed on the British sailors, and the explosion, owing to Spanish mismanagement, of the *Iris*, frigate, having on board some thousand of barrels of powder, and of a powder-ship. Sir Sydney Smith and his brave men were exposed to imminent risk from the falling timbers, and

* By the end of October the allies had 17,000 men at Toulon, including 2,114 British, and 6,840 Spanish, under General Valdez, the remainder being Italians and Royalists.

musketry fire from the ships and shore, but nevertheless, two 74-gun ships were burnt, and the mission on which he had been sent was successfully accomplished, notwithstanding the blundering of the Spanish officers and seamen appointed to assist him, who failed to destroy the ships in the basin before the town.

It appears from a statement by Lord Hood, that up to the 18th December, the date of the evacuation of Toulon, there were burnt or sunk one 80-gun ship, eight 74's, three frigates and two corvettes. In addition two 74's, four frigates, and two corvettes, being serviceable, were fitted out for use. The single frigate, *Alceste*, which fell to the lot of the Sardinians, was recaptured in May, 1794, by a French frigate, after a well-fought action. In all fourteen ships were destroyed and fifteen taken to England, where four of them subsequently did good service in the Navy. Of the unfortunate Royalists, 15,000 were embarked, one or two of the English ships-of-the-line having some thousands on board, but those who remained in Toulon suffered for siding with the British, and nearly 6,000 souls, it was said, perished or were ruthlessly executed by order of the Committee of Public Safety, in spite of the entreaties of General Dugommier, who urged the deputies to adopt a lenient course towards those who had aided the enemies of their country. Much blame was attributable to the British Government for despatching to hold Toulon only two regiments, the 1st Royals and 18th Foot, which, with the wholly unreliable Spanish, Sardinian, and Neapolitan troops, were expected to hold the extensive city and fortifications against the brave and enthusiastic soldiers of the Republic, daily receiving accessions of strength, and animated by the memories of their recent victories at Valmy and Jemappes.

Lord Hood and the officers and men of the British fleet did all that was possible under the circumstances, and no discredit for the failure incurred attaches to either the Army or Navy. As for the Spanish allies, Nelson declared that they were a terror only to the inhabitants of Toulon, and it may be said of our brave soldiers and sailors in the words of Addison's "Cato":—

> "'Tis not in mortals to command success,
> But we'll do more, Sempronius, we'll deserve it."

During the time that Toulon remained in the possession of the allied forces, Lord Hood carried on operations in the Mediterranean against the enemy. A Royalist insurrection broke out in Corsica, and, in response to an urgent request of General Paoli, commanding the insurgents, the British admiral, in September, sent to his assistance the *Alcide*, *Courageux*, and *Ardent*, 74's, and the frigates *Lowestoft* and *Nemesis*. Commodore

Linzee appeared off Calvi and San Fiorenzo, and despatched the frigates, under Captain William Wolseley, of the *Lowestoft*, to attack the tower of Mortella, which commanded the only secure anchorage in the Gulf of San Fiorenzo. After a couple of broadsides the *Nemesis* silenced the tower, when Captain Wolseley landed and took possession of the abandoned work. Instead of immediately attacking the tower and redoubt of Fornelli, situated about two miles in advance of the town, the commodore delayed until the garrison had completed their preparations, and the result was a repulse. At daybreak on the 1st October, the *Ardent* opened fire and was assisted by the *Courageux*, which sustained a raking fire from the town of San Fiorenzo, and less effectively by the *Alcide*. But the fire of the enemy's guns, including thirteen 24-pounders and six mortars, was heavy and well directed, and the British squadron was obliged to haul off and abandon the attempt, the *Courageux* having lost her first lieutenant and one seaman killed and her second lieutenant and 12 men wounded, the *Ardent*, one midshipman and 13 men killed and 17 wounded, and the *Alcide*, 9 seamen wounded, three of them mortally.

Lord Hood sent ships in search of a portion of the Toulon fleet, reported as cruising in the Mediterranean, and on the 5th October the *Bedford*, 74, Captain Mann, *Captain*, 74, Captain Reeve, and 14-gun brig *Speedy*, Commander Cunningham, on arriving at Genoa, discovered lying within the Mole the French 36-gun frigate *Modeste* and two small armed vessels, called tartans. Though the port belonged to a neutral power, it was resolved to bring off the French ships, and the *Bedford* and *Captain* were warped in alongside the *Modeste*, which, as well as the tartans, were boarded and brought out, and the frigate was purchased into the Navy. It having come to the knowledge of the captains of the British ships that the French frigate *Impérieuse*, 38, was lying in Spezzia Bay, on the 11th the *Captain* proceeded thither, and on the following day boarded and took possession of the frigate, which had been scuttled and abandoned by her crew. The *Impérieuse* was weighed, and on arriving in England was purchased into the service, but there being a ship of that name already in the Navy, she was rechristened the *Unité*.

Many actions between squadrons of frigates and single ships were fought this year and throughout the war. These encounters afforded, perhaps, the most remarkable opportunities for the display of the superior gunnery and dash of British seamen over other nations.

The first in order of date was the action between the brig-of-war, *Scourge*, carrying only 8 guns and seventy men and boys, and the French privateer, *Sans Culotte*, 12 guns (all of superior calibre) and a crew of 81 men. The action was fought on the

13th March near Scilly, and at the end of three hours the *Sans Culotte*, which lost nine men killed and 20 wounded, became the prize of the British brig. Two days later, a detachment of seamen from the *Syren*, 32, Captain Manley, who commanded the small squadron which accompanied the military expedition to Holland under the command of the Duke of York, embarked, under the orders of Lieutenant Western, on board three gun-boats, and attacked five batteries, which had been erected to bombard Willemstadt, a fortress situated on a small island about thirty miles east of Helvoetsluys. The fire of the gun-boats was so destructive that the French defenders of the batteries abandoned them, leaving the guns in possession of the British naval lieutenant and his men. Only a few days later, as this gallant young officer was in the act of pointing one of the twelve-pounders in his gun-boat against the enemy's entrenched camp, he was killed by a musket-ball through the head. He was the first British officer who fell in the long and sanguinary struggle with France, and the Duke of York testified his appreciation of his gallantry by attending the funeral, and ordered the erection of a monument to his memory in the church of Dordrecht, where his remains received interment.

The only other occasion in which the Navy participated in operations that had a disastrous termination, was on the 31st October, when a squadron, consisting of two frigates, a sloop and a floating battery, mounting twenty 68-pounder carronades, under the orders of Rear-Admiral Macbride, assisted Sir Charles Grey's division in expelling the French from the important posts of Ostend and Nieuport, and compelled them to retire upon Dunkirk.

The *Iris*, a 32-gun frigate, belonging to Admiral Gell's squadron, then on its way to Toulon, on the 13th May fought an indecisive action with the *Citoyenne Française*, a French privateer of equal force, a result due to the British frigate being unable to make sail in pursuit of the privateer, owing to the loss of her foremast and main and mizen topmasts. The action lasted for an hour and a half, and was hotly contested on both sides, as appears by the losses of the combatants, that of the *Iris* being four seamen killed and 30 wounded, besides her first lieutenant and master, the latter mortally, while the *Citoyenne Française* lost her captain and 15 men killed and 37 wounded.

On the 27th of the same month, the *Venus*, carrying 38 guns and 192 men and boys, commanded by Captain Faulknor, engaged the *Sémillante*, mounting 40 guns and having a crew of about 300 men. The action commenced at long range at 8 A.M., and by 10, the two ships were scarcely half a cable's length from each other, equal to about 120 yards. The French frigate had suffered greatly and her guns were almost silenced, when a strange sail appeared in sight, which proved to be the French 36-gun frigate *Cléopatre*, and the opponent of the *Venus* got away, while the latter, being well to windward, was enabled to escape by crowding all sail. In this affair the *Venus* had two killed and twenty wounded, and the *Sémillante*, twelve and twenty respectively. Not so fortunate was the *Hyæna*, mounting 30 guns, some of small calibre, and having a crew of 120 men, in her engagement with the *Concorde*, a heavy frigate, carrying 44 guns. The Frenchman was one of a squadron and chased the *Hyæna*, which she overtook, and after a brief action, the latter struck her colours. Captain (afterwards Sir William) Hargood, was tried by a court-martial for the loss of his ship, and was honourably acquitted.

Very brilliant was the gallantry displayed by the officers and men of the frigate *Nymphe*, carrying 40* guns, commanded by Captain Edward Pellew, so well-known in our naval history as Sir Edward Pellew, and later as Lord Exmouth, one of the most successful frigate captains in the service. The *Nymphe* and *Venus* had chased the *Cléopatre* and *Sémillante*, already mentioned, into Cherbourg, and early in the morning of the 18th June the former British frigate, when cruising off the Start, sighted a sail to which she gave chase, and which proved to be the *Cléopatre*. Finding that he could not escape, the Frenchman hauled up his foresail and lowered his top-gallant-sails, and awaited his antagonist. The action commenced at 6.15, when the *Nymphe's* foremost guns bore on the *Cléopatre's* starboard quarter. So near were the ships that their respective captains had hailed each other, hat in hand, the crews cheering them, and by a preconcerted signal the British frigate opened fire when Captain Pellew replaced his hat upon his head. A furious action now ensued, the ships running before the wind, at close range, and in a quarter of an hour the *Cléopatre's* mizen-mast and wheel were shot away. The French frigate, which had just before hauled up with the wind abeam, paid off, in consequence of this double disaster, and shortly fell aboard her antagonist, her jibboom passing between the fore and main-masts of the *Nymphe*, and fortunately breaking short off, thus preserving the already wounded main-mast from carrying away. The two ships now fell alongside each other, head and stern, the

---

* In all the accounts of these frigate actions, we shall, as far as possible, give the actual number of guns carried, rather than those for which the ships were pierced, as the latter method gives an incorrect view of the relative strength of the combatants. This we are generally enabled to do by the detailed accounts given by James in his "Naval History." Ships-of-the-line and frigates usually carried between four and six, or even eight, guns more than they were classed for.

cannonade furiously proceeding, and while thus locked the British seamen boarded the French frigate, and at 7.10 one of them hauled down her colours, and the *Cléopatre* became the prize of H.M.S. *Nymphe*.

As regards guns the ships were well matched, each carrying twenty on a side, and though the British frigate threw a heavier broadside by 36 pounds, her crew numbered 240 to 320 carried by her antagonist. The *Nymphe* had three midshipmen, her boatswain, master's mate, and eighteen men killed, and her second lieutenant, two midshipmen, a lieutenant of marines, and 23 men wounded. The *Cléopatre* lost 63 killed and wounded, among the latter being three lieutenants, and the former included her captain. This officer, whose name was Mullon, had displayed signal gallantry throughout the action, and even in the agonies of death, his thoughts were of his country's service. A round shot had torn open his back, and carried away part of his left hip, but desirous of preserving from capture the list of coast-signals adopted in the French Navy, he pulled out of his pocket a paper which he thought was the one in question, and actually died while trying to chew and swallow it!

Captain Pellew brought his prize to Portsmouth, and, together with his brother, Commander (afterwards Sir Israel) Pellew, who was a passenger on board the *Nymphe*, was introduced to George III., who knighted the one brother and promoted the other to the rank of captain. The first lieutenant of the *Nymphe*, Mr. Morris, also received a step in rank. The prize was purchased into the Navy, and was re-named the *Oiseau*, there being a *Cleopatra* already in the service.

Another memorable action, though having a different result, was that between the British frigate *Boston*, Captain Courtenay, carrying 38 guns and 204 men and boys, and the *Embuscade*, Captain Bompart, of the same force, but having a crew of 327 hands, and being nearly one-third larger. The meeting between these champions of their respective navies was preconcerted, Captain Courtenay—who had, by a ruse, taken prisoner the first lieutenant and a boat's crew of twelve men belonging to the French frigate—having sent a challenge to Captain Bompart to meet off New York, and the action actually took place within sight of a great concourse of American citizens.

The *Embuscade* stood out from the land at daybreak on the 31st July, and after various manœuvres bore up and ranged along the *Boston's* weather-side, when the British frigate fired a broadside, which was promptly returned by her antagonist as she lay with her main-topsail to the mast. The *Boston* then wore, and coming to on the starboard tack, soon after five, laid her main-topsail to the mast, and a desperate action ensued. The fire of the French frigate was directed with fatal effect chiefly at the spars and rigging of the *Boston*. Within an hour of the commencement of the duel, her cross-jack-yard, jib, and fore-topmast stay-sail, as well as the stays, and all her braces and bow-lines, were shot away, so that she became unmanageable under sail, and soon after her main-topmast, carrying the yard with it, fell over the port side, rendering some of the guns useless. At 6.20, Captain Courtenay and Lieutenant Butler, of the Marines, were killed by the same round shot on the quarter-deck, and at the same time the mizen-topmast, with the spanker and mizen-staysail, were shot away, and the mizen-mast was tottering to its fall. Lieutenants Edwards and Kerr were wounded, the latter being blinded, and the former rendered senseless by a contusion on the head, but finding that the crew were in confusion for want of officers to give orders, he returned to the deck as soon as he had somewhat recovered, and took command of the ship. The *Embuscade*, discovering that her enemy was at her mercy, dropped a little astern and took up a position for raking her, but the *Boston* fortunately managed to wear round before she could effect this, though in coming to the wind on the port tack the wreck of the main-topmast, with its cordage and sails, prevented her from using her port guns. Finding himself unable to fight or defend his ship, Lieutenant Edwards put before the wind under all the sail he could set in the direction of Newfoundland, and was pursued by the *Embuscade*, which, however, soon gave up the chase and made the best of her way to New York.

Out of the crew of 204, all told, the *Boston* had two officers and eight men killed, and both her lieutenants, one master's mate, two midshipmen, and 19 seamen and marines wounded. The *Embuscade* had 50 killed and wounded out of her crew of 327, which included many Americans recruited at New York. During the action the British frigate expended 842 rounds of shot, 72 of grape, and 70 of case shot. The action was unequal as regards the strength of the respective crews, and the size of the ships, one being 676 and the other 906 tons, and though the *Boston* had the worst of the conflict, her officers and crew were not disgraced, but displayed a courage and tenacity in defending their ship which probably no other European nation would have shown. Though the *Embuscade* lost no masts during the action, on arriving at New York she hoisted them all out, and was engaged between the 2nd August and 9th October repairing damages. In acknowledgment of the gallantry displayed by Captain Courtenay, the king settled pensions of £500 on his widow and £50 on each of his two children.

More successful was Captain James Saumarez and the officers and men of the *Crescent*, carrying 42 guns and 257 men, in their engagement with the 36-gun frigate *Reunion*, the former thus having the superiority in weight of metal. The frigates met off Cape Barfleur, at daybreak on the 20th October, and early in the action the *Crescent* lost her fore-topsail-yard, and soon afterwards her fore-topmast, but putting her helm hard a-starboard, she came round on the opposite tack, bringing her port guns to bear on her adversary. Meantime the *Reunion* had lost her foreyard and mizen-topmast, and being unmanageable, was exposed to a terrible raking fire, and after a gallant resistance of two hours and ten minutes, hauled down her colours, having lost 33 officers and men killed and 48 wounded out of her crew of 300 men, while the *Crescent* had no casualties. Captain Saumarez, like Captain Pellew, was knighted for this brilliant victory, which was especially welcome to the nation at the beginning of a war which had every appearance of being protracted and bitter, and the first lieutenant, Mr. George Parker, was promoted to the rank of commander. The prize was purchased for the Navy, retaining her name.

At this time Captain Horatio Nelson, England's greatest naval hero, performed good service in the Mediterranean, and added to the reputation he had already achieved as a daring and ambitious officer. While cruising off the Sardinian coast in the *Agamemnon*, 64, on the 22nd October, at daybreak he sighted five sail standing to the westward. These were the *Melpomene*, 40, the 36-gun frigates *Minerve* and *Fortunée*, the *Mignonne*, 28, and *Hasard*, 14. On coming close to one of the frigates Captain Nelson hailed her, and receiving no answer, fired a shot ahead of her and crowded all sail in pursuit, being followed by the four other ships. As the chase continued the *Agamemnon* and frigate fired at each other, as they could bring their bow or stern guns to bear, until about 9 A.M., when, having run into a calm, the four other ships came up. But they made no attempt to attack the British 64, which was much damaged aloft, and pursued their way, leaving her unmolested.

On the 24th October an action, without a decisive result, was fought between the British frigate *Thames*, carrying 32 guns and 187 men, and the *Uranie*, of 44 guns and 320 men, and double the tonnage of her antagonist. The French frigate fired a gun to windward at 10.30, and soon the ships neared each other on contrary tacks, when the *Uranie* fired a broadside and wore round. A spirited action ensued, and about 2.30

the Republican frigate, getting under the stern of the *Thames*, poured in two or three raking broadsides and attempted to board. But the crew of the British frigate, nothing daunted by their critical situation, managed to retaliate by giving the *Uranie* some double-shotted rounds from a few of their main-deck guns, right through her bows, when she gave up the attempt, and throwing all her sails aback, hauled off, greeted by the hearty cheers of the British sailors.

In this action the *Thames* lost eleven men killed, and her second lieutenant, master, master's mate, one midshipman, and nineteen seamen and marines wounded. She was unable to pursue, owing to her shattered state aloft, all her lower masts being shot through in several places, and all her stays and main rigging cut to pieces. The main-topsail-yard was shot away at the slings, and the main-yard hung by the trusses about a third of the way down the masts, while the fore and mizen masts were almost equally damaged, the rigging being all shot away. Had the *Uranie* continued the action with the ship, practically a wreck, the result must have been disastrous, but she had doubtless also suffered greatly, and lay to about two miles off, repairing damages. The British seamen, expecting her to renew the action, busied themselves in refitting their ship, but the *Uranie* stood off as soon as she was in a condition to carry sail.

Hardly had the *Thames* made some sort of attempt to move under head sails before the wind, her mizen-mast being so damaged that she could spread no canvas on it, than four strange sail were descried coming up rapidly with the freshening breeze. These proved to be three French frigates, one the *Sémillante*, and a 16-gun brig. The *Carmagnole*, of 40 guns, ranged up under the stern of the *Thames* and gave her a broadside, on which Captain Cotes hailed that she was in a defenceless state, and struck his colours. The *Carmagnole* sent a boat to take possession, those of the *Thames* being all shattered, together with the gear for hoisting them out or lowering them, and taking the prize in tow, the French frigate steered for Brest, where she arrived on the following day, when the officers and men were placed in confinement as prisoners of war.

Brief mention need only be made of the capture, in the West Indies, of the French frigate *Inconstante*, 36, by the 32-gun frigate *Penelope*, Captain Rowley, and *Iphigenia*, Captain Sinclair, when the prize was purchased for the Navy under her own name. But a more detailed account is due of the gallantry displayed by the packet *Antelope*, carrying six 3-pounders and 21 men, exclusive of passengers, in her action with the privateer *Atalante*, mounting eight guns of the same calibre and having a crew of 65 men. The action was fought off Cuba on the 2nd December, when the wind having fallen, the privateer, being confident of success, rowed up to her antagonist, and grappled her on the starboard side. A long and stubbornly contested action ensued, and the *Antelope's* crew, assisted by the passengers, defeated every attempt of the enemy to board. The captain, Mr. Curtis, was killed, and the chief mate was shot through the body, but the boatswain, on whom the command devolved, continued the defence, repeatedly repulsing the boarders, and at length the privateer sheered off. But the turn of the gallant boatswain, Mr. Pasco, and his men was now come. Running aloft, he lashed the yard of the schooner's square sail to the fore shroud of the packet, and the privateersman, after receiving a volley of musketry, called for quarter, which was given them, though they had fought with the red flag at the mast-head, denoting that none would be granted. In this action the *Antelope* lost three killed and four wounded, and the *Atalante* had no less than her captain, chief officer, and 30 seamen slain, and 17 officers and men wounded. For their gallantry the Jamaica House of Assembly voted the sum of 500 guineas for distribution among the crew of the packet.

On the outbreak of war, hostile operations were undertaken by the British Navy in both the East and West Indies, and generally with success, the distracted condition of France, divided as the nation was between royalists and republicans, conducing to this result.

Throughout the early part of the Revolutionary War, until the superiority of the British Navy was established over that of France and Spain by the battles of St. Vincent and Trafalgar, the West India Islands, long considered the most valuable colonial possession of the crown of England, were the scene of constant and sanguinary strife. Mr. Froude describes in eloquent terms, in his "English in the West Indies," the relations subsisting between the mother country and her possessions in those seas, and the fearful sacrifice of life and treasure by which her hold on the West Indies was retained. He says:—"They had been regarded as precious jewels, which hundreds of thousands of English lives have been sacrificed to tear from France and Spain. The Carribean Sea was the cradle of the naval empire of Great Britain. There Drake and Hawkins intercepted the golden stream which flowed from Panama into the exchequer at Madrid, and furnished Philip with the means to carry on his war with the Reformation. The Pope had claimed to be Lord of the New World as well as of the Old, and had declared that Spaniards, and only Spaniards, should own territory and carry on trade within the tropics. The seamen of England took up the challenge, and replied with cannon shot. . . . In those waters the men were formed and trained who drove the Armada through the Channel into wreck and ruin. In those waters, in the centuries which followed, France and England fought for the Ocean Empire, and England won it—won it on that day when her own politicians' hearts had failed them, and all the powers of the world had combined to humiliate her, and Rodney shattered the French fleet, saved Gibraltar and avenged York Town. If ever the naval exploits of this country are done into an epic poem—and since the Iliad there has been no subject better fitted for such treatment, or better deserving it—the West Indies will be the scene of the most brilliant canto."

The West Indies was divided into two naval commands, called the Leeward Islands, whose headquarters were at Barbados, and the Windward Islands, with Jamaica for its chief station. Sir John Laforey, commanding on the former station, in conjunction with General Cuyler, undertook an expedition against the island of Tobago, where, on the 14th April, some troops were landed. The French Governor was summoned to surrender, but refusing to do so, the works were attacked and carried after a spirited resistance. But the commanders were not equally successful in their next enterprise. About the middle of June, Admiral Alan Gardner, who succeeded Sir John Laforey in the command, embarked 1,100 British and 800 French Royalist troops, under General Bruce, and proceeded to attack St. Pierre, in the island of Martinique, where they hoped to have the co-operation of the Royalist inhabitants. But they miscalculated the strength of this faction, and the Republicans made so determined a resistance that the troops were re-embarked with considerable loss. A terrible fate awaited the Royalists, of whom the majority, over 2,000 in number, were left behind on the island.

In consequence of the divided state of parties, civil war raged in the French West India islands, especially in St. Domingo, where the Royalists applied to Jamaica for assistance. Commodore Ford, commanding the few ships on this station, sailed for St. Domingo on the 20th October, conveying a detachment of the 13th and 49th regiments, under Colonel Whitlock, and the British flag was hoisted amid popular rejoicings, in the towns of Jeremie and Cape Nicholas Mole, the latter French port mounting 100 pieces of cannon, and at the close of the year the remaining districts acknowledging French dominion surrendered to Commodore Ford.

On the North American station, where Vice-Admiral Sir Richard King, having his flag in the *Stately*, 64, was in command, no sooner had hostilities been declared than the small fishing islands of St. Pierre and Miquelon, off the coast of Newfoundland, were seized by a combined British military and naval force, the former consisting of detachments of the 4th and 65th regiments. These islands had been ceded to the French in 1763, taken from them in 1778, and restored to them by the treaty concluded five years later.

In the East Indies the French also lost Pondicherry and their possessions in Bengal and the Malabar Coast. At this time the British naval force consisted of only the *Crown*, 64, at Madras, and one or two frigates and sloops at Calcutta, the whole under the command of Commodore Hon. William Cornwallis, in addition to the East India Company's own ships-of-war, whose headquarters were at Bombay, and their armed merchantmen trading between England and China and the ports in India. The historian of the naval war mentions an incident, that had taken place two years before the time of which we are treating, which merits some notice. The right to search neutral vessels claimed by England, which gave rise to this incident, was the cause of a war with America some twenty years later, and was one which this country was compelled to abandon.

During the war we waged with Tippoo Sultan, successor to Hyder Ali, ruler of Mysore, the British ships were engaged watching the port of Mangalore, in order to prevent the supply of stores by the French, who favoured the cause of our enemy. Early in 1791, Commodore Cornwallis, carrying his broad pennant in the *Minerva*, 38, was lying at anchor at Tellicherry, accompanied by the *Phœnix*, 36, Sir Richard Strachan, and *Perseverance*, Captain Smith, when the French frigate *Résolue*, of 36 guns, in company with two coasting vessels, got under way from Mahé, a factory belonging to that power, about seven miles to the southward of Tellicherry, and steered for Mangalore, which lay a few leagues to the northward of that port of the Rajah of Mysore. The British commodore, on seeing the *Résolue* abreast of his anchorage, detached the *Phœnix* and *Perseverance* to search her for contraband of war. Sir Richard Strachan ran alongside the French frigate, and hailing the captain to lie to while he executed his orders, lowered a boat to search the coasting vessels which the *Perseverance* had brought to. The French captain replied to this demand by firing at the *Phœnix*, upon which a spirited action ensued. But it was brief, for at the end of about twenty minutes the *Résolue* hauled down her flag, having sustained a loss of 25 men killed and 40 wounded. The *Phœnix*, to which she surrendered, the *Perseverance* having taken no part in the engagement, lost only six killed and 11 wounded, but the conflict was an unequal one, as she carried heavier guns and the French frigate was unprepared for action.

A search showed that the *Résolue* carried no contraband of war, and her captain declined to resume command of his ship, which was, accordingly, towed into Mahé roadstead, and left there. Soon afterwards Commodore Saint Felix, commanding the French squadron, arrived in the *Cybele*, 40, and an acrimonious correspondence ensued between him and Commodore Cornwallis, in which the French officer threatened resistance if any of his ships were detained, but, nevertheless, harmony was apparently restored between the rival commanders, who cruised in company for some days.

On the 1st June intelligence was received at Madras of the declaration of war between France and England, and Commodore Cornwallis immediately took measures for seizing the French factories and settlements at Chandernagore, Karical, and Mahé, which were all occupied without resistance. The fortress of Pondicherry, being prepared for defence, refused to capitulate, and was besieged by a military force, under Colonel Braithwaite, Commodore Cornwallis co-operating with the *Minerva* and three of the East India Company's ships in blockading the place and driving the *Cybele* off the coast. After a bombardment lasting three days, Pondicherry, with its garrison of 645 Europeans and 1,314 Sepoys, surrendered on the 23rd October. The British loss during the brief siege was 37 Europeans and 56 native troops killed, and 49 Europeans and 82 natives wounded.

During the year 1793, British cruisers had captured or destroyed fifty-two ships of the French Navy, and ninety-eight privateers and armed vessels. Of the former thirty-five were captured, of which thirty were purchased into the British Navy, and six of the privateers were also added to the service. On the other hand, the Navy only sustained the loss of the *Scipion*, 74, accidentally burnt at Leghorn, and the *Thames*, 32, *Hyæna*, 24, and *Alerte*, 14, captured.

The year 1794 is chiefly memorable in our naval annals for Lord Howe's victory over the French fleet, which is generally known as the "Glorious First of June." Parliament and the nation were enthusiastic in the prosecution of the war, and supplies were voted for 85,000 seamen and marines.

Many changes were made in the *personnel* of the French Navy. All officers having Royalist proclivities were forced to retire, and some, including the captain and two lieutenants of the *Côte d'Or* and the captain of the *Jean Bart*, as well as several petty officers and seamen, were guillotined, and Admiral Kerguelen and other officers and men were thrown into prison. Monsieur Villaret-Joyeuse, relatively a junior officer, was promoted to the rank of rear-admiral, and raised to the command of the Brest fleet in succession to Admiral Morard de Galles. The new commander-in-chief hoisted his flag on board the *Côte d'Or*, renamed the *Montagne*, considered the finest man-of-war afloat, and the tri-coloured flag was adopted as the National emblem, and has since remained so. The French seamen of Brest and L'Orient were wrought up to the highest pitch of Republican and national ardour by addresses from deputies of the Convention sitting in Paris, which actually adopted a decree declaring that the death penalty should be inflicted on the captain and officers of any ship-of-the-line that struck her colours to any hostile force, however superior, unless she was actually sinking, and the same applied to the commander and officers of a frigate or smaller vesssel surrendering to a force double their strength.

The British Ministry assembled a vast fleet at Spithead, under command of the veteran seamen, Lord Howe, with the double object, besides the primary one of engaging the enemy, of convoying the East and West India and Newfoundland merchant fleets clear of the Channel, and of intercepting a French convoy returning from America, laden with the produce of the West India islands.

At length, on the 2nd May, the wind having shifted to a favourable quarter, Lord Howe stood down Channel with a fleet of 34 sail-of-the-line and fifteen frigates, convoying 99 merchantmen. Two days later, the vast armament arrived off the Lizard, when Lord Howe directed the different convoys to part company, and detached Rear-Admiral Montagu, with six 74's, and two frigates, to see them as far as the latitude of Cape Finisterre, when their protection was to be confided to Captain Rainier, of the *Suffolk*, 74, who had under his orders a 64-gun ship and four frigates. This reduced the fleet under his lordship's orders, for the prosecution of the great object of engaging the Brest fleet, to 26 sail-of-the line, seven frigates, and six small vessels. The fleet, as now constituted was commanded by seven flag-officers, and consisted of the following ships:—

100	Queen Charlotte	Admiral Earl Howe Captain Sir George Curtis „ Sir Andrew S. Douglas		Ramillies	Captain Henry Harvey
	Royal George	Vice-Admiral Sir Alexander Hood, K.B. Captain W. Domett		Audacious	„ William Parker
				Brunswick	„ John Harvey
				Alfred	„ John Bazeley
				Defence	„ James Gambier
	Royal Sovereign	Vice-Admiral Thomas Graves Captain Henry Nichols		Leviathan	„ Lord Hugh Seymour
			74	Majestic	„ Charles Cotton
98	Barfleur	Rear-Admiral George Bowyer Captain Cuthbert Collingwood		Invincible	„ Hon. Thomas Pakenham
				Orion	„ John T. Duckworth
	Impregnable	Rear-Admiral B. Caldwell Captain George B. Westcott		Russell	„ John W. Payne
				Marlborough	„ Hon. C. G. Berkeley
	Queen	Rear-Admiral Alan Gardner Captain John Hutt		Thunderer	„ Albemarle Bertie
	Glory	Captain John Elphinstone		Culloden	„ Isaac Schomberg
80	Gibraltar	Captain Thomas Mackenzie		**FRIGATES.**	
	Cæsar	„ Anthony J. P. Molloy	38	Phaeton	Captain William Bentinck
74	Bellerophon	Rear-Admiral Thomas Pasley Captain William Hope		Latona	„ Edward Thornborough
	Montague	Captain James Montagu	32	Niger	„ Hon. A. K. Legge
	Tremendous	„ James Pigott		Southampton	„ Hon. Robert Forbes
	Valiant	„ Thomas Pringle		Venus	„ William Brown
				Aquilon	„ Hon. Robert Stopford
			28	Pegasus	„ Robert Barlow

A 28-GUN FRIGATE, ABOUT 1794

There were many officers who subsequently acquired renown among the captains of Lord Howe's fleet, including Collingwood, Nelson's second-in-command at Trafalgar, Duckworth, who forced the Dardanelles in 1807, Gambier, and Stopford, who survived to command the fleet which bombarded Acre in 1840.

Lord Howe stood over for Ushant, when the *Phaeton* and *Latona*, covered by the *Orion*, proceeding round the island, discovered the enemy's fleet at anchor in Brest Roads. Satisfied on this point, Lord Howe stood for the latitude through which the merchantmen from America must pass, and between the 5th and 18th May, the fleet under his command kept crossing the bay of Biscay in various directions to intercept the convoy, but without sighting an enemy's sail. Lord Howe now returned off Ushant, and again despatched the same frigates to reconnoitre the port of Brest, when they rejoined him the same evening with the report that the birds had flown, and the harbour was empty. But the *Leviathan*, which, with the *Cæsar*, escorted the frigates, had spoken an American vessel from whose captain Lord Hugh Seymour learned that the French fleet had sailed from Brest a few days before.

It was on the 16th May that Admiral Villaret-Joyeuse, flying his flag on board the *Montagne*, 120, ventured out to sea with twenty-five ships-of-the-line and fifteen frigates, with the object of escorting the convoy of one hundred and seventeen sail, which had sailed from Norfolk in Virginia, having cargoes of provisions and West India produce. This convoy was under the escort of four 74's, two frigates and a brig, under Rear-Admiral Vanstabel, who was reinforced by a squadron from Rochefort of five ships-of-the-line and several frigates, under Rear-Admiral Nielly. On the day succeeding that on which he sailed from Brest, in a dense fog, Monsieur Villaret-Joyeuse passed so close to the British fleet that he could hear their signals, but on the morning of the 18th, when the fog had cleared off, the rival fleets were out of sight of each other. On the following day the French commander-in-chief was joined by one of Admiral Nielly's ships, with the information that he had captured the British 32-gun frigate *Castor*, Captain Thomas Troubridge, an officer destined to attain great fame as one of Nelson's most trusted captains, together with the greater portion of a convoy from Newfoundland he was escorting. On the same day Admiral Villaret fell in with the Lisbon fleet of fifty-three sail, chiefly Dutch ships, under the convoy of two Dutch men-of-war, which managed to effect their escape, leaving in his hands some eighteen or twenty of the merchantmen.

Meanwhile, Admiral Montagu, having, on the 11th May, parted with the East

Indiamen, cruised between Cape Ortugal and the latitude of Belleisle, as ordered by his instructions, in order to intercept the French convoy from America, and on the 15th was fortunate enough to recapture ten sail of the Newfoundland fleet, taken by Admiral Nielly, together with a 20-gun ship escorting them. From this source Admiral Montagu learned that the strength of the two French squadrons under Nielly and Vanstabel, if united, would outnumber his own by three sail-of-the-line, and detached a frigate to Lord Howe with a request for a reinforcement, continuing his cruise with his six 74's and remaining frigate.

The British commander-in-chief was joined by the frigate on the 19th, and fearing that his colleague might be overpowered by Admiral Villaret, on the following day sailed to effect a junction with him. Two days later he sighted part of the Lisbon convoy taken by the Brest fleet, and out of fifteen sail, managed to recapture ten, which were burnt, as his lordship did not wish to lessen his strength by detaching prize crews to take them into port. Lord Howe learnt from his prisoners the proximity of the main French fleet, and being of opinion that Admiral Montagu was far enough to the southward to be out of danger, he crowded sail in pursuit of the enemy. The greatest enthusiasm prevailed among all ranks of the British fleet to meet and engage the French, and they learned with satisfaction that Admiral Villaret-Joyeuse and his men were equally desirous of trying conclusions at close quarters. Further intelligence of the whereabouts of the French fleet was received from a Dutch ship on the 23rd, and two days later a French 74 was sighted to windward with a merchant vessel in tow. These were chased, when the line-of-battle ship, casting off her prize, escaped, but the brig was captured, and from her they learned that the former was on its way from Admiral Nielly's squadron to join the commander-in-chief. At the same time two smaller French ships-of-war were captured and all three were burnt. Nothing of importance occurred during the next few days, until, on the morning of the 28th May, the long expected and eagerly hoped for French fleet was discovered by the look-out frigates. At 9 A.M. the enemy changed their course and bore down on the British fleet under top-gallant sails, and Lord Howe made the signal to clear for action. An hour later Admiral Villaret, being now within nine or ten miles, hauled to the wind on the port tack, and laid to ready for battle.

The magnificent fleet of twenty-six sail-of-the-line and five frigates made an imposing display, and many hearts in both hostile arrays must have beat high, as for the first time in the war the relative efficiency of the British and French Navies was to be put to the only test which can be accepted as satisfactory, that of actual battle. If enthusiasm and the confidence inspired by victories on land, achieved at Valmy and Jemappes, not to mention the success at Toulon, could ensure success, the French officers and seamen might well count upon adding fresh glories to the Republican tricolour on the first occasion of its being displayed in battle at sea against the hereditary foe of their country; but the experienced officers afloat knew that more than this was required to ensure success, and here again the auguries, they considered, were favourable. The French fleet was well found in material and equipment, and the crews were carefully disciplined and well trained, and, indeed, no efforts had been spared to make the Brest fleet efficient for the ordeal of battle. Not less sanguine were the officers and men opposed to them. Defeat was an unknown word in the British Navy, and no fleet that had ever put to sea was in a better condition than that now waiting for the signal to engage. Though, after ten years of peace, most of the captains now, for the first time, commanded ships-of-the-line in action, they had all owed their selection to their professional qualifications. Above all they were led by a veteran admiral, who had often met and always triumphed over the enemy now before them, an officer whose skill in the handling of fleets was invariably acknowledged to be unrivalled since Hawke and Kempenfeldt had quitted the scene. Howe stood at the head of his profession, and his second-in-command, Sir Alexander Hood (afterwards Lord Bridport), was worthy to be his colleague.

Regarding the comparative force of the two fleets on the morning of the 28th May, the historian James, who made a careful analysis from official returns, makes the numbers of ships-of-the-line in each case the same, namely twenty-six. The guns of the British fleet numbered 2,170 against 2,214 carried by the enemy, and the aggregate crews were 17,241 in the former case, and 19,989 in the latter. The total tonnage of the French ships was about 5,000 more than that of Lord Howe's fleet, and, owing to the former carrying heavier guns, their broadside was as 28,126 pounds to 22,976. The fleets were thus fairly well matched, and what disparity there existed was in favour of the enemy.

There was some manœuvring between the hostile fleets until about 1 P.M., when the French ships filled and made sail, whereupon they were closely followed by the British fleet, to whom the commander-in-chief made a signal to engage the enemy as they overhauled them.

The first to fire a shot was the *Russell*, which was nearly a mile to windward, but the challenge was not accepted beyond a few rounds in return, and about three, the whole of the fleet went about on the starboard tack, on which the enemy were standing. About six o'clock the *Bellerophon*, 74, was near enough to open fire on the *Revolutionnaire*, 110, now the rearmost ship, but the heavy metal of her enemy was too much for her, and after sustaining her fire, unaided, for an hour and a quarter, Rear-Admiral Thomas Pasley, whose flagship she was, was obliged to bear up. By this time the *Russell*, *Marlborough*, and *Thunderer* were enabled to open a distant fire on the three-decker, which, having lost her mizen-mast and being otherwise disabled, wore round and put before the wind. But she was intercepted by the *Leviathan*, 74, which engaged her until the *Audacious*, 74, Captain William Parker, came up, when she passed on, and after firing a broadside at the ship next in the French line, in obedience to a signal from the commander-in-chief, dropped down towards the main division of the fleet.

The *Audacious* and *Revolutionnaire* were closely engaged until ten o'clock, when the great three-decker, having had her fore and main yards and main-topsail yard shot away, dropped athwart hawse the British 74, but the latter managed to extricate herself, when the Frenchman directed his course to leeward as best he could. Notwithstanding her crippled state the *Audacious*, owing to the fire of her huge adversary, was in no condition to compel her surrender, though she hailed the *Thunderer*, 74, to take possession of her, which, however, the latter failed to do. The *Audacious* passed the night in repairing her damages, but was in so shattered a condition that by daylight she had only her fore and main topmast staysails set, her foresail and three topsails being as yet "unbent," owing to her spars and rigging being almost shot away. In this helpless state she sighted nine French sail about three miles to windward, but fortunately rain and thick weather screened her from their view. The crew redoubled their efforts to refit their ship, but the weather soon cleared, and discovered in chase a frigate and a ship-of-the-line, which, by a coincidence, had the same name as herself. Setting all the sail that was "bent," the *Audacious* passed within a mile and a half of the *Revolutionnaire*, totally dismasted, and soon after she found the *Bellone*, a French 36-gun frigate, encouraged by her state and the proximity of her consorts, standing across her path. She, however, succeeded in shaking off this fresh antagonist, and hazy weather again supervening, the *Audacious* was enabled to make for Plymouth, and anchored in the Sound on the 3rd June. The *Revolutionnaire* was taken in tow by the *Audacieux*, and conveyed in safety to Rochefort. The loss of the French three-decker in her engagement with the *Bellerophon* and *Audacious* was, according to French accounts, no less than 400 *hors de combat*, while the latter ship, to which the chief credit of disabling her huge antagonist was due, had only three men killed and nineteen wounded.

During the night of the 29th May, the hostile fleets steered, under a press of sail, on the starboard tack, on a parallel course, and when daylight broke they were about six miles apart, the French ships being on the weather bow of their opponents. At seven o'clock the British fleet went about on the port tack, and then Lord Howe made the signal to pass through the enemy's line, the *Cæsar* and *Queen* firing as they performed this manœuvre. The French fleet wore in succession on the port tack, and as the two vans neared each other, the *Invincible, Royal George, Valiant, Russell, Queen,* and *Cæsar* exchanged broadsides with the French foremost ships.

Soon after noon Lord Howe gave the order to tack to starboard, and an hour later, to break through the enemy's line, himself leading in the *Queen Charlotte*, but the leading ship, the *Cæsar*, made the signal of inability to tack, and wearing, ran past the eighth ship of her own line, and her commanding officer, Captain Molloy, showed no disposition to engage. Meanwhile the *Queen*, 98, flying the flag of Rear-Admiral Alan Gardner, became closely engaged, and having passed the last ship in the French line, was disabled, and with difficulty succeeded in wearing on the port tack.

The *Queen Charlotte* was closely followed in her manœuvre of breaking the enemy's line, by the *Bellerophon* and *Leviathan*, and the commander-in-chief then went about on the port tack, and hoisting the signal for a general chase, left the rearmost French ships, *Tyrannicide* and *Indomptable*, which had been disabled by the *Royal George* and *Invincible*, to be brought to by his consorts astern, and pursued the *Terrible*, which had carried away her fore-topmast by heavy pitching; and the French van, having wore round on the starboard tack, reached near the centre of the fleet before the *Queen Charlotte* could approach her near enough to open fire. The *Orion* passed between the *Tyrannicide* and *Indomptable*, and being unable to chase, owing to her disabled state, bore up, and laying her main-topsail to the mast, engaged the latter 80-gun ship. Scarcely had the *Orion* poured two broadsides into her antagonist than the *Barfleur* arrived and also engaged the *Indomptable*.

Soon afterwards Admiral Villaret-Joyeuse made the signal for his fleet to wear in succession, but finding his signal disregarded, wore out of the line, and led the way to the rescue of the *Tyrannicide* and *Indomptable* in the rear. Lord Howe, having only near him, on the lee quarter, in a crippled state, the *Bellerophon* and *Leviathan*, was not in a condition to prevent the success of the French admiral's manœuvre, and all the *Queen Charlotte* could do was to wear, and with the other ships near her run down to cover the *Queen* and *Royal George*, towards which his antagonist had bent his course. This moment, says James, again brought the vans of the rival fleets within range of a distant cannonade, but Admiral Villaret-Joyeuse, having executed his design of relieving his two disabled ships, appeared disinclined to accept his adversary's challenge to a general engagement, and wearing round on the port tack, rejoined his rear. The British fleet followed motions, retaining the weather-gage, and a little after five all firing ceased. The hostile fleets now busied themselves in repairing damages.

During the action, which was of a partial character, twelve or fourteen ships only were engaged, and of these the *Queen, Royal George, Royal Sovereign*, and *Invincible* suffered considerably in killed and wounded, and were much cut up in their spars and rigging. The *Queen*, which had her mizen-mast and foreyard shot away, and her mainmast, bowsprit, and fore-topmast shot through, lost her master and 21 seamen and marines* killed, and Captain John Hutt, the sixth lieutenant, and 25 men wounded. The *Royal George* had her eighth lieutenant, one midshipman, and 15 men killed, and 23 wounded. The *Invincible*, which had her main-topmast shot away, lost 10 killed and 21 wounded, including a midshipman; and the *Royal Sovereign* had eight killed and 22 wounded. The total casualties of the British fleet were 67 killed, including the sixth lieutenant of the *Queen Charlotte*, and 128 wounded.

The 30th and 31st May were passed without a shot being fired, though the fleets were in sight of each other. The weather was foggy on the first-named day, but cleared on the 31st, and the fleets towards evening were less than five miles apart. A general action might have been brought on, but Lord Howe preferred to wait until daylight, when there could be no difficulty in understanding the signals. All that night the British carried a press of sail, in order to keep up with the enemy, and the *Phaeton* and *Latona* frigates were stationed about a mile to leeward, to watch the motions of the French ships, which had all apparently repaired damages, and were in a condition to renew the engagement on the morrow.

This was due to the circumstance that Admiral Villaret-Joyeuse had lost the services of the *Montagnard*, the captain of which had quitted the scene of conflict with

---

* Soldiers of the regular army served at this time in the fleet as marines, those under Lord Howe's command being from the 2nd Queen's and 29th regiments.

out orders, and had sent into port the *Indomptable*, escorted by the *Mont Blanc*, 74. But the places in his line of battle occupied by these three ships and the *Revolutionnaire* had been filled by four fresh ships. The following was therefore the strength of the French fleet on the eventful First of June :—

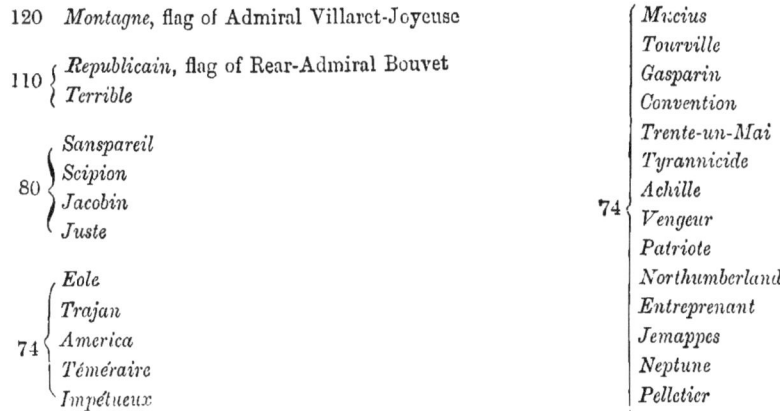

The order for breakfast was given at 7.30, and the British fleet, which had hove to while this necessary preliminary to an arduous day's work was completed, filled and bore down on the enemy's line, through which the commander-in-chief had by signal expressed his intention to pass, with the object of engaging to leeward. At 8.12 precisely the British fleet was in motion, and a few minutes later the *Queen Charlotte* displayed the signal for each ship to steer for and independently engage the ship opposite to her in the enemy's line.

With a view to his three-deckers being opposed to the heavy French ships, Lord Howe made some changes in his line, and when all had taken up their respective stations the British fleet, twenty-five sail-of-the-line, with the frigates as usual in the rear, was formed in line abreast. The French fleet, twenty-six battleships, was drawn up in a close head and stern line, and both fleets were under single-reefed topsails, with a fresh breeze, which carried the British ships at a speed a little over five knots an hour.

The first shot in this battle, so momentous in its results, was fired at 9.24 A.M. by the French van upon the British leading ships, the *Defence* being a little in advance. With the signal for close action flying at her mast-head, the *Queen Charlotte* steered for the great three-decker *Montagne*, 120, bearing the flag of Admiral Villaret-Joyeuse, and was saluted by the fire of the *Vengeur*, 74, the third ship in rear of the French admiral, but instead of returning the compliment, Lord Howe, in his anxiety to lead through the enemy's line, set his foresail and top-gallantsails, which brought him abreast of the next ship in the line, the *Achille*, which now opened fire.

The British commander-in-chief, intending to reserve his main attack for the *Montagne*, ordered that only the guns on the upper and quarter decks should reply to the *Achille*, but the guns' crews, stationed on the lower and middle decks, hearing the firing overhead, considered that they were at liberty to begin, and at a few minutes before ten poured a broadside into the French 74. Then with sailorlike promptness they reloaded their guns, and manned the port batteries in readiness to open fire on the *Montagne*. Passing close under the stern of the three-decker, so close indeed that the tricolour on her flagstaff brushed the main and mizen shrouds of the *Queen Charlotte*, the latter poured a tremendous broadside right into the stern of Admiral Villaret's flagship. Lord Howe intended to take up a position alongside the *Montagne*, but at this time the *Jacobin*, 80, which stood next in the line, afraid apparently of receiving her broadside, had stretched ahead, and was nearly abreast of the French commander-in-chief's flagship. Lord Howe expressed his regret at the *Jacobin* taking up a position he intended to occupy, when Mr. Bowen, master of the *Queen Charlotte*, observing by the motion of her rudder, that she was in the act of bearing up, by one of those intuitive acts which betoken the possession of genius, ordered the helm to be put "hard a-starboard," and the British flagship, luffing up, with her jib-boom grazing the port mizen shrouds of the *Jacobin*, directed her starboard guns into the stern and port quarter of the 80-gun ship, while her opposite battery poured in a close fire into the starboard quarter of the *Montagne*. The *Jacobin* was temporarily becalmed, as she lay under the lee of the British flagship, but dropping astern, was enabled soon to return the fire as her guns were brought to bear, and a lucky shot carried away the *Queen Charlotte's* fore-topmast. Meanwhile the *Montagne* had suffered terribly from the broadsides of the British three-decker. Her stern frame and starboard quarter were greatly shattered, and upwards of 100 men were killed and nearly 200 wounded, but soon after ten she was enabled to range ahead clear of the fire of her adversary.

The *Queen Charlotte* now found herself between the *Jacobin*, still on her starboard quarter, and the *Juste*, 80, the ship second ahead of the *Montagne*, but the former soon after disappeared in the smoke to leeward. The battle raged furiously between the *Juste* and the *Queen Charlotte*, which slowly drifted together towards the van of the two lines, both ships suffering severely. The former was totally dismasted, and the British flagship lost her main-topmast, and this, together with the loss previously experienced of her fore-topmast, and the damaged state of her rigging and lower yards, rendered her quite unmanageable.

Thus almost single-handed, save by the distant fire of the *Invincible*, Lord Howe engaged these three powerful ships-of-the-line. At this time a fourth adversary appeared in the *Republicain*, 110, carrying the flag of Rear-Admiral Bouvet, bearing down under all sail on the weather quarter of the *Queen Charlotte*. Just as the undaunted officers and seamen of the latter were expecting to receive, and preparing to return her fire, the main and mizen-masts of the French three-decker came down by the board from the distant fire of the *Gibraltar*. Instantly the *Republicain* bore up and passed within gunshot astern of the *Queen Charlotte*, but so great was the confusion on board that she neglected the opportunity of raking the flagship.

When the *Montagne*, followed by the *Jacobin*, crowding all sail, stood on, Lord Howe, fearing that they intended to escape, hoisted the signal for a general chase, but Admiral Villaret, on nearly reaching his van and being joined by nine other ships, wore round on the starboard tack and stood towards the *Queen*, which was almost defenceless owing to the loss of her mainmast and mizen-topmast. Seeing her danger, Lord Howe signalled his ships to close and form in line ahead and astern of her, and himself wore round with difficulty on the starboard tack. Followed by the *Barfleur*, *Thunderer*, *Royal Sovereign*, *Valiant*, *Leviathan*, and some others, the *Queen Charlotte* stood towards Admiral Gardner's flagship, when Monsieur Villaret gave up the attempt and stretched on to the support of his crippled ships. In this he succeeded almost beyond expectation, as he ought to have been repelled by those British ships which had taken little part in the action. The *Republicain*, which had lost her main and mizen-masts, and the *Mucius*, *Scipion*, and *Jemappes*, which were dismasted, were saved, and a fifth, the *Terrible*, which had also lost her main and mizen-masts, had previously joined him, having gallantly fought her way from out of the midst of her enemies. But there were six other dismasted French ships—the *Achille*, *America*, *Juste*, *Northumberland*, *Sanspareil*, and *Impetueux*,* (which had also lost her bowsprit)—and these were secured about 2.30, the firing, which had lasted since nine o'clock, having generally ceased about 1.15.

* The *Impetueux* caught fire on the 24th August following, while lying at her moorings in Portsmouth harbour. The flames spread with such rapidity as seemed to threaten the destruction of the whole dockyard, and the inhabitants of the town were so alarmed at the ship's nearness to the powder magazine, that they fled in all directions. The French prisoners at Porchester Castle, amounting to nearly 5,000, evinced feelings of quite an opposite kind. They shouted, "Vive la Republique!" and sang "Ça-ira" and the Marseillaise hymn all the while the flames were raging. To their disappointment, however, the proper precautions had been taken, and the *Impetueux*, after burning to the water's edge, drifted clear, and grounded upon the mud on the west side of the harbour.

Shortly after six, the *Vengeur*, 74, which had been engaged in a desperate conflict with the *Brunswick* of the same force, was taken possession of, but in so shattered a state, that she sank ten minutes afterwards, taking down with her 200 of her crew, mostly wounded.

The *Queen Charlotte*, in addition to the loss of her fore and main topmasts, with the yards, had her fore and main yards and all three lower masts wounded in several places, and her standing and running rigging much cut up. Her loss was the seventh lieutenant, a subaltern of infantry, and eleven men killed, and Captain Sir Andrew Douglas, one midshipman, and 27 seamen and marines wounded. Her antagonist, the *Montagne*, lost 300 killed and wounded, among the former being the flag-captain, two or three lieutenants, and several midshipmen, and among the wounded was a large number of officers. Though not injured aloft, she received over 250 shot in her hull, which was much shattered in every part, and among her injuries her rudder was unhung, two of the gun-room ports on the starboard side were knocked into one, the binnacle and wheel were destroyed, also the stern gallery, and all the boats, as well on the davits as on all the booms.

The British loss in the battle of the 1st June and the preliminary skirmishes of the 28th and 29th of May was 1,148, of whom 290 were killed and 858 wounded. Among the former was Captain Montagu, of the *Montague*, and the wounded included Rear-Admirals Bowyer and Pasley, Captain Hutt of the *Queen* (who lost a leg), and Captain Harvey of the *Brunswick* (mortally). The French placed their loss in killed and mortally wounded alone at 3,000, so that probably their total loss could not be much under 7,000 men.*

We will now give a detailed account of the part individually taken by each ship, in which we must express our acknowledgments to the naval historian James.

The *Cæsar*, 80, led the British van, but the conduct of Captain Molloy, who had misbehaved in the affair of the 29th May, was one of the unpleasant incidents of the day. Instead of bearing down under the stern of the enemy's van ship, as directed by signal, he brought to at a distance of over five hundred yards to windward. At a later period, anxious to retrieve his error and act in obedience to the signal flying on board the *Bellerophon*, his flag-officer's ship, Captain Molloy attempted to wear and make sail, but the tiller rope had become jammed by a shot, and the rudder would not move. The ship

---

* The six captured ships were stated to have lost as follows:—*Sanspareil,* 260 killed and 120 wounded; *Juste,* 100 and 145; *America,* 134 and 110; *Impetueux,* 100 and 75; *Northumberland,* 60 and 100; *Achille,* 36 and 30. Thus their loss was greater than that sustained by the whole British fleet.

dropped astern and when the accident was remedied, and she bore up to re-engage, was too late to be of much service, and her appointed opponent, the *Trajan*, had wore out of the line, having suffered a loss of only three men killed and a few wounded. During the action, the *Cæsar* had seven guns disabled by shot and one burst, and lost by the enemy's fire 14 men killed and 52 wounded, exclusive of five casualties caused by the bursting of a 24-pounder. Captain Molloy, having felt aggrieved by a passage in Lord Howe's despatch describing the partial action of the 29th May, demanded a court-martial, at which his conduct on the 1st June was also considered, when the court found a verdict that, while his personal courage was unimpeachable, he had not done his best to pass through the French line on the 29th May, nor taken a proper station for engaging the enemy on the 1st June, and adjudged him to be dismissed from the command of his ship.

The *Bellerophon*, 74, carrying the flag of Rear-Admiral Pasley, stood next in the British line to the *Cæsar*, and her part in the fray was much more honourable. With the flag for close action flying at her mast-head, and receiving the fire of three headmost French ships, the *Bellerophon* bore down on the *Eole*, 74, the ship opposite to her in the enemy's line, and taking up a position on her weather-quarter, engaged the French seventy-four within musket-shot range. Besides running the gauntlet of a portion of the French line, and engaging the *Eole*, the *Bellerophon* received the distant fire of the *Trajan*, which ought to have been engrossed by the *Cæsar*. About two hours after the commencement of the action, Admiral Pasley lost his leg, and the command devolved on Captain Wm. Hope, who continued to engage the *Eole* until about 11.45, when the latter wore out of action, but was closely followed by the *Bellerophon*, which carried away her fore and main-topmasts in effecting the manœuvre, the result of the heavy fire of her two opponents. All her boats were shot away, her main-mast was wounded, and all her rigging was cut to pieces so that she was unable to haul to the wind in pursuit of the fugitive. Her loss, however, in killed and wounded was small, only four being in the former category, and three officers and 24 men in the latter.

The *Leviathan*, Lord Hugh Seymour, the next ship in the line, engaged the *America*, 74, in close action, and at the end of about an hour shot away her adversary's foremast. Shortly before noon the *Trajan* and *Eole*, passing to leeward, fired upon the *Leviathan*, but soon passed on, when the British and French seventy-fours wore round together, and renewed the action. So severe had been the fire of the former that the main and mizen-masts of the *America* went by the board, and thus she lay dismasted, and rolled defenceless on the water. But the gallant crew, though they had lost more than one-third their number, and three of their guns were dismounted and burst, kept her flag flying on a stump, and the *Leviathan*, in obedience to a signal from the commander-in-chief, made sail to join his lordship. While inflicting this terrible loss on her opponent by the accuracy of her fire, the *Leviathan* had only her fore-topsail yard shot away, though her rigging was a good deal cut, and she lost 10 men killed and 33 wounded, including one midshipman (mortally).

The *Russell*, 74, Captain Payne, was opposed to the *Téméraire*, 74, and about ten o'clock lost her fore-topmast, but this did not prevent her, when the *Téméraire* made sail to leeward, from following her through the line, but she was compelled (owing to her fore-topmast, which hung through the top, preventing her from trimming sail in any other direction) to come to the wind again on the port tack. The *Russell*, after receiving a broadside from the *Trajan* and *Eole*, and giving a couple to the mastless *America*, passed to the assistance of the *Leviathan*, and accompanied her to the new line forming astern of the *Queen Charlotte*. About 2.45, in compliance with a signal to stay by prizes, Captain Payne stood for the *America*, which, not being in a position to offer resistance, hauled down her colours. The *Russell's* loss was only eight killed and twenty-six wounded.

The *Royal Sovereign*, 100, bearing the flag of Vice-Admiral Thomas Graves, engaged the *Terrible*, 110, flagship of Admiral Bouvet. Soon after the commencement of the action, Admiral Graves was severely wounded, and the command devolved on Captain Nichols. The *Terrible* had her main and mizen-masts shot away, and immediately bore up, in doing which she was repeatedly raked by the *Royal Sovereign*, which followed in pursuit, whereupon the *Montagne* and *Jacobin* came to the rescue. At a quarter before twelve, the British three-decker commenced a close action with the French commander-in-chief's flagship, which bore up in about half an hour, and was followed a short distance by the *Royal Sovereign*, but hauled up as well as the disabled state of her rigging would permit. In the action the *Royal Sovereign* had all three top-gallant-masts shot away, and lost one midshipman and 13 sailors and marines killed, and 41 wounded, exclusive of the admiral and two military officers.

The next ship to the *Royal Sovereign* in the British line was the *Marlborough*, 74, Captain Hon. Grantley Berkeley, which was opposed to the *Impetueux*, of the same force. Passing under the latter's stern, she ranged up alongside of her to leeward, and soon the two ships became entangled. In this position a most deadly conflict ensued.

An hour later, the *Mucius*, astern of the *Impetueux*, which was engaged with the *Defence*, made sail to get clear of her adversary, and fell on board the bow of the *Marlborough*, "the three ships thus forming a triangle, of which the *Marlborough* was the base." The gallant captain of the British seventy-four maintained the unequal contest with the spirit of his race, but soon his mizen-mast went over the side, and was followed by his fore and main-masts. His persevering gallantry was rewarded by the dismasting of both his opponents, the *Impetueux*, in addition, losing her bowsprit, so that she had not a "stick" standing. It was stated that both ships surrendered, but a diversion was created by the arrival on the scene of the great 120-gun ship, *Montagne*, which poured in a raking fire, as she passed under the *Marlborough's* stern, by which Captain Berkeley was wounded. Lieutenant Monckton assumed command of the *Marlborough*, and continued the defence of his ship with unabated vigour and skill. At length he made the signal for assistance, and was taken in tow by the *Aquilon*. Meantime the *Mucius* effected her escape, but the *Impetueux*, which had lost 100 killed and 75 wounded, was taken possession of by the *Russell*, which had yielded up the *America* to the *Royal Sovereign*. The *Marlborough* had also suffered severely, having one midshipman and 28 men killed, and her captain, second and fifth lieutenants, one master's mate, four midshipmen, and 82 seamen and marines wounded.

The *Defence*, 74, which, being in advance, was the first to cut through the enemy's line, was soon so hotly engaged with the *Mucius* and *Tourville*, that she lost her main and mizen-masts. Her two antagonists made sail from her, but other French ships approached, including the *Republician*, 110, which had only her foremast standing, and Captain Gambier was compelled to make the signal for assistance. The *Republicain* having run to leeward, the *Phaeton*, frigate, arrived to take the *Defence* in tow, her remaining mast having gone over the side. She lost in this stubborn defence her master, boatswain, and 15 men killed, and two officers and 34 wounded.

The British ships *Impregnable*, *Tremendous*, *Barfleur*, *Culloden*, and *Gibraltar* kept too much to windward for their fire to have much effect, but the *Invincible*, 74, Captain Hon. Thomas Pakenham, whose station in the line was between the *Barfleur* and *Culloden*, engaged the *Juste*, 80, which bore up, and encountering the overwhelming fire of the *Queen Charlotte*, struck to that ship. None of these six ships lost any spars, except the *Impregnable*, who had her three top-gallant masts and fore topsail-yard shot away; but the *Barfleur* and *Invincible* suffered aloft, their sails and rigging being much cut, and their masts wounded. The *Impregnable* had her master and six men killed, and a lieutenant, the boatswain, and 22 wounded. The *Tremendous* lost her first lieutenant and two men killed, and eight wounded. The *Barfleur*, flagship of Rear-Admiral Bowyer, had nine men killed, and the admiral, one lieutenant, two midshipmen, and 21 seamen and marines wounded. The *Invincible* lost four killed and ten wounded; the *Culloden*, two killed and a lieutenant and four seamen wounded; and the *Gibraltar*, two killed and 12 wounded.

Very brilliant, on this well-named "Glorious 1st of June," was the part played by the *Brunswick*, 74, Captain John Harvey, the ship next in the line to the *Queen Charlotte*, which found a foeman of equal metal in her opponent, the *Vengeur*, 74, commanded by Captain Renaudin, names not likely to be forgotten in the annals of France, as long as devoted gallantry holds a high place in the estimation of a chivalrous nation.

The *Brunswick*, like the British flagship, was exposed to a heavy fire as she bore down to the attack, and before the ship fired a shot she had experienced serious losses. Captain Harvey's right opponent was the *Jacobin*, but when she ranged ahead, and the *Achille* closed up with her, he bore up and steered for the interval between the latter ship and the *Vengeur*. Captain Renaudin, divining his purpose, took up a position closing the space. Thereupon Captain Harvey ran foul of the *Vengeur*, her three anchors on the starboard side hooking in the port fore chains* of the French seventy-four. At this time, it is said, Mr. Stewart, the master, asked Captain Harvey whether he should cut the ship clear of the enemy, when the latter replied in the true British spirit, "No, we have got her and we will keep her."

The two ships now swung close alongside of each other, and paying off before the wind, dropped out of the line, cannonading each other furiously. The British seamen, we are told, unable to open the eight lower deck starboard ports from the third abaft, blew them off; and the *Brunswick* and *Vengeur*, with their heads pointing to the northward, and with some considerable way upon them, both ships having squared their yards on coming in contact, commenced a furious engagement. The *Vengeur's* musketry and her 36-pounder poop-carronades loaded with langridge (old nails and pieces of iron) soon played havoc on the *Brunswick's* poop and quarter-deck, killing in a little while a captain of foot and several officers and men, and wounding, among others, Captain Harvey

---

* Chains, or channels, are broad and thick planks, projecting horizontally from the ship's side, to which they are bolted, and from which the iron chain-plates are projected to give the lower rigging greater spread and support. To these chain-plates are fastened the "dead eyes," wooden blocks with three holes for setting up the rigging.

himself, but not so severely as to occasion him to go below; the wound was by a musket-shot, which tore away three of the fingers from his right hand. But the courage and endurance of the crew of the *Brunswick* were to be put to a severe test. Through the smoke of battle could be seen a ship bearing down on the *Brunswick's* larboard quarter, having her gangways and rigging crowded with men, as if with the intention of boarding the British seventy-four. Quickly the men stationed at the starboard battery were turned over to the port side, and to each of the latter guns, already loaded with a single 32-pound shot, was added a double-headed shot. Presently the enemy, which proved to be the *Achille*, advanced to within musket-shot; when five or six rounds from the *Brunswick's* five after guns on deck brought down by the board the former's only remaining mast, the foremast.* The wreck of this mast, falling, where the wreck of the main and mizen masts already lay, on the starboard side, prevented the *Achille* returning the fire of the *Brunswick*, to which she struck. It was, however, wholly out of the *Brunswick's* power to take possession, and the *Achille* very soon rehoisted her colours, and, setting her spritsail, endeavoured to make off.

Meanwhile the two fast-locked combatants continued in hot action; feebly on the part of the *Brunswick* upon her quarter-deck, forecastle, and poop, from the superiority and already destructive effects of the *Vengeur's* musketry, but as vigorously as ever on the former's two principal batteries. On the lower deck the seamen, profiting by the rolling of the *Vengeur*, frequently drove home the quoins,† and depressed the muzzles of their guns, each of which was loaded with two round shot, and then again withdrew the quoins, and pointed the muzzles upwards; thus alternately firing into their opponent's bottom and ripping up her decks. This murderous conflict was at its height when Captain Harvey was knocked down by a splinter; but, although seriously hurt, he was presently on his legs again. Soon afterwards, however, the crown of a double-headed shot, which had split, struck his right arm, and he was compelled to go below. On

* On this disputed point James says:—"It is stated in other works, and is still contended by one of the *Brunswick's* surviving officers (although the master's log, minute as it is in other respects, notices no other ship, English or French, than the *Vengeur*), that the *Achille* had all three of her masts shot away by the *Brunswick's* partial fire. In opposition to this the log of the *Valiant*, the ship next in line to the *Brunswick*, states, that at a few minutes past 10 A.M. her opponent lost her main and mizen masts, and the log of the *Ramillies* says:—'10 h. 45 m. saw one of the enemy's ships opposed to our centre, with her main and mizen masts gone.' That this must have been the *Achille* is clear, because all the other dismasted ships in the French line, except the *Northumberland*, and she lost all three masts together, lay at or near to the two extremities. The end-on position in which the *Achille* approached the *Brunswick* in all probability led to what, from the most attentive review of the subject, we must still consider to be a mistake."

† "Quoins" are wooden wedges adjusted to support the breach of a gun, so as to elevate or depress the muzzle.

this occasion, the gallant officer is reported to have addressed his crew in the following words :—" Persevere, my brave lads, in your duty. Continue the action with spirit, for the honour of our King and country, and remember my last words—the colours of the *Brunswick* shall never be struck."

The command of the *Brunswick* now devolved upon Lieutenant Cracroft, who fought the ship in the spirit of his captain's orders. Shortly before, the two ships, having emainred three hours entangled, got clear, the *Vengeur* tearing away the three anchors from the *Brunswick's* bows. At this time the *Ramillies* ranged close up, and while waiting for the French ship to drift further from the British seventy-four, in order to have room to fire at her without injuring the latter, the *Brunswick*, by a few well-directed shots, split the *Vengeur's* rudder, and shattered her stern-post, besides knocking a large hole in her counter, through which the water rushed in a great volume. "At this spot," continues James, in his graphic account, "the *Ramillies*, now only forty yards distant, pointed her guns, and, assisted occasionally by her consort, reduced the gallant, but at this time overpowered, *Vengeur*, in a very few minutes, to a sinking state; when suddenly, as if perceiving the *Achille* making off in the distance, the *Ramillies* filled and made all sail from the two exhausted combatants; between whom, soon after 1 P.M., all firing ceased."

The *Vengeur*, now fast sinking, displayed a Union Jack over the quarter, to denote submission and a desire to be relieved. But the *Brunswick*, having all her boats destroyed, could afford her enemy no assistance, and soon her mizen-mast went over the side, which, with her shattered state and the damage done to the rigging, rendered it impossible for her to haul up for the British fleet, to leeward of which Monsieur Villaret was now leading a fresh line on the starboard tack, to recover as many as he could of his dismasted ships. The *Brunswick*, accordingly, put her head to the northward, with the intention of making the best of her way into port, should the French fleet, as, fortunately for her, proved to be the case, forbear from molesting her. All possible sail was therefore made upon the remaining wounded masts, and the crew set to work briskly to repair the damaged rigging, fish the masts, and secure the lower deck ports, through which the water was rushing at every roll. About 3 P.M. the *Brunswick* fell in with the *Jemappes*, wholly dismasted, but striving to make way with her spritsail—as the sail under the bowsprit, long since disused, is called. As the *Brunswick* edged up under her lee within hail, the *Jemappes* displayed a Union Jack over her quarter, and signified that she had struck to the *Queen*, then at a considerable distance to the south.

H. M. S. UNDAUNTED.
1ST CLASS CRUISER—BELTED.

During the action with the *Vengeur*, the *Brunswick*, besides losing her mizen-mast, and having her other masts with the yards and the bowsprit badly wounded, and the rigging and sails nearly cut to pieces, had 23 guns dismounted, her starboard quarter-gallery shot away, and her best bower anchor, with the "cat-head" to which it is secured, towing under her bottom. She had lost three officers—the captain of infantry, one master's mate, and one midshipman—and 41 seamen and marines killed, and her captain, second lieutenant, one midshipman and 110 seamen and marines wounded.

As for the *Vengeur*, her case was even more desperate. Shortly after the *Brunswick* left her, she continued rolling like a log on the sea, each time taking in water through the port-holes on the port side, the lids of which had been shot away during the action. Notwithstanding that she was fast sinking, the undaunted crew of the French seventy-four, it was said, rehoisted her colours, and set a small sail on the stump of the fore-mast. Fortunately for the survivors, for whom a watery grave appeared imminent, about 6.15, the *Alfred*, *Culloden*, and *Rattler*, cutter, approached her and lowered their boats to take the people off the wreck. Between them they removed the greater portion of the crew—the boats of the *Alfred* took 213, and those of the *Culloden* and *Rattler* nearly as many more—but nevertheless the *Vengeur* went down before all had been removed, though very few, besides the very severely wounded, were left behind. The legend of the *Vengeur* going down with her flag flying unconquered and the crew crying "Vive la Republique!" had no foundation in fact, but it was disseminated by the French authorities, and remains an article of belief to the present day in the French navy. Among the survivors of the crew were Captain Renaudin and his son, a boy twelve years of age. Each was ignorant of the fate of the other, having been rescued by different boats, but they met afterwards at Portsmouth, when the scene can be more readily imagined than described.

The *Valiant*, 74, Captain Pringle, the next ship in the British line to the *Brunswick*, first engaged the *Patriote*, 74, and after driving her to leeward, passed through the enemy's line ahead of her, and engaged the *Achille*, soon after the *Queen Charlotte* had quitted her. Soon the main and mizen-masts of the French two-decker, which had been injured by the fire of the flagship, went over the side, when the *Valiant*, stretching ahead, brought to to windward of the *Royal Sovereign*, which was engaged with the *Montagne*. Her opponent, the *Achille*, after striking her colours to the *Brunswick*, as already related, rehoisted them, but soon after four o'clock was overhauled by the *Ramillies*, which secured her, her loss during the battle having been 36 killed and 30 badly wounded. The *Valiant* suffered but little, having but two men killed and nine wounded; and the only spars she lost were the main-topsail and crossjack yards.

The *Orion*, 74, Captain Thomas Duckworth, had for her adversary the *Northumberland*, 74, firing an occasional shot at the *Patriote*, ahead of her, and the former, which had been partially engaged by the *Queen*, bore up, having lost all her masts, while the main-topmast of the *Orion* went over the side, carrying with it the main-top and main-yard. Captain Duckworth hauled up to the assistance of the *Queen Charlotte*, and the *Northumberland*, setting her spritsail, endeavoured to escape to leeward, but was secured, when it was found that she had lost 180 killed and wounded, including a large number of officers. The *Orion's* casualties were only two killed and 24 wounded.

The *Queen*, Captain Hutt, bearing the flag of Rear-Admiral Alan Gardner, was unable to close with her proper opponent, the *Northumberland*, owing to her sails and rigging having been greatly cut about while bearing down to the attack, but her foremost guns were brought to bear with effect on the French seventy-four, which got away, only to be engaged and reduced to a wreck by the *Orion*. The *Queen* now tackled the *Jemappes*, 74, when a hotly-contested action ensued, the Frenchman seeking to avoid the attentions of the British 98-gun ship, which would not be shaken off, but hung close upon her starboard quarter. First the *Jemappes*, which had her colours twice shot away, but hoisted them again at the mizen-top-gallant-mast-head, lost her mizen-mast, and then her main-mast went over the side, and finally her foremast followed suit. But the *Queen* also suffered considerably aloft. At 11, her main-mast was shot away, springing in its fall the mizen-mast, and carrying away the break of the poop; but the *Jemappes* at this time was a wreck, and her crew, having been driven from their quarters by the deadly fire of their enemy, waved their hats in token of surrender.

The *Queen*, however, was in too disabled a condition to take possession. Her mizen-topmast had been shot away, and her fore-mast, bowsprit, and mizen-mast had been shot through in several places, while her rigging and sails were cut to pieces. The crew set to work to repair damages, and the ship had begun to move through the water to leeward of the main line, when the *Montagne* and eleven other sail were descried standing towards her. Most of these ships opened a distant cannonade on the *Queen*, but the approach of the *Queen Charlotte* and the newly-formed line astern of her, induced the French commander-in-chief to keep away at a respectful distance.

Two frigates, however, presuming upon her disabled state, took up a position to engage her, but soon found that she was as dangerous a foe as when she was "all a-taunto." The loss sustained by the *Queen* in the action was 14 killed, and two lieutenants, one midshipman, and seven seamen and marines wounded.

Of the remaining seven ships of the British line, only the proceedings of the *Royal George*, 100, Captain Domett, bearing the flag of Vice-Admiral Alexander Hood, and the *Glory*, 98, Captain Elphinstone, merit special consideration. The *Montague*, 74, engaged the *Neptune*, and lost her captain, bearing the same name, and three men killed and two midshipmen and eleven men wounded. The *Alfred*, *Ramillies*, and *Majestic* took little part in the engagement and suffered proportionately, and the *Thunderer* did less and had no casualties. Far different was the conduct of the last two ships, whose proceedings we will briefly particularize.

The *Royal George* passed through the enemy's line, and was soon hotly engaged with the *Republicain* and *Sanspareil*, whose fore and mizen-masts she brought down by her fire. The *Glory*, meantime, which, like the *Royal George*, was a slow sailer, upon arriving on the scene, cut through the French line astern of the *Scipion*, 80, and engaging the latter to leeward, soon shot away all three of her masts, herself losing her fore-topmast and main and mizen-top-gallant-masts. After disabling her opponent, the *Glory* ranged ahead and engaged the *Sanspareil*, 80, flagship of Admiral Nielly, which had just lost her main and mizen-masts under the tremendously effective fire of the British three-decker. The *Republicain* was also raked by the fire of the two ships, and was glad to seek safety in flight, though soon afterwards her main and mizen-masts went by the board. The *Scipion* and *Sanspareil*, completely silenced, dropped astern, but the *Glory* and *Royal George*—which had lost her fore-mast and main and mizen-topmasts, and had her tiller ropes shot away—were in too disabled a state to take possession of the French ships. The *Royal George* had one midshipman and four men killed, and her second lieutenant, master, two midshipmen and 45 men wounded. The *Glory's* casualties were her master, one midshipman and eleven men killed, and 39 wounded.

The *Sanspareil* was stated to have lost 260 killed and 120 badly wounded, though some doubt has been thrown on the former estimate, but the carnage was great and was witnessed by a British officer, who happened to be a prisoner on board. Captain Thomas Troubridge, commanding the frigate *Castor*, an officer who was destined to attain great fame, had been captured by the *Sanspareil*, while convoying some merchantmen from Newfoundland, and, with a portion of his officers and men, was transferred to the French seventy-four. Captain Troubridge was therefore on board when the *Majestic*, 74, Captain Cotton, took possession of her, and remained to assist in navigating the prize into port. Captain Brenton, R.N., in his "History of the War," gives the following anecdote, which is discredited by James. The officers of the two-decker having entertained a belief—from Lord Howe's avoidance of a battle on the 31st May, and his refraining from bearing down to the attack on the following morning until the seamen of the fleet had breakfasted—that he was not eager to engage after the partial actions of the 28th and 29th May, twitted Captain Troubridge with the supposed timidity of the British admiral. The captain of the *Castor*, who knew his countryman better, after anxiously regarding the British line, replied, "Don't flatter yourselves. John Bull does not like fighting on an empty stomach, but see if he does not pay you a visit after breakfast."

The *Scipion*, which by some mischance escaped, was totally dismasted in her engagement with the *Glory*. Seventeen of her guns were dismounted, and she lost 64 men killed and 151 wounded. But nevertheless her crew managed to jury-rig her, and she effected her escape, though some of the British ships had scarcely lost a spar. Four others of the crippled ships joined the French admiral, and soon after six in the evening, Monsieur Villaret-Joyeuse had made good his escape with nineteen ships-of-the-line and his frigates, and all were out of sight.*

* Notwithstanding that the French commander-in-chief fled from the scene of conflict, towing his five dismasted ships, the French press claimed the battle as a victory and Barrère made a rhapsodical speech in the Assembly, describing the sinking of the *Vengeur*. But they could not disguise the loss of their ships, and Admiral Kerguelen wrote a more sober and truthful account of what his professional knowledge taught him was a disastrous defeat. He says:—"The action began with great spirit on both sides. The English captains, more accustomed than ours to manage ships-of-war, cut through our line in several places. Meanwhile the Republicans fought with infinite courage. Several ships were dismasted or disabled in the two fleets, and the action ceased before the victory was decided. One of our ships only, the *Vengeur*, disabled and sinking, had been taken possession of by the enemy. But what is incomprehensible is our abandonment, upon the field of battle, of six French ships, disabled but not subdued, which, lying together in a group, kept the tricoloured flag flying, as if stretching forth their arms towards the fleet, entreating to be succoured. To recover these six ships, and to take two disabled English ships (probably the *Queen* and *Brunswick*), at no great distance from them, it sufficed simply to put about. It is to be wished that we could blot out this disgraceful event." After alleging other complaints against the commanding officer of the French fleet, Monsieur Kerguelen proceeds as follows:—"We have thus sacrificed uselessly the men, the ships, and the interests of the Republic. But ignorance and presumption then presided over its destinies upon the ocean, and the most disgraceful defeat was transformed into a genuine triumph. We proclaimed a victory, after having lost seven fine ships, that mounted upwards of 590 pieces of cannon, and we gave to the commander-in-chief the rank of vice-admiral." An English writer, Admiral C. Ekins, who speaks with some authority in his "Naval Battles," a work embellished with seventy plates, criticises with undue asperity the veteran British admiral's conduct of the battle. He says: "On the 1st June, had Lord Howe attacked the centre and rear of the French line with his whole force, he would have gained a complete and easy victory." But he hit an undoubted blot when he adds:—"Not to follow up his success I hold to be a great and inexcusable error."

But the victory was a glorious one, and the fighting of the most determined character, as is apparent from the disabled condition of the ships that had taken a prominent part in the action, evidenced by the fact that it was not until five in the morning of the 3rd June that Lord Howe was in a position to make sail on his ships, and the six prizes that had been secured. Fortunately the weather remained fine, and the fleet, with the exception of nine ships, which proceeded to Plymouth, anchored at Spithead at 11 A.M. on the 13th June.

For his crushing defeat of the finest fleet possessed by France, Lord Howe, then in his seventieth year, was loaded with honours, and he and his gallant officers and men were greeted with every demonstration of welcome and applause by all classes, from the King to the meanest of his subjects. His Majesty, accompanied by members of his family and some of the Ministers, journeyed down to Portsmouth, and paid the admiral a visit on board his flagship at Spithead, when he presented Lord Howe with a diamond-hilted sword, valued at 3,000 guineas, and a valuable gold chain. The King also honoured the victorious admiral by dining with him on board the *Queen Charlotte*. Sir Alexander Hood was created Viscount Bridport, and Vice-Admiral Graves also received an Irish peerage; Rear-Admirals Gardner, Bowyer, and Pasley were created baronets, the two latter receiving pensions of £1,000 a year for their wounds, and Sir Roger Curtis, Captain of the Fleet, had a similar honour conferred on him. The first lieutenants of all the ships-of-the-line, including the *Audacious*, which had so gallantly engaged the *Revolutionnaire* on the 28th May, were promoted to the rank of commander, and several other lieutenants of the flagships also received a step in rank. Mr. Bowen, master of the *Queen Charlotte*, whose seamanlike conduct in the action has been mentioned, was promoted to the rank of lieutenant, as the rules of the service prevented his rising to a higher rank than that he held in the navigating branch of the service, which offered no chance of earning distinction or honour. All the admirals and captains of ships-of-the-line, with the exception of the officers commanding the *Cæsar*, *Impregnable*, *Tremendous*, *Culloden*, *Gibraltar*, *Alfred*, *Majestic*, and *Thunderer*, were awarded gold medals, but the captains of the *Montague* and *Brunswick* did not survive to receive the honour. All the subordinate officers of the fleet, together with the gallant seamen and marines, received a vote of thanks, passed by both Houses of Legislature, and the Trinity House, the merchants at Lloyds, and the citizens of London, Dublin, and Edinburgh subscribed liberally for the relief of the wounded, as well as for the widows and children of those who fell in the action.

As the first great battle between the fleet of England and that of her enemy, the success achieved by Lord Howe was hailed with enthusiasm by the nation, and though nothing finer is recorded in our annals than the stubborn valour displayed by the officers and crews of the ships, yet there was some remissness in securing the fruits of the victory, and the five dismasted ships, which escaped under the escort of the French commander-in-chief, ought to have been pursued by those of the English ships that had scarcely been engaged, and then instead of six sail-of-the-line captured and one sunk, the list would have stood at twelve. In that case the victory would have been ranked with those achieved by a greater commander than Howe, and the battle of the "Glorious First of June" would have been as memorable and complete as those of the Nile and Trafalgar.

CHAPTER V.

Admiral Montagu's Escape from the French Fleet—Lord Howe's Last Cruise—Capture of the *Alexander*—Mutiny on Board the *Culloden*—Operations in Corsica—Capture of San Fiorenzo—Captain Horatio Nelson at Bastia—He is Wounded at Calvi—Engagement between Sir John Borlase Warren's Squadron and some French Frigates—Action between the East India Company's Ships and French Privateers—Capture of the *Duguay-Trouin* and Action off Mauritius—The *Swiftsure* and *Atalante*—Actions between the *Carysfort* and *Castor*, *Romney* and *Sibylle*—Destruction of the *Volontaire* by Sir John Warren's Squadron—Expedition to the West Indies—Capture of Martinique, St. Lucia, and Guadaloupe—Loss of St. Lucia, St. Vincent, Guadaloupe and Grenada—Operations at St. Domingo — Daring Reconnaissance of Brest made by Sir Sydney Smith — Admiral Cornwallis's masterly Retreat before a Superior French Fleet—Lord Bridport's Action of the 23rd June, 1795—The Expedition to Quiberon Bay—Disastrous Gale in the Channel—Loss of the *Berwick* off Corsica.

IT will be remembered that on the 19th May, Rear-Admiral Montagu, after parting with the East India fleet he had been sent to convoy, cruised with his six ships-of-the-line and a frigate between Cape Ortugal and the latitude of Belleisle, to intercept the French convoy of 100 ships from America, but being unsuccessful, returned to Plymouth, where he anchored on the 30th May. As the Admiralty declared it of the first importance that the convoy, which was laden with provisions, should be captured, and the *Audacious* having arrived in port on the 3rd June with the news of the partial action between the British and French fleets on the 28th May, Admiral Montagu sailed on the following day with eight sail-of-the-line and two frigates. On the fourth day out, being about thirteen leagues off Ushant, the British fleet sighted a squadron of eight ships, under the command of Rear-Admiral Cornice, who made all sail to escape into the bay of Bertheaume, in which he succeeded, closely chased by Admiral Montagu. On the following morning the British admiral sighted Monsieur Villaret-Joyeuse's fleet of nineteen sail and three frigates, five of the former—the *Republicain*, *Terrible*, *Mucius*, *Scipion*, and *Jemappes*—being in tow. Rightly considering it would have been folly to attempt to engage this fleet, superior, notwithstanding its state, with another powerful squadron of equal strength within sound of the guns, Admiral Montagu stood to the southward, pursued by the French fleet, but late in the afternoon Monsieur Villaret gave up the chase, and made the best of his way to Bertheaume Bay, where he anchored on the 11th June, and on the following day was joined there by the whole of the convoy, consisting of 116 sail, escorted by Admiral Vanstabel with three ships-of-the-line. On the same day, Admiral Montagu, having missed this valuable fleet, arrived at Plymouth.

On the 22nd of the same month, Rear-Admiral Cornwallis, having his flag in the *Excellent*, 74, sailed from Plymouth with twelve ships-of-the-line, to escort the East India merchant fleet and cruise in the Bay of Biscay, and on the 7th September Lord Howe, having refitted his fleet, proceeded to sea from Torbay with thirty-four sail, including five Portuguese ships, and stood over to Ushant, but the weather being thick and stormy, the admiral bore up and returned to Torbay. Early in November the veteran admiral again put to sea, but his health had broken down, and before the close of the year he finally returned to port, hauled down his flag from the masthead of the *Queen Charlotte*, and went no more to sea.

At this time the Navy sustained a loss by the capture of the *Alexander*. This ship, commanded by Captain Bligh, and another 74, the *Canada*, Captain Hamilton, were returning to England, after escorting the Lisbon and Mediterranean convoys, when, on the 6th November, they fell in with a squadron of five 74-gun ships and three frigates from Brest, under the command of Admiral Nielly.

The two British seventy-fours passed the French squadron at four in the morning, and on ascertaining their nationality crowded all sail to escape. The *Canada* outsailed her consort, and two ships-of-the-line and two frigates went in pursuit of her, and the remaining three ships and one frigate in chase of the *Alexander*. Firing began between the hostile ships with the bow and stern chasers, as the pursuit and flight were continued, and about 11 A.M. the *Jean Bart* was compelled to sheer off, when the *Tigre*, bearing a commodore's pennant, took her place. Again the *Alexander* disposed of her assailant, whose mizen-topmast and main-yard she shot away, and a third ship engaged her. Captain Bligh continued the unequal combat until past one o'clock, when the *Alexander's* main-yard being shot away, all her masts and yards shot through, and her sails in tatters, with the other ships rapidly coming up, he surrendered his ship, which was carried into Brest. The *Alexander* had about 40 killed and wounded, including two officers, whereas, according to the French papers, her two principal opponents sustained between them no less than 450 casualties. The *Canada*, being a better sailer, managed to effect her escape.

Before the year 1794 closed, the first act of mutiny took place in the British Navy which, three years later, developed into so serious and wide-spread a revolt that the safety of the kingdom was imperilled. On the 3rd December the crew of the *Culloden*, one of the ships of Lord Howe's fleet which took so distinguished a part in his great victory, now commanded by Captain Troubridge, late of the *Castor*, broke out into open mutiny, and barricaded themselves below. On calling the muster on the following morning, the officers, petty officers, all the marines (except six) and 86 of the seamen returned to their duty, but the remainder, some 250 men, refused to fall in. The mutineers turned a deaf ear to the remonstrances of Admirals Cornwallis, Colpoys, and Lord Bridport, and matters continued in this state until the 11th, when the men listened to the expostulations of Captain Hon. Thomas Pakenham and returned to their duty. The ten ringleaders were made prisoners, and by the verdict of a court-martial two of them were acquitted and eight sentenced to be hanged. On the 13th January in the following year, five of the culprits were executed on board the *Culloden* at Spithead, the other three receiving the King's pardon.

We will now return to the proceedings of the Mediterranean fleet, still under the command of Lord Hood, and distinguished by the brilliant services rendered by Captain Horatio Nelson, in the *Agamemnon*, 64. After the evacuation of Toulon, Lord Hood detached some ships to cruise off Corsica to prevent the landing of provisions and reinforcements on the island. Among the ships thus engaged was the *Ardent*, 64, Captain Robert Manners Sutton, which met with a terrible fate. By some means she caught fire and blew up with every soul on board, and the only vestige of her seen was her quarter-deck. The British fleet had been in the Bay of Hyères, in the group of small islands of that name near Toulon, but Lord Hood—being determined, in conjunction with General Dundas, commanding the troops then in the fleet, to afford assistance to the Royalists in Corsica, under General Paoli, in an attempt to expel the Republican forces from the island—sailed thither from his anchorage on the 24th January, 1795, with his flag on board the *Victory*. The fleet encountered a severe gale on the following day, and was driven to take refuge at Porto Ferrajo, in the island of Elba. On the 5th February the admiral detached Commodore Linzee with the *Alcide, Egmont*, and *Fortitude*, 74's, and two frigates, with several transports, conveying 1,400 troops, to the Bay of San Fiorenzo in Corsica, and the soldiers, under General Dundas, were landed near Cape Mortella. The town of Mortella, which some French frigates had recaptured in October, 1793, was attacked from batteries on shore, and by the *Fortitude* and *Juno*, frigate, but the ships were beaten off, the former with the loss of six killed and 56 wounded, and a fire that broke out on board from a red-hot shot nearly caused her total destruction. The attack from the battery guns on shore was more successful, and the fort being set on fire the garrison surrendered.

The next operation attempted was an attack on the Convention Redoubt, mounting 21 heavy pieces, and regarded as the key of San Fiorenzo. By the exertions of the officers and men of the squadron, several 18-pounder ships' guns were dragged up a rocky ascent commanding the redoubt, 700 feet above sea level, deemed inaccessible, and therefore left unprotected, and from hence a cannonade was kept up for 48 hours, and upon the fire of the redoubt being nearly silenced, on the 17th February, the work was stormed by the troops and seamen. The squadron now anchored in perfect security in the Bay, and the French, having set on fire or sunk their two frigates,* evacuated San Fiorenzo, with its formidable batteries, mounting 25 guns, and retreated to Bastia.

General Dundas decided that he was not in sufficient strength to attack Bastia, the capital of the island, but Lord Hood, acting on the advice of Captain Horatio Nelson, who had reconnoitred the place, determined to make the attempt, which the gallant captain of the *Agamemnon*, who had actually engaged the batteries with his ship and the *Romulus* and *Tartar*, frigates, declared was feasible with a few ships and 1,000 troops. General Dundas, on account of his difference with the admiral, resigned the command, but his successor, General D'Aubant, declined to assist Lord Hood, who sailed for Bastia on the 2nd April, taking with him the soldiers placed under his orders to assist as marines, and two military officers and 30 artillerymen, with stores and entrenching tools. The squadron arrived off the town on the 4th, and the same evening the troops and a detachment of seamen, commanded by Captain Nelson, were disembarked under the superintendence of that officer, whose energy and skill were already acknowledged, at a point a little to the northward of the town. The total strength of the combined force was 1,248 officers and men, and General Paoli co-operated with about an equal number of Corsicans, while the garrison of Bastia consisted of 3,000 troops. The squadron took up a position out of range of the guns, while the soldiers and seamen set to work, with praiseworthy alacrity, to erect batteries, which were armed with five 24-pounders, two 13-inch and two 10-inch mortars, and two heavy carronades.

* The frigate that was sunk, named the *Minerve*, of 38 guns, was weighed by the British seamen and taken into the service, when she was renamed the *San Fiorenzo*. This and the other frigate, the *Fortunée*, were the two ships which, with the *Melpomene*, were engaged by the *Agamemnon* in the preceding October.

On the 11th, the batteries being ready, Lord Hood summoned the military governor to surrender, but that officer having refused, the guns opened fire, and were answered by the enemy's forts and batteries. A vessel converted into a floating battery also kept up a hot cannonade on the enemy's works, but she was set on fire by round shot and had to be abandoned. The siege was prosecuted for some weeks, but gradually the British fire overcame all resistance, and at length, on the 11th May, forty days after the commencement of hostilities, the town and citadel of Bastia were surrendered. The loss experienced in achieving this success was small, being only 14 killed, including a lieutenant of the *Victory*, and 33 wounded, and the honour acquired by the Army and Navy was chiefly due to the energy and example of Captain Nelson. General Paoli induced the inhabitants of Corsica to withdraw their allegiance from France, and on the 19th June the formal surrender of the island and its annexation to Great Britain was made, and Sir Gilbert Elliott was appointed viceroy.

Soon after troops arrived from Gibraltar, under Lieutenant-General Hon. Charles Stuart, who offered a marked contrast to Generals Dundas and D'Aubant, and preparations were at once made to attack Calvi, on the western side of the island, a little to the south of San Fiorenzo, which still remained in possession of the Republican troops. Lord Hood, who had sailed with thirteen battle-ships and four frigates to look after the French squadron of seven sail-of-the-line, which had put to sea on the 5th June, left Nelson to conduct the naval operations. That officer conveyed the troops to a small cove about three miles from Calvi, and by the 19th June the whole were disembarked and had taken up a strong position on a neighbouring ridge. Lord Hood, returning to Mortella Bay on the same day, despatched a detachment of seamen from the *Victory*, under Captains Hallowell and Serocold, with guns and stores, to assist in forming and working the batteries, and himself arrived on the 27th June, with the *Victory* and two 74's, in order to assist by his presence in the prosecution of the siege. Under Nelson's superintendence the batteries were completed and armed, Lord Hood having landed seven guns from his flagship to assist in the attack, and after a siege extending over fifty-one days, General Casa Bianca, the commandant, surrendered the town and forts on the 10th August. The British loss was five officers, including Captain Serocold, and 25 soldiers and seamen killed, and 53 wounded. While directing the fire of the batteries, Nelson received a wound, caused by a round shot driving some particles of stone and sand into his right eye, but he did not report the wound, or absent himself a day from duty, though he never recovered the sight of the eye. Among the ships taken at Calvi were the French frigates *Melpomene* and *Mignonne*, the two remaining ships of the squadron encountered by Nelson in the *Agamemnon*.

Early in November Lord Hood returned to England in the *Victory*, leaving Vice-Admiral Hotham in command of the fleet on the Mediterranean Station. Only a few days after his lordship resigned the command, a mutiny—the second that had lately taken place in the Navy, betokened a serious state of affairs which, a few years later, had a most alarming development in the outbreaks at the Nore and Spithead—broke out on board the *Windsor Castle*, 98, Captain Shield, the flagship of Rear-Admiral Robert Linzee. Admiral Hotham, Rear-Admiral Sir Hyde Parker, and several captains proceeded to the *Windsor Castle*, and remonstrated with the men, but they refused to return to duty until the admiral, captain, first-lieutenant, and boatswain were removed. An investigation was held into the conduct of Captain Shield, at his own request, but the result was a vindication of him from all blame. Nevertheless the commander-in-chief removed this officer as well as the first-lieutenant and the boatswain, and the mutineers were pardoned.

Several actions were fought between single ships during the year 1794, of some of which we will proceed to give details. In order to check the depredations of several French frigates in the Channel, which worked in small squadrons, the Admiralty despatched several frigates in search of them, and some severe actions were fought.

On the 23rd April, Sir John Borlase Warren was cruising near Guernsey, with the following five ships—*Flora*, 42, bearing the commodore's broad pennant, *Arethusa*, 44, Sir Edward Pellew, *Melampus*, 42, Captain Wells, *Concorde*, 42, Sir Richard Strachan, and *Nymphe*, 40, Captain G. Murray—when he sighted and gave chase to four strange ships, which proved to be the *Pomone*, 44, *Engageante*, 38, *Résolue*, 40, and *Babet*, 22. The *Flora*, which was the leading British ship, being abreast of the sternmost Frenchman, opened fire at 6.30 A.M., and pushing on, received in succession the fire of the three other French ships. Within an hour she had lost her main-topmast shot away, and her foremast was injured and her rigging and yards much cut up. As she dropped astern, her place was taken by the *Arethusa*, which, together with the *Melampus* and *Concorde*, neared the enemy's ships, which set every stitch they could carry in order to get away. The *Arethusa* and *Melampus*, who were in advance, engaged the *Pomone* and *Babet*, and at 8.30 the latter, having lost her fore-topmast, hauled down her colours, and was taken possession of by the *Flora*. Both the British frigates now directed their fire on the *Pomone*, the *Engageante* and *Résolue* having got out of range, and after a gallant resistance, during which she lost her main and mizen-masts, the French frigate surrendered at about 9.30 to the "saucy *Arethusa*," and Sir Edward Pellew sent a boat to take possession of her.

The *Concorde* and *Melampus*, followed by the *Nymphe*, gave chase to the *Résolue* and *Engageante*, and the former, being a good sailer, soon overhauled them sufficiently to enable her to receive and return their fire. Sir Richard Strachan hoped to tackle the two frigates in detail, leaving the first, after disabling her, to be dealt with by the *Melampus* and *Nymphe*, but they kept together and frustrated his intention by so disabling him aloft that he was compelled to drop astern. Having refitted, the *Concorde* resumed the pursuit, and about noon brought the *Engageante*, bearing the broad pennant of the French commodore, to close action. Shortly before two, the French frigate being completely disabled and her guns silenced, her crew called out that they had surrendered. The *Concorde* was in too damaged a state to pursue the *Résolue*,* and the *Melampus* and *Nymphe* being too far astern, she made good her escape into Morlaix.

The four British frigates which were engaged—*Flora*, *Arethusa*, *Melampus*, and *Concorde*—suffered considerably aloft in their spars and rigging, but their loss in killed and wounded was trifling. On the other hand the *Pomone* had between 80 and 100 casualties, and the *Babet* between 30 and 40, but the loss of the *Engageante*, which must have suffered seriously, does not appear. All three ships were taken into port, and added to the British Navy, and the *Pomone* proved a great acquisition from her excellent sailing qualities.

The next frigate action in chronological order was that fought on the 5th May in Indian seas. Early in the year, the *Centurion*, 50, Captain Osborne, *Resistance*, 44, Captain Pakenham, and *Orpheus*, 32, Captain Newcome, arrived on the India station, where, on the return to England of Admiral Cornwallis with his squadron in August, 1793, soon after the surrender of Pondicherry, the valuable trade and possessions of the East India Company were left without efficient protection against the depredations of the French privateers, fitting out at Mauritius, and a squadron of two frigates and two or three corvettes under Renaud, an officer of resource and enterprise. Indeed the Company's Indiaman, *Princess Royal*, carrying 30 guns, was captured in the Straits of

---

* This was the same ship that Sir Richard Strachan, when commanding the *Phœnix*, had encountered and captured, in conjunction with the *Perseverance*, off the Malabar coast, in November, 1791, but which was returned by Captain Strachan, he having engaged her under the impression that she was carrying contraband of war to Mangalore.

Sunda, in September, 1793, after a protracted and desperate defence against three French privateers, each nearly equal in force to a British 28-gun frigate. In the following May, four others of their armed Indiamen, and the brig-of-war *Nautilus*, of the local marine, captured near the Straits of Banca, after a spirited action, the French privateer *Vengeur*, carrying 34 guns and 250 men, and the *Résolue*, mounting 26 guns and having a crew of 230 men. Two days after this the same ships discovered, off Saint Nicholas Point, Java, the French frigates *Prudente*, 36, and *Cybele*, 40, the 14-gun brig *Vulcain*, and the late Indiaman *Princess Royal*, renamed the *Duguay-Trouin*, now carrying 34 guns, and a partial action ensued, but Captain Renaud seemed disinclined to fight, and as the Indiamen had among them a greater number of prisoners than their united crews, while with so many absent manning the prizes they had barely enough to work their guns, Commodore Mitchell, commanding the Indiamen, was not very eager to press on an encounter, and the French squadron stood away without molestation. Captain Renaud, however, succeeded on the 9th February in capturing the *Pigot*, Indiaman, as she lay at anchor off the Java coast, repairing damages received in repelling the attack of two French privateers, but this was his only triumph, and the arrival in Eastern seas of the three British frigates put him on the defensive.

While this squadron was cruising off Mauritius, on the 5th May, two strange sail were observed approaching, which proved to be the *Duguay-Trouin* and the *Vulcain*. Chase was given, and about noon the *Orpheus* got within range of the former, and a close action ensued. The British frigate took up a position on the starboard quarter of her antagonist, and a few minutes after one, had wrought such havoc by the accuracy and rapidity of her fire, that the Frenchman surrendered. Her bowsprit had been shot away, and she had lost, out of 403 persons, including sick and passengers on board, 21 killed, and 60 wounded. The *Orpheus*, which from having some men absent in a prize had a crew of only 194 men and boys, lost a midshipman killed, and a master's mate and 12 seamen wounded. On the 22nd October, the *Centurion* and *Diomede*, 44, Captain Matthew Smith, observed off Mauritius four strange sail, which proved to be the *Cybele*, *Prudente*, *Jean Bart*, corvette of 20 guns, and the 14-gun brig *Courier*, under the orders of Commodore Renaud, in the *Prudente*, who put to sea from Port Louis with the object of engaging the British frigates. Accordingly, the French commodore soon brought to in line ahead, his own ship leading, and the *Centurion* engaged the two frigates, while the *Diomede* took up her position between the *Jean Bart* and *Courier*. The action commenced at 3.30, within half musket-shot, and continued with unabated vigour until the *Centurion*, showing signs of being much damaged aloft, the *Prudente* bore up and ran to leeward, out of cannon-shot range, and signalled to her consorts to follow motions. In obeying the signal, the *Cybele* found herself, owing to a lull in the breeze caused by the heavy firing, becalmed close to the *Centurion*, which engaged her with great spirit. At length, taking advantage of a light air, the French frigate edged down towards the *Prudente*, which took her in tow, her fore-topmast and main-topgallant-mast having been shot away. The *Centurion* also had suffered considerably in her spars, and Captain Osborne was unable to chase, but had to keep his ship's head to the sea, to prevent the masts from going overboard. The *Diomede* had suffered but little by the enemy's fire, and sustained no loss of life, and might have followed up the crippled frigate, and perhaps have forced her consort to abandon her, but Captain Smith displayed a backwardness, which was attributed to private motives of jealousy. For his conduct on this occasion, the captain of the *Diomede* was brought to a court-martial and condemned to be dismissed, but owing to a technical informality in the proceedings, was only placed on the retired list.

In this action,—which was not specially creditable to the French ships engaged, though the writers in the official "*Victoires et Conquêtes*," according to their wont, magnified it into a triumph over "two ships-of-the-line,"—the *Centurion* lost only three killed and 24 wounded, while the *Prudente* had 15 killed, including the two senior lieutenants, and 20 wounded, including Commodore Renaud, and the *Cybele* lost her first lieutenant and 21 men killed and 62 wounded, showing where the victory lay had it been followed up.

On the 5th May, the same day that the *Duguay-Trouin* was recaptured in the East, the *Swiftsure*, 74, Captain Boyles, when a few days out from Cork, chased the 36-gun French frigate *Atalante*. The pursuit was continued all night and the following day, and not until 2.30 on the morning of the 7th was the British seventy-four able to bring her gallant opponent to action at long range. This continued for an hour, when Captain Linois, commanding the *Atalante*, struck his colours, having lost ten killed and 32 wounded, out of a complement of 274 hands. The *Swiftsure* had only one man killed. The *Atalante* was an excellent sailer, and this quality was soon again put to the proof, and stood her in better stead than when fleeing from her persistent adversary. Hardly had the rigging of the two ships been refitted than three French seventy-fours appeared in sight, and gave chase. The *Swiftsure* and her prize separated and both escaped. The *Atalante* was purchased into the British Navy, and was rechristened *Espion*, there being a ship-of-war of her name already in the service.

Mention has been made of the capture by a 74-gun ship of Admiral Nielly's squadron, early in May of this year, of the British 36-gun frigate *Castor*, Captain Thomas Troubridge, along with a portion of a convoy from Newfoundland which she was escorting. She did not, however, remain long under the tricolour. On the 29th of the same month, the *Carysfort*, Captain Laforey, carrying 32 guns and 180 men, encountered the *Castor*, now mounting 36 guns, with a crew of 200 hands, having in tow a Dutch brig she had captured a few days before, which had caused her to part company with Admiral Nielly's squadron. A spirited action ensued between the fairly-well matched adversaries; but at the end of seventy-five minutes the *Castor* was forced to haul down her colours, with the loss of 16 killed and nine wounded, that of the *Carysfort* being only one killed and four wounded. On board the prize were found an officer and eighteen seamen, the remainder of her crew, together with Captain Troubridge, having been removed, as already stated, to the *Sanspareil*, which was captured by Lord Howe in his great victory of the 1st June. The *Castor* was repurchased* into the Navy, and was commissioned by Lieutenant Richard Worsley, first of the *Carysfort*, who was promoted to the rank of commander as a reward for his gallantry.

Sir James Saumarez, who has before been mentioned in these pages, displayed great daring and seamanship by the skilful manner in which he eluded the pursuit of a superior French squadron. While cruising off the island of Jersey, on the 8th June, in the *Crescent*, 36, with the *Druid*, 32, Captain Elliston, *Eurydice*, 24, Captain Cole, in company, he fell in with two cut-down seventy-fours—*rasés*, as they were called—two 36-gun frigates and a brig, and being anxious for the safety of the *Eurydice*, which was a bad sailer, he gallantly kept the enemy at bay, and otherwise manœuvred in so masterly a way, that he succeeded in securing her escape into Guernsey, and, steering for an intricate passage known to the pilot he had on board, but never before attempted by a ship-of-war, he took his own ship, followed by the *Druid*, into the port in safety. The Lieutenant-Governor issued an order expressing his admiration of the conduct of Sir James Saumarez and the officers and men of his squadron. It was under such circum-

---

* The Admiralty claimed the *Castor* on payment of the usual salvage, upon the principle that, not having entered an enemy's port, she had not been adjudicated a prize, but Captain Laforey contested this claim, and the Judge of the Admiralty Court gave a decision in his favour.

H.M.S. LATONA.
2ND CLASS CRUISER.

stances that the superiority of British seamen to those of all other nations was evidenced in the days when steam was unknown, and the now lost art of seamanship saved from capture many valuable ships of the British Navy.

In the Archipelago, in Greek waters, British prowess also received an illustration. As Captain Hon. W. Paget, commanding the *Romney*, carrying 50 guns and 266 men, was convoying some English and Dutch merchantmen, she espied, on the 17th June, the French 44-gun frigate *Sibylle*, having a crew of 380 men, at anchor inshore of the island of Miconi, accompanied by three trading vessels. Leaving his convoy under the protection of his consorts, three British frigates, Captain Paget dropped his anchor at about a cable's length (240 yards) from the *Sibylle*, which carried the pennant of Commodore Rondeau. The commodore, when summoned, refused to surrender, but placed the frigate between the *Romney* and the town of Miconi, upon which Captain Paget warped his ship to a position further ahead, and anchoring with a spring on his cable, commenced an action which lasted for an hour and ten minutes, at the end of which, being in an almost defenceless state, the French frigate struck her colours and was taken possession of by the *Romney*, together with the three merchantmen under her protection. The *Romney*, which was 74 men short of her complement, had eight killed and 30 wounded, and the *Sibylle* had two officers and 44 seamen killed, and 112 officers and men wounded. The defence of their ship against a vessel of slightly superior force was very creditable to all concerned, but it was somewhat detracted, as regards Captain Rondeau, by his bombastic averment when refusing to surrender, that he had registered a solemn oath "never to strike his colours." The *Sibylle*, being a fine new ship, was purchased into the Navy under her own name.

Sir John Borlase Warren put to sea from Plymouth on the 8th August, with the *Flora*, flying his broad pennant, the 38-gun frigates *Arethusa*, Sir Edward Pellew, *Diamond*, Sir Sydney Smith, *Artois*, Captain Edmund Nagle, *Diana*, Captain Faulkner, and the *Santa Margarita*, 36, Captain Eliab Harvey—a group of as smart frigate captains as the Navy has ever boasted. The squadron sailed in quest of some French frigates reported to be infesting the Channel in the vicinity of the Scilly Isles; and on the 23rd the *Diamond* and three of her consorts sighted and chased the *Volontaire*, 36, and having overtaken her, drove her on shore near the Penmarck rocks, where they left her, "disabled and irretrievably lost," as the commodore wrote in his despatch. In the meantime, the *Flora* and *Arethusa* had started in chase of two 18-gun corvettes, *L'Espion* and *Alert*, both recently-captured prizes from the British Navy, which ran aground on the French coast, under the protection of three batteries. The two frigates engaged the batteries and grounded vessels until they had shot away their masts, when a great portion of their crews made their escape on shore. Sir Edward Pellew proceeded with the boats of the *Flora* and *Arethusa* to destroy the corvettes, but finding that there were from 20 to 30 killed and wounded in the *Alert*, and a greater number in the *Espion*, and that it was impossible to remove the wounded to the frigate, he brought away 52 prisoners, and left the corvettes to their fate. Subsequently, the *Espion* was got off the rocks by the French and refitted, but on the 3rd March in the following year (1795) she was recaptured by the *Lively*, Captain Burlton, and restored to the Navy.

On the 21st October, as the *Arethusa*, *Artois*, *Diamond*, and *Galatea*, 32, Captain Richard G. Keats, were cruising in company about 30 miles off Ushant, they sighted and gave chase to a French frigate, which proved to be the *Revolutionnaire*, carrying 44 guns and 351 men. The *Artois*, having the same number of guns, and a crew of 281 men, being the fastest sailer of the squadron, first came up with the enemy and brought her to action. A well-contested contest ensued for forty minutes, when the *Diamond* having taken up a position under her stern, and the two other British frigates being near at hand, the *Revolutionnaire* hauled down her colours. The *Artois* lost only one marine officer and two men killed and five seamen wounded, and the French frigate had eight men in the former category and five, including her captain, in the latter. Captain Nagle received the honour of knighthood, and Lieutenant R. D. Oliver, first of the *Artois*, was promoted to the rank of commander, and doubtless both these gallant officers, together with the crew, regretted that they had not been permitted to fight out their action unassisted. The *Revolutionnaire*, which had just been launched and only left port a week before on her first cruise, was purchased into the Navy, and was the finest yet captured from the French, with the exception of the *Pomone*.

Operations against the French possessions in the West Indies were conducted by the Navy in combination with the Army, during the year 1794, on a considerable scale, and with success. Vice-Admiral Sir John Jervis, having his flag in the *Boyne*, 98, Captain George Grey, arrived at Barbados in January to assume the command-in-chief, accompanied by General Sir Charles Grey in command of the forces, and sailed again on the 2nd February for Martinique with some 6,000 soldiers, and the following ships-of-the-line, in addition to the flagship :—*Vengeance*, 74, Captain Lord Henry Paulet, bearing the broad pennant of Commodore Charles Thompson; *Irresistible*, 74, Captain John Henry, and the 64-gun ships *Asia*, Captain John Brown, and *Veteran*, Captain Charles E. Nugent. Also eight frigates, four sloops, and a bomb-vessel.

The expedition arrived off Martinique on the 5th February, and operations were commenced against the island, which was held by General Rochambeau and 600 men, according to French statements, by disembarking the British troops in three divisions. By the 16th March the whole island had been conquered, except Forts Bourbon and Royal, with a loss of 71 killed and 193 wounded. The seamen of the fleet participated in the operations, dragging the guns and mortars for several miles over difficult country to commanding positions for reducing the enemy's fire, and 200 of them assisted in storming the important post of Monte Mathurine. In particular the exertions of 300 seamen, under the command of Captain Eliab Harvey of the *Santa Margarita* frigate, were most praiseworthy. This detachment dragged a 24-pounder and two mortars a distance of five miles, cutting a road for nearly a mile through a wood, and bridging two rivers, and then hoisted the ordnance to the summit of the hill of Sourriere. On the 17th March, a battery and some gunboats, commanded by Lieutenant Richard Bowen, of the *Boyne*, opened fire upon Fort St. Louis, as did the ordnance on the top of the hill, served by the sailors, on Fort Bourbon, commanding the town of Fort Royal. At the same time Lieutenant Bowen, taking the boats of the squadron, made a dash for the *Bienvenue* frigate, lying moored within fifty yards of the shore, and under a hot fire of musketry from the walls of Fort Louis, boarded and captured the ship with little opposition, the major portion of the crew escaping to the shore. As the frigate's sails were unbent, the gallant officer was unable to bring the ship off, but he made good his return, taking with him 22 of her crew as prisoners, with the loss of only three killed and five wounded. It was now determined to assault the town and Fort Royal, and a number of scaling ladders made from long bamboos having been prepared, the troops were directed to advance, with field-pieces, along the side of the hill under Fort Bourbon, over the canal at the back of Fort Royal, while the *Asia*, Captain Brown, and *Zebra*, sloop, Captain Faulknor, moved to batter the lower and more exposed part of Fort Louis, and cover the flotilla of flat-bottomed boats, barges, and pinnaces, containing 1,200 men, under the command of Commodore Thompson and Captains Nugent of the *Veteran* and Riou of the *Rose*.

The attack was successful, the *Asia* only being unable to participate owing to the French officer refusing to pilot her, but Captain Faulknor, with the brilliant gallantry that he had before displayed, took the *Zebra* in the teeth of a shower of grape close under the walls of the fort, which was carried by storm, with the assistance of the men in the boats, Captain Nugent himself hauling down the tricolour and hoisting the British flag. General Rochambeau, cowed by the loss of Fort Louis, surrendered Fort Bourbon, which received the Saxon names of George and Edward. The British troops lost during the operations three killed and four wounded, and the Navy had Captain Milne, of the *Avenger*, sloop, and 13 seamen killed, and Captain Tatham, of the *Dromedary*, store-ship, two lieutenants, a surgeon, and 24 seamen wounded. Captain Faulknor, who had displayed such conspicuous gallantry, was appointed to the command of the *Bienvenue*, which was added to the Navy as a 28-gun frigate, and received the name of the *Undaunted*, and Lieutenant Bowen was placed in command of the *Zebra*.

A sufficient garrison, under the orders of General Prescott, appointed governor, with a small squadron, commanded by Commodore Thompson, was left to hold the island of Martinique, and a detachment of troops proceeded, with the remaining ships of war, to undertake the reduction of Saint Lucia. The troops were disembarked on the 1st April, and between that date and the 3rd were engaged in attacking the enemy's works, and on the 4th General Ricard surrendered the island. Sir Charles Gordon, a military officer, was left in charge, and on the following day the remainder of the troops returned to Martinique.

The British commanders lost no time in undertaking the more difficult task of reducing Guadaloupe, where Sir John Jervis, in the *Boyne*, with two other ships-of-the-line and some frigates and transports, arrived on the 10th April. Soon after midnight a detachment of soldiers was landed, under cover of the fire of the 32-gun frigate *Winchester*, Captain Lord Garlies, who was wounded. Early on the 12th the troops, commanded by General Dundas, assisted by a party of seamen, under the energetic Captain Faulknor, advanced to the attack of the strong fort of Fleur d'Epée, which was carried after severe fighting. This success was quickly followed by the abandonment of the other fortified positions of Grand-terre, the British casualties being 15 killed and 58 wounded, while the enemy lost, in defending Fort d'Epée, 67 slain and 55 wounded, and 110 prisoners. Meanwhile the small neighbouring islands, called the Saintes, were captured without loss by a party of seamen and marines from the frigates *Quebec* and *Ceres*. The next enterprise was the attack of the town and works of Basse-terre, which was surrendered by General Collot on the 20th April, after two or three batteries defending the town had been captured with slight loss by the troops.

Thus the whole of the island of Guadaloupe fell to British arms, but it was not suffered long to remain an appanage of the Crown. General Dundas was placed in command of Guadaloupe with what was considered an adequate garrison, and the naval and military commanders-in-chief quitted the island.

But a French squadron of two frigates, one corvette, two large ships, and five transports, having troops on board, under the command of Victor Hugues, had been enabled to make their escape from Rochefort, some time in April, and on the 3rd June anchored off Gosier near Fort d'Epée, where 300 men were disembarked. Colonel Drummond, commanding the post, permitted some 180 French royalists to march out to attack the enemy, but on encountering them they fled panic-stricken. By the 6th, the Republicans, now being between 1,200 and 1,500 men, commenced their march on the fort, held by only 160 men of the 43rd Regiment and Artillery, who after a resolute defence, retreated. Collecting the small garrisons at the other forts, Colonel Drummond proceeded to Grande-terre. On hearing of this unexpected irruption, Sir John Jervis, who was at St. Kitts, sailed for Guadaloupe, accompanied by Sir Charles Grey, with the *Boyne* and *Veteran*, having despatched the *Winchester* and *Nautilus* to Antigua and Martinique for reinforcements.

On their arrival off Guadaloupe, the two commanders were joined by Commodore Thompson, with the 74-gun ships *Vengeance* and *Vanguard*, which latter, now carrying his broad pennant, under command of Captain Sawyer, had joined in place of the *Irresistible*. Sir Charles Grey landed at Basse-terre, which still remained in possession of the British troops, and Sir John Jervis proceeded with the *Boyne*, *Vanguard*, *Vengeance*, and *Veteran* to Pointe-à-Pitre. Troops, with a strong detachment of seamen, under Captain Robertson, of the *Veteran*, and Sawyer, of the *Vanguard*, were landed on the 19th June, to attempt the recapture of Grand-terre, and from the 25th to the end of the month skirmishes with varying success took place between the British and French forces, but after the repulse on the 2nd July of an attack on Pointe-à-Pitre, and the abandonment in consequence of an assault on Fort Fleur d'Epée, General Grey withdrew from before Grand-terre. The loss experienced by the troops in these operations was seven officers and 93 rank and file killed, 11 officers and 319 wounded, and 56 missing, and the Navy lost Captain Robertson and six men killed, two officers and 27 wounded, and 16 missing.

In September, Victor Hugues received reinforcements from France, and proceeded to attack the English camp at Berville, where General Graham was in command.

Finding his effective force reduced to 125 combatants, and being without hope of succour, while his provisions were nearly all consumed, Graham was compelled to capitulate, and the French thus became masters of the whole of Guadaloupe, except Fort Matilda. General Prescott held this post until the 10th December, when he effected a safe retreat with his garrison of 621 men, on board of the frigate *Terpsichore*, Captain Richard Bowen, who received a severe wound in the face from a musket-ball while bringing off in his own boat the last men from the fort. Thus the English were dispossessed of the island of Guadaloupe, and as soon as the French Government heard of the great success achieved by Victor Hugues, they strained every nerve to send him supplies and reinforcements.

On the 17th November, the *Hercule*, 50, *Astrée*, 36, two corvettes, and about ten transports, having on board 3,000 troops and carrying military stores of every description, sailed from Brest. They managed to elude discovery till the following 5th January, when they were discovered by the *Bellona*, 74, Captain Wilson, and *Alarm*, 32, Captain Carpenter, which were cruising off the islands. After a chase lasting all day, the weather being hazy and squally, Captain Wilson prepared to engage the five ships formed in rear of the convoy, and signalled Captain Carpenter to attack the latter. The *Bellona*, which was one of the fastest ships-of-the-line in the service, soon overhauled the sternmost of the ships, which was found to be the *Duras*, of 20 guns and 70 seamen and having on board 400 soldiers. Leaving the *Alarm* to take charge of the prize, Captain Wilson made chase after the other transports which had stood away under all sail. Favoured by the darkness and unfavourable weather, and still more, perhaps, by mismanagement on the part of the commodore, the whole of these, with the convoy, succeeded in reaching Guadaloupe in safety. The Republican general, Victor Hugues, who had displayed equal skill and daring in his past operations, made good use of the reinforcements he had received. Troops were landed at St. Lucia, St. Vincent, and Grenada, and a sanguinary war of races ensued. The Negroes and many of the old French inhabitants revolted, and fearful atrocities were perpetrated, while plantations were fired in all directions. The British troops, badly distributed and few in number, were enfeebled by disease and fatigue, and could offer no effective resistance. On the 19th June, St. Lucia was evacuated by its garrison, numbering 2,000 men, which were embarked on board an armed store-ship and transport, and this island, as also Grenada and St. Vincent, again came under the French flag. But no long time elapsed before the tables were once more turned, and the see-saw of events found England again triumphant, as we shall show in a later chapter.

The loss of Guadaloupe was, in a measure, counterbalanced by a success achieved in the island of St. Domingo. On the 3rd February in this year (1794), the British troops captured a strong post at Cape Tiburon, and on the last day of May a joint expedition of 1,465 troops, with the *Irresistible*, 74, Captain James Dacres, the 64-gun ships *Belliqueux*, Captain Richard Dacres, and *Sceptre*, Captain Brine, *Europa*, 50, Captain Gregory, and three frigates and three sloops, under the command of Commodore Ford, sailed from Cape Nicholas-Mole to attack the town and defences of Port-au-Prince. On the first day of June the *Belliqueux* and *Sceptre*, with the *Penelope*, frigate, attacked Fort Brissoton, while the *Irresistible* and *Europa*, flying the commodore's broad pennant, co-operated by their fire, and covered the disembarkation of the troops. The fort was carried by assault, and the other posts being cannonaded by the frigates *Hermione* and *Iphigenia*, were abandoned by the enemy, and Port-au-Prince was surrendered, and thus all the possessions in the French half of St. Domingo were lost to that power. The British post at Cape Tiburon was, however, attacked on Christmas day by a strong body of French and Colonial troops, assisted by three vessels, and an armed merchantman, which was the only naval protection, after making a determined defence, was set on fire and blown up with all on board, and the fort was abandoned, the garrison losing about 100 of their number. Thus the result of the West India enterprises, though generally unfavourable to England, was of a chequered nature.

In Africa a French squadron of five ships from Brest attacked the unprotected town of Sierra Leone, and set on fire and destroyed a great part of the place; thence they sailed for other settlements along the coast between Senegal and Bonny, which they devastated, and there being no English ships-of-war in these seas, returned in safety with their spoil to France.

During the year 1794, the British Navy captured thirty-six ships-of-war, of which twenty-seven were added to the service. On the other hand the country lost seventeen ships, including the *Alexander*, 74, captured on the 6th November by a French squadron of eight ships. The number of seamen voted by Parliament for the service of the ensuing year was 85,000, with 15,000 marines, being 25,000 in excess of the preceding year, and the total supplies, exclusive of the charge for ordnance, was £6,315,000.

The new year was signalised, before it was many days old, by a daring exploit by Sir Sydney Smith, one of the most dashing officers of the British Navy in this its palmiest days. The British Admiralty having learned that the Brest fleet of thirty-five sail-of-the-line, with thirteen frigates, under Admiral Villaret-Joyeuse, with Rear-Admirals Nielly, Vanstabel, Bouvet, and Renaudin, had proceeded to sea on the last day of the year, on the 2nd January, 1795, despatched a squadron of frigates, consisting of the *Flora*, *Arethusa* and *Diamond*, under their titled and distinguished captains, Sir John Borlase Warren, Sir Edward Pellew, and Sir Sydney Smith, to the bay of Brest to ascertain the truth of the report. On arriving off the port on the following day, the *Diamond*, with the wind easterly, commenced beating up towards the entrance of the harbour, in which, under French colours, she was engaged all that day and the succeeding night. At daybreak on the 4th, Sir Sydney saw two ships coming out of the harbour, there being fifteen small vessels at anchor in Canaret Roads, and a ship-of-the-line on shore, supposed to be the *Republicain*, which had been stranded a week before, when the fleet was driven back while attempting to leave the port. Not finding any ships-of-war in Brest Roads, Sir Sydney bore up towards Pointe St. Matthieu. A corvette, which had been running along Bertheaume Bay to the westward, shortened sail, and apparently had some suspicion of the *Diamond*, though she was under French colours, for she hoisted some signals, and hauled close under the lee of the castle there. Sir Sydney Smith, however, stood on, and passed within hail of a line-of-battle-ship, which lay at anchor with jury yards and topmasts. The captain of the *Diamond* hailed the French commander in French, of which language he was a master, and asked if he wanted assistance. To this he received an answer in the negative, and also the information that the ship was the *Nestor*, and having been dismasted in a gale of wind, had parted from the fleet three days before. With this information, and having accomplished his object, Sir Sydney Smith rejoined his consorts in the offing.

The cruise of Monsieur Villaret-Joyeuse's fleet, extending over thirty-four days, was a stormy one. Scarcely had he got out to sea than he encountered a heavy gale of wind, in which several ships were damaged, and the *Nestor*, as above stated, lost her masts and returned to port. A few days later Rear-Admiral Vanstabel's division of eight sail and some frigates returned to Brest, and on the 28th January the remainder of the fleet met with a terrific gale, when about 150 leagues from land, in which the line-of-battle-ships *Jacobin*, *Scipion*, and *Superbe* foundered, and nearly the whole of the crew of the *Jacobin* perished, a large number on account of the fore and main-masts falling on the quarter-deck, but the crews of the two other ships, except 21 men in the *Superbe*, were rescued from a watery grave. The *Neptune*, a 74, which, like the *Jacobin* and *Scipion*, had been engaged with Lord Howe's fleet on the 1st June, was wrecked on a point of the coast about twelve leagues from Brest, and the *Téméraire* and *Convention* reached port with great difficulty. The remainder of the fleet found its way to Brest, having inflicted, during this disastrous cruise, considerable loss on the British mercantile marine, of which about 100 sail were captured or destroyed, including the frigate *Daphne*, mounting 30 guns.

Lord Howe put to sea from Torbay, on the 14th February, with the Channel Fleet, consisting of thirty-seven sail-of-the-line, together with five Portuguese seventy-fours, under Admiral de Valle, and a large number of frigates, and, having escorted the East and West India trading fleets safely out of the Channel with their convoys, ascertained that his adversary, Monsieur Villaret-Joyeuse, had returned to Brest with his crippled ships, and sailed for Spithead. The French authorities displayed such activity and despatch, that by the 22nd of the month Rear-Admiral Renaudin was enabled to sail from Toulon with six sail-of-the-line, and within a fortnight the remaining twelve ships were ready for sea. Admiral Hon William Cornwallis, carrying his flag in the *Royal Sovereign*, 100, with four seventy-fours, two frigates, and a sloop-of-war, sailed from Spithead for a cruise off Ushant, and on the 8th June sighted off the Penmarcks the squadron of Rear-Admiral Vence, consisting of three seventy-fours, and six or seven frigates, forming part of the Brest fleet, which, with a numerous convoy, was returning from Bordeaux. The British admiral gave chase, the French ships standing for Belleisle under a press of sail, and, having succeeded in capturing eight vessels laden with wine and brandy, steered for the Channel, and when a few leagues from Scilly directed the *Kingfisher*, sloop, to take the prizes into port, while he returned to look after Admiral Vence's squadron. But that officer had taken advantage of the absence of Admiral Cornwallis to quit Belleisle and make for Brest, and on the way was met by Admiral Villaret, flying his flag in the *Peuple* (late *Montagne*) of 120 guns, with nine sail-of-the-line, two 50-gun *rasés*, seven frigates, and four corvettes.

On the 16th June, when working back towards Brest, the French commander-in-chief, having now twelve battle-ships, sighted Admiral Cornwallis' squadron, which, being in greatly inferior force, hauled to the wind under all sail to retreat. All that day the respective fleets manœuvred, the one to close, and the other to avoid an engagement, but owing to the bad sailing of the *Bellerophon* and *Brunswick*, at daylight on the 17th the French fleet, in three divisions, was approaching the British squadron, the weather division being nearly abreast of the British rear. At about nine o'clock the leading French ship opened fire upon the *Mars*, which returned the compliment, and shortly before noon the cannonade became general on the part of the British ships, which fired their stern and quarter guns as they could be brought to bear. The van ship engaging the *Mars* having suffered aloft, dropped astern, and the ship next to her in the line took up the position she had occupied. But the *Mars* was seriously crippled, on observing which Admiral Cornwallis bore up to her assistance in company with the *Triumph*, 74, and by this bold and well-executed manœuvre saved her from further molestation, and brought her into close order of battle, when the four French ships which had borne up to secure the *Mars* hauled their wind on being baulked of their anticipated prey. The enemy continued the pursuit, keeping up partial and desultory firing, but soon after six they gave up the chase and stood to the eastward. In this affair the *Mars* was much damaged aloft, and had twelve men wounded, and the *Triumph*, the only other ship engaged, suffered but little in her sails and rigging. The retreat of Admiral Cornwallis, with five ships from twelve sail-of-the-line and fourteen frigates, without abandoning the *Mars*, was a very masterly performance, and commanded general admiration, but the French officers sought to give a sufficient reason for their retreat, when they had almost surrounded so inferior a force, by declaring that they mistook some strange ships, sighted on the horizon, for Lord Bridport's squadron, and this view, it has been stated, originated by a *ruse de guerre*, practised by the British frigate, *Phaeton*, Captain Hon. Robert Stopford, which, being detached ahead of the squadron, made the signal for a fleet, known to the enemy, by letting fly her topgallant sheets and firing two guns in quick succession.

Vice-Admiral Cornwallis and his squadron received the thanks of Parliament for their cool and courageous conduct in the face of the enemy, and the admiral enhanced his own share in the exploit by the modest terms of his despatch, and the brief mention made of the part played by the *Royal Sovereign*. He says:—

"Indeed I shall ever feel the impression which the good conduct of the captains, officers, seamen, and marines, and soldiers in the squadron has made on my mind; and it is the greatest pleasure I ever received to see the spirit manifested by the men, who, instead of being cast down at seeing thirty sail of the enemy's ships attacking our little squadron, were in the highest spirits imaginable. I do not mean the *Royal*

Sovereign alone; the same spirit was shown in all the ships near me; and although, circumstanced as we were, we had no great reason to complain of the conduct of the enemy, yet our men could not help repeatedly expressing their contempt of them. Could common prudence have allowed me to let loose their valour, I hardly know what might not have been accomplished by such men." Of his flagship's individual share he merely says:—"In the evening they made a show of a more serious attack upon the *Mars*, and obliged me to bear up for her support."

Meantime Lord Bridport, in succession to Earl Howe, who was indisposed, had sailed from Spithead with the Channel fleet on the 12th June—the same day that Admiral Villaret had quitted Brest—consisting of the 100-gun ships *Royal George* (bearing his flag) and *Queen Charlotte*, the 98's *Queen*, Vice-Admiral Sir Alan Gardner, *London*, Vice-Admiral John Colpoys, *Prince of Wales*, Rear-Admiral Harvey, *Prince*, *Barfleur*, and *Prince George*, the *Sanspareil*, 80, Rear-Admiral Lord Hugh Seymour, and the *Valiant, Orion, Irresistible, Russell* and *Colossus*, 74's; in all fourteen ships-of-the-line, besides four frigates, a 20-gun sloop, and two fireships. The admiral's object was to afford protection to an expedition, consisting of three ships-of-the-line and some frigates, and transports with troops, bound to Quiberon Bay, under the command of Commodore Sir John B. Warren, flying his broad pennant in the *Pomone*, 40-gun frigate, in company with which he remained until the 19th June, when the wind being fair for their destination, he stood off the coast in readiness to engage the Brest fleet, of whose departure he had no knowledge. The same day Admiral Villaret, quitting Belleisle where his fleet had taken shelter from a severe gale, sighted Commodore Warren's expedition, who despatched a frigate to recall Lord Bridport, with whom, on the following morning, having altered his course, he effected a junction.

The French admiral apparently showed no desire to engage, whereupon Lord Bridport threw out a signal for a general chase, which was continued all night, the wind being light, until the following morning, when the *Queen Charlotte*, Sir Andrew Douglas, was nearest the rearmost of the enemy's ships, the majority of which lay in a cluster ahead. Next to the *Queen Charlotte* was the *Irresistible*, with the *Orion, Sanspareil, Colossus*, and *Russell* in support, with the island of Groix nearly due east about eight miles on the lee bow of the flagship.

The first of the enemy's ships to open fire, about 6 A.M., was the sternmost, the *Alexandre*, 74, captured by the French squadron on the 6th November in the preceding year, which was replied to by the *Irresistible* and *Orion*. Soon afterwards the *Formidable*, the next ship ahead of the *Alexandre*, returned the fire of the *Queen Charlotte*, which had brought her heavy starboard broadside to bear on her, and the *Sanspareil*, in passing ahead of the French 74, to engage other ships, gave her a taste of her metal. The *Formidable* suffered severely from the broadsides of the *Queen Charlotte*, and catching fire, dropped astern, and soon afterwards, on her mizen-mast going over the side, she hauled down her colours.

In addition to the ships named, the *Colossus, Russell, London*, and *Queen*, of the British fleet, and the *Peuple, Mucius, Redoutable, Wattigny*, and *Nestor*, of the hostile squadron, were more or less engaged, the remaining ships of both nationalities being too far ahead or astern to participate in the action. The *Queen Charlotte* had her rigging and sails much cut up by the fire of the enemy, but managed, nevertheless, as she dropped astern, to repair damages, and compel the *Alexandre* to strike her colours in token of surrender. The *Tigre*, 74, with which she had been engaged, ranged ahead, hotly fired upon by the *Sanspareil*, and on the *Queen* and *London* opening their broadsides on her, she surrendered.

Lord Bridport now signalled to the *Colossus* and *Sanspareil* to cease firing, and directing some ships to take the three prizes in tow, the commander-in-chief, in the *Royal George*, followed by the other British ships, wore round from the land and the French fleet, which, being thus unexpectedly relieved from further danger, took shelter between Groix and the entrance to Lorient, and then retreated into the latter port.

The *Queen Charlotte* took the most prominent part in the action, and was the chief sufferer aloft of the eight British ships that were engaged, her fore and main-masts being badly wounded, as were also the main-masts of the *Sanspareil* and *Irresistible*. The loss in the British fleet was inconsiderable, the total casualties being 31 killed and 113 wounded. The French loss is not known, but of the three prizes, the *Tigre*, out of a complement of 726 men, had 130 killed and wounded; the *Alexandre*, 220 out of 666, being exactly one-third her crew; and the *Formidable* had no fewer than 320 casualties, including three lieutenants killed and Captain Linois, her second captain, and her remaining three lieutenants wounded. Under these circumstances it must be allowed that the officers and men of the Republican Navy maintained the reputation for devotion and gallantry that had always distinguished the service under such Royalist commanders as De Suffren and Thurot.

Having disposed of the Brest fleet and sent home the prizes, which were taken into the British Navy, and renamed respectively *Alexander* and *Belleisle*, the *Tigre* retaining her name, Lord Bridport remained off the coast until the 20th September, to assist Sir John Warren, whose ill-fated expedition to Quiberon merits some record.

On the 25th June this squadron—consisting of the 74's *Robust*, Captain Thornborough, *Thunderer*, Captain Albemarle Bertie, the *Standard*, 64, Captain Ellison; and the frigates *Pomone*, bearing the commodore's broad pennant, *Anson*, *Artois*, *Arethusa*, *Concord*, and *Galatea*, with some transports, carrying 2,500 French *émigrés*, as the expatriated Royalists were called,—entered the Bay of Quiberon, a capacious and secure anchorage, and two days after their arrival the troops were landed with slight opposition, and were joined by 16,000 of their compatriots, for whom arms and the munitions of war had been brought in the transports. The fort of Penthièvre, situated on the peninsula of Quiberon, was surrendered by its garrison of 600 men, but an attack made on the 16th July, by the Comte D'Hervilly at the head of about 5,000 men, including 200 British marines, on the right flank of the Republican army, commanded by the celebrated French General Hoche, posted on some heights, was repulsed with loss, and the Royalist troops only made good their retreat to the fort by the fire of some armed launches, stationed close to the beach. Only a few days after, a greater disaster befel the cause of the French monarchical party. During the night of the 20th July, while a storm of wind and rain swept the country, the enemy, introduced into the fort by some traitors in the Royalist camp, suddenly made their entry, and a scene of confusion and massacre ensued, all who did not respond to the cry of " *Vive la Republique* " being put to the sword. A party, under De Sombreuil, obtained terms of capitulation, which were afterwards violated, and that gallant young officer and other aristocrats were shot, the rank and file being permitted to join the Republican forces. Some 1,100 men of the garrison of Fort Penthièvre, led by the Comte de Puisaye, succeeded in making their way to the shore, where, on the following morning, they were embarked with about 2,400 Chouans, as the inhabitants of the peninsula were called, by the boats of the squadron, under the superintendence of Captain Goodwin Keats, of the *Galatea*. The whole of the vast supply of military stores and clothing for an army of 40,000 men, together with 10,000 stand of arms, and 150,000 pairs of shoes, were left behind, and fell into the hands of the enemy, and in addition, six transports that had arrived on the previous evening with provisions were seized by them.

Commodore Warren now took possession of two small islands off the peninsula, and having disembarked, at their own request, near Lorient, 2,000 of the Chouans brought from Quiberon, he occupied the small island of Eu, about five leagues from the island of Noirmontier, at the mouth of the Loire. Early in October Sir John Warren was joined at Isle D'Eu, by the *Jason*, 38, Captain Stirling, convoying some transports with 4,000 British troops, under the command of General Doyle, on board the frigate being the Comte D'Artois (afterwards Charles X., King of France), the Duc de Bourbon, and several French nobles. The troops were landed on the island, but though something might have been effected had they been brought to co-operate with the *émigrés*, the Royalist cause was now in a desperate state, and after remaining here until the end of the year, the British soldiers were re-embarked in the transports, and returned to England *re infecta*. The Quiberon expedition was only less disastrous than that to Toulon by reason of its being on a smaller scale, and was almost equally remarkable in giving the young and talented Republican General Hoche an opportunity for displaying military talents second only to those of Napoleon Buonaparte, as exhibited in the repulse of the allied attack on the great French port and arsenal in the Mediterranean. Both expeditions equally showed that the Republican fever had seized on almost the entire French nation, and that there was no room for the Royalist revival, which was to replace the Bourbons on the throne of the Capets, which the British Government, and a majority of the people, believed was capable of realisation, an opinion which led to the restoration of Louis XVIII. and his brother, with results that are now historical.

Before the close of the year 1795, on the 17th and 18th November, a westerly gale swept the Channel with disastrous results. A fleet of 200 transports and West Indiamen, having on board over 16,000 troops, convoyed by eight ships-of-the-line, under Admiral Christian, had just quitted Spithead, when they were exposed to this furious storm, which scattered the vast armament, and several of the transports and merchantmen foundered, and the wrecks of others strewed the shore. The fleet put back to their anchorage, and it was the 5th December before the ships were in a condition to put to sea again, but it was only for the second time to encounter a gale which lasted for over a fortnight, and again scattered the convoy.

Vice-Admiral Hotham fought an action off Genoa with Admiral Martin, commanding the Toulon fleet, which, by great exertions, had been increased to fifteen sail-of-the-line and six frigates, fully equipped for service. The French admiral, on hearing that the British fleet had sailed from San Fiorenzo Bay, in Corsica, and retired to Leghorn, embarked about 5,000 troops, with the object of attempting the recovery of that island, and sailed on the 3rd March from Toulon. On the 7th, Admiral Martin arrived off San

Fiorenzo Bay, from which the *Berwick*, 74, Captain Littlejohn, which, being dismasted, had been left behind at the anchorage by Admiral Hotham, was then issuing to make her way to Leghorn. Captain Littlejohn made every endeavour to escape, but was brought to action by the *Alceste*, frigate, assisted by the *Minerve* and *Vistula*, until the line-of-battle ships began to draw near, when the colours of the *Berwick* were struck by order of Lieutenant Palmer, who succeeded Captain Littlejohn, when that officer was killed by a cannon-shot. During the action the *Alceste* also lost her captain. The *Berwick*, escorted by a frigate, was despatched to Toulon, to be refitted, and Admiral Martin continued his cruise, which the members of the French "Committee of Public Safety" on board the flagship declared was "to seek the enemy, fight the English wherever they were to be found, drive them out of the Mediterranean, and restore for that sea a free navigation," objects which could not have been gathered from the subsequent manœuvres of the Republican fleet.

CHAPTER VI.

Vice-Admiral Hotham's Action off Genoa with the French Fleet and Capture of the *Ca Ira* and *Censeur*—His engagement off Hyères and Capture of the *Alcide*—Loss of a British Convoy and the *Censeur*—Rupture with Holland and Seizure of Dutch Ships—Action between the *Blanche* and *Pique*, and Death of Captain Faulknor—The *Lively* and *Tourterelle*—*Astræa* and *Gloire*—The *Thetis* and *Hussar* with Five French Store-ships—The *Dido* and *Lowestoft* with the *Minerve* and *Artemise*—The *Southampton* and *Vestale*—The *Rose* and Three Privateers—The *Mermaid* and Two Corvettes—Loss of the *Boyne*—Capture of the Cape of Good Hope and of a Dutch Squadron sent to its Relief—Also of the Dutch Possessions in Ceylon and India.

ADMIRAL HOTHAM was lying in Leghorn Roads, where, on the 8th March, 1795, he heard of the departure of the French fleet from Toulon, and divining that their object was an attack on Corsica, he at once weighed anchor and put to sea with the following ships:—

100	*Britannia*	{ Vice-Admiral William Hotham { Captain Holloway		*Captain* *Fortitude*	Captain Samuel Reeve „ William Young
98	*Princess Royal*	{ Vice-Admiral S. C. Goodall { Captain Purvis	74 {	*Illustrious* *Terrible*	„ Thomas L. Frederick „ George Campbell
	St. George	{ Vice-Admiral Sir Hyde Parker { Captain Thomas Foley		*Courageux* *Bedford*	„ Augustus Montgomery „ David Gould
	Windsor Castle	{ Rear-Admiral R. Linzee { Captain J. Gore	64 {	*Agamemnon* *Diadem*	„ Horatio Nelson „ Charles Tyler

Also the frigates *Inconstant*, *Lowestoft*, *Meleager*, and *Romulus*, besides two sloops and a cutter. He had likewise under his command the Neapolitan ship, *Il Tancredi*, 74, commanded by Prince Carraccioli, and two frigates of the same nationality. On the 11th the enemy were sighted working back to Toulon. The following were the ships-of-the-line under the command of Admiral Martin:—

The French fleet was descried again on the following day, the 12th March, but there was so little wind that Admiral Hotham could do no more than close up his line and form in order of battle. The night of the 12th was squally, and the French *Mercure*, 74, lost her main-topmast, and was directed to return to port, escorted by a frigate. On the following morning, as Admiral Martin evinced no desire to engage the British fleet, which it was his avowed intention "to drive from the Mediterranean," Admiral Hotham signalled his fleet to chase, and an accident soon put it into the power of some of his frigate-captains to test the quality of the enemy. The *Ca Ira*, third ship from the rear, fouled her second ahead, the *Victoire*, and carried away her own fore and main-topmasts. Thereupon, Captain Fremantle, commanding the 36-gun frigate *Inconstant*, who was far advanced in the chase, ranged up close to the port quarter of the *Ca Ira*, and giving her a broadside, stood on. Having tacked, the British frigate again passed under the lee of the French 80-gun ship, which was now in tow of the *Vestale*, frigate, and fired into her, but the two-decker retaliated by a broadside from her lower deck guns which killed three and wounded 14 of the *Inconstant's* crew, and a 36-pound shot striking her between wind and water, the frigate was forced to bear up. Shortly before 11, Captain Horatio Nelson, in the *Agamemnon*, got upon the quarter of the *Ca Ira*, and opened a distant fire on her, but several French ships coming to the aid of their crippled consort, the British sixty-four ceased firing about 2.45, and took up her station in the line. The desultory firing kept up by the *Bedford* and *Egmont* on the three rearmost French ships terminated for the day about the same time.

The chase was continued throughout the night, and soon after daybreak on the 14th March the *Captain* and *Bedford* overhauled and engaged the dismasted *Ca Ira*, now towed by the *Censeur*, 74, which were a considerable distance astern and to leeward of the French fleet. The *Captain*, being ahead of her consort, sustained for a quarter of an hour the concentrated fire of the two French ships, without being able to return a shot, and when she had got into position to do so was considerably damaged. The two British seventy-fours engaged the *Ca Ira* and *Censeur* for about eighty minutes, when both were so disabled that they were obliged to cease firing, and were towed out of action. Their loss was small, the *Captain* having three men and the *Bedford* seven killed, and the former her first lieutenant and master wounded, and the latter her first lieutenant and seventeen seamen wounded. But they were both rendered unmanageable by reason of their shattered condition aloft. The *Captain* had her sails cut to pieces, most of her stays and shrouds were shot away, and her fore and mizen yards and fore and main topmasts were disabled. The *Bedford* had been equally a sufferer. Her standing and running rigging and sails were cut, and her foremast, fore-yard, bowsprit, mizen topmast, and main top-sail yard were shot through.

The *Illustrious* and *Courageux* coming up to the aid of their consorts, about eight o'clock, engaged the *Duquesne*, the leading French ship, and the *Victoire*, at a range of about six hundred yards, and soon the *Tonnant*, 80, opened fire on the two British seventy-fours. At the end of an hour's conflict the fore-topmast of the *Illustrious* went over the bow; a few minutes later the main-mast fell over the poop, carrying away the mizen-mast in its fall, and her fore-mast and bowsprit were shot through, and her hull pierced in many places. The *Courageux* also lost her main and mizen-masts, and neither ship, owing to there being almost a dead calm and their shattered condition, could escape from the destructive fire of the French ships-of-the-line, with their superior weight of metal. In this unequal conflict the *Illustrious* had 20 men killed and 70 wounded. The *Courageux* had one midshipman and 14 men killed, and her master and 32 wounded.

The firing ceased about 2 p.m., and a breeze springing up, the *Duquesne*, *Victoire*, and *Tonnant* abandoned the *Ca Ira* and *Censeur* to their fate, and the French fleet made sail, Admiral Hotham making no effort to renew the action or pursue them. These two French ships surrendered after making a most gallant resistance, their united loss being about 400 men; and both were greatly shattered, while the *Ca Ira* lost her fore and mainmasts, and the *Censeur* her mainmast. The total loss in the British fleet was 74 killed and 284 wounded, the *Illustrious* and *Courageux* being the principal sufferers.

The capture of two French ships-of-the-line entitles Admiral Hotham's action to be ranked technically as a victory; but in view of the fact that there was small disparity in the strength of the two fleets, and what there was on the last day, the 14th March, was on the side of the British commander—he having fifteen ships to his adversary's thirteen, while the *Sans Culottes* was their only three-decker—taking, we say, these circumstances into account, and the fact that there was no pursuit, the action must be considered as somewhat indecisive, and little credit was due to the British admiral, who displayed a lack of enterprise.

Nelson in vain sought to induce Hotham to pursue the enemy. The admiral replied to the fiery captain of the *Agamemnon*, "We must be content; we have done very well," an answer upon which Nelson observed in a letter to his wife: "Now had he taken ten sail and allowed the eleventh to escape, when it had been possible to have got at her, I could never have called it well done." Before many years the great sailor put in practice his views of the duty of a British admiral.

The British fleet, taking in tow the dismasted ships and the two prizes, bore up for Spezzia, but on the night of the 17th the *Illustrious* and *Meleager*, frigate, which had her in tow, were separated from the rest of the ships, and the hawser parting, the seventy-four, after using every effort to get off the land, drifted ashore in Valance Bay between Spezzia and Leghorn. Here she became a total wreck, and was set on fire and destroyed, but by the aid of the frigates and the boats of the fleet, then at anchor in Spezzia Bay, the crew and some of the stores were removed in safety. The fleet repaired to San Fiorenzo Bay on the 26th, where it lay refitting until the 18th April, when Admiral Hotham sailed for Leghorn. Admiral Martin made the best of his way to the Bay of Hyères, where he was joined by the *Mercure* and *Sans Culottes*, and the *Berwick*, prize, and sent for repairs to Toulon the *Victoire*, *Timoleon*, and *Berwick*, and the frigates *Alceste* and *Minerve*. A few days later the French commander-in-chief was joined by Rear-Admiral Renaudin from Brest, with the 80-gun ship *Formidable*, and the 74's *Jupiter*, *Mont Blanc*, *Jemappes*, *Revolution*, and *Tyrannicide*, three frigates, and three corvettes, which raised his fleet to seventeen sail-of-the-line, without reckoning the three ships refitting at Toulon, whither the French fleet now proceeded.

Admiral Hotham sailed from Leghorn on the 8th May, on a cruise off Minorca, where, on the 14th June, he was joined by nine sail of the line* from England, under Rear-Admiral Mann, flying his flag on board the world-renowned *Victory*, and on the 29th the whole fleet anchored in the bay of San Fiorenzo. On the 4th July Admiral Hotham despatched Commodore Nelson, with the *Agamemnon*, and the *Meleager* and *Ariadne* frigates, *Moselle*, sloop, and *Mutine*, cutter, to cruise along the coast to the northward of Genoa, and on the 7th that indefatigable officer discovered the Toulon fleet, which had put to sea on the 7th June. Admiral Martin gave chase, Commodore Nelson making sail to escape, and on the following morning he began firing guns as signals to the British fleet in San Fiorenzo Bay, which the French ships in pursuit discovered to the number of twenty-two sail, and several frigates, about 9.30 A.M., when they gave up the chase, and in turn sought safety in flight. Most of the ships of the

* These ships, excluding the *Victory*, were the following:—

98	*Blenheim*	Captain John Bazeley		*Cumberland*	Captain Barth. S. Rowley
80	*Gibraltar*	" John Pakenham	74	*Defence*	" Thomas Wells
74	*Bombay Castle*	" Charles Chamberlayne		*Culloden*	" Thomas Troubridge
	Saturn	" James Douglas		*Audacious*	" William Shield

British fleet were engaged refitting and watering, but notwithstanding this, and the state of the wind, which blew right into the bay, Admiral Hotham, by dint of great exertion, was enabled by 9 o'clock in the morning to take advantage of the land wind which then set in, and got his fleet under way.

The British fleet, numbering twenty-three sail-of-the-line, inclusive of the two Neapolitan ships, pursued all night in the direction taken by the enemy, and on the evening of the 12th received information that they had been seen that day to the southward of the Hyères Isles, whereupon the fleet stood in that direction. A heavy westerly gale set in during the night, and at daybreak on the 13th the French fleet was discovered on the lee beam, about five miles distant. Admiral Hotham threw out his signal for a general chase, and to engage, on each ship arriving up with the enemy, in succession, and the British fleet gained so much on the French, that at noon their rear was only three-quarters of a mile distant from the van English ships, which were the *Victory*, *Culloden*, and *Cumberland*. The enemy opened fire shortly afterwards on these ships, which returned the compliment, and with such effect that the *Alcide*, the rearmost French ship, was disabled, and about two o'clock was compelled to strike her colours to the *Cumberland*, Captain Rowley, which, without stopping to take possession, crowded all sail and pushed on to engage the second rear French ship. The gallant captain of the *Cumberland* had taken up an advantageous position for closely engaging this ship, when the commander-in-chief made a signal to discontinue the action. At this time the *Blenheim*, *Gibraltar*, *Captain*, and other ships were closing with the enemy. By this unaccountable conduct Admiral Martin was enabled to take advantage of a shift of wind, which gave him the weather-gage, and made his way unmolested into Frejus Bay, where he anchored that night.

The only British ship that lost a mast was the *Culloden*, whose main-topmast was shot away, but the *Victory* and *Cumberland* suffered severely aloft, the former having her stays shot away and all her lower masts and bowsprit wounded, and the latter suffered almost equally. The casualties, however, were small, only eleven, including two midshipmen of the *Victory*, being killed, and twenty-seven wounded, of whom four were officers of the same ship. The French losses were probably not greater, except as regards the *Alcide*, which unfortunately caught fire soon after her surrender and blew up, when 315 officers and men, out of 615, were killed, the remainder being saved by the boats of the British fleet.

In commenting upon this action, Captain Brenton justly remarks:—" In this action

A 74-GUN SHIP-OF-THE-LINE, ABOUT 1794.

there was a total misapplication of tactics, neither recommended by a Clark or justified by experience. The French fleet should have been attacked by a general chase as soon as discovered; the bending new top-sails, when the enemy was dead to leeward, was at best a useless measure; and it is much to be regretted that time was lost in forming a line of bearing which could not be preserved with any effect; as the admiral observes in his despatches, 'the calms and shifts of wind in that country rendered all naval operations peculiarly uncertain.' With this knowledge it was incumbent on him to have dashed upon his enemy, who he knew would not wait for him, and who must have been in a great measure unprepared; by an immediate chase he would have compelled them to engage, or have increased their distance from the land, which would, in a great degree, have ensured their capture or destruction. The delay of making the signal gave them time to recover from their confusion; and when, after a lapse of four hours, the British admiral made sail in chase, the wind failed, and the opportunity was irrecoverably lost."

Admiral Hotham made his way to San Fiorenzo and Leghorn, but put to sea again on the 6th August, and two days later was off Toulon, where he found Admiral Martin lying at anchor with his fleet. Standing away to the eastward, he detached Commodore Nelson, in the *Agamemnon*, with the frigates *Inconstant*, *Meleager*, *Tartar*, and *Southampton*, the *Ariadne*, 20, and *Speedy*, 14-gun brig, to cruise along the Italian coast with the object of assisting the Austrian and Sardinian armies in expelling the Republicans from the Genoese territories. While thus engaged, the commodore, on the 26th August, cut out with the boats of his squadron two brigs, two armed galleys, and five merchantmen, laden with provisions, without the loss of a man.

Under instructions from the French Government Admiral Martin, on the 14th September, detached Rear-Admiral Richery from Toulon to cruise on the Newfoundland coast, and reinforced the Brest fleet with the *Victoire*, 80, and the 74's *Barras*, *Jupiter*, *Berwick*, *Resolution*, and *Duquesne*, and three frigates. On hearing of this event, the commander-in-chief sent Rear-Admiral Mann, on the 5th October, in pursuit with the *Windsor Castle*, 98, now flying his flag, and the 74's *Cumberland*, *Defence*, *Terrible*, *Audacious*, and *Saturn*, and the frigates *Blonde* and *Castor*. But there had been a delay of thirteen days in despatching this squadron after the enemy, and the result was disastrous.

On the 25th September, the *Fortitude*, 74, Commodore Taylor, and *Bedford*, Captain Montgomery, with the French prize *Censeur*, of 74 guns, jury-rigged, the *Lutine*, frigate, and *Tisiphone*, fire-ship, sailed from Gibraltar for England, escorting sixty-three ships, forming the valuable Levant fleet. Thirty-two of these parted company the same night, under the convoy of the *Juno* and *Argo*, frigates, but the others remained under the protection of the commodore, and on the 7th October Rear-Admiral Richerry's squadron was sighted, bearing down on them. Commodore Taylor made the signal for the merchantmen to disperse, and formed his ships into line of battle to engage the enemy, so as to give his convoy an opportunity of escaping. But the *Censeur* rolled away her fore-topmast, and having only a frigate's mainmast, was soon left astern, and being at the mercy of the enemy, was compelled to strike after making a spirited resistance, in which she lost her two remaining topmasts, and expended nearly all the little powder she had in her magazine. The other four ships of the British squadron effected their escape, but all the convoy, with the exception of one ship, were captured by the frigates, and Admiral Richerry entered the port of Cadiz with his thirty prizes and the recaptured *Censeur*.

But Rear-Admiral Richerry was not alone in effecting his escape from Toulon. A fortnight after his departure, Rear-Admiral Gauteaume got to sea with the *Mont Blanc*, 74, and the 40-gun frigates, *Junon* and *Justice*, the *Artémèse* and *Sérieuse*, of 36 guns, the *Badine*, 28, and *Hasard*, 16. Monsieur Gauteaume made his way to the Levant with the object of intercepting the merchant fleet which accidentally fell into the hands of Admiral Richerry, and—having captured many trading ships of different European nationalities, and released the 36-gun frigate *Sensible* and corvette *Sardine*, which, along with their prize, the *Nemesis*, of 28 guns, had been blockaded by the British frigates, *Aigle*, Captain Samuel Hood, and *Cyclops*, Captain William Hotham,—managed to evade two British squadrons sent in pursuit of him, and arrived in safety at Toulon on the 5th February, 1796. Admiral Hotham returned to Leghorn on the 13th October, and on the 1st November struck his flag and proceeded to England, resigning the command to Vice-Admiral Sir Hyde Parker until the arrival from Portsmouth of Admiral Sir John Jervis, who hoisted his flag as commander-in-chief on board the *Victory* on the 3rd December, and sailing a few days later for Toulon, cruised between that port and the island of Minorca.

Admiral Hotham, notwithstanding his considerable services, cannot be regarded as among our great naval commanders. He incurred Nelson's censure by his remissness in the action of the 14th March, and again in the following July he delayed chasing the enemy when lying in San Fiorenzo Bay, and when the *Cumberland* and other ships were closing with the enemy he recalled them by signal, thus enabling the enemy to escape. Finally, in September, he delayed for thirteen days in sending a squadron to intercept Rear-Admiral Richerry's squadron, by which act of neglect the *Censeur* and the whole of her valuable convoy were captured.

In addition to her other enemies, this country found herself involved in hostilities with Holland, which, after the country had been overrun by the French armies in 1794, discarded her Stadtholder, and threw in her lot with the Republican Government, under the newly-acquired name of the Batavian Republic. The British Ministry laid an embargo on all Dutch ships in English ports, and seized the *Zeeland*, 64, *Brakel*, 54, *Thulen*, 40, and two brigs-of-war, besides seven Indiamen and over fifty sail lying in Plymouth Sound. Active measures were also set on foot to conquer the colonial possessions of Holland, which, as well as her captured ships, were to be held in trust for the exiled Stadtholder, and a squadron, under the command of Vice-Admiral Adam Duncan, was despatched to sea to watch the movements of the Dutch squadron in the Texel. Associated with the British admiral was a Russian fleet of twelve sail-of-the line and seven frigates, but they were of little service, being scarcely seaworthy. During the year 1795 some actions between frigates and small squadrons took place, which are worthy of chronicle.

Notable among these was the duel between the *Blanche*, Captain Robert Faulknor, of 38 guns and 198 men, and the *Pique*, of like force, but having a crew of 279. The captain of the *Blanche*, one of the most gallant and successful in the British service, while cruising off the island of Guadaloupe, had, on the 30th December preceding, silenced the guns of a fort on the neighbouring island of Desirade, under which a French schooner, carrying eight guns, had taken refuge, and then sent in his boats and cut her out. Early on the 4th January, the *Blanche* was cruising off Pointe-à-Pitre, a harbour in Grande-terre, Guadaloupe, when she descried the *Pique* lying at anchor outside the harbour. The French frigate got under weigh in company with a schooner, and the *Blanche* made sail to meet her, but finding that the *Pique* was apparently disinclined to engage her, brought to an American schooner, which she boarded, and taking her in tow, steered for the harbour in the Saintes, two small islands close to Guadaloupe, where her other prize was lying. Finding, however, that the *Pique* was standing towards her, the *Blanche* shortened sail, but the former would not accept the challenge, and, after much manœuvring, the British frigate cast off the schooner and made all sail in chase.

Shortly before midnight the *Blanche* passed under the lee of the Frenchman, and returned her distant broadside, and a little before one, on the 5th January, she was within musket-shot range, and both frigates wore in succession, the *Pique* with the intention of crossing her opponent's hawse and raking her ahead, and the *Blanche* to frustrate this manœuvre. The rival frigates now became closely engaged, and a furious cannonade ensued, broadside to broadside, until the *Blanche*, having shot ahead, carried away her wounded main and mizen-masts, while in the act of luffing up to rake the *Pique*. The latter, seeing the British frigate at this disadvantage, fell on board her port quarter, and made several attempts to board, but the gallant British seamen beat back the Frenchmen, and from their port quarter-deck guns, and such of those on the main-deck as would bear, poured a destructive fire into the *Pique's* bow, which she returned from her tops and from some quarter-deck guns run in amidships fore and aft.

It was at this time that the gallant captain of the *Blanche* was killed. A few minutes before three, he was assisting his second lieutenant, Mr. David Milne, and one or two seamen, to lash the bowsprit of the *Pique* to the capstan of his ship, when a musket-ball pierced his heart and he expired immediately.

The lashings broke adrift, and the French frigate, crossing the stern of the *Blanche*, fell on board her a second time on the starboard quarter. Instantly the British seamen, seizing the hawser which had been brought up on deck the more securely to fasten the ships when they were last in contact, lashed the bowsprit of the Frenchman to the stump of their own main-mast. Thus held in her antagonist's relentless grasp, the *Pique* was towed by the British frigate before the wind, while the marines of the latter by their close fire defeated every attempt to cut away the lashings. The crew of the *Pique* behaved with exemplary gallantry under these trying circumstances, and defended their ship without thought of surrender. "The constant stream of musketry poured upon the quarter-deck of the *Blanche* from the forecastle and tops of the *Pique*," says James, "and a well-directed fire from the latter's quarter-deck guns pointed forward, gave great annoyance to the former, particularly as having, like many other ships in the British Navy at this period, no stern-ports on the main-deck, the cannonade on the part of the *Blanche* was confined to two quarter-deck six-pounders. The carpenter having in vain tried to cut down the upper transom beam, no alternative remained but to blow away a part of it on each side. As soon, therefore, as the firemen with their buckets were assembled in the cabin, the two after guns were pointed against the stern-frame. Their discharge made a clear breach on both sides, and the activity of the bucketmen quickly extinguished the fire it had occasioned in the woodwork. The two 12-pounders of the *Blanche*, thus brought into use, soon played havoc upon the *Pique's* decks."

The French frigate had lost her fore and mizen-masts at an earlier period of the action, and about a quarter past three in the morning her main-mast went over the side, leaving her in a defenceless state, as the wreck of her masts, falling over the guns, rendered them unserviceable, and she was unable to return the murderous raking discharges of her enemy. At length, soon after five, some of the crew called from the bowsprit that the ship had surrendered. There was a difficulty in taking possession of the prize, as all the boats in both ships had been destroyed by shot, but Lieutenant Milne, accompanied by ten seamen, managed to gain the deck of the *Pique* by partially swarming along the hawser, and partially swimming when their weight brought the bight of the rope into the water.

During this memorable action the *Blanche*—which fought with a diminished crew, two officers and 12 seamen being absent in prizes, thus reducing her crew to 198 men and boys, or 81 less than her antagonist—lost her captain, one midshipman, and six men killed, and one midshipman and 20 men wounded. Accounts differ as to the strength of the crew and the losses of the *Pique*. Admiral Caldwell, in two letters which appear in the *Gazette*, places the total of killed, wounded, and prisoners at 360, and Schomberg gives the number at a hundred higher, but the French officers deposed to the crew numbering between 260 and 270, though the actual strength on board, as stated in documents transmitted along with the certificates on which head-money was paid to the captors, was 279, and is so estimated by James, the most reliable and painstaking of all Naval historians. Of this total no less than 76 officers and men were killed and 110 wounded, making the carnage proportionally greater than in almost any other well-authenticated action. The heroism of the French captain, Conseil by name, who was mortally wounded, and his gallant crew, in fighting their ship until she was dismasted and defenceless, and their numbers were reduced to nearly one-third their original strength, is striking and deserving of special record. Equally worthy of praise was the valour, and more commendable the skill of the victors, who stuck to their enemy throughout the long and dark hours of the night with a bull-dog pluck worthy the best traditions of the service. It was this tenacity of purpose, manifest on this occasion in victory, but not less brilliantly displayed in defeat, that wrung from De Witt, the great "Pensionary" of Holland, after the memorable three days' battle in June, 1666, when Admiral Monk was overpowered and beaten by De Ruyter in the Channel, the expression of opinion, that "the English defeat did them more honour than all their former victories. The Dutch had discovered that Englishmen might be killed and English ships might be burnt, but that English courage was invincible."

A handsome monument was erected by his countrymen, in St. Paul's Cathedral, to commemorate the services and glorious death of Captain Faulknor, than whom the British Navy, fertile as it was at this time in heroes, possessed none more deserving of admiration. In the pride with which the nation received the details of his brilliant exploit and untimely death other feelings had place,

> "And mingled with her cup
> The tear that England owes."

The *Pique* was taken in tow by the *Veteran*, 64, Captain Kelly, which arrived at the conclusion of the action, and carried to the harbour in the Saintes. Subsequently she was added to the Navy, and Lieutenants Watkins and Milne were promoted to the rank of commander. An action between the *Lively*, Captain George Burlton, carrying 38 guns and 251 men, and the *Tourterelle*, Captain Montalan, of 30 guns and 230 men, resulted in the capture of the latter, though, owing to her inferiority, this was to be anticipated. The two frigates were cruising off the coast of France, in the neighbourhood of Ushant, when they sighted each other, and Captain Montalan showed no disinclination to engage. The firing commenced about 10.30 A.M., and continued for three hours, latterly at close range, when the *Tourterelle*, having all her topmasts shot away and her hull and rigging much shattered, hauled down her colours. Her loss was 16 officers and men killed and 25 wounded, while the *Lively* was little damaged aloft, though her antagonist employed red-hot shot, for which there was a furnace on the lower deck, and had only one officer, Lieutenant Otway Bland, and one seaman wounded. Two prizes, in company with the *Tourterelle*, which escaped during the action, were taken by the *Lively* a few days afterwards, and the captured frigate was bought in for the Navy.

More creditable to the service, from the disparity of force being against the British ship, was the capture of the French 42-gun frigate *Gloire*, having a crew of 275 men, by the *Astræa* (Captain Lord Henry Paulet), of 32 guns and 212 men. The latter formed part of a squadron of five ships-of-the-line and three frigates, under command of Rear-Admiral Colpoys, which sighted and gave chase to three French frigates. The *Astræa*, having overhauled the *Gloire*, about 6 P.M. on the 10th April, brought her to close action four hours later, and within an hour compelled her to lower her colours, with the loss of 40 officers and men. The British frigate had only eight wounded (one mortally), but was so much cut up aloft that her main-topmast fell over the side after the action, and the two other topmasts had to be sent down and shifted. Mr. Talbot, first lieutenant of the *Astræa*, brought the prize, which was purchased into the service, to Portsmouth, and was promoted to the rank of commander. Of the *Gloire's* two consorts, the *Gentille* was captured on the following day by the *Hannibal*, 74, but the other escaped.

Sir Richard Strachan inflicted some loss on the French mercantile marine. While lying at anchor off the Island of Jersey, on the 9th May, with the *Melampus*, carrying his broad pennant, and the 38-gun frigates *Diamond*, Sir Sydney Smith, and *Hebe*, Captain Minchin, and the 32-gun frigates, *Niger*, Captain Foot, and *Syren*, Captain Graham Moore, he descried thirteen sail on the French coast, and gave chase. The vessels, which were laden with military stores, succeeded in getting under the protection of two gunboats, each armed with three long 18-pounders, and a small battery, but the boats of the squadron boarded and took possession of the whole convoy, including the gun-vessels, with the loss of only one midshipman and one marine killed, and two officers and 15 seamen wounded. On the 3rd July, the *Melampus* captured off St. Malo six more vessels, carrying stores, and an armed brig.

On the coast of America, off Chesapeake Bay, the *Thetis*, Captain the Hon. Alexander Cochrane, having 42 guns and 261 men, and *Hussar*, Captain Beresford, carrying 34 guns and 193 men, sighted and gave chase to five French armed ships, which hauled up and showed fight. The *Hussar* drew up opposite the two van ships, while the *Thetis* engaged the others, of which the centre vessel was the largest. The *Hussar* compelled her antagonists to quit the line and make sail to escape, when she directed her fire on the three other ships, all of which surrendered, but one managed to get away. The *Prevoyante*, the larger of the prizes, which were both purchased into the Navy, mounted 24 guns, and made a good defence, losing her fore and main-masts, and the *Raison*, the other, carried 18 guns. Their losses are not stated, but the *Thetis* had eight men killed and nine wounded, and the *Hussar* only three wounded.

In the West Indies, the *Thorn*, Captain Otway, 16 guns and 80 men, captured, on the 25th May, after a brief and spirited action of thirty-five minutes, with the loss of only five wounded, the 18-gun ship *Courier National*, which lost seven killed and 20 wounded out of her complement of 119.

More memorable was the action on the 24th June between two frigates of Admiral Hotham's fleet,—the *Dido*, 32, Captain Towry, and *Lowestoft*, 36, Captain Middleton,—with the *Minerve*, 42, and *Artemise*, 40, the rival frigates having been sent by their respective admirals from Minorca and Toulon to reconnoitre the positions of the enemy. After a brief chase, the French frigates, having discovered their own superior force, wore round and stood on under easy sail to meet the *Dido* and *Lowestoft*. The *Minerve*, being the headmost ship, commenced the action about 8.30 A.M., by firing on the *Dido*, which did not return the compliment until she had taken up a position close under the former's lee beam. Suddenly the French frigate bore up and attempted to run her adversary on board, but the *Dido* put her helm hard aport, thus avoiding a direct blow on her beam, which might have sent her to the bottom, but, nevertheless, so great was the shock of the *Minerve's* starboard bow on her port quarter, that the former's jib-boom was carried away, and her bowsprit became locked in the *Dido's* mizen rigging. The crew of the French frigate attempted to board while in this position, but were repulsed by the pikemen on the *Dido's* quarter-deck, and after the two ships were thus locked together for about fifteen minutes, the *Minerve's* bowsprit snapped short off, carrying overboard eight or ten of her crew, as well as the *Dido's* mizen-mast. The British ensign went over the side with the gaff, but the signal quartermaster, Henry Barling—his honest Anglo-Saxon name should be perpetuated—nailed a Union Jack to the stump of the mast.

The ships hung together broadside to broadside for a few minutes, and then the *Minerve* tore herself clear, carrying away the *Dido's* two remaining topsails, and ranged ahead. Here she was closely engaged by the *Lowestoft*, which shot away her antagonist's foremast, and her main and mizen-topmasts, and then, in obedience to a signal from the *Dido*, Captain Middleton quitted the *Minerve*, and made sail in pursuit of the *Artemise*, which, after firing a broadside into each of the British frigates, had left her consort to her fate. Meantime the *Dido's* crew were busied refitting their ship, and bending new fore and main-topsails, and this completed, Captain Towry headed for the *Minerve*, which the *Lowestoft*—having failed to gain on the *Artemise*, owing to an unlucky shot received through her mizen-mast—had again engaged. Before the *Dido* was in a position to complete the conquest she had so nearly effected, the *Minerve* surrendered to the *Lowestoft*.

Out of 193 men and boys the *Dido* had her boatswain and five seamen killed, and her first lieutenant, another officer, and 13 men wounded. The *Minerve*, out of a complement of 318, had twenty casualties, including her captain wounded, exclusive of those drowned when her bowsprit went over the side. The *Lowestoft* had only three wounded. In this action Captain Towry displayed distinguished gallantry in engaging a ship whose broadside weight of shot was superior to both the British frigates, and his coolness and skill at the critical time when the *Minerve*—whose tonnage in comparison with the *Dido's* was as 1,102 to 595—bore down to sink his ship, saved the little frigate and was worthy of the highest admiration.

The *Minerve* was added to the Navy and received Captain Towry as her commander, and the *Dido's* first lieutenant, Mr. Bucknoll, was promoted, as was also that of the *Lowestoft*.

A Dutch frigate, the *Alliance*, of 36 guns and 240 men, struck to the *Stag*, 38 guns and 250 men, commanded by Captain York, off the coast of Norway, after about an hour's action, in which the British frigate had four men killed and 13 wounded, but the loss of her prize was not stated. This action occurred on the 22nd August, and on the 29th of the following month, to take the actions in their chronological order, the *Southampton*, 32, Captain Macnamara, while standing in towards Genoa, encountered the French 36-gun frigate *Vestale*, which was in company with the 28-gun corvette *Brune* and 14-gun brigs *Alerte* and *Scout*. The action began at 10 P.M., but the *Vestale*, after returning the *Southampton's* broadside, sought to escape, and was promptly followed by the British frigate, which, just as she got within point-blank range of the Frenchman, carried away her mizen-mast, which had received a shot through it. With surprising smartness the crew cleared away the wreck and rigged a jury-mast and bent fresh sails, but the time thus gained gave the *Vestale* a lead which enabled her to effect her escape, with the loss, as was afterwards ascertained, of eight killed and nine wounded.

Lieutenant Walker, commanding the cutter *Rose*, having 8 guns and only 13 men, on the 28th September, while on his passage between Leghorn and Bastia, with specie, displayed great courage in attacking three French lateen-rigged privateers, each of which carried more men than the crew of the *Rose*. The gallant young commander himself steered his little craft for the largest of the privateers, and carrying away her mizen-mast and part of her stern, poured into her a destructive raking fire as he passed to leeward. Coming round on the other tack the *Rose* gave her a second broadside, setting on fire her foresail and mizen, on which the privateer called out that she had struck. Lieutenant Walker made sail after the second privateer, and by a well-directed broadside sent her to the bottom. Meantime the third vessel had escaped, and Mr. Walker, leaving the crew struggling in the water to their fate, as he considered they deserved no pity, and his numerical weakness prevented his taking them on board his little craft, secured his prize. She mounted one long brass 6-pounder, four swivels in her bow, and twelve musketoons on her sides, and had on board 29 men, exclusive of 13 killed. The vessel that was sunk was reported to have had a crew of 56 hands, and the one that escaped 48, making a total of 146 against 14. Forcing his prisoners below hatches in their vessel, and battening them down there, Lieutenant Walker proceeded with his prize to Bastia, where he received the warm encomiums of Admiral Hotham and Sir Gilbert Elliot, Governor of Corsica, but owing to the non-publication of his despatch, the gallant officer was never promoted for a deed of heroism which redounded much to the credit of the British Navy.

On the 10th October, Captain Warre, commanding the 32-gun frigate, *Mermaid*, while cruising off the island of Grenada, sighted the French 18-gun corvette, *Republicaine*, and 10-gun brig, *Brutus*, at anchor off La Baye, and made sail for them, when they got under weigh. Finding that the British frigate was gaining on her, the *Brutus* bore up for the land and anchored, when the *Mermaid* followed motions, anchoring close to her. The brig now landed her crew, consisting of 50 sailors and 70 soldiers, upon which Captain Warre manned and armed his boats and took possession of her. The *Mermaid* then stood out of the bay with her prize, and at daybreak on the 14th, sighted and chased a strange sail, which proved to be the *Republicaine*. The British frigate came up with the enemy at noon, and after a running fight, which lasted three and a half hours, and a close engagement of ten minutes, the *Republicaine* surrendered, having lost, out of a crew of 250, about 20 killed and many wounded. Among the passengers was a French general who was about to assume command of the troops in Grenada. The loss of the *Mermaid* was only nominal, being one killed and three wounded.

The capture of the *Eveillé*, 16 guns, off Rochefort, by Sir John Borlase Warren's squadron, was the last made in the year 1795. Against these gains must be set the loss of the *Boyne*, 98, on the 1st May. This fine three-decker caught fire as she lay at anchor at Spithead, and notwithstanding every effort made to save her by her crew and the boats of the fleet, the ship was totally destroyed, but her crew, with the exception of 11 men, were saved. All the ships to leeward of the *Boyne* got under weigh, and escaped injury from the fire, but two men were killed and three wounded on board the *Queen Charlotte* by the discharges from her guns, which, being loaded, went off as they became heated. The ship drifted slowly to the eastward till she grounded opposite Southsea Castle. About 6 P.M., the fire having then lasted seven hours, her magazine caught fire, and she blew up, offering a splendid spectacle, in a clear sky and perfect calm. "The flames," says Brenton, "which darted from her in a perpendicular column of great height, were terminated by an opaque white cloud-like round cap, while the air was filled with fragments of wreck in every direction, and the stump of the foremast was seen far above the smoke descending to the water."

When the people of Holland threw in their lot with the French Republican government, the English ministry resolved to punish them by the despatch of expeditions against their possessions in South Africa, as well as in the East and West Indies. Accordingly Vice-Admiral Sir George Keith Elphinstone sailed for the Cape of Good Hope with the following ships:—

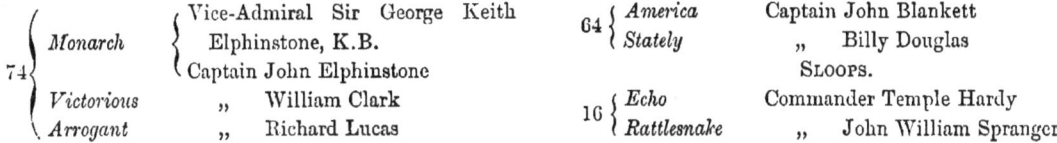

On board the squadron was embarked a detachment of 500 men of the 78th Highlanders, commanded by Major-General Craig. The squadron anchored in Simon's Bay early in August, and the admiral made proposals to the Dutch governor, General Sluysken, to surrender the settlement, but this he declined to do, and sent away the inhabitants of Simon's Town, preparatory to burning the place. Before this could be accomplished, the 78th regiment and 350 marines from the fleet were landed and took possession of the town, which was evacuated by the Dutch militia and native levies, who occupied the pass of Muyzenburg, about six miles from Cape Town, having the sea on the one side and a steep mountain on the other. To assist the troops in dislodging them from this strong position, the admiral landed 1,000 seamen, who were formed into two battalions, under the command of Captains Hardy and Spranger, and to co-operate in the attack from the sea, the launches of the fleet were equipped with 18 and 24-pounder carronades.

Everything being prepared, at noon of the 7th August the *America* and *Stately*, with the two sloops, stood in shore as close as the shallow water would permit, and assisted the armed launches in covering the march of the troops. The ships first drove the enemy from two advanced positions, and then opened fire on their camp, and long before the troops could co-operate, the Dutch militia were driven in flight from all their works, and took post on some rocky heights. By 4 o'clock General Craig had taken possession of the camp, and the same evening the enemy were driven off the ridge by the British troops, with the loss of Captain Scott of the 78th regiment. On the following day, being reinforced from Cape Town, the Dutch advanced, with eight field-pieces, to regain possession of the position, but were compelled to retire. During these operations, says General Craig, "the seamen manœuvred with a regularity which would not have discredited veteran troops."

Soon after, the Dutch, encouraged by some partial successes, advanced with all the force they could muster, together with 18 guns, on the night of the 3rd September, to make an attack on the British camp; but just at the critical moment, 14 Indiamen arrived with strong reinforcements, under Sir Alured Clarke, and further resistance appeared hopeless. All the troops, together with the guns, ammunition, and stores, were disembarked by the 14th, when the army began its march for Cape Town, each man carrying four days' provisions, the sailors dragging the guns through the deep sand, while the *America*, the two sloops, and the Indiaman, *Bombay Castle*, proceeded round to Table Bay to make a diversion on that side. This so alarmed the Dutch general, whose troops were retiring before the British army, that he sent in a flag of truce, and within twenty-four hours terms were arranged, by which the troops, numbering 1,000 regulars, surrendered, and the colony became a possession of this country; and so, with the exception of a short interval, before it was re-conquered in 1806, it has ever since remained.

Before the capitulation of Cape Town, five Dutch Indiamen were seized in Simon's Bay, and the ship *Castor* and armed brig *Star* were also taken possession of in Table Bay, and the latter was added to the British Navy and christened the *Hope*.

The Government of the Dutch Republic made an attempt to recover their possessions in South Africa, and misled as to the strength of the British squadron that had captured Cape Town and Simon's Bay, despatched with that object the following ships, under the command of Rear-Admiral Lucas: *Dordrecht* and *Revolutie*, 66; *Van-Tromp*, 54; *Casthor* and *Braave*, 40; *Sirene*, 26; *Bellona*, 24; *Havik*, 18; and *Maria*, store-ship.

On the 3rd August Sir George Elphinstone received intelligence at Simon's Bay of the arrival off the coast of these nine men-of-war. The British admiral had the following ships under his command: the *Monarch*, 74, bearing his flag; *Tremendous*, 74, flag-ship of Rear-Admiral Pringle; and the 64-gun ships, *America*, *Ruby*, *Stately*, *Sceptre*, and *Trident*. Also the *Jupiter*, 50; *Crescent*, 36; *Sphynx*, 20; and the sloops *Moselle*, *Rattlesnake*, *Echo*, and *Hope*.

Admiral Elphinstone put to sea, but was driven back to Simon's Bay by stress of weather, and here he was compelled to remain until the 15th August, when he sailed for Saldanha Bay, where Admiral Lucas had put in. On descrying the enemy in the bay on the evening of the 16th, Sir George Elphinstone sailed in, and anchoring within gun-shot, summoned the Dutch commander to surrender, as resistance would cause unnecessary bloodshed, considering the disparity of force. Within twenty-four hours a capitulation was arranged, and the Dutch squadron of nine sail passed under another flag. The surrender was in no way disgraceful to Admiral Lucas, as the total complement of his ships was only 1,972, and that of the British squadron 4,291. In the following October, Sir George Elphinstone sailed for England, leaving Admiral Pringle in command. Before the close of the year the *Crescent*, accompanied by the *Braave*, late Dutch frigate, and *Sphynx*, took possession of and destroyed the French settlement on Foul Point in the island of Madagascar, bringing away five merchant vessels lying in the roads.

The Dutch also suffered for their adhesion to the cause of the French Republic by the loss of their possessions in the East Indies. When Lord Howe sailed on the cruise which resulted in his great victory of the 1st June, 1794, he was accompanied by the *Suffolk*, 74, Rear-Admiral Peter Rainier, and some other vessels of war, escorting a convoy to the East Indies, which parted company with the main fleet off the Lizard, on the 4th May. The squadron arrived at Madras in the following November, without either touching anywhere on the voyage, or losing a ship of the great convoy committed to their charge.

In June, 1795, Rear-Admiral Rainier sailed to attack the Dutch settlements and forts in the island of Ceylon, with the *Suffolk*, Captain Lambert, and *Centurion*, 50, Captain Samuel Osborne, and a squadron of ships of the Indian Navy, including the *Bombay*, 38, Commodore Pickle, *Swallow*, 24, and some smaller vessels, together with several transports, carrying a detachment of troops, commanded by General James Stuart, with the necessary stores and munitions of war. Off Negapatam the admiral was joined by the *Diomede*, 44, Captain Matthew Smith,* with a transport, having on board some more troops, and the expedition, which was still further strengthened by the *Heroine*, 32, Captain Alan Hyde Gardner, anchored on the 1st August off Trincomalee. The Dutch governor of Ceylon was summoned to surrender, but refused compliance; but the troops were landed at a spot about four miles to the north of the town, though it was ten days before the whole of the stores with the provisions and guns were landed, the transport of which, over three miles of sandy ground, was accomplished by the seamen. But a serious loss was experienced in the destruction of the *Diomede*, which, while working into the bay, struck on a sunken rock, and went down with all her stores. The construction of batteries was commenced on the 18th, and five days later eight 18-pounders and some smaller guns opened fire on the fort of Trincomalee; and a breach being effected on the following day, the commandant surrendered the work, with its garrison of 679 men and nearly 100 guns. In achieving this success, the British loss was 16 killed and 60 wounded. The fort of Oostenburg, commanding the harbour, capitulated on the 31st, and the fort of Batticaloe, on the 18th September. A few days later, General Stuart embarked with some troops on board the *Centurion*, *Bombay*, *Swallow*, and some storeships, and on landing the detachment on the north side of the island, the important post of Jaffnapatam was surrendered without opposition. On the 1st October, the *Hobart*, 18, Captain Page, having on board a detachment of the 52nd regiment, took possession of the post and factory at Molletive.

The Indian Government resolved to complete the conquest of the whole island, and in the following February an expedition was despatched against Colombo, consisting of the *Heroine*, 32, Captain Alan Hyde Gardner; the 16-gun sloops *Rattlesnake*, Commander Ramage, *Echo*, Commander Todd, and *Swift*, Commander Rainier, with five armed ships of the Indian Navy, having on board some troops under the command of General Stuart. The fort was occupied without opposition, and stores and merchandise to the value of a quarter of a million sterling fell into the hands of the victors. The troops were now disembarked, and marched to Colombo, about twenty miles distant, while the *Heroine* and squadron took up a position close to the fortress in readiness

---

* This was the same officer who behaved so badly in the action, on the 22nd October, off Mauritius, between the *Centurion* and *Diomede*, and a French squadron under Commodore Renaud, for which he was eventually brought before a court-martial and cashiered, but owing to an informality in the proceedings, was restored to his rank in the Navy, but not again employed.

to land the guns. But Colombo surrendered without resistance, and thus the island passed into possession of England.

About the same time a smaller expedition, consisting of the *Orpheus*, 32, Captain Newcome, with transports, having on board some troops under the orders of Major Brown, soon after strengthened by the *Resistance*, 44, Captain Edward Pakenham, sailed to reduce Malacca. This important place surrendered on the 17th August, and on the capitulation of Chinsura, near Calcutta, Cochin, on the Malabar coast, and other factories, the whole of the Dutch possessions in India fell under the dominion of England before the close of the year.

During this year, 1795, the French had lost by capture six ships-of-the-line, of which five were added to the British Navy, and seven frigates, of which five were purchased into the service. The Dutch had one of each class taken, and both were utilised in the Navy, which, during the same period, lost the seventy-fours *Censeur* and *Berwick*, and four other vessels, the *Nemesis*, 28, captured at Smyrna (which soon again changed hands), *Daphne*, 20, by the Brest fleet, and the schooners *Flying Fish*, 6, and *Shark*, 4. Thus, while the States allied against England carried all before them on the Continent, and a British army was expelled from Holland, the state of hostilities brought increased glory and gain to the British Navy, which lost nothing of its proud pre-eminence on the sea.

CHAPTER VII.

Commodore Nelson's Services in the Mediterranean—War with Spain—Evacuation of Corsica—Retreat of the British Fleet to Gibraltar before the United Navies of France and Spain—Loss of the *Courageux* and *Bombay Castle*—Services of Sir Sydney Smith in the *Diamond*—Capture of the *Etoile* and *Unité*—Sir Sydney Smith is made Prisoner—His Escape from Paris—Capture of the *Virginie*—Cutting Out of a Lugger at the Penmarcks—Capture of the *Argo*—Action between the *Santa Margarita* and *Tamise*—The *Unicorn* and *Tribune*—*Dryad* and *Proserpine*—*Southampton* and *Utile*—The *Glatton* and a French Squadron—The *Aimable* and *Pensée*—The *Mermaid* and *Vengeance*—Admiral Sercey's Cruise in the East Indies—Action between his Squadron and the Seventy-fours *Arrogant* and *Victorious*—The *Pelican* and *Medée*—The *Lapwing* at Anguilla—*Terpsichore* and *Mahonessa*—*Terpsichore* and *Vestale*—The *Minerve* and *Sabina*, and the *Blanche* and *Ceres*—Capture of the Dutch Settlements in the West Indies, and of the Islands of St. Lucia, St. Vincent, and Grenada—Attack on St. Domingo—Capture of the Dutch Possessions in the Moluccas, and of a Squadron in Simon's Bay.

THE first event of importance in the year 1796 was the escape on the 23rd February, during the temporary absence of the British fleet under Admiral Duncan, blockading the Texel, of a Dutch squadron of two sixty-fours, two 54-gun ships, and several frigates. It was known that the French Ministry was preparing a great armament at Brest, the destination of which, however, could only be conjectured, but the Channel fleet was divided into three squadrons, to be prepared for all eventualities, one to cruise to the westward, one off Brest, and the third to be ready for despatch to any threatened point. In the Mediterranean Sir John Jervis, the brave and experienced commander-in-chief, kept watch and ward off Toulon, where a French fleet of fifteen sail-of-the-line, under Admiral Brueys, lay ready to proceed to sea at a favourable opportunity, and a squadron of seven battle-ships rode at anchor at Carthagena, in Spain, with which the English Government had strained relations.

Sir John Jervis sent Admiral Hon. W. Waldegrave, with his flagship, the *Barfleur*, 98, and four seventy-fours, to Tunis, to bring away the *Nemesis*, which lay there with one of her captors, the *Sardine*, and the *Postillon*. This service was effected without loss on the 9th March, by the boats of the squadron, under Captain Sutton, of the *Egmont*, and the admiral rejoined the commander-in-chief off Toulon. Commodore Nelson repeatedly displayed the professional skill of which he was so great an exponent, and whenever any operations demanding zeal and smartness were to be executed, Sir John Jervis was sure to select the gallant captain of the *Agamemnon*.

Towards the end of March, when the fleet was cruising off Vado, the commodore was directed, with his ship, and the *Diadem*, 68, Captain Towry, *Meleager*, 32, Captain George Cockburn, and sloop, *Peterel*, Captain John Temple, to blockade the port of Genoa, and harass the coast. On arriving off Laona Bay, Nelson discovered four vessels laden with stores for the French army, lying under the batteries at the bottom of the bay. He sent in his boats and the *Peterel*, to cut them out, a service which was gallantly performed under a heavy fire from the batteries. The squadron, reinforced by the *Blanche*, 32, Captain Preston, and 16-gun brig *Speedy*, Commander Thomas Elphinstone, was cruising off Oneglia, when it chased six French vessels, which took shelter under a battery, upon which Nelson stood in shore to less than four fathoms of water, with the *Agamemnon*, *Meleager*, *Peterel* and *Speedy*, and silencing the batteries, sent his boats to cut out the two armed vessels, and four transports in company, laden with military stores, which was successfully accomplished, with the loss of only one killed and three wounded. The loss of the ordnance and stores, destined to be employed in the siege of Mantua, greatly conduced to the failure of the attack on that city. Nelson now shifted his broad pennant into the *Captain*, 74, and after the *Inconstant*, 36, with some store-ships, on the 27th June, had removed the British residents and their property from Leghorn, in the dominions of the Grand Duke of Tuscany, when the French army took possession of the town, Commodore Nelson remained off the place to warn any ship ignorant of the change of masters. On the 10th of the following month, he took possession of the fort of Porto Ferrajo, in the island of Elba, also belonging to the Court of Tuscany, and landed some troops to hold the place.

Before the end of July, Spain entered into an offensive and defensive treaty with France, by which she placed at the disposal of the latter power, nineteen sail-of-the-line and ten frigates. England's reply to the treaty concluded between the two powers was a declaration of war on the 5th October, and an embargo on all Spanish ships in her ports. The first use made of the Spanish fleet, which lay at Cadiz, was to escort out of the bay, on its way to America, Admiral Richery's squadron of seven line-of-battle ships and three frigates.

Admiral Mann, who was then on his way from San Fiorenzo Bay to England with seven sail-of-the-line, and a convoy of three transports and a brig, at sunset on the 1st October discovered the Spanish fleet, which had passed through the Straits, becalmed off Cape de Gata, but a breeze springing up before midnight, the Spanish admiral, Don Juan de Langara, gave chase and captured a transport and the brig, though the British squadron succeeded in reaching Gibraltar. Admiral de Langara stood back to the eastward, and off Carthagena was joined by seven sail-of-the-line, making his fleet twenty-six battle-ships, besides frigates, when he cruised up the Mediterranean, and on the 15th was seen by the frigates of Sir John Jervis's fleet, numbering fourteen sail-of-the-line, then lying in Mortella Bay. Notwithstanding the disparity of force, the Spanish admiral steered for Toulon, where he found at anchor twelve French sail-of-the-line and several frigates.

Owing to the extraordinary success of Napoleon Buonaparte in his wonderful Italian campaign, the power and prestige of France were unchallenged in the peninsula, and the kings of Savoy and the Two Sicilies submitted to the conqueror and signed humiliating terms of peace. A consequence of these victories was the evacuation of Corsica, which was only effected in time to prevent the capture, by the partisans of France, of the British garrisons in the island. Off the port of Bastia, Nelson lay with the *Captain* and *Egmont*, 74's, and some other vessels, which embarked the British troops. Marshall says of this event:—"Commodore Nelson, who was appointed to superintend the evacuation, frustrated these projects. On the 14th October, 1796, he sent word to the committee that, if the slightest opposition was made to the embarkation and removal of British property, he would batter the town down. A privateer, moored across the Mole head, pointed her guns at the officer who carried this message, and muskets were levelled against him from the shore. Hereupon Captain Sutton, pulling out his watch, gave them a quarter of an hour to deliberate upon their answer. In five minutes after the expiration of that time, the ships, he said, would open fire. Upon this the very sentinels scampered off, and every vessel came out of the Mole. During the five following days, the work of embarkation was carried on; the property of individuals was saved, and public stores to the amount of £200,000. On the 22nd, after having, as the French accounts say, taken prisoners the British rear-guard, consisting of 700 or 800 men of Dillon's regiment, the Corsican general quitted Bastia for the town of San Fiorenzo, and in the face of a destructive discharge of grape from two British seventy-fours moored off the beach, made themselves masters of it, taking prisoners a part of the garrison. The same evening, Bonifacio was occupied by the French, and the garrison also made prisoners.

In the meanwhile, General Gentili marched upon Ajaccio, the birth-place of Buonaparte, the capture of which restored the whole island to the French Republic."

On the completion of the evacuation of Corsica, Sir John Jervis set sail for Mortella Bay on the 2nd November, with fifteen ships-of-the-line and some frigates, and on the 11th December anchored off Gibraltar; and thus, for the first time, perhaps, for more than a century, the Mediterranean was destitute of the presence of a single English ship-of-the-line. The Spanish fleet sailed from Toulon to Carthagena, and Admiral Villeneuve, who accompanied it, proceeded thence with the *Formidable*, 80, the 74's *Jean-Jacques*, *Jemappes*, *Mont Blanc*, and *Tyrannicide*, and three frigates, and favoured by a gale of wind from the south east, passed without hindrance the rock of Gibraltar, off which the British fleet lay.

The gale which saved Villeneuve from attack caused a great disaster to the British fleet. The *Courageux* parted from her anchors on the 10th November, and drove nearly under the Spanish batteries on the opposite side of the bay. Setting close-reefed topsails, Lieutenant Burrows, in temporary command, stood over to the Barbary coast, but the gale increased to a furious storm, and the ship struck on the rocks at the back of Ape's Hill, and in a few minutes became a total wreck. Of her crew of 593 officers and men, 464 perished, the remainder escaping by passing along the main-mast to the rock-bound coast. The *Gibraltar*, 80, Captain Thomas Pakenham, and *Culloden*, 74, Captain Thomas Troubridge, narrowly escaped sharing the fate of the *Courageux*, and the former struck several times on a bank off Cabrita Point, actually driving over it, and lost her fore-topmast and split her courses and stay-sails. The *Gibraltar* anchored in Tangier Bay, on the opposite side of the Straits, at noon of the following day, but she was so much injured that she was sent to England, and on docking her at Plymouth it was discovered that a large piece of rock had pierced her bottom, and had it not fortunately remained there the ship would probably have foundered.

On leaving Gibraltar for Lisbon on the 16th December, Sir John Jervis entrusted the command of the small naval force still retained at Porto Ferrajo to Commodore Nelson, who shifted his broad pennant from the *Captain* to the *Minerve*, frigate. A series of accidents befell the British fleet at this time. The *Zealous*, 74, struck on a sunken rock in Tangier Bay, and was much damaged, and the *Bombay Castle*, 74, was swept by the tide on a sand bank at the mouth of the Tagus, where she remained beating in the heavy weather from the 21st to the 28th, and all the efforts to get her off were unavailing. These casualties reduced Sir John Jervis's fleet to fourteen sail-of-the-line, including the *Zealous*, which was temporarily effective, and the *St. Albans*, 64, bearing the flag of Rear-Admiral Vandeput, which was lying in the Tagus when he arrived.

Among the most successful frigate captains during the year 1796 was Sir Sydney Smith, commanding the *Diamond*, 38. This enterprising officer, having chased a corvette and six smaller vessels into the port of Herqui, near Cape Fréhel, on the French coast, determined, notwithstanding its narrowness and intricacy, to make an attempt to cut them out. Accordingly, on the 18th March, the *Diamond*, accompanied by the *Liberty*, brig, of 14 guns, Lieutenant McKinley, and hired lugger *Aristocrat*, Lieutenant Gossett, stood for the port, and soon became exposed to a heavy fire from four 24-pounders, erected on commanding positions at the entrance. Finding that he could not silence them, Sir Sydney sent a party of men, under Mr. Horace Pine, first lieutenant of the *Diamond*, to storm the batteries. Some French troops descended to the beach to prevent the landing, but the party, climbing the steep precipices in front of the guns, before the soldiers could return to the heights, spiked the guns, and regained the boats with the loss of Lieutenant Carter, of the Marines, mortally wounded. The British ships then attacked the *Etourdie*, of 16 guns, and in spite of the fire from her and the troops on shore, captured the corvette, four brigs and two sloops, all of which were set on fire and destroyed. In this affair two seamen were killed and Lieutenant Pine and five seamen wounded.

Two days after this brilliant exploit, good service was performed by a squadron of frigates, under Sir John Borlase Warren, consisting of his ship, the *Pomone*; the *Anson*, 44, Captain Charles Durham; *Artois*, 38, Sir Edmund Nagle, and *Galatea*, 32, Captain Richard G. Keats. Off the Saintes they sighted thirty-nine strange sail, and gave chase and overhauled some sixty sail, convoyed by a French squadron, consisting of the *Proserpine*, 40, 36-gun frigates *Unité*, *Coquille* and *Tamise*, and corvette *Cigogne*, of 20 guns, together with the armed store-ship *Etoile* and a brig. Four vessels were captured, and Sir John Warren made sail in chase, engaging the enemy as the squadrons passed on opposite tacks. In this cannonade the *Galatea*, which was the rearmost of the British ships, suffered the most, and on the squadron tacking, she led the line, when the French ships crowded all sail to escape. The *Etoile*, store-ship, of 28 guns and 159 men, struck to the *Galatea*, but the five ships-of-war effected their escape through the narrow and intricate Passage du Roy, while the bulk of the convoy had taken shelter among the Penmarck rocks. The *Galatea* lost during the day a midshipman and one seaman killed, and a lieutenant and five wounded, and was cut up a good deal aloft.

One of the French frigates, the *Unité*, only postponed her capture by a few weeks. On the 13th April, as Sir Edward Pellew was cruising off Ushant in the *Indefatigable*, 44, with the *Argo*, 44, Captain Burgess, *Revolutionnaire*, 38, Captain Cole, and 36-gun frigates *Amazon*, Captain Reynolds, and *Concorde*, Captain Hunt, he sighted and chased a frigate. The *Revolutionnaire* closed with the stranger shortly before midnight, and hailed Captain Linois, commanding the *Unité*, which she proved to be, to haul down his flag, but that officer refused, though after a feeble resistance, just as Captain Cole had ported his helm to run her on board, the crew called out that they had surrendered. The *Revolutionnaire*, though rated as a 38-gun frigate, carried 46 guns and had a crew of 287 men, while her prize, which was purchased into the service, carried only 38 guns and 255 men, of whom she had nine killed and 11 wounded, the British frigate suffering no loss.

The Navy at this time had to deplore the capture of Sir Sydney Smith, who, however, lived to meet and defeat the great Emperor Napoleor who bitterly declared that he was baulked of his destiny by a British post-captain.

The *Diamond*, commanded by this officer, came to anchor in the outer roads of Havre on the 17th April, and finding in the inner road the *Vengeur*, privateer, carrying 10 guns and 45 men, noted for her success, Captain Smith determined to cut her out. Accordingly, at ten o'clock on the same night, the *Diamond's* launch, armed with an 18-pounder carronade, and four other boats—manned with nine officers (six of them midshipmen between twelve and sixteen years of age) and 43 men, under the personal command of Sir Sydney Smith, the three lieutenants of the frigate being either absent in England or indisposed—pushed off from the *Diamond*, and on arriving within sight of the lugger, the boats lay on their oars while the captain reconnoitred the position. This done and the order communicated to the commanding officers, the boats took a broad sweep between the lugger and the shore, with the object of allaying suspicion, and then pulled straight for the *Vengeur*, with orders to reserve their fire until she had opened on them. This she did at half pistol-shot, when they returned the fire, and in a few minutes the British seamen had gained the deck, and obtained possession of the object of their attack. But the crew had cut the cable, and the prize, under the influence of the strong tide flowing into the Seine, drifted on shore, although sail was made on her, and the boats started towing. At length a small kedge anchor was discovered and let go, but it failed to hold the *Vengeur*, which at length brought up nearly two miles higher up the river than Harfleur. Sir Sydney Smith resolved to defend his prize until the tide turned, or a favourable breeze sprang up, but the means to do so were but scanty, and there was no grape-shot on board. First, the prisoners were landed at Honfleur, on the southern side of the river, opposite to Harfleur, and then the prize was got under weigh to receive the attack of another large lugger advancing against her. The *Vengeur* beat off this vessel, but others filled with soldiers surrounded her, and at length the gallant captain of the *Diamond*, overpowered by numbers, was compelled to surrender, having lost four men killed and seven wounded, out of about 20 or 30 altogether engaged, as the launch, after landing the prisoners, and, it is said, another boat, had returned to the frigate.

The British seamen and officers were taken to Rouen, but Sir Sydney Smith and a midshipman, named Wright, were sent on to Paris, and were confined in separate cells in the Temple prison. Here they languished for two years, when the two officers, by the connivance, it is thought, of the French Government, effected their escape, and arrived in London in May, 1798.

Only a few days after this failure of Sir Sydney Smith at Harfleur, Sir Edward Pellew captured a French frigate. On the 20th April, the *Indefatigable*, in company with the *Concorde* and *America*, was off the Lizard, when she sighted and gave chase to a strange sail, which proved to be the *Virginie*. After a run of 168 miles in 15 hours, the *Indefatigable*, one of the swiftest vessels in the Navy, came up with the enemy, and a spirited action began shortly after midnight. For one hour and three quarters the two frigates, running close alongside under a press of sail, engaged each other, until at length the *Virginie* lost her mizen-mast and main-topmast, and the *Indefatigable*, which had shot ahead, after reeving new braces, was about to renew the action, when the *Concorde* arrived on the scene and took up a position astern to rake her. The French captain thereupon surrendered his ship, which had four feet of water in the hold and was greatly crippled aloft. The *Virginie* carried 44 guns and 339 men, and the *Indefatigable* 44 and 327, but the broadside of the latter was more than double that of her opponent, being as 702 pounds to 342, so that she was incalculably the more powerful ship, and the defence of Captain Bergeret was creditable and commanded the admiration of his brave antagonist. The *Virginie*, which was purchased into the service, lost in the action 15 killed and 27 wounded, but the British frigate had no casualties.

The *Niger*, 32, Captain Foote, performed good service off the coast of France. The frigate was cruising off Brest with Admiral Colpoys' squadron on the 27th April, when she was detached to pursue a large French lugger, the *Ecureuil*, carrying 18 guns and 105 men. The chase took place among the rocks of the Penmarcks, and after dark Captain Foote sent his boats, under Lieutenants Long and Thompson, Mr. Morgan, master's mate, and Mr. Patton, midshipman, to cut her out. This service was gallantly performed, and after an obstinate resistance, the lugger, with her commander and 28 men (the rest having gained the shore), was captured and set on fire, the British casualties being seven wounded, including Lieutenant Long (severely) and Mr. Patton.

Early in May the British sloop, *Spencer*, of 14 guns and 80 men, captured, after an action lasting an hour and a quarter, the French brig *Volcan*, of 12 guns and over 80 men, which lost heavily owing to the explosion of some powder prepared for use when boarding the English ship. A few days after this exploit the *Argo*, 36, was captured. Admiral Duncan, commanding in the North Sea, detached the *Phœnix*, 36, Captain Halsted, accompanied by the *Leopard*, 50, *Pegasus*, 28, and brig *Sylph*, to intercept the Dutch frigate and three brigs on their way from Norway to the Texel. The latter were sighted on the 12th May, and the *Phœnix* coming up with the *Argo*, engaged her, and at the end of twenty minutes compelled her to strike her flag. The British frigate, which was of greatly superior force, had only one man killed and three wounded, and the *Argo* lost six in the former category and 28 in the latter.

The British 14-gun brig *Suffisante*, Commander Tomlinson, captured off Brest, after a chase of eleven hours, and a close action lasting thirty minutes, the French brig, *Revanche*, of 12 guns and 85 men, but the loss of the combatants was trifling.

A more sanguinary action was that between the *Santa Margarita*, carrying 44 guns and 237 men, and the *Tamise* (late British frigate *Thames*) of the same force, but having 69 more men. The *Santa Margarita*, Captain Byam Martin—afterwards Admiral Sir Byam Martin, one of the most distinguished officers of the Navy—was cruising off Scilly in company with the *Unicorn*, 32, Captain Williams, when, on the 8th June, she sighted the *Tamise*, the *Tribune*, 36, and the 18-gun corvette *Légère*, which had left Brest a few days before. The three French ships made sail to escape, but opened fire with their stern chasers soon after noon with considerable effect on the *Unicorn* and *Santa Margarita*. The *Tamise* bore up about 4 o'clock to pour a broadside into the latter frigate, which, however, succeeded in laying herself alongside her opponent, and after a very spirited engagement lasting twenty minutes, the French frigate struck her colours, having suffered considerably aloft and in her hull. Of her crew of 306 hands, she had 32 killed and 19 wounded, while the *Santa Margarita* suffered the nominal loss of two seamen killed and three wounded. The victory was creditable to Captain Martin and his officers and men, and the first lieutenant, Mr. George Harrison, received promotion to the rank of commander. Later in the year Captain Martin succeeded in capturing the *Vengeur*, of 16 guns and 120 men, from Brest, and a merchant ship, her prize, from Poole bound to Newfoundland. The *Santa Margarita*, while cruising in the Channel, also took the privateer *Buonaparte*, of 16 guns and 137 men. During the twenty months the *Tamise*, which was now reinstalled in the British navy under her old name, was in the French service, she is stated, in the official journal, *Le Moniteur*, to have captured twenty prizes.

Meantime the *Tribune* made sail to escape, closely pursued by the *Unicorn*. The former was commanded by Commodore Moulston, stated to have been a native of the United States, and after a chase extending over 210 miles, during a great part of which a running fight was maintained, at 10.30 P.M. the *Unicorn* brought her antagonist to bay. On ranging up alongside the *Tribune*, the gallant British tars gave three hearty cheers, and a close action commenced, the ships, owing to the light airs that prevailed, continuing in almost the same position for thirty-five minutes. At length the *Tribune* fell astern, when she tried to cross the *Unicorn's* stern, and get to windward of her, but this manœuvre was thwarted in the most seamanlike way by the British frigate throwing her sails flat aback and dropping astern when she crossed the Frenchman's weather bow, and regaining her old station, continued the action. This was quickly decided by a few well-directed broadsides, which brought down the fore and main-masts and mizen-topmast of the *Tribune*, which then hauled down her colours, having lost out of her complement of 339 men, 37 killed, and her captain and 14 men wounded, while her antagonist, which began the action with 240 hands, suffered no loss. This extraordinary circumstance, as in the similar instances of the *Indefatigable* and *Revolutionnaire*, is almost inexplicable, but the result of the action was due to the superior gunnery of the British seamen of that time, which was more marked a feature than even their greater skill in seamanship. Captain Williams was deservedly knighted, and his first lieutenant, Mr. Thomas Palmer, received a step in rank. The *Tribune* was added to the Navy, and retained her name. The only remaining ship of Commodore Moulston's squadron, the *Légère*, 18-gun corvette, surrendered later in the month of June to the British frigates *Apollo* and *Doris*, and was added to the Navy under her own name.

A few days before this event, on the 13th June, the *Dryad*, of 44 guns and 254 men, Captain Lord Amelius Beauclerk, engaged and captured the *Proserpine*, carrying 42 guns and 346 men. On sighting the British frigate off Cape Clear, the *Proserpine* made sail to escape, but was chased by the *Dryad*, until about 9 P.M. she ranged close up to the lee, or port, quarter of the French frigate, and a close action ensued for an hour and forty-five minutes, when the captain of the *Proserpine* hauled down the tricolour. The disparity of loss, as in the other frigate actions, was great, the *Dryad* losing only two men killed and seven wounded, and the *Proserpine*, 30 and 45 respectively. The senior lieutenant of the former was promoted to commander, and the *Proserpine* was added to the service under the name of *Amelia*, after the noble lord who captured her, there being a ship of her name already in the Navy list.

In the Mediterranean, off Toulon, the 32-gun frigate *Southampton*, Captain Macnamara, was detached on the 9th June by Sir John Jervis to effect the capture of the French corvette *Utile*, as she was seen working up towards the Hyeres roadstead, and in very gallant style did that fine officer execute his mission. The *Southampton*, from the boldness of her movements, was mistaken by the French artillerymen in the batteries for a French frigate, and taking advantage of this error, Captain Macnamara stood across the roads, and at 8.30 P.M. got within pistol-shot range of the *Utile*, when he called upon the French commander to surrender, but the latter replied by snapping his pistol in his face. Thereupon the frigate, backing her main-topsail, poured in a broadside, and her captain, finding that she was drifting near a heavy battery, hauled athwart the hawse of the corvette, and lashing her bowsprit to his main rigging, poured a division of boarders on the deck under Lieutenant Charles Lydiard. After a brief struggle, in which the French commander was killed, the *Utile* was carried with the loss, out of her crew, of eight killed and 17 wounded, the *Southampton* losing only one man. Captain Macnamara had a difficult task in getting his prize clear of the batteries, which opened fire on both ships, but he effected his object with seamanlike skill, and the *Utile* was added to the Navy, and commissioned by the gallant young officer who had boarded her, with the rank of commander. A fearless deed such as this showed the contempt entertained by British seamen of that day for Frenchmen.

The *Glatton*, Captain Trollope, fought a spirited action with some French frigates.

The *Glatton* was one of nine ships purchased by the Government from the East India Company, and was armed with 56 guns and received a complement of 320 men and boys. She sailed from Sheerness on the 13th July to reinforce the North Sea fleet, and two days later sighted off the coast of Flanders a squadron, which proved to consist of four frigates and two corvettes. Captain Trollope, in no way daunted by the disparity of force, stood towards the enemy, who were nothing loth to meet him. The action commenced at 10 P.M., when the *Glatton* engaged the French commodore's ship, and on the van ship arriving within hail poured a broadside into her with destructive effect. The latter passed on, leaving the *Glatton* in close action with the commodore upon her lee bow, another large frigate on her lee beam, and the three smaller vessels on her lee quarter. At the end of twenty minutes the combatants approached the shoal, upon which the French commodore tacked to prevent his going ashore, and Captain Trollope followed motions. So successfully did the gallant officers and crew of the *Glatton* keep up the unequal combat that the frigates soon sheered off, as did also the smaller vessels and a 16-gun brig and a cutter, which had arrived towards the close of the action and taken up a position under her stern. By 11 P.M. all firing had ceased, and the *Glatton* remained master of the field, though so cut up aloft as to make pursuit impossible. There was no loss of life, and that on board the enemy's ships was not accurately known, though it was reported by fishermen that one of the ships had sunk in the harbour, and had lost 70 men killed and wounded. Captain Trollope's conduct merited and received the commendation of his countrymen, and the merchants of London presented him with a handsome piece of plate. Much of the success achieved was due to the action of Captain Trollope in fitting his ship on the lower deck with twenty-eight 68-pounder carronades, the remainder of her guns being long 18-pounders on her first, and 32-pounder carronades on her second deck. The havoc wrought by these great projectiles at short range was terrible, and had the *Glatton* been a swift-sailing ship, she might have succeeded in cutting off one or more of her antagonists from making good their retreat to Flushing, though she was much cut up aloft, and every brace and stay, except the mizen, had been shot away, and so had all the running and the greater part of the standing rigging, while her courses and jib were in ribands.

An action off Guadaloupe, fought between the *Aimable*, 32, Captain Mainwaring, and the French 36-gun frigate *Pensée*, was spirited but indecisive. The two frigates came into action at 6.45 on the 22nd July, about a mile and a half off the shore, and a breeze springing up, the British frigate made an attempt to board the *Pensée*, but the latter evaded her, and the firing ceased for that night. On the following morning the action was renewed at short range, the two captains, it is stated, exchanging salutes by raising their hats. After an interchange of broadsides, the *Aimable* tried, but ineffectually, to rake her opponent, which, putting her helm aport, succeeded in pouring a raking broadside into her. But the *Pensée*, having by this time had enough, made sail, chased by the *Aimable*, and about noon succeeded in shaking off her pursuer. The British frigate escaped without loss, but the *Pensée*, as was afterwards ascertained when she was blockaded at St. Thomas's by the *Mermaid*, had 90 killed and wounded.

The same frigate, commanded by Captain Otway, and carrying 32 guns and 275 men, was engaged a few weeks later off Guadaloupe with the *Vengeance*, mounting 52 guns. The *Mermaid* pursued a strange sail, by orders of the admiral, and about noon on the 8th August came up with the *Vengeance*, when the ships exchanged broadsides. The action continued with varying success, but about 1.30 the French frigate twice missed stays when trying to tack, thus exposing herself to heavy raking broadsides from her adversary, which, from her proximity to the shore, occasionally received a shot from the batteries. About 3.40, the wind having fallen very light, the *Vengeance* ran close in under the batteries, when the *Mermaid* stood off; the former made sail for Basse-terre, which she reached in safety, pursued by the British 40-gun frigate *Beaulieu*, Captain Laforey. In this action the *Mermaid* suffered no loss, but her rigging and sails were much cut about. The *Vengeance*, on the other hand, as was stated by Victor Hugues to some British dragoon officers, prisoners at Basse-terre, lost 12 men killed and 26 wounded. Considering the disparity of force, the action was in every way creditable to the officers and men of the British frigate.

The next naval event we have to chronicle was not very creditable to the commanders of certain transports. The *Quebec*, 32, Captain John Cooke, encountered two French frigates while convoying four transports and a merchant ship from Martinique to Cape Nicholas-Mole, in St. Domingo. The strange sail were sighted late on the evening of the 6th July, and on the following morning, when Captain Cooke made the signal for his convoy to disperse, and exchanged broadsides with one of the frigates, the captains of the transports surrendered to the other, without making an effort to escape.

The destruction of the French frigate *Andromaque*, off the mouth of the river Gironde by the *Galatea*, 32, Captain R. Goodwin Keats, one of the finest officers in the service, and 18-gun brig *Sylph*, Commander White, belonging to Sir Borlase Warren's squadron, was a smart affair. The *Andromaque* was chased by the *Galatea*, and when she ran ashore, Captain Keats sent his boats, and those of the *Sylph* and *Artois*, 44, Captain Durham, to effect her destruction. The crew got safely on shore and the *Sylph*, running in, riddled the frigate's bottom with shot, and then set her on fire. The British 30-gun ship *Raison*, Captain Beresford, offered a stout resistance to the *Vengeance*, 52, the *Mermaid's* old opponent, which discovered the truth of the old naval maxim, "A stern chase is a long chase." The *Raison* cut away her jolly-boat, and fitted four stern-chasers, with which she kept up a fire on her pursuer, and ultimately, thanks to a fog, made good her escape with the loss of only three killed and six wounded, besides being much cut up aloft. The *Vengeance*, which was three times the tonnage of her opponent, was also considerably damaged, and six of her crew were killed.

The French Government having resolved on despatching an expedition to East Indian waters, to harass British trade in that part of the world, Rear-Admiral Sercey sailed on the 4th March, 1796, with the *Forte*, 52, *Régénérée*, 36, *Seine*, 44, *Bonne-Citoyenne* corvette, and *Mutine* brig, having on board 800 troops and a quantity of military stores. But bad weather overtook the squadron in the Bay of Biscay, and the *Bonne-Citoyenne*, being damaged, was captured by the *Phaeton*, Captain Hon. Robert Stopford, and soon after the *Mutine* shared the fate of her consort. At Santa Cruz, in the Canaries, the squadron was joined by the *Virtu*, 44, and continuing the voyage round the Cape, made some prizes, and on the 18th June arrived at Mauritius, where they found the French frigates *Prudente*, 36, and *Cybèle*, 44. Admiral Sercey sailed with his six frigates on the 24th July for the Coromandel coast, taking with him as a despatch boat the privateer schooner *Alerte*. This vessel, being detached from the squadron to give information of the strength and disposition of the British ships on the station, was captured by the 28-gun frigate *Carysfort*, Captain James Alexander, which, mistaking her for an Indiaman, she sought to capture by boarding, and thus placed the papers of the French admiral, with his plan of route, in the hands of the British.

Meanwhile Admiral Sercey cruised off the coast of Sumatra, making some captures, but on the 8th September found himself in the presence of two British seventy-fours, the *Arrogant*, Captain Lucas, and *Victorious*, Captain Clark. The admiral adopted the usual French course of avoiding an action unless in overwhelming force, or in the event of absolute necessity,* but the captains of the British seventy-fours, who had agreed

---

* The author of the great French work on the Revolutionary and Napoleonic wars, "Victoires et Conquetes," distinctly implied this guiding precept of the French Navy in the following passage :—" In the weak state of the French marine, the greatest of all follies is to send ships to sea to seek and offer battle to those of the enemy. It was

H. M. S. COLOSSUS.

1st CLASS BATTLE-SHIP.

to dog the six French frigates, and bring them to action when a favourable opportunity offered, were not so easily to be shaken off. The British ships continued the chase throughout the day, and at length Admiral Sercey, finding escape impossible, signalled his ships to form in order of battle. The *Arrogant* began the action at 7.25, by opening fire on the *Virtu*, and a brisk cannonade ensued. The *Arrogant* lost her fore-topsail yard and received other injuries aloft, which rendered her quite unmanageable, and ceased firing. The *Victorious*, which lay astern of her consort, fired on the French frigates as they successively got abreast of her, and a little later sustained the united fire of the enemy, and at 10.15, having suffered severely in her hull and had her three lower masts and bowsprit, as well as her yards and topmast, badly wounded, she ceased firing and wore to rejoin the *Arrogant*, which lay about a mile and a half distant. For some time, owing to the prevalence of a dead calm, the British seventy-four was exposed to the united raking fire of the enemy's three ships, but a light breeze springing up, she brought her starboard broadside to bear on them. The *Virtu* and *Cybèle* now made off, and about eleven the remaining frigates bore up under a press of sail, and a few minutes later the *Victorious* ceased firing, the enemy being out of range.

In this action the *Arrogant*, out of a complement of 584, lost a midshipman and six men killed and 27 wounded, and the *Victorious*, which had absent in prizes her first lieutenant and 90 men, had 17 killed, and her captain, one midshipman, and 53 seamen and marines wounded. The French squadron did not escape without much damage in hull, masts, and rigging, and the casualties sustained among their crews—which had an aggregate nearly double of ours—were 52 killed and 104 wounded; among the former being Captain Latour, of the *Seine*.

On the conclusion of the action, the *Arrogant* and *Victorious*, the latter in tow, steered for Madras, where they arrived on the 6th October, and the French ships

done, however, at the commencement of the war, and we have witnessed the ill consequences arising from it. This fatal experience, moreover, was unnecessary to prove that such are not the proper tactics of the weaker party. To deceive the vigilance of the stronger, escape his pursuit, strike unawares upon a point which he had left unprotected (and it is impossible for him to protect all) is the proper way to compensate for great inequality of force; even were the forces of two enemies equal, he who acted thus would soon triumph over the other. In naval matters, an engagement is not always the aim to be proposed, unless a party possesses a force so superior that he may hope very soon to annihilate his enemy. Ships of war have thus always an object, other than of fighting the ships of an enemy, and it often happens that, whatever may be the issue of the combat, this first and principal object fails to be fulfilled. The important point to the state is, that a naval commander should execute the mission with which he is charged, and not neglect to do so in order to afford a proof of his courage and acquire a trophiless glory for his country. According to these principles the different governments which succeeded each other in France during the war of the Revolution have almost all of them, and very wisely, given a formal order to their flag officers and captains, to avoid an action except in a case of absolute necessity, and to devote the whole of their energies towards the accomplishment of their mission."

bent their course for Mergui, where they refitted, and thence sailed for the coast of Ceylon, but the state of the hulls of three of his frigates determined Admiral Sercey to repair to Batavia for a thorough overhaul.

Mention should be made of the gallant manner in which the 18-gun brig *Pelican*, Captain Searle, engaged and beat off the *Médée*, mounting 40 guns, with a crew of 300 men. The *Pelican* sighted the French frigate off Guadaloupe, on the 22nd September, and the crew, numbering only 97 out of a complement of 121, hesitated at first to engage a ship of such force, but responded with three cheers to Captain Searle's appeal to stand by him and not discredit the good name they had earned, by fleeing from a Frenchman. The action commenced at seven, the brig's first broadside killing the helmsman, wounding three men and disabling a gun. The action was continued on both sides with spirit for two hours, when the *Médée* made sail and left her plucky adversary to repair damages, which were very extensive, and included every brace and bowline, all the after back-stays, the main-stay, several shrouds, and her mainmast, main-topsail yard, and foreyard. Strange to say, the *Pelican* had no casualties, while the French frigate, it was afterwards learned, from an officer of the 60th regiment who was a prisoner on board during the action, had 33 men killed and wounded.

Captain Searle captured on the following day a large ship, late a British army victualler, the prize of the *Médée*, and put a prize crew on board her, but as she lay becalmed off the shore of Guadaloupe, with the *Pelican* close at hand, the boats of the *Médée*, which came up with the land breeze, regained possession of her, and the brig had some difficulty in escaping from her former antagonist, which had been joined by another French frigate.

Captain Barton, of the 28-gun frigate *Lapwing*, while lying at St. Kitts, received information of an attack on the island of Anguilla, by two French ships-of-war and a body of troops. On seeing the *Lapwing* off the island, the French commander re-embarked his troops on board the *Decius*, 26, and brig *Vaillante*, 6 guns, to which the *Lapwing* gave chase, and about 10 P.M. brought them to action on the 26th November. After an hour's action the ship struck her colours, when Captain Barton went in pursuit of the brig, which ran ashore and was destroyed by the fire of the British frigate. The latter had only the nominal loss of one killed and six wounded, while the *Decius*, which had on board, including troops, 336 men, lost no less than 80 killed and 40 wounded. The loss of the brig, whose complement, with the soldiers, was about 135, was not known, but must have been heavy. On the following day the *Lapwing* was chased by two French frigates, when Captain Barton, taking his men and prisoners out of the *Decius*, set her on fire, and reached St. Kitts in safety, when the inhabitants presented him with an address of congratulation.

In the Mediterranean, off the port of Carthagena, a Spanish 34-gun frigate, the *Mahonesa*, surrendered to the *Terpsichore*, 32, commanded by Captain Richard Bowen. The latter was not particularly anxious to engage, because of his proximity to a Spanish fleet, and the sickly state of his crew, of whom only 182 were able to attend at their quarters. But Captain Bowen disdained to fly, and as the *Mahonesa* hauled to the wind on his weather beam, he fired a gun, to which the Spanish captain replied by a broadside, and an action ensued. At the end of one hour and twenty minutes, Captain Don Tomas Ayaldi had had enough of it, and tried to sheer off, but the crew of the *Terpsichore*—which was considerably cut up aloft, and had all her lower masts and bowsprit wounded—having repaired damages, with sailor-like promptness, in twenty minutes, made sail in pursuit. Soon she was alongside the *Mahonesa*, which had suffered even more than the British frigate, when the Spanish captain hauled down his colours, having lost, out of his complement of 275, 30 killed and the same number wounded, the casualties of the *Terpsichore* being confined to only four wounded. Captain Bowen refitted his prize, which had scarcely a shroud left standing, and carried her to Lisbon, and she was subsequently added to the Navy.

On the 12th December, two months after her action with the *Mahonesa*, the *Terpsichore* espied, about sixty miles off Cadiz, a strange sail, to which, notwithstanding the fresh gale that was blowing, she gave chase. This proved to be the *Vestale*, 36, Captain Foucaud, which had parted company a few days before from Admiral Villeneuve, while on his way from Toulon to Brest. Persevering in the chase, though with his fore and main-topmasts sprung, Captain Bowen and his gallant crew had their reward, when at 9.30 in the evening of the 13th December, Cadiz being then only a few miles distant, the captain of the *Vestale* hauled up his courses, and backed his main-topsail in readiness to engage his persistent adversary. The *Terpsichore* ranged alongside the *Vestale*, and a hot cannonade ensued at a range of only ten yards. At one time the British frigate had to suspend her fire owing to her braces getting foul, but it was only to resume it with redoubled vigour, and within twenty minutes of midnight the *Vestale* hauled down her colours, all her three masts and bowsprit being shot through.

The resistance offered by the ship's company was of a determined character, but their skill was not equal to their courage. Out of a complement of 270 men, she lost her captain, two officers, and 27 men killed, and 37 wounded, including her first lieutenant. The *Terpsichore* also suffered considerably. All her boats, her bowsprit, fore and main-masts, main-topmast, and her sails and rigging were much damaged, and out of 166 men and boys on board (six officers and 100 men of her crew being away in prizes or sick on shore) she had four killed, and her only lieutenant, Mr. George Bowen, brother of the captain, and 17 men wounded.

Directly after the action, all the three masts and bowsprit of the *Vestale* went overboard, and the position of the ship, as well as that of her consort, on a treacherous shore, close to windward of the shoals that lie between Cape Trafalgar and Cadiz, was one that called for all the energies and boundless resource of British seamen. By the great exertions of Mr. Elder, master of the *Terpsichore*, and one midshipman and seven seamen, all that Captain Bowen could spare in the reduced state of his crew and the dangerous condition of his spars and rigging, the prize was anchored in eighteen feet of water, and the *Terpsichore* succeeded in weathering the rocks of San Sebastian, and getting out to sea. It was a trying night for all hands on board the British frigate and her prize, the greater portion of the crew of which were lying helplessly drunk about the decks; but on the following morning Captain Bowen stood back in search of his prize, and anchored close to her in twenty fathoms of water, about four miles off the land.

Owing to the shattered condition of the boats of both frigates, and the swamping of the *Terpsichore's* cutter alongside the prize, none of the prisoners, except the second lieutenant, had been removed from the *Vestale*. Darkness set in before the British frigate could get her prize out to sea. Standing off for the night, she was drifted by the currents, the wind having fallen light, into the Straits. At daybreak she again stood towards her prize, but had the mortification to see her, with her colours flying, steering for Cadiz. During the preceding evening, the crew, having recovered from their state of inebriation, had overpowered the master and prize crew, and hoisted out the launch to make for the shore. Soon afterwards some Spanish boats came alongside, and setting what sail they could on a pair of shears, the *Vestale* was towed into Cadiz, and the captain and the gallant seamen of the *Terpsichore* lost the prize they had fought so hard to gain; but none the less, the honour they had acquired remained to them.

Before the close of the year, Commodore Nelson had an encounter with the enemy, in which he came off victorious. On being left in the Mediterranean by Sir John Jervis, he had shifted his flag from the *Captain*, 74, to the *Minerve*, 42, Captain George Cockburn, the same ship that had been captured by the *Dido*, as already related. The *Minerve* was proceeding, in company with the *Blanche*, 32, Captain Preston, from Gibraltar to Porto Ferrajo, to bring away the stores left there, when on the 19th December they fell in with two Spanish frigates. Commodore Nelson ordered Captain Preston to attack the smaller ship to leeward, while he directed Captain Cockburn to bring the other frigate to action. The latter, named the *Sabina*, carried 44 guns and 286 men, and was commanded by Captain Jacobo Stewart, who made a gallant defence, especially for a Spanish officer, as Lord Cochrane would have said. The action, which was maintained at close quarters, lasted two hours and fifty minutes, and at the end of that time the Spanish frigate hauled down her flag, her mizen-mast being over the side, and her other masts shot through in several places, while out of her complement of 286 men, being the same as her victorious opponent, her casualties, according to Commodore Nelson's despatch, were no less than 164, though the Spanish captain only acknowledged to 10 killed and 45 wounded. The *Minerve*, on the other hand, had one midshipman and six seamen killed, and Lieutenant Noble, who had accompanied Nelson from the *Captain*, the boatswain, and 32 seamen and marines wounded.

Nelson placed in charge of his prize his first and second lieutenants, John Culverhouse and Thomas Masterman Hardy (captain of the *Victory* at Trafalgar), with 40 seamen, and took her in tow; but at four o'clock another Spanish frigate was seen coming up. Casting off the *Sabina*, which stood to the southward, the *Minerve* engaged the enemy, which proved to be the 34-gun frigate *Matilda*. There is little doubt Nelson would have captured his second antagonist, which wore and stood off, at the end of half an hour, had not three other Spanish ships, one of the line and two frigates, hove in sight. It was necessary now to consider his own safety by a timely flight, and it was with the utmost difficulty that the British frigate, which was chased throughout the whole of the following day, succeeded in eluding her pursuers at nightfall. During this second action her loss was ten men wounded, including the gunner, and her rigging and sails, which had suffered much previously, were further cut up considerably. The *Sabina* fell into the hands of the enemy, but not until Lieutenant Culverhouse had made every effort to escape, and lost in the attempt both her remaining masts.

Meantime the *Blanche* had engaged the other 40-gun Spanish frigate, named the *Ceres*, and compelled her to haul down her colours with the loss of seven killed and 15 wounded. But the advent on the scene of the *Matilda* and *Perla*, 34, obliged her to wear and seek safety in flight.

Commodore Nelson anchored in the harbour of Porto Ferrajo on the 26th December, and having in three days embarked on board his squadron all the troops and stores, sailed thence, accompanied by the *Romulus*, *Southampton*, and *Dido*, frigates, *Dolphin* and *Dromedary*, storeships, two sloops, and twelve transports, which made sail for Gibraltar. On the same evening Commodore Nelson proceeded with the *Minerve* and *Romulus* towards the coast of France, and having reconnoitred Toulon roadstead and the ports of Barcelona and Carthagena, he rejoined the other ships of his squadron at Gibraltar.

When Rear-Admiral Richery was released from his blockade in Cadiz by the Spanish Admiral Langara, he sailed across the Atlantic with his squadron of seven seventy-fours and three frigates, and did considerable damage to the fishing stations in Newfoundland and the adjacent islands of St. Pierre and Miquelon, as well as the coast of Labrador, but did not care to attack the batteries in the harbour of St. John, which were reinforced by a portion of the crew of the 32-gun frigate *Venus*, Captain Graves, the ship herself being moored across the entrance of the port, which had a width of only 160 yards. Admiral Richery, having executed all the damage in his power on the defenceless fishing-stations, ruined the poor fishermen, and destroyed upwards of one hundred merchantmen, set sail on his return across the Atlantic, and all the ships of his squadron had entered the ports of Rochefort and Lorient by the 15th November.

On the other hand the commanders of our ships-of-war were very successful in the West Indies. In April Sir John Laforey, commanding on the Leeward Islands station, sent the *Malabar*, 54, Captain Parr, with some frigates and transports, on board of which was embarked a detachment of 1,200 troops, under General Whyte, to take possession of the Dutch settlements of Demerara, Esequibo, and Berbice in Guiana, which were surrendered without resistance. At Demerara, the Dutch ship *Thetis*, 24, and a 12-gun cutter, were captured, together with several richly laden merchantmen.

In our account of the operations of the previous year, we have described the loss of the islands of St. Lucia, St. Vincent, and Grenada. The British Government resolved to attempt the recapture of these colonial possessions, and on the 21st April Rear-Admiral Christian arrived in Carlisle Bay, Barbados, with two ships-of-the-line and five frigates and sloops, convoying a large fleet of transports, with a strong body of troops, under the command of Sir Ralph Abercrombie. On the following day Sir John Laforey sailed with his augmented squadron to Marin Bay, in Martinique, when he resigned the command to Admiral Christian and sailed for England in the *Majestic*, 74. Thence the expedition stood across to St. Lucia, when the troops, together with a small brigade of 800 seamen and 320 marines, under the command of Captains Lane, of the *Astrea*, 32, and Ryves, of the bomb-vessel, *Bull-dog*, were landed at three different points, under the protection of the guns of the fleet. The post of Morne Chabot was first attacked on the night of the 28th April, and carried by the troops with the loss of 13 killed, 49 wounded, and nine missing. Then occurred two sanguinary repulses, one, on the 3rd May, while attempting to dislodge the enemy from their batteries near the Grand Cul de Sac, and a second, on the night of the 17th, before the post of Vigie. But the fire of the ships' guns, mounted in batteries, caused the Republicans severe loss, and on the 25th the garrison, numbering 2,000 men, capitulated, and the whole island surrendered, the entire British loss achieving this great success being 66 killed, 378 wounded, and 122 missing. Sir Ralph Abercrombie acknowledged, in a General Order, the aid rendered by the Navy, especially in establishing batteries on commanding eminences deemed impregnable.

The next attack was directed on the island of St. Vincent, where the troops were disembarked on the 8th June, under cover of the *Arethusa*, 38, Captain Wolley, who landed a detachment of seamen to serve on shore. After some fighting the island was surrendered on the 11th, the British loss being 38 killed and 145 wounded. Grenada was reduced with the loss of only nine killed and 60 wounded, but the *Mermaid* had seven seamen killed and five badly injured by the bursting of a main-deck gun, while covering the landing of the troops, in conjunction with the *Hebe*, frigate, and *Pelican* and *Beaver*, sloops. In March of this year, troops were embarked from the garrison of Port au Prince, in the island of St. Domingo, under the command of General Forbes, and were landed in two divisions to attack the town and fort of Leogane, in the same island. The western division was covered by the *Ceres*, frigate, Captain Newman, and *Lark*, sloop, Captain Ogilby; and the eastern division, by the frigate *Iphigenia*, Captain Gardner, and sloops *Cormorant*, Captain F. Collingwood, and *Sirene*, Captain Guerin, while the town was cannonaded by the *Swiftsure*, 74, Captain Parker, and the fort by the *Leviathan*, 74, Captain Duckworth, and *Africa*, 64, Captain Home. The combined attack, however, was not successful, as the defences of the town and fort were stronger than was anticipated, and the troops were withdrawn on the following day. The *Africa* had one killed and seven wounded, and the *Leviathan* five killed and 12 wounded, and both ships suffered considerably aloft, and were compelled to proceed to Jamaica to refit. The fort of Bombarde was, however, captured with its garrison of 300 men. In the following May, a French squadron arrived at Cape François from Rochefort and Brest with 1,200 troops, besides arms and ammunition, which were safely landed on the island, when the French ships, consisting of two seventy-fours, three frigates, two corvettes, and eight transports, eluded the British fleet, and returned to France without encountering any opposition.

At the same time an expedition was undertaken by the British admiral in the East, against the Dutch possessions in the Moluccas. On the 16th February, Admiral Rainier arrived off Amboyna, the chief island of the group, with the *Suffolk*, 74, Captain Lambert, bearing his flag, *Centurion*, 50, Captain Osborne, *Resistance*, 44, Captain Pakenham, *Orpheus*, 32, Captain Newcome, some armed Indiamen, and three transports, having on board a detachment of troops. The island was surrendred without firing a shot, and the British troops took quiet possession, when the rich store of cloves fell into the hands of the victors. The squadron then sailed for the Banda group, which were also occupied, after the exchange of a few shots between some batteries and the *Orpheus* and one of the Indiamen. The settlement of Nassau, in Banda Neira, and the other islands surrendered, and the warehouses, stored with nutmegs and mace, became prize to the British Army and Navy. This expedition, though remarkable for the bloodless character of its operations, is not less distinguished for the value of the booty acquired by the services, and the five naval captains present at the surrender of Amboyna and Banda each received £15,000 prize money.

Before the close of the year 1796, one of those sad catastrophes happened which darken the annals of the British Navy. The *Amphion*, 32, Captain Israel Pellew, was lying at Plymouth, lashed to a sheer-hulk, close to the dockyard jetty, when she suddenly blew up. At the time of the accident there were on board, in addition to the crew, over 100 women and children, visiting their friends, as the frigate was under orders to sail on the following day. Captain Pellew was sitting at dinner, with his first lieutenant and Captain Swaffield, of the *Overyssel*, when the shock warned him of the coming catastrophe, and the two former officers, though much bruised, retained sufficient presence of mind to jump out of the cabin windows into the sea and were saved, but their companion shared the fate of 390 men, women and children, whose mangled remains were strewed over the town and port.

During the year the British Navy had captured twenty-five ships—three Dutch sail-of-the-line and nine French, eleven Dutch, and two Spanish frigates—of which twenty-two were added to the service. On the other hand, only the 10-gun brig *Experiment* was lost by capture to the British Navy, though the loss by stress of weather or accident was considerable. Thus two ships-of-the-line were wrecked and one was burnt, while of smaller vessels, eleven were wrecked, six foundered, and two were burnt. On the whole the Empire was increased by the conquest of Cape Colony, Ceylon, the Moluccas, and other groups of islands in the East, and in the West Indies by the acquisition of many important settlements belonging to the Republican Governments of France and Holland.

CHAPTER VIII.

The Invasion of Ireland—Dispersion of the French Fleet—Action between the *Droits de l'Homme* and the *Indefatigable* and *Amazon* Frigates—Shipwreck of the French Seventy-four and *Amazon*—The Mutiny at Spithead and the Nore—Disaffections on other Stations—Sir John Jervis's Victory over the Spanish Fleet off Cape St. Vincent—Sir Horatio Nelson at Cadiz—Repulse of his Attack on Santa Cruz—Admiral Duncan's Victory over the Dutch Fleet off Camperdown—Frigate Actions During the Year 1797—Loss of the *Tribune*—Capture of Trinidad—Cutting-out Affairs in the West Indies—Action between the *Mars* and *Hercule*—Repulse of the French Channel Flotilla.

THE French Directory turned their serious attention to the invasion of England, in which attempt Holland and Spain promised their assistance; but the plan fell through, and the less difficult operation of landing an army in Ireland to co-operate with the Irish insurgents, under Lord Edward Fitzgerald and the other leaders, was adopted. The execution of this great venture was entrusted to Vice-Admiral Morard-de-Galles, in conjunction with the distinguished Republican General Hoche, who was nominated to the supreme command of the troops. The English Government strained every nerve to meet the coalition against this country, and 120,000 seamen and marines were voted for the service of the Navy. Indeed to the vigilance and activity of England's "first line of defence" was attributable the defeat of the well-planned scheme for the conquest of Ireland, which was to have the active co-operation of the Irish patriots, or insurgents, as they were indifferently called.

On the 26th December, 1796, Admiral Morard-de-Galles, with Admirals Bouvet, Nielly, and Richery, all except the latter flying their flags in frigates, got under weigh from Brest, with a fleet consisting of seventeen ships-of-the-line, thirteen frigates, six corvettes, seven transports, and a powder ship, forty-four sail in all, conveying 8,000 troops, under the command of Generals Grouchy (whose name is inseparably connected with Waterloo), Borin, and Humbert. Misfortune marked the course of this expedition from its start, and Admiral Morard, who with General Hoche had embarked in the frigate *Fraternité*, after giving his fleet orders to proceed by the Channel du Raz, in order to avoid discovery by the British fleet cruising off Ushant, signalled the ships while under sail to steer for the Passage d'Iroise, as being more directly in front. Thus, what with this change of plan and the darkness, confusion ensued, the ships got scattered at the outset, and the *Séduisant*, 74, struck on a rock near the entrance of the Channel du Raz and was lost, together with her captain and many officers, and 680 seamen and soldiers out of 1,300 on board the ill-fated ship.

The movement of the French fleet had been closely watched by a squadron of Vice-Admiral Colpoys' fleet off Ushant, consisting of the frigates *Indefatigable*, 44, Sir Edward Pellew; *Revolutionnaire*, 38, Captain Cole; 36-gun frigates, *Amazon*, Captain Reynolds, and *Phœbe*, Captain Barlow; and the commodore sent two of his frigates in succession to apprize the admiral of the departure of the French fleet from Brest, and with the *Indefatigable* alone, hung about close to the enemy, being at times half gun-shot only from the leading ships. During the evening and night he continued firing guns and signal lights, which distracted the French admirals and captains, and then made sail for Falmouth to report the departure of this great armament from the French port.

At daybreak of the 17th, Rear-Admiral Bouvet found himself with nine sail-of-the-line, six frigates, and one transport in company; and in order to avoid encountering the British fleet, steered to the westward until the 19th, when he changed his course to north, and soon afterwards was joined by 16 French ships, which raised his strength to 15 sail-of-the-line, ten frigates, three corvettes, and five transports, only the *Nestor* and three frigates, including the *Fraternité*, with the naval and military commanders-in-chief, being absent. The fleet anchored off the entrance to Bantry Bay, when the pilots, mistaking them for British, came off and were all detained, thus providing one for almost every ship. Admiral Bouvet continued to beat against an easterly wind for two days, but made little way, and on the 22nd anchored, with eight battle ships and seven other sail, off Great Bear Island. The weather continued too boisterous to permit of landing General Grouchy's division of 6,000 troops. Several of the ships-of-the-line drove from their anchors and stood out to sea, and the *Immortalité*, having on board Admiral Bouvet and General Grouchy, having parted one cable, was obliged to cut the other to prevent herself from going on shore. The frigate scudded before the gale for three days, but when the wind moderated, Admiral Bouvet decided on returning to Brest, as his provisions were almost consumed, and he was fearful of finding none of his ships in Bantry Bay. Accordingly, the *Immortalité* steered for Brest, where she cast anchor on the 1st January, and was joined the same day by the *Indomptable*, 80, and the seventy-fours *Fougueux*, *Mucius*, *Redoutable*, and *Patriote*.

Meantime the *Fraternité*, with the *Nestor*, 74, and *Romaine* and *Cocarde*, frigates, sailing in company, were dispersed by a fog, and the frigate, carrying the two commanders-in-chief, had a narrow escape of capture by a British frigate, which chased her until darkness shrouded her movements. On her way to Bantry Bay, the *Fraternité* encountered the *Resolution*, 74, which had been compelled to embark the crew of the *Scévola*, which was in a sinking state, and relieved her of some of the seamen and troops; but the additional burden of feeding so many mouths proved beyond the resources of the two ships, and ultimately Admiral Morard-de-Galles and General Hoche decided on returning to Brest. On their way they were chased by the British frigates *Unicorn*, 32, Sir Thomas Williams, and *Doris*, 36, Captain Hon. C. Jones, and when they escaped this danger, found themselves in close proximity to Admiral Bridport's fleet. The foggy and stormy weather, which had wrought such havoc with the plans of the commander-in-chief, now saved them from capture, and on the 14th January the *Resolution* and the *Fraternité* entered the port of Rochefort.

Meanwhile, the French ships that had reached Bantry Bay suffered even more than their consorts. On the 30th December the *Justine*, transport, was captured, and the *Impatiente*, frigate, was wrecked on the coast near Crookhaven, when all on board, except seven men, were drowned. A few days later, the *Surveillante*, frigate, went on shore at Bantry Bay, and a portion of her crew were made prisoners; the *Ville de l' Orient*, transport, was captured by the *Druid*, 32, Captain King; the *Tortue*, frigate, by the *Polyphemus*, 64; and the *Fille Unique*, transport, foundered in the bay. At length eight or nine of the French ships managed to reach the mouth of the Shannon, but only to abandon the enterprise and steer for Brest; but on the way the *Suffren* and *Allegro*, transports, and the *Atalante*, brig, were captured. The line-of-battle ships had all reached port by the 14th, except one, the *Droits de l' Homme*, 74, and also all the frigates, except those mentioned as captured or lost.

On the 5th January, the *Droits de l' Homme*—bearing the broad pennant of Commodore La Crosse, and having on board the famous General Humbert, commanding a division of troops, when about four leagues off the mouth of the Shannon, captured the *Cumberland*, British privateer, and after cruising about for eight days, and again looking into Bantry Bay, where there were no signs of the French fleet, steered for Belleisle, on the coast of France. When about 15 miles from the land on the 13th January, thick weather set in, and the French seventy-four sighted the British frigates, *Indefatigable*, 44, Sir Edward Pellew, and *Amazon*, 36, Captain Reynolds. The wind continued to increase until it blew a gale, and the *Droits de l' Homme* carried away her fore and main topmasts, so that at about 5.30 in the afternoon the *Indefatigable* was enabled to overhaul her sufficiently to pour in a raking fire, to which the seventy-four replied by a broadside. The two combatants continued to manœuvre, the Frenchman to run her on board, and the British frigate to rake her adversary, which, owing to the heavy sea and the want of sails to steady her, rolled so heavily as to render her lower-deck guns useless. An hour after the commencement of the action the *Amazon* arrived on the scene, and poured a broadside into the quarter of the two-decker within pistol-shot range. The cannonade was continued with spirit till 7.30, when both ships shot ahead, the *Indefatigable* to repair damages, which gave the crew of the *Droits de l'Homme* a little breathing time.

Having refitted, the British frigates recommenced the action, one on either bow of the Frenchman, and by regulating their speed, were enabled to rake her by turns, while their unwieldy and almost disabled opponent strove to board one or the other of her persistent enemies, but managed only, by yawing on one tack and then the other, to return an ineffectual fire. At 10.30, the main-mast of the seventy-four, being on the point of falling, was cut away to prevent its encumbering the deck, and the frigates took up a position on either quarter, and continued to pour their broadsides into the crowded decks of the enemy, who made no sign of surrender, fresh bodies of men taking the places of those that fell at their quarters. Thus the conflict, with only a second brief interval to repair damages, raged until daylight, when suddenly the land was seen close at hand, and the cannonade, after being protracted over thirteen hours, ceased, while the combatants, worn out with their exertions, concentrated their efforts to save themselves from imminent death. At this time the *Indefatigable* had four feet of water in her hold, and all her masts were wounded. The *Amazon* also made three feet of water, her mizen-topmast, main-topsail yard, and other spars were shot away, and her fore and main-masts and yards were wounded, and all her sails and rigging damaged. Throughout the action the gallant seamen of both ships had fought with the water up to their waists on the main deck, and the violent straining had carried away the breechings and drawn the ring-bolts of many of the guns.

The casualties were comparatively small, the *Indefatigable*, out of 330, having only her first lieutenant, Mr. Thompson, and 18 men wounded, and the *Amazon*, whose complement was 260, losing only three killed and 15 wounded. On the other hand, the loss of life on board the *Droits de l'Homme* was appalling. Out of 1,350 sailors and soldiers, she had 103 killed and 150 wounded, and it cannot be gainsaid that Commodore La Crosse made a gallant defence when it is considered that he was unable to use his lower-deck battery of 36-pounders.

On seeing the land and the breakers ahead, Sir Edward Pellew got his tacks on board, and wearing ship, made all sail to the southward, and with difficulty about 11 A.M. succeeded in weathering the much-dreaded Penmarck rocks. His consort, the *Amazon*, wore to the southward, but being more crippled, was unable to get clear off shore, and soon afterwards struck the beach. The crew, with the exception of six seamen, reached the shore in safety on rafts, but it was only to find themselves prisoners in the hands of a party of French soldiers who took them to Quimper, where they remained in confinement until they were exchanged in the following September.

The crew of the *Droits de l'Homme* met with an even worse fate. Seeing that he could not hope to claw off, Commodore La Crosse let go his anchor, but it failed to hold, and the ship struck on a sandbank, when the main-mast went by the board. A terrible scene presented itself to some English officers and 48 men, prisoners on board the two-decker, who were told to save themselves as best they could. The decks were cumbered with the dead and dying and slippery with blood, the masts had fallen over the side, and the wind and the breakers roared around the devoted ship, as though thirsting for the lives of all on board. The shore was lined with people, who, however, could render no assistance, but witnessed repeated attempts of the crew to gain the shore by boats and rafts, which were destroyed in the angry surge, a portion only of their occupants reaching the land in safety. Thus the day wore on and night set in, during which the sea stove in the ship's stern. The dawn of the second day only revealed more plainly the harrowing condition of affairs to the spectators on the beach, who could render no aid; and thus the day dragged along, and night again set in, the people having been nearly thirty hours without food or water. Repeated attempts had been made to gain the shore in boats and rafts, and an English officer and eight seamen had actually reached the land by means of a small boat, but a huge raft, having on board some wounded, two women and six children, was upset by a rush of people, and over 120 souls were drowned.

An English officer, a prisoner on board the *Droits de l'Homme*, Lieutenant Pipon, writes of the situation when the third night set in, by which time nearly 900 people had perished:—"Weak, distracted, and wanting everything, we envied the fate of those whose lifeless corpses no longer needed sustenance. The sense of hunger was already lost, but a parching thirst consumed our vitals. Recourse was had to wine and salt water, which only increased the want. Half a hogshead of vinegar floated up, and each had half a wine-glass full. This gave a momentary relief, yet soon left us again in the same state of dreadful thirst. Almost at the last gasp, everyone was dying with misery; the ship, which was now one-third shattered away from the stern, scarcely afforded a grasp to hold by to the exhausted and helpless survivors. The fourth day (the 17th) brought with it a more serene sky, and the sea seemed to subside; but to behold, from fore and aft, the dying in all directions, was a sight too shocking for the feeling mind to endure. Almost lost to a sense of humanity, we no longer looked with pity on those who were the speedy forerunners of our own fate, and a consultation took place to sacrifice some one to be food for the remainder. The die was going to be cast, when the welcome sight of a man-of-war brig renewed our hopes. A cutter speedily followed, and both anchored at a short distance from the wreck. They then sent their boats to us, and by means of large rafts about 150, of near 400 who attempted it, were saved by the brig that evening; 380 were left to endure another night's misery, when, dreadful to relate, above one half were found dead next morning." Mr. Pipon thus concludes his thrilling narrative of one of the saddest disasters even the annals of the sea can show:—"I was saved at about 10 o'clock on the morning of the 18th with my two brother officers, the captain of the ship, and General Humbert. They treated us with great humanity on board the cutter, by giving us a little weak brandy and water every five or six minutes, after which a basin of good soup. I fell on the locker in a kind of trance for nearly thirty hours, and was swelled to that degree as to require medical aid to restore my decayed faculties. We were taken to Brest almost naked, having lost all our baggage. There they gave us a rough shift of clothes, and, in consequence of our sufferings and the help we afforded in saving many lives, a cartel was fitted out by order of the French Government, to send us home without ransom or exchange. We arrived at Plymouth on the 7th March following."

The failure of the great armament for the invasion of Ireland, from which so much was expected, was as complete as in the case of the Spanish Armada, and the cause was much the same. The British frigates, by the vigilance they displayed, had done good service, cutting off four transports and three ships-of-war, but the elements had dispersed the expedition and was accountable for the loss of two ships-of-the-line, three frigates and a transport. It was a singular circumstance that though the fleet, commanded by Lord Bridport and Admiral Colpoys, were traversing in every direction the English and Irish Channels during the three or four weeks the enemy were at sea, they never came into actual contact with the French expedition, of which 31 sail out of 44, including 15 battle-ships, returned safely to port. This strange immunity from capture was not due to any remissness on the part of those distinguished admirals, and Lord Bridport actually looked into Bantry Bay on the 9th January, when the enemy were not there, and on the following day chased the *Révolution* and *Fraternité*. Having ascertained on the 19th that the enemy were all safe in port, his lordship detached Rear-Admiral Parker to Gibraltar with five sail-of-the-line and a frigate, and putting in at Torbay, on the 3rd February cast anchor at Spithead.

But a greater danger than even the designs of the enemy could inflict upon the country at this time threatened the nation, and so desperate was the situation at one time that the Funds fell to a price they had never touched before or have been quoted at since. The seamen of the British Navy had long entertained a feeling of disaffection, but on the 15th April it suddenly burst into flame. On that day, when Lord Bridport—who had held only temporary command of the Channel fleet during the indisposition of Lord Howe, but was now appointed to the substantive charge—made the signal for the fleet to weigh anchor, the seamen of the *Royal George*, flagship, instead of yielding a ready compliance, ran up the shrouds and gave three cheers, a preconcerted signal which found a response throughout the fleet. In vain the captains and officers of the respective ships strove to awaken the men to a sense of their duty. On the following day each of the sixteen ships appointed two delegates, who met and deliberated in the admiral's state cabin on board the *Queen Charlotte*, and on the following day all the seamen were sworn to support the demands of the leaders, and ropes were rove at the fore-yard-arm of each ship, and such of the officers as had been guilty of oppression or were obnoxious were put on shore.

The thirty-two delegates drew up and signed two petitions, couched in respectful language, one to Parliament and the other to the Admiralty, in which they prayed "that the wages of the seamen should be increased, that their provisions should be increased from fourteen to sixteen ounces to the pound (the remaining two being retained by the purser to allow for waste) and to be of a better quality; that their measures should be the same as those in general use; that vegetables, instead of flour, should be served with fresh beef; that the sick should be better attended to and the "medical comforts" for their use should not be embezzled; and finally

H. M. S HERO.
2ND CLASS BATTLE-SHIP.

that the men might have, on returning from sea, a short leave to visit their families."*

On the 18th, a Committee of the Board of Admiralty, consisting of Lord Arden (first Lord), Rear-Admiral Young, and Mr. Marsden, the second secretary, arrived at Portsmouth, and in answer to the petition of the seamen declared that the Board would recommend the King to propose to Parliament an increase of four shillings per month to the wages of petty officers and seamen, three to the wages of ordinary seamen, and two of landsmen, and that the Board had resolved that seamen wounded in action should be continued in pay until their wounds were healed, or until, being declared unserviceable, they should be pensioned, or received into Greenwich Hospital. The delegates, however, urged that the distinction between ordinary and landsmen was new; and demanded that the wages of able seamen should be raised to one shilling a day, and of petty officers and ordinary seamen and marines, while serving on board, in the same proportion. Further, that the Greenwich pension should be raised to ten pounds per annum; that, to maintain the additional fund, every merchant seaman should thereafter pay one shilling, instead of sixpence a month, and that the regulation should extend to the seamen of the East India Company. The seamen then repeated their former demands for an increased weight and measure and an improved quality of provisions, and a supply of vegetables instead of flour with fresh beef; concluding with a declaration that until their grievances should be redressed and an Act of Indemnity passed they were determined not to lift an anchor.

On the next day, the 20th, the Admiralty Committee sent, through Lord Bridport, a letter to the seamen, agreeing to the increase of wages demanded and to the full weight and measure of provisions, and promising pardon, but taking no notice of any increase in the Greenwich pensions or any additional allowance of vegetables when in port. On the same, or the following day, the seamen returned a reply, expressing in very grateful terms their thanks for what had been granted them, but persisting in their demands, failing which they would not lift an anchor; unless, indeed,

* A simple statement of these demands will create a feeling of incredulity as to their existence, but of this there can be no doubt; and further that the Admiralty had refused to redress the grievances. The pay of the sailors had not been raised since the time that the Duke of York, afterwards James II., was Lord High Admiral, neither were their pensions increased from the amount at which they stood at that date, while those to which soldiers became entitled were so increased. More extraordinary than all was the rule by which provisions were served out to the sailors on the scale of fourteen ounces to the pound, instead of sixteen! The demand also that the "comforts" to the sick should not be embezzled was one that entailed disgrace on the Government of England for having permitted such an iniquity.

as had been already stated, the enemy's fleet should put to sea. On the 21st, Vice-Admirals Sir Alan Gardner and Colpoys and Rear-Admiral Pole went on board the *Queen Charlotte* to confer with the delegates, who, however, assured the admirals that no arrangement would be considered as final until sanctioned by the King and Parliament, and guaranteed by a proclamation of pardon. This so incensed Admiral Gardner that he seized one of the delegates by the collar, and swore he would have them all hanged, together with every fifth man in the fleet.

On the return of the offended delegates to their respective ships, says James, to whose account of these proceedings we are indebted, those of the *Royal George* resolved to summon a meeting on board their ship, and immediately hoisted the preconcerted signal of the red flag, a signal which alarmed all the well-disposed in the fleet. The officers of the *Royal George*, ashamed to see it flying with Lord Bridport's flag, hauled down the latter. The seamen of the fleet now proceeded to load the guns, ordered watches to be kept, as at sea, and put their ships in a complete state of defence. They also prevented their officers from going on shore, but otherwise put no constraint upon them.

On the 22nd, having become somewhat pacified, the seamen caused two letters to be written, one to the Lords of the Admiralty, in which they stated the cause of their conduct on the two preceding days, the other to Lord Bridport, in which they styled him their father and friend, and disclaimed offering him any intentional offence. This induced Lord Bridport on the following day to go on board the *Royal George*, the crew of which immediately hoisted his flag. The admiral then, at the close of an energetic address, informed the men that he had brought with him a redress of all their grievances, and the King's pardon for the offenders. After a short deliberation these offers were accepted, and every man returned with cheerfulness to his duty. All disputes were now considered as settled, and the fleet dropped down to St. Helen's, except the *London*, flagship of Vice-Admiral Colpoys, *Minotaur*, and *Marlborough*. The crews of the two latter refused to go to sea under their present officers, and the *London* had been directed to remain in company with them, to afford to Vice-Admiral Colpoys an opportunity of exerting his influence in restoring the disobedient ships' companies to a sense of their duty.

A foul wind detained the ships at St. Helen's until the morning of the 7th May, when, having just received intelligence that the French fleet had dropped into the outer harbour of Brest preparatory to sailing, Lord Bridport made the signal to weigh and put to sea, but every ship in the fleet, as on the 15th of the preceding month, refused to obey the signal, alleging as a reason for this second act of disobedience the silence that Government had observed respecting their complaints, by which they were led to suspect that the promised redress of grievances would be withheld.

At about 1 P.M. it was discovered on board the *London*, at Spithead, that boats were pulling to and fro among the ships at St. Helen's, and that yard-ropes were rove in the same manner as on the 17th of the preceding month. Convinced that a renewal of the mutiny had taken place, Vice-Admiral Colpoys addressed the crew of the *London*, and asked them if they had any grievances remaining, to which they replied in the negative. He then, as a measure of security, ordered the seamen below, and the officers and marines to arm themselves. On observing the boats of the delegates from the fleet at St. Helen's approaching the *Marlborough*, the *London's* crew below began to unlash the second-deck guns, and to point them aft and up the hatchways. Under orders from the admiral the officers fired on those that were forcing their way on deck, when five men were mortally, and six others badly wounded. The marines throwing down their arms, the seamen soon rushed in crowds up the hatchways; and the vice-admiral, unwilling to spill more blood, ordered the officers to cease firing. The seamen now seized the first lieutenant, Mr. Bower, and were proceeding to hang him, when Vice-Admiral Colpoys, interfering, told them that Lieutenant Bower had acted in conformity to his, the vice-admiral's, orders, received from the Admiralty. These instructions the seamen, whom the delegates from the fleet had now joined, demanded and obtained; when they ordered the admiral, Captain Griffiths, and the whole of the officers to their respective cabins. Matters remained in this state until the 11th, when Vice-Admiral Colpoys and Captain Griffiths were sent ashore, and during these five days of renewed discontent many unpopular captains and other officers were also landed. At length, on the 14th, the venerable Admiral Lord Howe arrived from London, with plenary powers to settle all matters in dispute, together with an Act of Parliament, which had been passed on the 9th, and a proclamation granting the King's pardon to all who should immediately return to their duty.

On the 15th the delegates from the fleet landed at Portsmouth, and proceeded to the Governor's house, whence they marched in procession to the sally-port, and there, accompanied by Lord and Lady Howe, and several officers and persons of distinction, embarked on board the men-of-war's barges. After visiting the ships at St. Helen's, the party proceeded to Spithead, where the squadron, under Rear-Admiral Sir Roger Curtis, had just anchored from a cruise, the seamen of which, on a representation of what had taken place, became reconciled to their officers. The boats then returned to Portsmouth, and the delegates carried Lord Howe on their shoulders to the Governor's house. On the succeeding day, the 16th May, all matters in dispute having been amicably adjusted, Lord Bridport put to sea, with his fleet of fifteen sail-of-the-line.

But notwithstanding the concessions, which were extended to the seamen of the entire navy, the disaffection seized on the ships lying at Sheerness and the Nore, whose especial duty it was to guard the Medway and Thames. This ill-feeling displayed itself in an overt act of mutiny on the 20th May, when the ships hoisted the flag of defiance. The ringleader in the mutiny was a seaman of the name of Richard Parker, one of that class of men denominated by sailors "sea-lawyers." This Parker was a bad character, having been discharged from several ships in disgrace on account of misconduct, and had only joined the *Sandwich*, 90, flagship of Vice-Admiral Bucknor, commander-in-chief at the Nore, in the preceding March, having been sent from Perth as "quota-man," the name by which those men raised from each district or county were called. The delegates from the ships at Sheerness, with Parker as president, transmitted a statement containing eight articles, most of which were frivolous and inadmissible, to which the Admiralty replied, pointing out how far the Legislature had already complied with their wishes, and refusing to accede to any further demands, but promising forgiveness if they would return to their duty. On the following day the mutineers struck Vice-Admiral Bucknor's flag, hoisting in its stead the red flag of mutiny, and they compelled all ships which lay near Sheerness to drop down to the Nore. On the 24th the offer of pardon was repeated, and again rejected. The delegates went on shore and, headed by Parker, marched in procession, and also sent deputations inviting the crews of other ships to join them. The mutineers went to greater lengths than the Spithead malcontents, and even flogged and otherwise maltreated some of the officers.

By the end of the month the outbreak assumed the most alarming proportions; eleven ships-of-the-line belonging to the North Sea fleet, with which Admiral Duncan was about to sail from Yarmouth to blockade the Texel, turned back to the mouth of the Thames and joined Parker. Notwithstanding this defection, the gallant admiral proceeded to his destination with his own ship, the *Venerable*, 74, and the *Adamant*, 50, Captain Hotham, and by adopting the device of causing the *Adamant* to make signals in the offing, induced a belief in the Dutch fleet of fifteen sail-of-the-line that he lay off the coast in force. The greatest alarm now seized upon the inhabitants of the capital, as the mutineers moored their ships in line across the river, and detained all merchantmen bound up or down, and threatened to force their way up the Thames towards London. The Government, on their part, acted with vigour; the buoys were taken up, and the forts manned and armed to open fire on the fleet should it advance towards the capital. But nothing could stay the panic, and the Funds fell to an unheard of price. Parker treated with insolence a Committee of the Lords of the Admiralty who went down on the 29th May to confer with the delegates, and at length the Government, driven to desperation, took courage of despair, and brought in Bills to Parliament (which were passed in two days), authorising the infliction of the utmost penalties of the law on the mutineers, and all who should give them aid and comfort.

This severity had the desired effect. Early in June the fleet at Portsmouth and Plymouth disowned all complicity with Parker and his acts, and, notwithstanding that he hanged Mr. Pitt and Mr. Dundas in effigy at the yardarm of the *Sandwich*, two of the ships, the *Leopard* and *Repulse*, hauled down the red flag of mutiny, and retreated into the Thames. Parker fired upon these ships, but the contagion of their good example spread, and ship after ship deserted, until, on the 14th, the crew of the *Sandwich* brought her also under the guns of the fort at Sheerness, and gave up Parker as a prisoner to the authorities. This notorious ringleader was tried, convicted, and hanged on the 29th, on board the ship that had been the scene of his misdeeds. Some of the mutinous men were also executed, and others were flogged through the fleet or sent to prison. The mutiny was not, however, confined to the ships on the home stations. Some of the crew of the *Venerable* had caught the contagion of disaffection, but Duncan nipped the attempt in the bud.

In the Mediterranean fleet, then off Portugal, Lord St. Vincent had more trouble, but acted with great promptitude. The ringleaders were seized and tried by court-martial, which sentenced three of them to death. The execution was directed to be carried out on board the *St. George*, 98, the admiral declining to accede to the petition of the crew, among whom the disaffection had first shown itself, to grant a reprieve. The men of the *St. George* thereupon entered into a conspiracy to seize the ship and liberate the prisoners under sentence of death, but Captain Peard and his first-lieutenant, Mr. Hatley, seized two of the ringleaders and, dragging them out of the crowd of mutinous seamen, put them in irons, which overawed the crew. On the following morning, the 7th July, the three mutineers were hanged at the fore-yard-arm of the *St. George*, and on the 9th the culprits seized by Captain Peard, who had been sentenced to death by court-martial, were likewise executed.

A like attempt on the Cape of Good Hope station by the men of the *Tremendous*, the flagship of Admiral Pringle, was suppressed by a similar display of timely severity, and the execution of the worst of the ringleaders brought matters back to their normal condition of discipline and obedience to orders.

Captain (afterwards Admiral) Billy Douglas, commanding the *Stately*, 64, at St. Helena, nipped in the bud the mutiny which broke out on board his ship. A relative of the gallant officer gives us the following account of the incident:—Captain Douglas was on shore dining with Governor Brook at St Helena, when his first-lieutenant came on shore and informed him that a ship had arrived from England with news of the mutiny, and that his men had come aft, and demanded the command of the ship, and were in a state of mutiny. Captain Douglas received the intelligence very coolly, and as the ship was under the guns of the forts, and the sails unbent, he said to the governor, "I will go immediately on board, and if in five minutes after I am in the ship, they do not return to their duty you will fire on her, for better that I go down with the ship than the men should command her." On reaching his ship he communicated this spirited determination to the men, and added that if the ringleaders were not given up unconditionally they knew what they were to expect. The allotted time expired and the fort began to fire, when the ringleaders were given up, and two of them hanged at the yard-arm. Thus by his intrepidity this gallant officer, who was at a later period of his career offered knighthood, which he declined chiefly on account of his singular baptismal name, crushed the incipient spirit of mutiny in his ship.

Notwithstanding the mutinous spirit that was abroad in the fleet at this time, it is singular to note the affection and respect in which the seamen held the immortal hero of Trafalgar. Nelson, who had been promoted to the rank of rear-admiral in March, had shifted his flag from the *Captain* to the *Theseus*, taking with him Captain Miller, and he had not been long in her when one night a paper signed "Ship's Company," and couched in the following terms, was dropped on the quarter-deck:—"Success attend Admiral Nelson! God bless Captain Miller! We thank them for the officers they have placed over us, we are happy and comfortable, and will shed every drop of blood in our veins to support them, and the name of the *Theseus* shall be immortalised as high as the *Captain's*."

A mutiny of quite a different character, as it arose from the tyranny of the captain, and having different results, took place in the West Indies, and merits a brief record. The *Hermione*, 32-gun frigate, had the misfortune to be commanded by Captain Hugh Pigot, who was one of the most cruel and oppressive officers in the service. On the 21st September, when cruising off Porto Rico, Captain Pigot, when reefing topsails, called out that he would flog the last man off the mizen-topsail-yard. "The poor fellows," says Captain Brenton, "well knowing that he would keep his word (and though the lot would naturally fall on the outermost and consequently the most active), each resolved at any rate to escape punishment; two of them, who from their position could not reach the topmast rigging, made a spring to get over their comrades within them, they missed their hold, fell on the quarter-deck, and were both killed." This being reported to the captain, he is said to have made answer, "Throw the lubbers overboard." It appears also that all the other men on coming down were severely reprimanded and threatened with punishment. On the night succeeding this act of brutal tyranny, the men broke out into open mutiny, and commenced throwing the shot about the deck. The first lieutenant went forward to inquire into the disturbance, and received a wound on the arm with a tomahawk. He retired, but soon went forward again, when they cut his throat and threw him overboard. Says Captain Brenton:—"The captain hearing the noise ran on deck, but was driven back with repeated wounds; seated in his cabin he was stabbed by his coxswain and three other mutineers, and, forced out of the cabin windows, was heard to speak as he went astern. Not satisfied with this retaliation on the object of their hatred, the mutineers murdered the two other lieutenants, purser, surgeon, the officer of marines, one midshipman, the captain's clerk, and boatswain. The only officers spared were the master, one midshipman, and the gunner. The murderous crew then navigated the ship into La Guayra, and gave her up to the Spanish governor, who sent the ship to sea as a national frigate. But they did not escape punishment for their crimes, and many of the crew were afterwards apprehended and executed."

Lord Bridport, on arriving off Brest at the latter part of May, found the enemy's fleet still there, but with his fleet, now strengthened to 21 sail, he continued to cruise to the westward throughout the summer months, only returning to port to refit or revictual. Meanwhile the French Directory made preparations on a grand scale for a second invasion of Ireland, which was to be undertaken in conjunction with the Dutch fleet lying at the Texel, under Admiral de Winter, and General Hoche, who was again to be commander-in-chief, proceeded thither to inspect the fleet and the troops, under General Daendels, that were to assist in the enterprise. The expedition was, however, postponed owing to the removal of the energetic Minister of Marine, Monsieur Truguet, and the crushing defeat of the Texel fleet, by Admiral Duncan, in the following year, robbed the attempt of much of its force.

The year 1797 was signalised by two decisive victories, one gained on St. Valentine's Day by Sir John Jervis over the Spanish fleet, and the other, later in the year, by Admiral Duncan, over the Dutch at Camperdown.

On the 18th January, Sir John Jervis sailed from the Tagus to convoy some Portuguese and Brazilian ships, and on the 6th February was joined off Cape St. Vincent by five battle-ships and one frigate from the Channel fleet, when his strength stood as follows:—

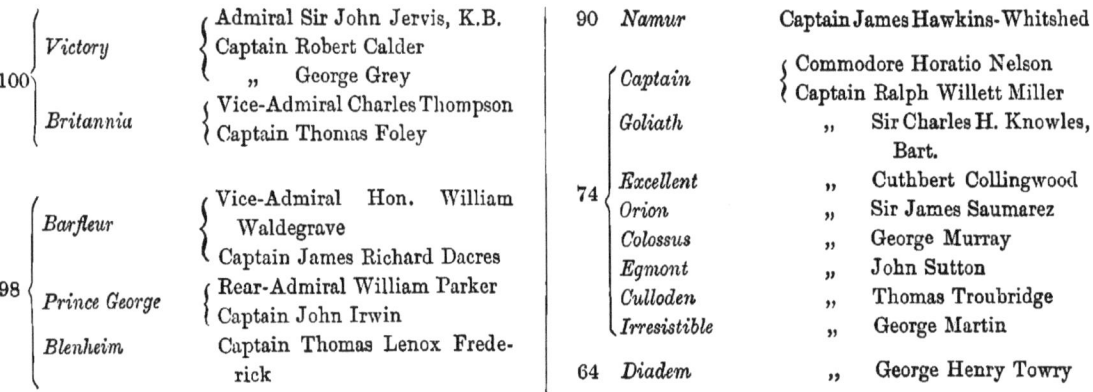

100	Victory	Admiral Sir John Jervis, K.B. / Captain Robert Calder / ,, George Grey	90	Namur	Captain James Hawkins-Whitshed
	Britannia	Vice-Admiral Charles Thompson / Captain Thomas Foley		Captain	Commodore Horatio Nelson / Captain Ralph Willett Miller
98	Barfleur	Vice-Admiral Hon. William Waldegrave / Captain James Richard Dacres		Goliath	,, Sir Charles H. Knowles, Bart.
	Prince George	Rear-Admiral William Parker / Captain John Irwin	74	Excellent	,, Cuthbert Collingwood
				Orion	,, Sir James Saumarez
	Blenheim	Captain Thomas Lenox Frederick		Colossus	,, George Murray
				Egmont	,, John Sutton
				Culloden	,, Thomas Troubridge
				Irresistible	,, George Martin
			64	Diadem	,, George Henry Towry

Also the following frigates and sloops:—

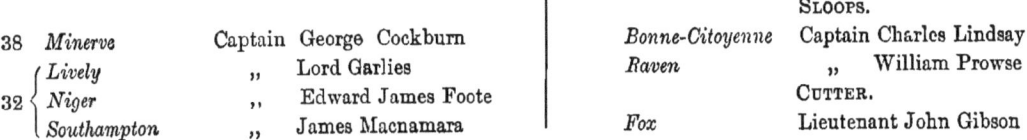

38	Minerve	Captain George Cockburn			Sloops.
32	Lively	,, Lord Garlies		Bonne-Citoyenne	Captain Charles Lindsay
	Niger	,, Edward James Foote		Raven	,, William Prowse
	Southampton	,, James Macnamara			Cutter.
				Fox	Lieutenant John Gibson

On the 13th February Sir John Jervis was joined by the *Minerve*, Captain George Cockburn, then bearing the broad pennant of Commodore Nelson, and having on board Sir George Elliot, late Governor of Corsica. The *Minerve* had been chased by two Spanish ships-of-the-line soon after quitting Gibraltar, and sighted the enemy's fleet. This was welcome news to the officers and men of the British fleet, who were longing to engage, and Commodore Nelson, who was anxious to fight in the line of battle, shifted his broad pennant into the *Captain*, 74, Captain Miller. The exact strength of the Spanish fleet was not ascertained, but it was known to exceed twenty sail-of-the-line, while of Jervis's fifteen line-of-battle-ships, two, the *Colossus* and *Culloden*, had come into collision and sustained considerable damage; indeed, few officers except Captain Troubridge, commanding the *Culloden*, would have refrained from going into port to repair damages. More than once during the night of the 13th the signal guns of the Spanish fleet were clearly audible, and at 6.30 the *Culloden* made the signal for five sail, and later twenty-five sail-of-the-line were descried through the haze. The following was the composition of the Spanish fleet of twenty-seven sail, under the orders of Admiral Don Josef de Cordova:—

also twelve frigates and a brig.

There was no hesitation or doubt as to the result of the impending battle among the hearts of oak that manned our ships, who had confidence in such officers as Nelson, Troubridge, Saumarez, Towry, Calder, and Collingwood.

Much of the success of the British Navy during the Revolutionary war was due to the vigilance and professional ability of Sir John Jervis. The officers and crews of the Mediterranean fleet had been trained under his own eye, and the ships were in a remarkably efficient condition, for the veteran admiral was a strict disciplinarian, and insisted, above all, on good gunnery. Nelson said, "I have never seen any fleet that could compare with those ships that served in the Mediterranean. In comparison with the officers brought up in that school all others betray a want of resources that surprises me." Sir John Jervis was the greatest naval reformer of his day, and it should never be forgotten that the officers and men whom Nelson led to victory were trained under his supervision. On the paramount importance of good gunnery, a falling off in which, more than anything else, led to our disasters in the war with the United States in 1812, he would say to his captains, "It is of the greatest importance that our crews should be perfect in the use of their guns; I therefore wish that every day, whether in harbour or at sea, a general or partial exercise should take place on board every ship in the squadron."

Admiral Jervis, whose impatience had been extreme lest the enemy should escape him, at daybreak summoned his captains on board the *Victory* to receive his final instructions, when he said to them, "I wish we were at this moment well up with the Spaniards. A victory is all important to England, and we could never be better prepared to meet the enemy than now."

At early dawn, as the strength of the Spanish fleet became gradually apparent, Captain Calder successively reported their numbers, "Ten sail-of-the-line, Sir John." "Very well, Sir." "Fifteen sail-of-the-line, Sir John." "Very well, Sir." "Twenty sail-of-the line, Sir John." "Twenty-seven sail-of-the-line, Sir John; against such a force is it advisable to— ?"

"Enough, Sir, enough," broke in the veteran admiral, " were there fifty sail-of-the-line, Sir, I'd go through them all."

There breathed the true spirit that has made old England invincible on the sea; and so thought Captain Halliwell, a passenger on board the *Victory*, who, forgetting the requirements of naval etiquette, in his delight actually clapped the redoubtable admiral and rigid disciplinarian on the shoulder, exclaiming, "That's right, Sir John! and by heaven we'll give them a good licking."

The British fleet stood straight for the opening between the two divisions of the Spanish fleet in the following order, Captain Troubridge having the honour of leading the van :—*Culloden, Blenheim, Prince George, Orion, Colossus, Irresistible, Victory, Egmont, Goliath, Barfleur, Britannia, Namur, Captain, Diadem,* and *Excellent.* The action was commenced at 11.30 A.M. by the *Culloden*, which, having arrived abreast of the Spanish weather division, opened fire with her starboard guns, to which the enemy's van ships replied, as they brought their guns to bear.

It is related that as the commander-in-chief marked the seamanlike manner in which the gallant captain of the *Culloden* led the attack, he exclaimed :—"Look at Troubridge, does he not manœuvre as if all England was looking at him? Would to God all England were present to appreciate, as I do, the gallant captain of the *Culloden*."

At this time, five ships of the Spanish weather division stood across the head of the British line, and joined the five forming the lee division, which had hauled sharp up on the port tack to weather the whole British fleet, the two divisions being thus eight and sixteen respectively, taking the actual strength of the Spanish fleet at the lower number of twenty-four sail, at which Sir John Jervis places it in his official account.* A few minutes after noon, the *Culloden*, having passed the sternmost of the Spanish weather ships, tacked to port, as did in succession the *Blenheim, Prince George, Orion, Colossus*— which, having her fore and fore-topsail yards and her fore-topmast shot away, was compelled to wear—and *Irresistible*, when the last-named became exposed to the fire of the two leading ships of the lee division, which had shortly before put about on the port tack, and stood towards the head of that portion of the British line still on the starboard tack. Just before the *Victory*, the ship next to the *Irresistible*, tacked, Vice-Admiral Moreno, commanding the lee division, steered so as to cut the British line ahead of the flagship, but was thwarted by the rapid advance of the *Victory*, which forced the three-decker bearing his flag, supposed to be the *Principe de Asturias*, to tack close under her lee, pouring in a tremendous raking broadside as she did so. All the ships of the division now bore up, except the *Oriente*, which continued on the port tack, and succeeded in joining her van.

About 1 P.M. came a critical period in the action, which caught the observant eye of Commodore Nelson, who acted with his wonted decision. The rearmost ship of that part of the British line which was still on the starboard tack had advanced so far ahead as to leave an open space to leeward of the Spanish weather division, then passing in the contrary direction, when the advanced ships of the latter bore up together in order to join the lee division. Nelson, whose ship, the *Captain*, was in the rear of the line, and had not yet fired a shot, divined the object of Admiral de Cordova, and acting up to the spirit, if not the letter, of the commander-in-chief's signal, then flying, "to take suitable stations for mutual support, and engage the enemy as coming up in succession," directed Captain Miller to wear the *Captain*. This was quickly done, and the British seventy-four, passing between the *Diadem* and *Excellent*, the two rearmost ships, ran athwart the bows of the huge four-decker, the *Santissima Trinidada*, the most advanced ship, being sixth from the rear, the other five being the three-deckers *San Josef, Salvador del Mundo*, the *San Nicholas*, 80, *San Isidro*, 74, and another three-decker, believed to be the *Mexicano*. The *Captain* opened fire on the *Santissima Trinidada* and the ships near her, when, seeing the manœuvre frustrated, and other ships

* There is some discrepancy as to the actual strength of the Spanish fleet. It is given as 25 sail-of-the-line in the log of the *Victory*, and in Sir John Jervis' letter, but Captain Brenton, in his "Naval History," gives the number at 27, and quotes the admiral's letter at that figure. Before the action commenced, one Spanish two-decker crowded sail to escape, so that the number actually engaged was probably 24 sail, as opposed to the British 15.

advancing against him, Admiral de Cordova gave up the design of running to leeward of the British fleet, and hauled upon the port tack. Nelson had been nobly seconded by the *Culloden*, which took off some of the fire of the four-decker and her consorts, as did also the *Blenheim*, thus giving him time to repair damages and replenish his shot-lockers.

Meantime, the *Victory*, after disposing of the *Principe de Asturias*, tacked to port, followed by the *Barfleur*, *Namur*, *Egmont*, and *Goliath*, and stood to windward of the Spanish fleet, which was already in confusion. The *Excellent*, being now ahead of the weather division, at 2.15, in compliance with a signal from the flagship, advanced to pass through the enemy's line, if the term could be applied to the broken squadrons, and within twenty minutes had arrived abreast of the disabled Spanish three-decker, *Salvador del Mundo*, which she engaged for a few minutes, and then passed on to the *San Isidro*, which had lost her three topmasts, both ships having suffered severely from the accurate fire of the *Captain* and *Culloden* and, at a later period, of the *Prince George*, *Orion*, and other ships. The *San Isidro* was the first to strike to Captain Collingwood, and at 3 o'clock, the *Salvador del Mundo*—which also lost her topmasts, having been hotly engaged with the *Irresistible* and *Diadem*, when these ships took up their stations on her weather bow and lee quarter—struck her flag to the *Victory*, which was about to rake the ship as she passed under her stern. Pushing on into the thick of the fight, Captain Collingwood closely engaged the *San Nicholas*, 80, which had lost her fore-topmast in the hot action with the *Captain*. Indeed, it was time that Commodore Nelson should receive support, for he wrote:—"The *Captain* had lost her fore-topmast; she had not a sail, shroud, or rope left her which was not shot away; and she was incapable of further service in the line or in chase." Collingwood interposed his ship between the *San Nicholas* and the disabled British seventy-four, thus allowing the harassed crew a respite to replenish their lockers, and, pouring in a broadside at a range of ten feet, stood on ahead. In luffing up to avoid the *Excellent*, the 80-gun ship ran foul of the *San Josef*, 112, which had already lost her mizen-mast, under the fire of the ubiquitous *Captain*, and of the *Culloden*, *Blenheim*, and *Prince George*, which had all engaged her in succession, the latter having inflicted most of the damage.

In luffing up close to the wind, the *Captain* carried away her fore-topmast, which had been shot through, upon which Nelson, taking into consideration her helpless condition, her wheel having been shot away, and also her sails, shrouds, and rigging, resolved to board the *San Nicholas* as the only alternative. Firing her port broadside into the two-decker at 20 yards range, which was returned with spirit, the *Captain* suddenly put her helm hard-a-starboard, and, on coming to, hooked with her port cathead the starboard quarter-gallery of the *San Nicholas*.

What ensued is best told in Nelson's own words:—"The soldiers of the 69th, with an alacrity which will ever do them credit, and Lieutenant Pearson, of the same regiment, were almost the foremost in this service. The first man who jumped into the enemy's mizen-chains was Captain Berry, late my first lieutenant (Captain Miller was in the act of going also, but I directed him to remain), and he was supported from our spritsail-yard, which hooked in the mizen rigging. A soldier of the 69th regiment having broke the upper quarter gallery window, I jumped in myself and was followed by others as fast as possible. I found the cabin doors fastened, and some Spanish officers fired their pistols; but, having broke open the doors, the soldiers fired; and the Spanish brigadier (commodore with a distinguishing pennant) fell, as he was retreating to the quarter-deck. I pushed immediately onwards for the quarter-deck; where I found Captain Berry in possession of the poop, and the Spanish ensign hauling down. I passed with my people and Lieutenant Pearson, on the larboard gangway, to the forecastle, where I met two or three Spanish officers, prisoners to my seamen; they delivered me their swords. A fire of pistols, or muskets, opening from the admiral's stern-gallery of the *San Josef*, I directed the soldiers to fire into her stern; and calling to Captain Miller, ordered him to send more men into the *San Nicholas*, and directed my people to board the first-rate, which was done in an instant, Captain Berry assisting me in the main chains. At this moment, a Spanish officer looked over the quarter-deck rail and said they surrendered. From this most welcome intelligence, it was not long before I was on the quarter-deck, where the Spanish captain, with a bow, presented me his sword, and said the admiral was dying of his wounds. I asked him, on his honour, if the ship was surrendered. He declared she was; on which I gave him my hand, and desired him to call on his officers and ship's company, to tell them of it; which he did. And on the quarter-deck of a Spanish first-rate, extravagant as the story may seem, did I receive the swords of vanquished Spaniards, which, as I received, I gave to William Fearney, one of my bargemen, who put them, with the greatest *sang froid*, under his arm. I was surrounded by Captain Berry, Lieutenant Pearson, of the 69th regiment, John Sykes, John Thompson, Francis Cooke, all old *Agamemnon's*; and several other brave men, seamen and soldiers. Thus fell these ships."

Few more intrepid actions are recorded in history than this, by which a seventy-four carried by boarding two ships of superior force, and every Englishman is familiar with the picture representing the immortal Nelson, on the deck of the *San Josef* receiving, and handing over to the nearest pig-tailed seaman, the swords of the Spanish officers. It should, however, be noted that the *San Josef* was closely engaged by the *Prince George* at the time she got foul of the *San Nicholas*, and Admiral Parker's flagship continued to fire on both ships until she was hailed from the *Captain* that they had struck.

Meantime the *Excellent* engaged the *Santissima Trinidada*, then hotly attacked by the *Blenheim*, *Orion*, and *Irresistible*, and after sustaining for an hour the concentrated fire of these ships, during which she lost her fore and mizen-masts and was otherwise much crippled, Admiral de Cordova surrendered by hoisting an English flag, but was saved by the lee division and some others bearing down to his assistance. The *Victory*, observing the approach of these ships, eleven sail in all, about 3.40 o'clock, signalled the fleet to form a line in her wake, and for the frigates to take the prizes in tow, and soon after, all firing ceased.

The only ship in the British fleet that lost a mast was the *Captain*, while the *Colossus* suffered considerably aloft, having lost her fore-yard, and the *Culloden* had her fore and main-masts, as also her main-topmast and other spars, shot through. The *Captain* had many shot-holes in her hull, and the *Culloden* had her boats shot to pieces, and her hull was so much damaged that she was very leaky. The *Blenheim*, likewise, suffered greatly in her hull, having received 105 shots, many at the water's edge, and two of her ports were knocked into one by the fire of the enemy's ships, five of which were at one time engaged with her. Her masts, bowsprit, and yards were much cut up, and she had 12 men killed and three officers and 46 seamen and marines wounded. The *Captain* lost Major Morris, of the marines, a midshipman, 19 seamen and three soldiers killed, and 56 of all ranks were wounded, including Commodore Nelson—who received a contusion in the groin from the effects of which he never recovered—the boatswain and a midshipman. Among the other ships the chief sufferers were the *Excellent*, with her boatswain and ten men killed, and one officer and 11 seamen and marines wounded; and the *Culloden*, which lost a lieutenant of marines and nine men killed, and 47 wounded. The total loss on board the fleet was 73 killed and 227 wounded, exclusively of the slightly wounded, who were not enumerated in the return.

According to the Spanish account the *Santissima Trinidada* lost upwards of 200 killed and wounded, but the loss in the other ships was not known, except on board the four prizes. Of them, the *Salvador del Mundo*, which had lost her three topmasts, had five officers and 37 men killed, and three officers and 121 wounded; the *San Isidro*, whose three topmasts were also shot away, lost four officers and 25 men killed, and eight officers and 55 wounded; the *San Josef*, which had lost her mizen-mast and main-topmast, had two officers and 44 seamen killed, and five officers and 91 wounded. The casualties of the *San Nicholas* were even heavier. This 80-gun ship, whose fore-topmast was shot away in the action, had no less than four officers and 140 of her crew killed, and eight officers and 51 wounded. Thus the loss in the four prizes alone amounted to 261 killed and 342 wounded. The Spaniards acknowledge that ten of their ships, exclusive of those captured, suffered materially, chief among them being the flagship and the three-deckers, *Principe de Asturias* and *Mexicano*.

The battle fought on St. Valentine's Day was, in many ways, memorable, and chiefly so for the intrepidity of Sir John Jervis, in attacking, with 15 sail-of-the-line, a fleet of 24 battle ships, and for the dash with which Commodore Nelson, who was the true hero of the day, carried into effect his memorable manœuvre of wearing out of the line in order to engage the four-decker, and prevent the Spanish commander-in-chief and his advanced ships from joining the lee division. Sir John Jervis knew that he might rely on his officers and men in attacking so greatly superior a force,* for while the former were trained to a high pitch of excellence, the Spanish ships, with all their advantage in numbers and weight of metal, were manned chiefly by soldiers and pressed landsmen, who had no stomach for the fight. A word of praise is due to Captain Troubridge, commanding the *Culloden*, the leading ship of the British fleet, and, to Captain Collingwood, of the *Excellent*, that truly noble specimen of a British naval officer. Two finer seamen the navy never possessed.

The rival fleets lay to during the night of the 15th February repairing damages, and when daylight broke, they were discovered formed in line of battle on opposite tacks, but though the Spanish fleet, consisting of 22 sail, had the weather-gage, they made no effort to renew the battle. On the following day the British fleet, with its prizes, anchored in Lagos Bay, in Portuguese waters, and on the 23rd made sail for the Tagus.

* The six three-deckers in the Spanish fleet were all larger than the *Ville de Paris*, the biggest ship in the British Navy, and the *Victory*, the largest in Sir John Jervis's fleet.

The greatest exultation prevailed at home on receipt of the news of the victory. Sir John Jervis was raised to the peerage as Baron Jervis of Meaford and Earl St. Vincent, after the promontory off which he achieved his victory, with a pension of £3,000 a year; Vice-Admiral Thompson and Rear-Admiral Parker were created baronets, and Vice-Admiral Hon. W. Waldegrave received a lucrative appointment abroad. Commodore Nelson was offered a baronetcy, but preferred the ribbon of the Bath, a distinction more coveted, because more rare, in those days.

In his public letter, Sir John Jervis had not mentioned any officer for special praise, because, he said, if all had not been equally prominent, all were equally desirous of being foremost in the honourable rivalry of battle, but in a private letter to the Admiralty, he did justice to the heroism of Nelson, and paid the tribute of praise to the conduct of some of his captains. He had previously, in person, made his acknowledgments to Nelson for his important share in the victory. It is related that when the latter presented himself on board the flagship, Sir John embraced him, and refused to accept the sword of the Spanish vice-admiral. "Keep it," he said, "it justly belongs to you who took it from your prisoner." Upon Captain Calder directing his attention to Nelson's evolution as a disobedience of orders, the veteran admiral sarcastically replied, "I saw it, and if ever you commit such a breach of orders, depend upon it you shall be forgiven."

This officer, who held the post of Captain of the Fleet, also received the distinction of K.B., and all the lieutenants were promoted. The thanks of Parliament were voted to the fleet, and gold medals were conferred on the flag officers and captains. The brave but unfortunate Spanish admiral, on the other hand, was degraded by his Government from his rank in the navy for his want of success; his second in command, Count Morales, and the captains of the four captured ships were al deprived of their rank, but Admiral Winthuyson, more fortunate, died of the wounds he had received on board the *San Josef*.

Earl St. Vincent, having his flag in the *Ville de Paris*, of 110 guns, quitted Lisbon on the 31st March, with his fleet, now increased to 21 sail-of-the-line, and arrived off Cadiz, where lay the Spanish fleet, under Admiral Massaredo, numbering 28 sail, now reported fit for sea. Not succeeding in inducing the Spanish admiral to venture out of port, his lordship resolved to bombard Cadiz, as much to give occupation to his seamen, and divert them from following the example of the mutinous ships' crews at the Nore and Spithead, as for any expectation he entertained of effecting a great success. To Rear-Admiral Sir Horatio Nelson, who commanded the in-shore squadron, was entrusted the duty, and everything being in readiness, the *Thunder*, bomb-vessel, Lieutenant Gourley, took her station near the tower of San Sebastian, within 2,500 yards of the town, then garrisoned by 4,000 men, and defended on the sea face by 70 guns and eight large mortars. The *Thunder*, which was supported by the gunboats, launches, and barges of the fleet, under Nelson's immediate command, commenced to throw her shells with great precision, until an injury received by her thirteen-inch mortar compelled her to withdraw. On observing this, a number of Spanish gunboats and armed launches sallied forth to try and effect her capture, under Don Miguel Tyrason, when a desperate hand-to-hand conflict ensued between the Spanish commandant's barge, manned by 26 seamen, and that of Sir Horatio Nelson, with a crew of only ten, exclusive of Captain Fremantle and his coxswain, John Sykes, one of his old "*Agamemnon's.*"

Steering alongside the British admiral's barge the Spanish commandant tried to carry it by boarding, but was repulsed after a severe struggle, the most desperate, according to Nelson's account, in which he had ever been engaged. Twice the British admiral narrowly escaped death, on one occasion his devoted coxswain actually interposing his own head to receive the sword cut intended for his beloved master. At length when 18 out of the crew of 26 Spaniards had been killed, and Don Miguel Tyrason and the remainder wounded, the Spanish commander surrendered his sword to his illustrious conqueror. The other Spanish boats were driven back to the walls of Cadiz, leaving in the possession of the British seamen, two mortar-boats, beside the commandant's launch, with many prisoners. The loss in the British boats was only one killed and 20 wounded, including (besides the gallant Sykes,* who was severely wounded) Captain Fremantle, three lieutenants, a master's mate, and a midshipman. On the night of the 5th July, under Nelson's directions, Cadiz was bombarded a second time by the *Thunder, Terror, and Stromboli*, bomb-vessels, the covering ships being the *Theseus*, 74, Captain Miller, and the frigates *Terpsichore*, Captain Richard Bowen, one of the most promising officers in the Navy, and *Emerald*, Captain Waller. Much loss was caused both in the town and among the shipping, and the British and Spanish gunboats and launches again came into collision, with considerable loss to the enemy, while the British casualties were three killed and five officers and 11 men wounded.

* This typical British man-o'-war's-man, who always stood by his beloved master in the hour of danger, was killed later on by the explosion of a shell.

Under orders from Lord St. Vincent, Sir Horatio Nelson now undertook an attack on the town of Santa Cruz, in the island of Teneriffe, where it was rumoured a richly-freighted Manilla galleon had taken shelter. On the 29th of the preceding May, a gallant exploit had been performed at Santa Cruz, when the boats of the British frigates *Minerve* and *Lively*, under the command of Lieutenant Thomas Masterman Hardy, senior lieutenant of the *Minerve*, boarded and cut out, under a heavy musketry fire, the French brig *Mutine*, of 16 guns and having a crew of 113 men. After capturing the brig, the lightness of the wind required that she should be towed out by the boats, and this was done under an unremitting fire from the batteries, and from a large ship lying in the roads. In this brilliant affair the British loss was only 15 wounded, including Lieutenant Hardy and Mr. Edgar, midshipman.

On the 20th July, Admiral Nelson arrived at Santa Cruz, with the following ships, except the *Leander*, which joined him a few days later, in time to participate in the action:—

74	*Theseus*	Rear-Admiral Sir Horatio Nelson, K.B.	38	*Seahorse*	Captain Thomas Francis Fremantle
		Captain Ralph Willett Miller	36	*Emerald*	„ John Waller
	Culloden	„ Thomas Troubridge	32	*Terpsichore*	„ Richard Bowen
	Zealous	„ Samuel Hood		*Fox*, Cutter	Lieutenant John Gibson
50	*Leander*	„ Thomas Boulden Thompson			And a mortar-boat.

The enterprise in which Nelson had embarked was considered to be so desperate, that the Governor of Gibraltar declined to permit any of his soldiers to take part in it; but Nelson had reduced Bastia without the co-operation of the military commandant, and doubtless expected to be equally successful at Santa Cruz, where, moreover, Admiral Blake had achieved one of his most striking victories, the remembrance of which must have nerved him to rival his great predecessor. Having reconnoitred the place, the natural strength of which was increased by strong batteries, and made all his arrangements, Nelson decided to land about 1,100 seamen and marines, under the command of Captain Troubridge.

On the night of the 20th, the three frigates, accompanied by the cutter and mortar-boat, with the boats of the squadron, stood close in to land the men, but a gale of wind and a strong current prevented the boats from reaching the point of debarkation. The attempt was accordingly deferred until the 22nd, when the squadron stood in for the town, and the frigates landed the men, but owing to calms and contrary currents, the ships-of-the-line were unable to co-operate by battering a fort which commanded the town, and the attempt was abandoned for that day. But Nelson was determined to persevere, and at length, at 11 P.M. on the night of the 24th, about 1,100 seamen and marines, under the personal command of the admiral, embarked in the boats of the squadron, which lay some miles off, and other small craft, and pushed off for the shore. It was a desperate undertaking, owing to the darkness and the inclement weather, and it need scarcely be said that its failure was due to no want of gallantry on the part of the officers and men. About 1.30 in the morning, the *Fox*, cutter, which carried 180 men, accompanied by the admiral's barge and some boats, including those in which Captains Fremantle and Bowen had embarked, reached without discovery within gun-shot of the mole-head, when suddenly a heavy fire was opened from 30 to 40 guns, and from a strong body of troops drawn up on shore to receive the invaders.

A scene of death and carnage now ensued. An unlucky shot struck the *Fox*, which instantly sank, carrying to a watery grave 97 fine fellows, including her commander. Nelson was hit by a grape-shot in the elbow, shattering the joint, as he was in the act of drawing his sword and stepping on shore. He became insensible, and was taken back to his ship by his stepson, Lieutenant Nisbet, who saved his life by stanching the flow of blood. Captain Bowen's boat was sunk by another shot, and several of his men were killed. But notwithstanding these losses, the remainder of the party landed and carried the mole-head in the most gallant manner, though defended by over 300 men, with six 24-pounders. Spiking these guns, the seamen and marines continued to advance, but encountered a heavy fire from the citadel and the houses at the end of the mole, under which they suffered severely, among those who here met their deaths being Captain Richard Bowen and his first lieutenant, Mr. George Thorpe. In the meantime Captains Troubridge and Waller, with some of the boats, had missed the mole and landed under a battery close to the citadel, but the surf had wetted the ammunition in the men's pouches. Nevertheless the gallant captains of the *Culloden* and *Emerald*, collecting the crews of those boats that had effected a landing, boldly pushed on to the square of the town, the place of rendezvous appointed by Nelson, and Captain Troubridge actually had the audacity to send a sergeant of marines, with two gentlemen of the town, to summon the citadel to surrender, though the loss of the scaling ladders in the surf prevented any attempt to enforce the alternative of an attack. The sergeant did not return, and after waiting for an hour, Captain Troubridge marched to join Captains Hood and Miller, who had landed with a small party, the entire detachment now numbering 340 men. It was determined to make an attempt on the citadel without the ladders, but by this time daybreak discovered their weakness to the enemy, numbering upward of 8,000 Spaniards, who were approaching on all sides. Under these circumstances, the boats being all stove in by the surf, and the ammunition damaged, Captain Troubridge sent Captain Hood to treat for terms, which included the embarkation without molestation of his men, while he undertook on behalf of the British admiral, that the squadron should make no further attack on the town, or any of the Canary Islands. The Spanish governor acceded to the conditions, which were assuredly as favourable as men in the desperate condition of the English could have expected, and furnished the detachment with boats in which to embark, as well as a ration of biscuit and wine, and with great humanity caused the wounded to be removed to the hospital, and intimated to Admiral Nelson that he was at liberty to purchase provisions for the squadron under his command.

The total British loss in this ill-starred expedition was 141 killed and drowned, and 105 wounded and missing. Many officers of distinction fell, including Captain Bowen,* whose loss was irreparable to the country, four lieutenants, and two marine officers, and the wounded included Captains Fremantle and Thompson. "Of the survivors," says a writer, "no one was more severely wounded than Nelson himself. His arm was frightfully shattered, and the loss of blood which the wound occasioned might have proved fatal, had it not been for the presence of mind of his stepson, Lieutenant Nisbet, who was in the boat with him, and who bound up the wound with handkerchiefs, and, collecting four or five seamen, launched a boat and conveyed him back to the ship. Yet suffering and weak as Nelson was, he stopped the boat on her way, to aid the drowning crew of the *Fox*, and with his remaining hand himself saved many who were still struggling in the water, greatly increasing the pain and danger of his wound by these exertions. On reaching the *Theseus* his arm was amputated, but he did not allow the loss of the limb to interrupt his exertions for a single day. In a few days he even spoke of himself as quite recovered, but the hurry in which the operation had been performed had caused some mismanagement in taking up the arteries, which subsequently caused him severe suffering." Nelson rejoined Lord St. Vincent at Cadiz on the 16th August, and shortly afterwards proceeded to England for the recovery of his health, but the year expired before he was able again to report himself fit for service.

Throughout the year 1797 the British flag was scarcely seen in the Mediterranean,

* Nelson begged Earl Spencer, then First Lord of the Admiralty, to cause a monument to be erected to his memory in St. Paul's, and in his despatch said of him that "a more enterprising, able, and gallant officer does not grace his Majesty's service."

and Napoleon added the Republic of Genoa to the possessions of France, and conceded to Austria, by the treaty of Campo Formio, Istria, Dalmatia, and the Republic of Venice, which had existed for fourteen centuries. In June, Admiral Brueys, under the orders of Buonaparte, sailed from Toulon with six battle ships and several frigates, and took possession of Corfu and the Ionian Islands.

A victory scarcely less important or glorious than that gained by Sir John Jervis at St. Vincent, was achieved by Admiral Duncan over the Dutch fleet off Camperdown. This gallant admiral had long watched the enemy's ships at the Texel, and continued the blockade, even when the mutiny of his ships reduced his fleet to his flagship and the *Adamant*. Gradually Admiral Duncan was joined by his ships, but early in October he retired to Yarmouth to refit and take in provisions, leaving a small squadron of observation under Captain Trollope, off the Dutch coast. Early in the morning of the 9th an armed lugger brought intelligence that the enemy had quitted the Texel, and before noon the British fleet were at sea.

The following were the ships of Admiral Duncan's fleet:—

74	*Venerable*	Admiral Adam Duncan / Captain William George Fairfax		*Lancaster*	Captain	John Wells
	Monarch	Vice-Admiral Richard Onslow / Captain Edward O'Brien		*Ardent*	„	Richard Rundell Burgess
	Russel	„ Henry Trollope	64	*Veteran*	„	George Gregory
	Montagu	„ John Knight		*Director*	„	William Bligh
	Bedford	„ Sir Thomas Byard		*Monmouth*	„	James Walker
	Powerful	„ William O'Brien Drury	50	*Isis*	„	William Mitchell
	Triumph	„ William Essington		*Adamant*	„	William Hotham
64	*Belliqueux*	„ John Inglis	40	*Beaulieu*	„	Francis Fayerman
	Agincourt	„ John Williamson	28	*Circe*	„	Peter Halkett
				Martin, sloop,	„	Hon. Charles Paget

The Dutch fleet was sighted at 8.30 on the morning of the 11th October, and was soon made out to consist of the following 21 ships and four brigs, under the command of Vice-Admiral de Winter.

74	*Vryheid* / *Jupiter* / *Brutus* / *States-General*	64	*Haarlem* / *Hercules* / *Leyden* / *Wassenaer*	44	*Mars*
				40	*Monnikendam*
64	*Cerberus* / *Devries* / *Gelykheid*	50	*Alkmaar* / *Batavia* / *Beschemer* / *Delft*	32	*Ambuscade* / *Heldin*
					Two corvettes, and four brigs.

Admiral de Winter, so far from shunning a conflict, on sighting the British ships, squared his yards, and invited their approach. Admiral Duncan shortened sail until some of his bad sailers had come up, and soon after 11, hoisted the signal for each ship to engage her opponent in the enemy's line, and for the van to attack their rear. This signal was replaced about noon by one for close action.

The first ship to cut through the Dutch line was the *Monarch*, leading the port division, which, passing between the *Jupiter* and *Haarlem*, poured a well-directed broadside into each, and luffing up close alongside the 74, engaged her closely. The remaining ships of the port division quickly attacked the enemy's rear. The *Venerable*, flying the commander-in-chief's flag, ported her helm, and running under the stern of the *States-General*, flying the flag of Rear-Admiral Storey, poured into her a broadside, which compelled her to bear up; while the *Triumph*, the *Venerable's* second astern, engaged the *Wassenaer*, holding the same position as regards the *States-General*. The British admiral, meantime, ranged up on the lee side of the *Vryheid*, Admiral de Winter's flagship, which was engaged on the opposite side by the *Ardent* and ahead by the *Bedford*. The Dutch ships *Brutus*, *Leyden*, and *Mars* advanced to the assistance of their heavily-pressed admiral, and inflicted considerable damage on the *Venerable*, which was obliged to haul off and wear round on the starboard tack. So hotly was the flagship engaged that more than once her flag was shot away, upon which a seaman named Jack Crawford, a native of Sunderland, nailed the flag to the main-topgallantmast-head, using a pistol as a hammer.* The *Hercules* now caught fire, and drifted past the hotly-engaged ships, and to save her from being blown up, the crew threw over the gunpowder, which prevented her from participating further in the action, and shortly afterwards she surrendered. The *Wassenaer* struck to the *Triumph*, which turned her attention to the *Vryheid*, and at length the gallant Dutch commander-in-chief, who had received the fire of the *Ardent* and *Director*, as well as of the *Venerable* and *Triumph*, drifted out of the line and struck his colours. The *Jupiter*, which had been the first to engage, also surrendered, and besides these two ships, and the *Hercules* and *Wassenaer*, the trophies

---

* This heroic action has not been forgotten by his townsmen, and many years afterwards was commemorated by them. On the 8th April, 1890, Jack Crawford having died in his native town in 1831, a statue was unveiled by Lord Camperdown, descendant of Admiral Duncan, in memory of the gallant seaman, bearing the following inscription :— "The sailor who so heroically nailed Admiral Duncan's flag to the main-topgallantmast of his Majesty's ship *Venerable* in the glorious action off Camperdown on October 11th, 1797. Crawford was born at the Pottery Bank, Sunderland, 1775, and died in his native town in 1831, aged 56 years. Erected by public subscription." A monster procession of trade societies, military and Volunteer forces in the town, and a detachment of 300 bluejackets sent by the Admiralty and marines, paraded the principal streets, and then went to the park. Lord Camperdown delivered an interesting and appropriate address. The statue is the work of Percy Wood, and the height of the group is 20ft. 7in. The sculptor has selected the moment when Jack has ascended the mast of the *Venerable* as far as the truck, which rests on the summit of the pedestal. The colours are thrown over his left shoulder, and in his right hand he holds a pistol, with the butt end of which he drives in the nails.

of victory included the 64's *Devries*, *Gelykheid*, and *Haarlem*, the 50-gun ships *Alkmaar* and *Delft*, and the frigates *Monnikendam* and *Ambuscade*. The other ships of the Dutch fleet wore out of the line and escaped, and could not be pursued owing to the shallowness of the water, and the land between Camperdown and Egmont being only five miles distant.

Contrary to their experience in actions with the French and Spanish fleets, the chief damage sustained by the British ships was in the hulls, which were struck in some instances by nearly 100 cannon-shot, necessitating the employment of the pumps to keep them clear of water; but their masts remained intact, and the rigging and sails had suffered but little. Far different was the condition of the captured Dutch ships, which were all either dismasted during the action, or carried their spars away on the passage to an English port. Their hulls also were so riddled with shot-holes that they were rendered useless for further service.

The British loss, owing to the enemy's fire being directed at the hulls, was proportionately heavy. The *Venerable* had 15 seamen and marines killed, and two lieutenants, a marine officer, one midshipman, a master's mate, and 93 seamen and marines wounded. The *Bedford* lost two midshipmen and 28 men killed, and one lieutenant and 40 men wounded. The *Powerful* had 10 killed, and a lieutenant, a marine officer, a midshipman, the boatswain, and 74 men wounded. The *Ardent*, having taken a prominent part in the action, suffered very severely. She had her captain, master, and 39 seamen and marines killed, and two lieutenants, the captain of marines, four midshipmen, master's mate, the captain's clerk, and 99 foremast hands wounded. The *Belliqueux* had one lieutenant, a master's mate, and 23 men killed, and a lieutenant, the captain of marines, one midshipman, and 75 men wounded. The *Triumph* lost 29 men killed, and Captain Essington, two lieutenants, master, a midshipman, and 50 men wounded. Other ships suffered less considerably, and the total loss was, according to the *London Gazette*, 203 killed and 622 wounded, though the committee appointed to relieve the wounded and the families of the slain, placed the loss much higher, the killed being stated at 228, and the wounded (including 16 mortally) at 812.

The loss in the Dutch fleet amounted, according to the official report, to 540 killed and 620 wounded. Admiral de Winter died of disease shortly after his arrival in England, and the three other admirals were all wounded, and the captains of the *Vryheid* and *Wassenaer* died of their wounds.

Though the British fleet had a superiority of force in this sanguinary action, it was so slight as to be of small account, and cannot be considered to have detracted from the merits of Admiral Duncan's victory. According to an elaborate calculation made by James, the rival fleets had each sixteen ships engaged in the line-of-battle, the British broadside was 575 guns to 517 of the enemy, and the crews 8,221 to 7,157.

Scarcely was the action over than the hazy weather which had prevailed was succeeded by a gale of wind, and the *Delft*, which had lost 43 killed and 76 wounded, foundered, carrying with her the greater number of the wounded, and many of her officers and seamen. The *Monnikendam* was also wrecked, but without loss of life, and the *Ambuscade* frigate, being driven on the Dutch coast, was recaptured. The remainder of the prizes were safely brought into port, but as already mentioned, were too much damaged to be serviceable.

Admiral Duncan was created a Baron and a Viscount of Great Britain, by the titles of Baron Duncan of Lundie, and Viscount Duncan of Camperdown. Vice-Admiral Onslow was created a baronet, and Captains Trollope and Fairfax were knighted. Gold medals were also struck to commemorate the victory, and presented to the admirals and captains, and the thanks of both Houses of Parliament were voted to the fleet, while the City of London presented Lord Duncan with its freedom and a sword of the value of two hundred guineas, and the same, with a sword valued at one hundred guineas, to Sir Richard Onslow. As in the victories of Lords Howe and St. Vincent, the first lieutenants of all the ships engaged received promotion to the rank of commander.

During the year 1797, some frigate actions were fought with the usual successful results. On the last day of January, the *Andromache*, 32, Captain Mansfield, encountered an Algerian cruiser, of equal force, which, taking her for a Portuguese frigate, accepted battle, and was captured after an action of forty minutes' duration, with the loss of 66 killed and 50 severely wounded, the greater portion having fallen in an attempt to capture the *Andromache* by boarding, the loss of the latter being only three killed and six wounded.

The French 40-gun frigate, *Résistance*, and *Constance*, 22-gun corvette, were also captured by the British 36-gun frigates *San Fiorenzo*, Captain Sir Harry Neale, and *Nymphe*, Captain John Cooke. Towards the end of February the French ships and two others had landed in Fisgard Bay, on the coast of Wales, some 1,200 galley slaves dressed as soldiers, who surrendered without resistance to a detachment of Militia, under Lord Cawdor. After effecting this ill-advised mission the *Résistance* and *Constance* were returning to Brest, when they were sighted, on the 9th March, by the two British frigates, which formed part of Lord Bridport's fleet, then off Ushant. They brought the *Résistance* to action, within sight of the French fleet in Brest, and forced her to strike her colours after a brief resistance, and the *Constance*, coming up, was also captured, the running action having lasted half an hour. The enemy lost 18 killed and 15 wounded, and the *Constance* had her main-mast and fore-topmast shot away, but the British frigates suffered no damage or loss in either action. The *Résistance* was added to the Navy as a 36-gun frigate, under the name of the *Fisgard*, and the corvette *Constance* retained her name, and mounted 22 guns. Both were useful acquisitions to the service.

While returning from Gibraltar to Algiers, the 14-gun cutter *Viper*, Lieutenant Pengelly, on the 13th March sighted a Spanish 10-gun privateer, to which she gave chase. After a brief run she brought the privateer to action, and captured her after a smart resistance. On the 1st day of April the *Hazard*, 18-gun sloop-of-war, Commander Ruddach, took, after a long chase off the coast of Ireland, the privateer *Hardi*, of 18 guns and 130 men. The *Hazard*, in the preceding December, had captured, after a brief resistance, another French privateer, the *Musette*, of 22 guns and 150 men, for which success Captain Ruddach was promoted to post rank.

Two Spanish frigates were captured on the coast near Cape Trafalgar. These were the *Ninfa* and *Santa Elena*, of 34 guns and 320 men each, bound from Havana to Cadiz, with treasure on board. The *Irresistible*, 74, Captain Martin, and *Emerald*, 36, Captain Berkeley, chased the frigates, which took shelter in Conil Bay, near Cape Trafalgar, and succeeded in landing the treasure by some fishing boats before the British ships, which chased them into the bay, compelled them to surrender after a smart action. The *Ninfa* and *Santa Elena* lost 18 men killed and 30 wounded, and were brought off, though the greater portion of their crews escaped on shore. The *Ninfa* was purchased into the Navy, and received the name of *Hamadryad*.

Some good service was done in July by the 18-gun brig *Sylph*, Commander White, belonging to Sir John Borlase Warren's squadron, while cruising off Ushant. The squadron having chased some French vessels, under convoy of the 28-gun frigate *Calliope*, the latter ran ashore, when the *Sylph* anchored within 150 yards of her, and getting a spring on her cable, fired into her until the frigate was sunk, and six of her convoy were captured or destroyed by the squadron. In the following August,

Commander White engaged a French corvette and brig, which had anchored at the entrance of the river Sable d'Olonne, under the protection of a fort, and inflicted considerable damage on the latter and the corvette, and sunk the brig, her own loss being one officer and two men killed and three wounded. The British frigates *Pomone* and *Jason* joined in the cannonade, and later in the month captured five French merchant vessels near the entrance to the Gironde.

The British frigate *Arethusa*, 44, Captain Woolley, overhauled the French corvette, *Gaieté*, carrying 20 guns and 186 men, which had the temerity to show fight, but was forced to surrender at the end of half an hour. The *Gaieté* being a new ship, was bought into the Navy. The 6-gun schooner *Alexandrian*, Lieutenant Senhouse, when cruising off Martinique, engaged and captured, after a spirited action, the French privateer schooner *Coq*, of 6 guns and 34 men. In the following October the *Alexandrian* chased a schooner, and having brought her to close action, compelled her to haul down her colours at the end of fifty minutes. The prize, which lost 16 men killed and wounded, proved to be the privateer *Epicharis*, mounting 8 guns, and having a complement of 74 men. The 16-gun brig *Penguin*, Captain Pulling, captured, on the 16th August, two brigs, the largest of them named the *Oiseau*, of 18 guns, after a running fight of nearly two hours, and the other, the 14-gun privateer *Express*, of Dartmouth, prize to the *Oiseau*. The exploit was a creditable one to the officers and men of the *Penguin*, who had worked their guns knee-deep in water, as the *Oiseau* alone was her equal in armament and crew. The brig *Pelican*, 18, Lieutenant White, also captured off the Island of St. Domingo the French privateer *Trompeur*, of 12 guns and 78 men, which made a gallant resistance, the yard-arms of the two brigs being locked together. At length the after-part of the *Trompeur* blew up, and she went down, when the captain and sixty of the crew were rescued by the boats of the *Pelican*.

Among other captures was that of the *Hyène*, carrying 24 guns and 230 men—late the British corvette *Hyena*, captured in May, 1793, by the 40-gun frigate *Concorde*,—by the *Indefatigable*, 44, Sir Edward Pellew, and of the privateer *Epervier*, of 16 guns and 145 men, and *Renard*, of 18 guns and 189 men, by the *Cerberus*, 32, Captain Drew. Record should also be made of the gallantry of Mr. Middleton, purser of the 16-gun sloop *Fairy*, who, in her launch having only seven men, brought to action and carried by boarding a French privateer lugger, mounting six small guns and swivels, with a crew of 25 men.

On the other hand we have to chronicle the loss of the 10-gun brig *Growler*, Lieutenant Hollingsworth, having a complement of 50 men, by two privateer luggers, carrying respectively 10 guns and 80 men, and 8 guns and 70 men. The event took place off Dungeness one dark December night. and among the mortally wounded were the commander and his second officer.

A determined action was fought between the British frigate *Phœbe*, Captain Barlow, of 44 guns and 261 men, and the *Néréide*, mounting 36 guns, and having a complement of 330 hands. The action was fought at nightfall at close range, the frigates being at one time aboard each other, but the *Phœbe* got clear, and compelled her adversary to surrender, with the loss of 20 killed and 55 wounded, her own casualties being only three and ten respectively. The *Néréide* was added to the Navy, under her name, and Lieutenant Halliday, first of the *Phœbe*, was promoted to the charge of her with the rank of commander. The last capture in the year, effected on the 29th December, was that of the French corvette *Daphne*, of 20 guns and 276 men, by the British 44-gun frigate *Anson*, Captain Durham. The result was a foregone conclusion from the relative strength of the combatants.

The Navy sustained a loss in the wreck of the 36-gun frigate *Tribune*, Captain Barker. The ship was off Halifax on the 16th November, when the master, instead of waiting for a pilot, expressed his ability to take her in, and receiving permission from the captain, ran the ship on some shoals near the harbour. The *Tribune* got off, making much water, but the wind increasing to a gale, she drove before the storm on to the shore, and went down, leaving upwards of 240 men struggling in the water. During the night those of the crew who took refuge in the rigging, were all washed off one by one, and at length, in the morning, only 12 out of 240 or 250, including some people who had come off to render assistance, with several women and children, were saved, and two of these by the exertions of a lad of thirteen, who put off alone in the raging sea in a skiff, and brought off these seamen clinging in a half-conscious condition to the fore-top.

Of colonial expeditions during the year 1797, Rear-Admiral Harvey commanded one which captured the Spanish island of Trinidad. The squadron, consisting of four ships-of-the-line, two frigates, five sloops, and one bomb-vessel, with some troops under Sir Ralph Abercrombie, sailed from Port Royal, Martinique, on the 4th February, and the island was surrendered without resistance from the Spanish batteries and four sail-of-the-line, three of which and a frigate were set on fire by the enemy and totally destroyed, and the fourth was brought off by the boats of the British squadron. In

March the boats of the 32-gun frigate *Hermione*, Captain Pigot, brought out or burnt three small French privateers and their twelve prizes, which had run aground close to a battery on the west end of the island of Porto Rico, whither Admiral Harvey proceeded with his squadron and some troops to dispossess the Spaniards. The soldiers were landed, and the town was bombarded, but Sir Ralph Abercrombie met with so determined a resistance that the attempt was abandoned with the loss of 225 killed, wounded, and missing.

On the Jamaica station the 74-gun ships *Thunderer*, Captain Ogilvy, and *Valiant*, Captain Crawley, forced the French frigate *Harmonie*, 36, to run ashore, when she was abandoned by her crew, who set her on fire, and she blew up. Shortly after the boats of the frigates *Hermione*, *Quebec*, and *Mermaid* cut out from the small port of Jean Rabel nine vessels which lay under the protection of some batteries, and in the same month of April the boats of the *Magicienne*, 32, and *Regulus*, 44, entered the harbour of Cape Roxo, in the island of St. Domingo, and captured, sunk, or burnt thirteen square-rigged vessels and schooners, and both these exploits were performed without the loss of a man. The same ships captured a battery, and a privateer and four schooners at anchor in Carcasse Bay, which were about to attack the fort of Irois. In this affair the *Magicienne* lost four men killed and nine wounded.

The Channel fleet, under the command of Lord Bridport, was kept up to a great strength throughout the year 1798, owing to fears of the invasion of our coasts. In January a division of twelve sail-of-the-line and three frigates, under Admiral Sir Charles Thompson, sailed for a cruise in the Bay of Biscay; early in April a second division of six sail-of-the-line and three frigates, under Rear-Admiral Sir Roger Curtis, went for a cruise on the coast of Ireland, and a few days later the commander-in-chief himself sailed from Spithead with the remainder of his fleet, making ten ships-of-the-line, and took up his station off Brest.

On the 21st April, the 74-gun ships *Mars*, Captain Alexander Hood, and *Ramillies*, Captain Inman, and the *Jason*, 38, Captain Stirling, sighted three sail off Brest, and singled out the largest of the strangers, which proved to be the *Hercule*, 74, which had been launched at Lorient ten months before, and had only left port twenty-four hours on her first cruise. Her commander was Captain l'Heritier, the same officer who commanded the *America* in Lord Howe's action, a near relative of one of Napoleon's most famous cavalry generals at Waterloo.

The *Ramillies* carried away her fore-topmast and dropped astern, and the *Jason* was out-distanced, but the *Mars* continued the chase, and at 7.30 P.M. the *Hercule*, finding she could not make head against a strong current, anchored at the entrance of the Passage du Raz, about 21 miles from Brest. Laying out a spring abaft, she slewed her starboard broadside round so as to bring it to bear on the *Mars*, which hauled up her courses at 8.45 to engage her. The action was begun half an hour later by a broadside from the *Hercule*, to which a quick rejoinder was given by the *Mars*, which soon after anchored, and dropping astern her port anchor, caught that on the starboard bow of her opponent, the two ships being thus entangled yard-arm to yard-arm. The battle raged furiously, the enemy making two attempts to board the *Mars*, which were, however, repulsed, and at 10.30 the French seventy-four struck her colours.

So close had the ships fought, says James, that the guns on the lower deck of each could not, as usual, be run out, but were obliged to be fired inboard. With the exception of the jib-boom of the *Mars*, neither ship lost a spar, the damage to both ships being confined to the hulls. The *Mars* had her hammocks, boats, and spare spars shot through, and three or four of her first-deck ports unhinged in the collision of the ships; her hull, also, was hit in several places. The *Hercule's* starboard side was riddled from end to end. Several of her ports were unhinged, and in some instances, the spaces between them entirely laid open. The contrast between the two sides of the ship was, indeed, most remarkable; the port side of the *Mars*, which had been slightly injured, was of a bright yellow; while the starboard side of her adversary was burnt as black as a cinder. The five aftermost starboard lower-deck guns of the *Hercule* also were dismounted, and several of the others much damaged.

The loss sustained by the *Mars* in this long and close action was necessarily severe. Out of a crew of 634 men and boys, she had Captain Hood, nephew of Lords Bridport and Hood, the captain of marines, one midshipman, 15 seamen, and four marines killed, three seamen and five marines missing (how is not stated), and her third and fifth lieutenants, one midshipman, 36 seamen, and three marines wounded; total 30 killed and missing, and 60 wounded. The loss of the *Hercule*, whose complement was 680 of all ranks, was differently stated, some accounts putting it as high as 400, but her officers, who may be credited with placing it at as low a figure as possible, allowed that the total of killed and wounded was not less than 290, being more than two-fifths her complement. The victory was very creditable to the officers and men of the *Mars*, as the ships were well-matched, the broadside weight of each being within one pound the same, while the *Hercule* carried 50 more men.

Soon after the conclusion of the action, the *Jason* came and assisted in getting the prize out of the intricate passage in which she had anchored, but it was fortunate the weather was not stormy, or the *Hercule*, with her shattered side, could not have been navigated in safety to Plymouth, which she reached on the 27th April, and was purchased into the Navy under her own name. Lieutenant Butterfield, who brought the *Mars* out of action, received his well-merited promotion.

The Brest fleet did not venture out to sea, but meanwhile, a vast scheme,* worked

* Buonaparte's project, which attests his genius for combination, bears date the 13th April, 1798, and is to the following effect :—In our situation we ought to wage a sure war against England, and we can do so. Whether in peace or war we should expend from forty to fifty millions (francs) on re-organizing our navy. Our army need not be of greater or less strength ; so long as the war obliges England to make immense preparations, that will ruin her finances, and destroy the commercial spirit, and absolutely change the habits and manners of her people. We should employ the whole summer in getting the Brest fleet ready for sea, in exercising the sailors in the Roads, and in completing the ships that are building at Rochefort, Lorient, and Brest. With a little activity in these operations, we may hope to have by the month of September, thirty-five sail-of-the-line in Brest, including the four or five that may then be ready at Lorient and Rochefort. We shall have by the end of the month, in the different ports of the Channel, nearly 200 gun-boats. These must be stationed at Cherbourg, Havre, Boulogne, Dunkirk, and Ostend, and the whole summer employed in inuring the soldiers to the sea. In continuing to allow to the commissions for the coasts of the Channel 300,000 francs per decade (a period of ten days) we shall be enabled to build 200 gun-boats of large dimensions, capable of carrying cavalry. We shall then have, in the month of September, 400 gun-boats at Boulogne, and thirty-five sail-of-the-line at Brest. The Dutch can also have ready, in this interval, twelve sail-of-the-line in the Texel. We have in the Mediterranean two descriptions of line-of-battle ships, twelve of French construction, which, between this and the month of September, may be augmented by two new ships ; and nine of Venetian construction. We may perhaps be able, when the expedition which the Government projects in the Mediterranean is over, to send the fourteen ships to Brest, and to retain in the Mediterranean only the nine Venetian ships, which will give us, in the month of October or November, fifty ships-of-the-line at Brest, and almost an equal number of frigates. We may, perhaps, then be able to transport 40,000 men to any spot in England we wish, by avoiding, however, a naval action, if the enemy should be too strong ; in the meanwhile 40,000 men threaten to put off in the 400 gun-boats and about as many fishing-vessels of Boulogne, and the Dutch fleet and 10,000 men threaten a descent upon Scotland. The invasion of England, put in practice in this manner in the months of November and December, would be almost certain. England would waste herself by immense efforts, but these would not secure her from invasion. In fact, the expedition to the East will oblige England to send six additional ships-of-the-line to India, and perhaps twice as many frigates to the entrance of the Red Sea ; she would be obliged to have from twenty-two to twenty-five ships-of-the-line at the entrance of the Mediterranean, sixty before Brest, and twelve before the Texel, forming a total of 300 line-of-battle-ships, without reckoning those she now has in America and the Indies, and ten or twelve 50-gun ships, with twenty frigates, which she would be obliged to have ready to oppose the invasion from Boulogne. We should always remain masters of the Mediterranean, since we should there have the nine Venetian ships-of-the-line. There would yet be another way to augment our force in this sea ; to oblige Spain to cede three ships-of-the-line and three frigates to the Ligurian Republic. This republic cannot be considered otherwise than as a department of France ; it possesses more than 10,000 excellent seamen. It is politic in France to encourage the Ligurian Republic, and to take care also that it has a few ships-of-the-line. If any difficulties arise about Spain's ceding to us or to the Ligurian Republic three ships-of-the-line, I should think it would be proper for us to sell to the Ligurian Republic three of the nine ships we took from the Venetians, and we should require of them to build three others ; it would be a good squadron, manned with excellent sailors, which we should thus obtain. With the money received from the Ligurians, we ought to build at Toulon three good ships upon our own models ; for ships built after the Venetian plan require as many sailors as a good seventy-four ; and seamen—there is our weak point. As future events may turn out, it would be extremely advantageous to us, that the three republics of Italy, which ought to be equal in force to the King of Naples and Grand Duke of Tuscany, should have a stronger navy than that belonging to the King of Naples."

out by Buonaparte, was in preparation for the invasion of England, while at the same time, he was elaborating his project for the conquest of Egypt, with the ultimate design of wresting India from us, and securing French predominance throughout the East.

An enormous flotilla of gunboats and flat-bottomed boats was constructed in the French Channel ports, under the command of Admiral La Crosse. Early in April a division of this flotilla, consisting of thirty-three boats, embarking a detachment of troops, and some gunboats, made an attempt from Havre on the two small islands of St. Marcouf, lying off the coast of Normandy, which were held by 500 seamen and marines, under Lieutenant Price, of the *Badger*, a small vessel mounting 4 guns. But the flotilla was encountered by the British 38-gun frigates *Diamond*, Sir Richard Strachan, and *Hydra*, Captain Francis Laforey, and took refuge in the Caen River, where it was reinforced by 40 more boats with troops, and seven gun-brigs from Cherbourg, Admiral La Crosse's headquarters. Here the expedition was blockaded for three weeks, when it effected its escape. Taking advantage of a calm, when the squadron defending St. Marcouf, consisting of the *Adamant*, 50, Captain Hotham, *Eurydice*, 24, Captain Talbot, and *Orestes*, 18, Captain Haggitt, were not able to approach within six miles, the enemy, with 52 gunboats and flat-bottomed boats, having, it was said, 6,000 men on board, attacked the garrison at daybreak on the 7th May. The flotilla opened fire at a range of from 300 to 400 yards, to which Lieutenant Price replied with vigour from 17 guns that could be brought to bear, and after a brief action repulsed the enemy with the loss of six or seven boats, which were sunk.

Information having reached the British Government of the preparation of a flotilla at Flushing, for Dunkirk and Ostend, to be employed in the invasion of England, Captain Popham of the *Expedition*, 26, on the 14th May, sailed from Margate, with a squadron of 3 frigates, two 20-gun ships, and 20 sloops, bombs, and gun-vessels, after embarking a detachment of troops, under General Eyre Coote. About 1,140 officers and men with six guns were landed at Ostend before daybreak on the 19th, and some of the gun-brigs and bombs engaged the town batteries, but without inflicting much damage, though the *Wolverine* and *Ark* suffered considerably, and had to retire from the contest. The French troops now mustered in considerable force and attacked the British detachment with such success that General Coote, after losing 65 men, was compelled to surrender at discretion.

On the 30th May the *Hydra*, with the bomb-vessel *Vesuvius*, Captain Fitzgerald, and 12-gun cutter *Trial*, Lieutenant Garrett, sighted off Havre three sail, which proved to be the 36-gun frigate *Confiante*, the corvette *Vesuve*, 20, and an armed cutter, all bound to Cherbourg. The *Hydra*, leaving the *Vesuvius* and *Trial* to pursue the *Vesuve*, chased the frigate, and after a running fight drove her on shore about three leagues from Cherbourg, where she was cannonaded until the fall of the tide obliged Sir Francis Laforey to haul off into deeper water. On the following day, he sent the boats of the *Hydra*, under Lieutenant Acklom, covered by the guns of the *Trial*, to burn the *Confiante*, which had been abandoned by her crew. This service was effectually carried out in the face of a musketry fire from some troops, without the loss of a man, while from the number of slain found in the French frigate, she had suffered severely. The *Vesuve* was also run aground, but her crew got her afloat again, and took her into the River Dive, where a division of gunboats had taken shelter on its return to Havre from the attack on St. Marcouf.

These attacks on the flotillas at Cherbourg, Havre, and other French ports, testified to the admirable vigilance and sleepless energy which animated the officers and men of the squadron employed in preventing the threatened invasion of England. Buonaparte all this time was engaged at Toulon superintending the fitting out of the expedition destined for the conquest of Egypt.

H.M.S. RODNEY.
1st CLASS BATTLE-SHIP.

CHAPTER IX.

French Expeditions to Ireland—Capture of the *Hoche* and Consorts—*Mermaid* and *Loire*—*Anson* and *Loire*—*Fisgard* and *Immortalité*—Buonaparte's Expedition to Egypt—Nelson's Victory over the French Fleet at Aboukir Bay—Capture of the *Leander* by the *Généreux*—Results of the Battle of the Nile.

THE year 1798 is chiefly memorable in our naval annals for the glorious victory achieved by Nelson over the French fleet in Aboukir Bay, known as the Battle of the Nile. But before describing this memorable achievement, we will notice the French expedition to Ireland, a repetition of the abortive attempt made in December, 1796. The outbreak of a rebellion, which bathed that unhappy country in blood, appeared to offer a favourable opportunity for renewing the invasion of Ireland, and two expeditions were organized at Brest and Rochefort. The latter, which was the first to sail, consisted of the *Concorde*, 40, Commodore Savary, the 36-gun frigates *Franchise* and *Médée*, and the *Venus*, 28, on board which were embarked 1,150 soldiers, with four field-pieces, under the command of General Humbert, together with a considerable store of ammunition, arms, and equipments for 3,000 Irish rebels, or patriots, as they were indifferently called, according to the political proclivities of the rival parties.

The expedition sailed on the 6th August, and on the 22nd cast anchor in Killala Bay. The same evening the troops and military stores were landed, with feeble opposition from about 200 soldiers and yeomanry, and the squadron then set sail on its return to Rochefort, which was reached in safety. It is a matter of history that the attempt ended in failure. The bands of the United Irishmen failed to co-operate in sufficient numbers, and after some skirmishing, General Humbert and 843 of his troops surrendered at discretion, at Ballinamuck, on the 8th September, to a British force under Lieutenant-General (afterwards Lord) Lake.

The second expedition from Brest, which sailed on the 16th September, consisted of the *Hoche*, bearing the broad pennant of Commodore Bompart, who commanded the *Embuscade* in her action with the *Boston* earlier in the war, the 40-gun frigates *Immortalité*, *Romaine*, and *Loire*, the 36-gun frigates *Bellone*, *Coquille*, *Embuscade*, *Résolue*, and *Sémillante*, and the schooner *Biche*. At daybreak on the following morning, the French ships were descried by a British squadron of observation, consisting of the 38-gun frigates *Boadicea*, Captain Keats, and *Ethalion*, Captain Countess, and 18-gun brig *Sylph*, Commander White, on which Captain Keats crowded all sail to apprize Lord Bridport, leaving his consorts to watch the movements of the enemy. On the 18th Captain Countess was joined by the *Amelia*, 38, Captain Hon. Charles Herbert, and kept close to the enemy, who tried to throw them off the scent by steering a course as if for the West Indies. There was little wind on the following day, and on the 20th the *Anson*, 44, Captain Durham, joined company. Finding that these artifices had not the desired effect of shaking off the British frigates, Commodore Savary steered a course for the Irish coast, on which Captain Countess detached the *Sylph* to apprize the admiral commanding on that station. Two days after this, on the 25th September, Commodore Bompart sighted about 100 sail of English merchantmen, including some Indiamen, but for some reason suffered them to escape unmolested. The French squadron continued on their course, closely attended by the British frigates, which they tried to shake off by twice chasing them, but ineffectually. On the 4th October the weather came on thick and blowy, when the British squadron lost sight of the French ships.

Meantime, Sir John Borlase Warren, with the 74's *Canada* (flagship) and *Robust*, Captain Thornborough, *Foudroyant*, 80, Sir Thomas Byard, and *Magnanime*, Captain Hon. Michael de Courcy, sailed from Cawsand Bay on the 23rd September, on hearing of the departure of the French expedition from Brest, and on the 10th October was joined off the Donegal coast by the 36-gun frigates *Melampus*, Captain Graham Moore, and *Doris*, Lord Ranelagh, which while at Lough Swilly had received intelligence from the *Sylph* of the destination of the French squadron. On the following day Sir John Warren was joined by the *Ethalion*, when he had under his command three ships-of-the-line and five frigates, and kept a sharp look out for the enemy. Commodore Bompart meanwhile shaped his course so as to land the troops on Lough Swilly, according to instructions, but at noon on the 11th, when he bore up for Tory Island, having, as he thought, quite ridden himself of the persistent British cruisers, his leading ship signalled their approach. Sir John Warren threw out the signal for a general chase, and for the ships " to form in succession as they arrived up with the enemy." A heavy gale set in that evening, during which the *Anson* carried away her mizen-mast, mainyard, and main-topsail-yard, while the *Hoche* lost her main-topmast and fore and mizen-top-gallant-masts, and the *Résolue* sprung a leak. Commodore

Bompart now bore away to the south-west, with the intention of landing his troops at any practicable point on the coast, but at daylight on the 12th found his squadron nearly surrounded by the British ships.

In obedience to a signal from the commodore, the *Robust* edged down towards the rear of the French squadron, which was formed in an irregular single line ahead, followed closely by the *Magnanime*, and on arriving within gunshot range of the *Embuscade* and *Coquille*, received their fire, which the *Robust* returned, and bearing down to leeward of them, ranged alongside of the *Hoche*, with which she maintained a close action of a very determined character.

Meantime the *Magnanime* became exposed to a raking fire from the *Loire*, *Immortalité* and *Bellone*, which, however, soon made sail to escape, when the *Magnanime* took up a raking position ahead of the *Hoche*, which was also soon after subjected to the fire of the *Amelia* on her stern and port quarter. Thus assailed, the French commodore defended his ship with great gallantry until 10.50, when, her rigging being cut to pieces, her masts and hull riddled with shot, five feet of water in her hold, 25 of her guns dismounted, and a great portion of her crew *hors de combat*, he struck her colours, and on the boats of the *Robust* and *Magnanime* taking possession, presented his sword to Lieutenant Charles Dashwood, first of the frigate. Half an hour later, the *Embuscade*, which had received the fire of the *Magnanime*, and from the bow guns of the *Foudroyant*, surrendered to the former frigate, and the *Foudroyant*, *Canada*, *Ethalion*, *Amelia*, and *Melampus* made sail after the rest of the French squadron. The *Loire* and *Immortalité* succeeding in crossing the bows of the *Foudroyant*, the leading ship, but the *Bellone* was tackled by the *Melampus*, and though she got clear, was overtaken by the *Ethalion*, which got abreast of her about 2 P.M. A smart action now ensued, but at the end of two hours, when her masts, rigging and sails were much damaged, and she had five feet of water in her hold, the *Bellone* hauled down her colours, her loss in the action being 20 killed and 45 wounded, though the French accounts place it at 35. The *Coquille*, also, after an hour's chase and a brave resistance, surrendered. Thus the *Hoche* and three frigates were captured, but the remaining five frigates made every effort to escape. In doing so they passed close to the *Anson*, which, owing to the loss of her mizen-mast, had been unable to approach the scene of action. All the French ships exchanged broadsides with the British frigate on passing her, and she suffered severely aloft, having her fore and main-masts, fore-yard, fore-topmast and bowsprit shot through, and sustained the loss of 15 killed and wounded.

The casualties on board the other ships of the British squadron were trifling, except in the case of the *Robust*, which in her close action with the *Hoche* lost 10 killed and her first lieutenant, a marine officer, and 38 men wounded. The French flagship, on the other hand, had no less than 270 killed and wounded out of 1,237 on board her, including soldiers. The *Embuscade* lost 15 killed and 26 wounded, and the *Coquille*, 18 and 31.

The *Robust*, taking the *Hoche* in tow, steered for Lough Swilly, but owing to the injuries their spars had received in the action, the British seventy-four carried away her fore-topmast, and the prize her fore and main-masts. The tow rope parted during the heavy weather, and the *Hoche* was only kept afloat by the united exertions of the prize crew and prisoners. Ultimately the *Doris* hove in sight and taking her in tow, the three ships arrived at Lough Swilly without further adventure. While the *Amelia* and *Magnanime* stood by the *Coquille* and *Embuscade*, the *Ethalion* by the *Bellone*, and the *Anson* had enough to do to provide for her own safety, the *Canada*, *Foudroyant* and *Melampus* overhauled the *Résolue* at 1 A.M., on the 14th October, and after a brief interchange of broadsides, the latter hauled down her colours, having suffered severely from the accurate fire of her opponents. Her main-yard was shot away, and her mizen-mast and main-topmast wounded, and she made four feet of water, but she only lost 10 killed, besides the wounded, out of a total of 500 men on board. The next of the four remaining French frigates that fell to British prowess was the *Loire*. In company with the *Sémillante*, she was sighted by the 38-gun frigate *Revolutionnaire*, Captain Twisden, the *Mermaid* 40, Captain Newman, and 18-gun brig *Kangaroo*, Captain Brace, off the north-west coast of Ireland. While the *Revolutionnaire* chased the *Sémillante*, the *Mermaid* and *Kangaroo* made sail after the *Loire*, 46, and the brig engaged her with her stern-chasers on the 16th, but losing her fore-topmast, was left astern. Early on the following morning the French frigate, finding the *Mermaid* alone, shortened sail, and a severe action at pistol-shot range ensued. The *Loire* lost her fore-topmast and main-topsail-yard, and Captain Newman gave orders to steer athwart her hawse to rake her, when his mizen-mast went over the side, and was quickly followed by his main-topmast. Thus crippled, and with his shrouds, spars, rigging and sails cut to pieces, and the fore and main-masts wounded, Captain Newman felt compelled to discontinue the action, and the *Loire*, making sail, effected her escape. Out of her complement of 208 men, the *Mermaid* lost in this hardly-contested action with a superior enemy three killed (exclusive of the carpenter drowned while stopping a shot-hole outside), and 13 wounded. The *Loire*, whose broadside was nearly double that of her adversary, the relative weight being 442 and 252 pounds, lost heavily, her crew and the soldiers on board her numbering 624. A gale of wind quickly succeeded the action, and the fore-mast of the *Mermaid* went over the side, and the mainsail blew away, when the ship, making much water, fortunately succeeded in reaching Lough Swilly.

But the *Loire* had not yet got clear of the persistent and omnipresent British frigates. At daylight on the following day, the 18th October, she found herself close to leeward of the *Anson*, 44, Captain Durham. Both ships were in a crippled state. The *Loire* had lost her fore and main-topmasts, the latter having carried away during the previous night, and the *Anson*, her mizen-mast and main-yard, her bowsprit and fore-yard having also been shot through in the general action of the 12th. In company with the *Anson* was the *Kangaroo*, which, having been refitted since her previous encounter with the *Loire*, now bore down and again engaged her. The *Anson* had already been engaged for more than an hour with the French frigate, which lost her mizen-mast, and, having six feet of water in the hold, and being unable in her crippled state to make head against the fire of her two antagonists, hailed to say she surrendered, and was taken possession of by a boat from the brig. The *Anson* lost in the action only two killed, and three officers and 10 men wounded, and the *Kangaroo* had no casualties in her complement of 120 men and boys. The *Loire's* casualties, according to the French admission, were 46 killed and 71 wounded. She made a gallant defence, and no discredit attached to her surrender to a superior force.

The next frigate of Commodore Bompart's squadron to be captured was the *Immortalité*, carrying 42 guns and 330 men, besides troops.

On the 20th October, the *Fisgard*, of 46 guns and 284 men, a French prize commanded by that very gallant and distinguished officer, Captain Thomas Byam Martin, sighted the French frigate not far from her destination, the port of Brest, and after a distant fire between the bow-guns and stern-chasers of the ships, soon after noon, Captain Martin got close alongside his opponent, and a spirited action commenced. The *Immortalité's* fire, directed towards the *Fisgard's* rigging, was so accurate that the latter dropped astern, when the Frenchman made sail to escape. Refitting his ship with praiseworthy promptitude, Captain Martin gave chase, and overhauling the *Immortalité* at 1.30, was again closely engaged with her. In the destructive cannonade that raged between the combatants both suffered severely, but at length, at the end of an hour and a half, the French frigate hauled down her colours. The *Fisgard* was struck so low in the hull that she had six feet of water in her hold before the close of the action, but the *Immortalité* was not only reduced to a sinking condition by her opponent's close and deadly fire, but lost her mizen-mast close by the board, and her two other masts and all her spars and rigging were much cut up.

The British frigate, though having a slight superiority as regards guns, 46 to 42, was really inferior, the weight of her broadside being 425 pounds to 450, that of her adversary. Her loss, out of a complement of 281 men and boys, was 10 killed, and one officer and 25 men wounded. The *Immortalité*, which had a crew of 330 seamen, besides 250 soldiers as passengers, lost her Captain, Monsieur Legrand, and her first lieutenant, also General Monge, and seven other naval and military officers, and 44 seamen and soldiers killed, and 61 wounded.

Thus there remained only two of Commodore Bompart's frigates unaccounted for. The *Romaine*, without disembarking her troops, sailed for the coast of France, and reached Brest in safety on the 23rd, in company with the schooner *Biche*, and about the same time the *Sémillante* arrived at Lorient. The whole of the seven prizes, some after being refitted at the nearest port, were brought in safety to Plymouth.

The *Hoche* was purchased into the service under her new name of the *Donegal*, after the coast off which she was captured. The *Embuscade* was re-named the *Seine*, and the *Loire*, a fine frigate, presented to the Republican Government by the city of Nantes, was also bought for the navy, and so was the *Immortalité*. All these four ships being in excellent condition, and more or less new, proved useful additions to the service. The *Bellone* and *Résolue*, being old and worn out, never went to sea, though they were purchased into the Navy; and the *Coquille* unfortunately blew up while lying at anchor at Hamoaze, when three midshipmen, seven seamen, and three women lost their lives.

Sir John Borlase Warren and his officers and men received the thanks of both Houses of Parliament for their vigilance and success in averting an invasion of the sister island, and the first lieutenants of the *Canada*, *Robust*, *Fisgard*, and *Ethalion* were promoted to the rank of commander. The chief credit for the happy result achieved was due to Captain Countess, of the *Ethalion*, for his perseverance in dogging the French squadron; and to Captain Thornborough, of the *Robust*, who was chiefly instrumental in bringing about the surrender of the *Hoche*; also to the gallantry of the captain and crew of the *Mermaid*, in engaging a frigate of superior force, of the *Anson* and *Kangaroo*, and especially of the *Fisgard*, all notable incidents in this memorable episode in our naval annals.

Undeterred by his previous failure, Commodore Savary, on the 12th October, the same day the *Hoche* was captured, sailed from Rochefort, with the same four frigates, *Concorde*, *Médée*, *Franchise*, and *Venus*, having on board a detachment of troops, in order to ascertain what had become of Commodore Bompart's squadron, and of General Humbert's army. The squadron had the good fortune to arrive unmolested at Killala Bay on the 27th October, and after learning the fate of their countrymen, put to sea again the same afternoon, on their return to France. On the following day the four frigates, being then not far from Broadhaven, were sighted by the *Cæsar*, 80, Sir James Saumarez, *Terrible*, 74, Sir Richard Bickerton, and *Melpomene*, 38, Sir Charles Hamilton, which gave chase. At six o'clock in the evening, the *Terrible* exchanged shots with the four French frigates, and at eleven, the *Cæsar*, which was fast coming up with them, carried away her fore-topmast and main-topgallantmast, which caused her to fall astern. The chase was continued by the *Terrible* and *Melpomene*, and at noon on the following day the latter got within two or three miles of the *Venus*, when Commodore Savary signalled his ships to disperse. The *Melpomene* singled out the *Concorde* to chase, and the *Terrible* the *Médée* and *Franchise*, which were saved from capture by a squall of wind, which carried away the fore and main-topsail yards of the seventy-four and compelled her to discontinue the pursuit. Eventually all the French frigates gained the port of Rochefort, and thus abortively ended the last of four expeditions fitted out by the Republican Government to assist the insurgents in Ireland.

In order to ascertain the object of the great preparations at Toulon, on the 2nd May Lord St. Vincent, under instructions from the Ministry, detached thither Sir Horatio Nelson, who had returned to the fleet off Cadiz from England on the 29th April, after recovering from the wound he had received at Santa Cruz. Nelson sailed in his flagship, the *Vanguard*, with the 74-gun ships *Alexander* and *Orion*, the frigates *Emerald* and *Terpsichore*, and the *Bonne Citoyenne*, sloop. Entering the Mediterranean on the 17th, when off Cape Sicie, he learned that there were nineteen sail-of-the-line at Toulon, and that Buonaparte was expected to embark there with a powerful army for some unknown destination. A few days later the squadron, then off the Hyères isles, was overtaken by a severe gale, in which the *Vanguard* lost her fore-mast and main-topmast, and sprung her bowsprit, and was taken in tow by the *Alexander*, which sailed in company with the *Orion*, to the harbour of St. Pietro, in Sardinia.

Meanwhile, General Buonaparte arrived at Toulon on the 8th May, having under his orders an army of 36,000 men, and Generals Kléber, Dessaix, Regnier, and

Menou. The fleet, numbering thirteen sail-of-the-line, eight frigates, two Venetian sixty-fours, and smaller vessels, manned by 10,000 seamen, with 400 transports, was commanded by Vice-Admiral Brueys—having as his flagship the *Sans Culotte*, of 120 guns, re-named, in honour of the object of the expedition, the *Orient*, on board of which Buonaparte embarked—who was seconded by Villeneuve, Blanquet, Decrès, and Ganteaume. The Toulon portion of the great Armada sailed on the 19th May, and stopping off Genoa, where it was joined by a division of transports, ran along the coast of Corsica and Sardinia, and on the 7th June passed within gun-shot of the port of Mazara in Sicily. Two days later the fleet sighted Malta, off which the Civita Vecchia division of transports, some 70 sail, joined the French admiral, and three days afterwards Malta was surrendered, together with two 64-gun ships and some other vessels, with much ammunition and provisions for six months, and church plate valued at £140,000.

During this time Nelson had refitted the *Vanguard* with the assistance of the officers and men of the *Alexander* and *Orion*, and on the 27th May sailed for the rendezvous off Toulon, when the admiral heard of the departure of the armament under Buonaparte for some unknown destination. Here he was joined by the 16-gun brig *Mutine*, Commander Thomas Masterman Hardy, who reported that ten sail-of-the-line, under Captain Troubridge, were on their way to reinforce him, and brought him instructions to go in quest of the Toulon fleet,* and two days later, on the 7th June, the British squadron joined him. The force now under the command of Sir Horatio Nelson amounted to the following thirteen 74-gun ships, one of 50 guns, and the *Mutine* :—

74	*Vanguard*	{ Rear-Admiral Sir Horatio Nelson, K.B. / Captain Edward Berry	74	*Zealous*	Captain Samuel Hood
	Orion	„ Sir James Saumarez		*Audacious*	„ Davidge Gould
	Culloden	„ Thomas Troubridge		*Goliath*	„ Thomas Foley
	Bellerophon	„ Henry D'Esterre Darby		*Majestic*	„ George Blagden Westcott
	Minotaur	„ Thomas Louis		*Swiftsure*	„ Benjamin Hallowell
	Defence	„ John Peyton		*Theseus*	„ Ralph Willett Miller
	Alexander	„ Alexander John Ball	50	*Leander*	„ Thomas Boulden Thompson

It was the first time that England's greatest admiral was placed in a position of

---

* Lord St. Vincent's instructions, dated the 21st May, were to the effect that he was "to proceed in quest of the armament preparing by the enemy at Toulon and Genoa, the object whereof appears to be either an attack upon Naples or Sicily, the conveyance of an army to some part of the coast of Spain for the purpose of marching towards Portugal, or to pass through the Straits with a view of proceeding to Ireland." In some additional instructions of the same date the Rear-Admiral is told that he may pursue the French squadron to "any part of the Mediterranean Adriatic, Morea, Archipelago, or even into the Black Sea."

absolute independence, and he took advantage of the opportunity to show the world his quality. Assuredly he had nothing to complain of as regards the captains of ships under his command, whose names included many that will live for ever in our naval history.

Nelson had no clue as to the destination of the enemy's fleet, but from the fact of their having sailed with a north-west wind, he was of opinion that they had steered up the Mediterranean. He accordingly proceeded in that direction, and passing Corsica and Elba, dropped anchor in the Bay of Naples. Here Nelson could gain no information of the movements of the French fleet from the British ambassador, Sir William Hamilton, except that they had been seen off the coast of Sardinia, and setting sail on the 20th June, he entered the Straits of Messina, where he learned from the British consul at that port that Buonaparte had seized Malta and Gozo, and the French fleet was lying at anchor off the smaller island. But the admiral was again disappointed, for on the 22nd the captain of the *Mutine* heard from a brig that the French fleet had quitted Malta four days before. Nelson accordingly directed his course for Alexandria, which he was satisfied was Buonaparte's goal. Meanwhile, though all ranks in the British fleet were burning to engage the enemy, who had thus far eluded them, the interval before Alexandria was sighted, which was on the 28th June, was passed by the ships' crews in assiduous drill at the great guns. But a fresh disappointment was in store for the British fleet. On arriving off the Pharos no enemy was found in the harbour, and on the following day the fleet weighed anchor and stood to the northward, and on the 19th July arrived at Syracuse.

Buonaparte, meanwhile, in the game of hide and seek, had quitted Malta on the 19th June, leaving 4,000 troops, under General Vaubois, as a garrison, and sighting Candia on the 1st July, arrived off Alexandria two days after Nelson had sailed thence for the coast of Natolia and the island of Sicily. Anxious beyond everything to disembark his troops before the dreaded Nelson again made his appearance off the port, Buonaparte landed his army with the utmost despatch. It is related of the great French conqueror that, on the 1st July, just as a portion of his troops had been disembarked, and Buonaparte was stepping into the boat that was to land him, the look-out ships signalled an enemy's sail to the westward, when he exclaimed, "Fortune! wilt thou abandon me? What! only five days!" A minute or two more and he was reassured by the announcement that the approaching vessel was the French frigate *Justice*, from the island of Malta.

Buonaparte gained possession of Alexandria on the following day with trifling loss, and by the 3rd July the disembarkation was completed. The channel leading to the old harbour—which is divided from what is known as the new harbour by the strip of land on which the city is built—being narrow and intricate, Buonaparte directed Admiral Brueys to anchor his fleet in the Bay of Aboukir, about 20 miles to the north-east of the city, and thither accordingly the following ships proceeded:—

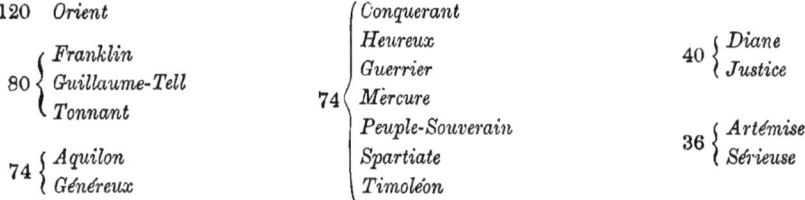

Brigs *Alcide* and *Railleur*; bomb-vessels, *Hercule* and *Salamine*, and several gun-boats.

We will now turn to Nelson's movements. Having re-victualled his fleet, he sailed on the 24th July for the Morea, being of opinion that as all accounts agreed in representing that the French fleet had not gone down the Mediterranean, it must be somewhere about the Levant or on the Egyptian coast. At Coron Captain Troubridge learned that the enemy had been seen four weeks before on the coast of Candia, steering south-east. This course the British admiral adopted, and on the 1st August, that ever-glorious anniversary, once again sighted the port of Alexandria, where was presented to his view a forest of masts of the French transports, and eight ships-of-war, the *Causse*, *Dubois*, and six Venetian frigates. Almost immediately after the report was received, the *Zealous* signalled the presence in Aboukir Bay of seventeen ships-of-war. Instantly Nelson steered to the eastward in the direction indicated, and all hearts were gladdened by the sight of the French fleet at anchor, formed in line of battle. To apprehend the special features of the battle that ensued, one of the greatest and most masterly victories achieved by any British admiral, it is necessary that some description of the scene of conflict should be given, for which we are indebted to the pages of James, that most accurate and painstaking of naval historians. Aboukir Bay extends from the castle of that name, in a semicircular direction, to the westernmost or Rosetta mouth of the Nile, distant from the castle about six miles. Aboukir Bay has no depth for line-of-battle ships nearer than three miles from the shore, a sand-bank, on which there is four fathoms, running out to that distance. Owing, also, to the width of its opening, the bay affords very little shelter, except on its north-west side, by a small island, situated about two miles from the point whereon the castle stands, and connected with it by a chain of sandbanks and rocks, and surrounded by a continuation of the shoal that runs along the bottom of the bay.

At a council of war, summoned by Admiral Brueys, all the officers, except Rear-Admiral Blanquet, approved of the fleet remaining at anchor in case of attack, but that officer maintained that it was only when a fleet could be supported by the cross-fire of strong forts, that any advantage was gained by anchoring. However, he was over-ruled, and the ships were formed in line ahead in the following order:— *Guerrier, Conquerant, Spartiate, Aquilon, Peuple Souverain, Franklin* (Blanquet's flagship), *Orient* (commander-in-chief's flagship), *Tonnant, Heureux, Mercure, Guillaume Tell* (Villeneuve's flagship), *Généreux, Timoléon;* with, in an inner line, about 350 yards from the first, and about midway between that and the shoal, the *Sérieuse* frigate, nearly abreast of the opening between the *Conquérant* and *Spartiate,* the *Artemise* abreast of the *Heureux,* and the *Diane* of the *Guillaume Tell.* The van ship bore from Aboukir Island south-east, distant about two miles. Between the *Guerrier* and her second astern, and between all the other line-of-battle-ships successively, the distance was about 160 yards, so that, reckoning each of the thirteen ships to occupy, upon an average, a space of 70 yards, the length of the line was rather under a mile and five-eighths. But this line was a curve, or rather, a very obtuse angle, having its projecting centre towards the sea. The edge of the shoal at the back of the line, on the contrary, was concave; so much so, that the centre ship, the *Orient,* was nearly twice the distance from it that either the van or rear ship was, particularly the latter. To protect his flanks, the French admiral, besides giving suitable stations to his bomb-vessels and gun-boats, erected a battery on Aboukir Island.

On first sighting the British fleet Admiral Brueys made preparations to get under weigh, but observing some of the advanced ships bring to, he concluded that an attack would be deferred till the following morning, and signalled that he should remain at anchor. But he was soon undeceived, when he issued orders to each ship to lay out an anchor on the south-south-west, and to send a stream cable to the ship next astern of her, making a hawser fast to it, in such a manner as to spring her broadside to the enemy. This measure was rendered the more necessary by the state of the wind, which blew from north-north-west, the direction of the line formed by the six van-ships. Meantime Nelson, only too eager to engage, hoisted the signal for battle at 3 P.M., and an hour later ordered his ships to prepare to anchor by the stern. Each ship, accordingly, made fast a stream cable to her mizen-mast, and passing it out of one of her gun-room ports, carried it along her side just below the first deck ports, to several of which it was slung by a slight rope-yarn lashing, and then bent it to an anchor at her bow, so that when the anchor was let go, the ship ran over her main cable, or that out of the hawse-hole, and brought up by the cable from her stern. This was to avoid the risk of being raked while swinging head to wind, as well as to enable the ship, by slackening one cable and hauling upon the other, to spring her broadside in any direction she pleased. Shortly after the signal to prepare to anchor, another was made, that the admiral intended to attack the enemy's van and centre, thus passing with his fourteen seventy-four's the French line on its outer side, down to the seventh ship, the *Orient;* so that these seven French ships might each have a British ship on her bow and quarter.

Admiral Brueys now detached two brigs, one of which, on arriving nearly within gun-shot of the leading British ships, bore away directly across the rocky shoal of Aboukir Island, with the object of decoying the *Zealous*, or one of the seventy-four's, in chase of her, and thus getting her on shore, but the ruse was seen through, and the British fleet steered a safe course. The *Zealous*, with the *Goliath* on her port quarter, was the first to round the shoal, when she bore up, bringing the wind on her starboard beam, and the other ships followed in succession, ranged in the following order:—*Goliath, Zealous, Orion, Audacious, Theseus, Vanguard, Minotaur, Defence, Bellerophon, Majestic, Leander;* the *Culloden* being at some distance to the northward, and still farther to the westward, the *Alexander* and *Swiftsure*. The rapidity and precision with which the eleven British ships formed line elicited the encomiums of the French officers, and about 6.20 the battle was commenced by the *Conquérant* and *Guerrier* opening fire upon the *Goliath* and *Zealous*. Ten minutes later, just as the sun was sinking below the horizon, the former crossed the head of the French line, and pouring a raking broadside into the *Guerrier*, the headmost ship, anchored abreast of the inner or port quarter of the next ship, the *Conquérant*. The *Zealous* brought up within musket-shot of the *Guerrier*, which was the ship Captain Foley intended to engage, and in a few minutes shot away her fore-mast, an event which was greeted with three cheers by the British fleet. Following the *Zealous*, the *Orion* rounded her starboard quarter, and ran past her and the *Goliath*, but the *Audacious* and *Theseus* arrived first at their respective stations; the former steering for the opening between the *Guerrier* and *Conquérant*, brought up within seventy yards of the bows of the *Conquérant*, into which she poured a broadside from her port battery, and swinging round, head to wind, came to again on the port side of the French seventy-four. The *Theseus*, crossing the bows of the *Guerrier*, ran down along the line between the *Zealous* and *Goliath*, and their opponents, to each of which she administered a broadside, and anchored by the stern abreast of the *Spartiate*, at a range of about 300 yards.

The *Orion*, meanwhile, while making a sweep outside the French line, was fired upon by the *Sérieuse*, frigate, when she retaliated by such destructive broadsides as to dismast her puny antagonist, and so damage her hull that she drifted further upon the shoal and sank. The *Orion*, thereupon, brought up a little abaft the beam of the *Peuple Souverain*, which she engaged, occasionally firing into the port bow of the *Franklin*, 80, flagship of Rear-Admiral Blanquet.

Nelson, in the *Vanguard*, in execution of his plan to complete the capture or destruction of the van ships before attacking the rear division, which, being to leeward, could not afford them any immediate support, edged away towards the outer side of the French line, from which he received a raking fire, and at 6.30, a few minutes after the *Theseus* had taken up her position abreast of the *Spartiate*, anchored within eighty yards of that ship's starboard beam. A few minutes later the *Minotaur* brought to opposite the *Aquilon*, and about seven, the *Defence* anchored abreast of the *Peuple Souverain*, while the *Bellerophon* and *Majestic* passed on for the purpose of attacking the enemy's centre and rear, and soon the former, anchoring by the stern, was engaged with the *Orient*, and the *Majestic* brought up abreast of the *Tonnant*, 80, flagship of Rear-Admiral Villeneuve.

By the time these ten British ships were hotly engaged with seven sail of the enemy, darkness had set in, but there was no confusion, for in accordance with Nelson's orders, each ship had hoisted at her mizen-peak four lights horizontally, and also the St. George's ensign, the white cross of which was distinctly visible.

Unfortunately, the *Culloden* grounded on the reef off the north-eastern extremity of Aboukir Island, and notwithstanding every endeavour of her captain, the gallant Troubridge, to get her afloat, she remained there immovable. But her misfortune saved the *Alexander* and the *Swiftsure*, which rounded the shoal in safety shortly after, and bore down to participate in the action, guided by the flashes of the guns. In describing the incidents of this memorable battle, we will adopt the course taken by James, and begin with the foremost ship of the British line, the *Zealous*.

So heavy were the raking broadsides the *Zealous* was enabled to bring to bear on her antagonist, the *Guerrier*, with little damage to herself from her station on the port bow of that ship, that within a quarter of an hour of the commencement of the action the French seventy-four lost all three masts. Captain Hood, receiving but a languid return from the guns that could be brought to bear, hailed to ask if she had surrendered, but there was no reply, and he resumed the work of slaughter. More than once the humane captain of the *Zealous* challenged his brave opponent without receiving a response, and at length, soon after nine, he sent his first lieutenant on board, who made the agreed signal of submission by hoisting and hauling down a light.

The following was the condition of the *Guerrier* when she became a prize to the *Zealous*. Her bowsprit and the whole of her head were shot away, and the two anchors cut in two, while both bows, particularly the port one, were much shattered, and from the latter to the gangway, her maindeck ports were nearly knocked in one, and her gunwale totally cut away. This had caused two of her main-deck beams to fall upon her guns; and most of the masts, having fallen in-board, lay along with the rigging over the dead and wounded seamen, estimated at more than half her complement, or at from 350 to 400 men. On the other hand, the loss on board the *Zealous* amounted to only one killed and seven wounded, and the ship was quite as perfect in her masts, and nearly so in her rigging, as when, three hours before, she entered into action.

The *Goliath* and *Audacious* engaged the *Conquérant*, the latter raking her frequently, without receiving much return from the position she had taken up, and at length the French seventy-four, having lost her fore and mizen-masts, and her main-mast tottering to its fall, struck her flag, further resistance only entailing useless slaughter. The *Conquérant*'s loss is not stated, but was said to have been nearly as severe as that of the *Guerrier*, and among her wounded was her captain. The *Goliath* did not share the immunity from loss of the *Zealous*, but had 21 killed and 41 wounded, while all her masts were much damaged, and her main and mizen rigging was nearly all shot away. The *Audacious* suffered aloft in her fore and main-masts, but lost only one killed and 35 wounded.

The *Theseus* at first attacked the *Spartiate*, but dropped a little farther down the line, on the arrival of the *Vanguard*, Nelson's flagship, which was closely engaged with the Frenchman, which also became exposed to an occasional fire from the *Minotaur*, and on the surrender of the *Conquérant*, from the quarter guns of the *Audacious*. Thus severely handled, the *Spartiate* lost all her masts, and was compelled to surrender, having lost heavily, her captain being among the severely wounded, though the exact number is not stated. The *Vanguard* suffered greatly, as she was exposed to a destructive raking fire from the *Aquilon*, until the *Minotaur* brought her powerful broadsides to bear upon her. The *Vanguard* had 30 killed and 76 wounded, including Sir Horatio Nelson, who was struck by a splinter over the eye he had lost at Calvi.

The *Minotaur*, assisted by the occasional fire of the *Theseus*, on the inner side, reduced her opponent to the dismasted condition of her three consorts ahead, and the *Aquilon* surrendered about 9.25, having sustained great loss in killed and wounded, including among the former her captain, Monsieur Thevenard. The *Minotaur* lost in the action 23 killed and 64 wounded, and her second, the *Theseus*, which was only partially engaged, had five killed and 30 wounded.

The *Defence* was equally successful in her engagement with the *Peuple Souverain* Assisted by the raking broadsides of the *Orion*, as the latter lay on the French seventy-four's quarter, she shot away her adversary's fore and main-masts, and also her cable, when the *Peuple Souverain* dropped out of the line, having lost heavily in killed and wounded, including her commander among the latter. The *Defence*, on the other hand, had only four killed and 11 wounded, and the *Orion*, which lost her fore-top-mast, and suffered considerably in all three lower-masts and rigging, had 13 killed and 29 wounded.

The greatest sufferer of all the British ships was the *Bellerophon*, which had the temerity to engage the three-decker *Orient*. Shortly before eight, so destructive was the fire of her great antagonist, that her mizen-mast was shot away, and was quickly followed by her main-mast. At length, being disabled, Captain Darby cut his cable, and setting his spritsail, wore clear of the *Orient*, but in the act of setting his fore-topsail and foresail, the fore-mast went over the side, and thus the *Bellerophon* drifted helplessly along the rear of the French line, receiving a broadside from the *Tonnant*. The loss of the British seventy-four was no less than 49 killed and 148 wounded, including Captain Darby, but she had played a glorious part on this ever-memorable day.

The *Majestic* had almost as formidable an opponent as the *Bellerophon* in the *Tonnant*, of 80 guns, and soon after commencing the action she lost her commander, the gallant Captain George Blagden Westcott, who was killed by a musket-ball. The command devolved on her first lieutenant, Mr. Cuthbert, who proved himself not unworthy of the trust. Soon after eight, finding she was drifting athwart-hawse the *Heureux*, the *Majestic* slipped her stern cable, and brought up with her bower anchor. She still continued to receive the fire of the *Tonnant,* and about three o'clock on the following morning her main and mizen-masts were shot away close to the deck. The *Majestic* had 50 killed, including Captain Westcott, and 146 wounded. Her adversary, which had been the only French ship to keep up her fire after midnight, soon afterwards lost all three masts, but by veering her cable, she had drifted so far to leeward that she had now no opponent, and also ceased firing. Soon after the *Tonnant* took up a station ahead of the *Guillaume Tell* and the two French ships in her rear.

About midnight a great calamity befell the flagship of the commander-in-chief, the circumstances of which we will proceed to describe. After rounding the shoal soon after eight, the *Swiftsure* brought up close astern of the spot just quitted by the *Bellerophon*, and opened fire with her foremost guns, at a range of about 200 yards, on the starboard bow of the *Orient*, while her after guns were brought to bear on the starboard quarter of the *Franklin*, on whose port bow the *Leander*, 50, was keeping up a hot fire with but little return. Soon after the *Alexander* anchored so as to bring her starboard broadside to bear on the *Orient's* port quarter, and the *Defence* fired into the *Franklin*. Suddenly a terrific explosion shook the sea and silenced the fire of the contending fleets. The crew of the *Orient* had been vainly striving since nine o'clock to extinguish a fire which first broke out in the poop and admiral's cabin, and ascending the rigging and spreading along the decks, about 10 P.M. caught the magazine, when the noble three-decker blew up with a tremendous explosion. The effect produced was electrical, but our powers of description would be at fault in attempting to depict the grandeur of the scene and the effect it had in hushing the warring elements that raged within the breasts of the combatants. The catastrophe produced a calm and cessation of strife, which, however, was but momentary, for hardly had the illumination given place to darkness that seemed Cimmerian in the contrast, and the wreckage ceased to fall on the decks of the contending ships, than the battle was renewed with redoubled energy by such of the enemy's ships as had not already struck.

The crews of the nearest ships to the *Orient*, the *Alexander, Swiftsure,* and *Orion*, foreseeing the result of the impending explosion, had provided to the best of their ability to prevent a conflagration, by closing the ports and hatchways, removing all combustibles from the decks, and having firemen with buckets in readiness to extinguish the flames. The vibration shook the hostile fleets to their keelsons, opening the seams, and flaming masses of wreckage fell on the *Franklin*, the nearest French ship, and on the three British seventy-four's, but all danger was quickly averted by the promptitude of the seamen. The *Franklin* was the first to recommence hostilities, but she brought on herself the fire of the *Defence* and *Swiftsure*, which lay on her starboard bow and quarter, and after bravely continuing a hopeless contest till her main and mizen-masts went over the side, and most of her guns were silenced, she hauled down her colours, having lost more than half her crew in the action.

At daybreak, about 4 A.M., the *Heureux* and *Mercure* having withdrawn from the line, the *Tonnant, Guillaume Tell, Généreux* and *Timoléon* resumed firing on the *Alexander* and *Majestic*, who were soon supported by the *Theseus* and *Goliath*, which came up to the scene of action and anchored, but the four French line-of-battle ships, and the two remaining frigates—the *Artemise* having caught fire and blown up—dropped out of gunshot, and the *Timoléon*, being too far to leeward to escape, ran herself ashore. Meantime the *Goliath, Theseus, Alexander,* and *Leander* stood towards the *Heureux* and *Mercure*, which had now run ashore to the southward of the bay, and on being summoned, struck their colours. The absence of the British ships afforded a favourable opportunity for the *Généreux, Guillaume Tell*, and frigates *Diane* and *Justice* to escape, and making sail they hauled close on the port tack, but encountered the *Zealous*, which made a gallant attempt to check their flight, receiving a destructive fire within musket-shot range. Nelson now recalled Captain Hood by signal and congratulated him on his spirited action in engaging these four ships.

Early on the following day, the 2nd August, the *Tonnant*, which lay a mere wreck, hauled down her colours when the *Theseus* and *Leander* approached, and about noon the *Timoléon*, which was on shore, was set on fire by her crew, when they abandoned her, and she blew up.

This was the last incident of the battle of the Nile, by which name the conflict in Aboukir Bay is known in our history. The victory was one of the most complete and splendid in its tactical arrangements recorded in history. Of thirteen French sail-of-the-line nine had been captured, two were destroyed, and two only, with two frigates, escaped, and these were all ultimately taken.

The *Bellerophon* was the only British ship that was entirely dismasted, but the *Majestic* lost her main and mizen-masts, the *Defence* her fore-topmast, the *Alexander* her mizen-topmast, and on the day following the action the latter's and the *Goliath*'s main-topmasts went over the side, having been wounded in action. All the ships suffered greatly in their yards and rigging, and among those that were most injured in their hulls were the *Bellerophon*, which was much shattered, the *Vanguard, Swiftsure, Theseus,* and *Majestic*, especially the last. The *Bellerophon* also had seven of her quarter-deck guns and eight on her other decks disabled.

The total British loss was 218 killed and 678 wounded, out of 7,401 seamen and marines.*

The loss sustained by the French ships was not reported in the *Gazette*, but according to one account it amounted to 2,000, and another placed it as high as 5,000. The commander-in-chief, Admiral Brueys, was wounded in the face and on the hand, and as he was descending from the poop to the quarter-deck a shot cut him in two, the last words of the gallant officer being a request that he might die on his quarter-deck as became an admiral of France. Commodore Casa Bianca, of the flagship, was severely wounded, and perished in the explosion. He was accompanied by his son, a child ten years of age, who also perished. His untimely fate was commemorated in Southey's well-known lines commencing:—

"The boy stood on the burning deck."

What was the loss of the *Orient* from the British fire before she blew up, was never ascertained, but after that event only 70 officers and men were saved by the boats of the English ships, and the captain of the fleet, Rear-Admiral Ganteaume, escaped to the French brig *Salamine*, which joined the *Guillaume Tell* when she got away.

Of the captured ships, the *Guerrier, Conquérant, Spartiate, Aquilon,* and *Tonnant* were totally dismasted, the *Peuple Souverain* lost her fore and main-masts, and the

---

* This loss was distributed as follows:—The *Goliath* had one master's mate, one midshipman, and 19 men killed, and one lieutenant, two midshipmen, and 38 of all ranks wounded. The *Zealous* had only one killed and seven wounded. The *Orion*, the captain's clerk and 12 men killed, and Captain Sir James Saumarez, three midshipmen, the boatswain, and 11 men wounded. The *Audacious* had only one seaman killed, and a lieutenant, the gunner, and 33 men wounded. The *Theseus* had five killed, and a lieutenant and 29 men wounded. On board the *Vanguard* the loss was heavy. Her captain of marines, two midshipmen, and 29 seamen were killed, and Sir Horatio Nelson, two lieutenants, the admiral's secretary, two midshipmen, the boatswain, and 68 men were wounded. The *Minotaur* had one lieutenant, one master's mate, and 21 men killed, and one lieutenant, a marine officer, her second master, one midshipman, and 60 men wounded. The *Defence* had no casualties among her officers, and only four killed and 11 wounded forward, but the *Bellerophon* suffered severely. Her loss was three lieutenants, one master's mate, and 45 seamen and marines killed, and Captain Darby, the master, captain of marines, one midshipman, the boatswain, and 143 men wounded. The *Majestic* had 50 killed, among whom were Captain Westcott, in whose memory a monument was set up in St. Paul's Cathedral, one midshipman, and the boatswain; and 143 wounded, including two midshipmen and the captain's clerk. The *Swiftsure* lost seven killed, and a midshipman and 21 men wounded, and the *Leander* had only 14 seamen wounded; while the *Alexander* had one lieutenant and 13 seamen killed, and her commander, Captain Ball, the captain of marines, master, two midshipmen, and 53 seamen and marines wounded.

Franklin her main and mizen-masts, and the hulls of all were greatly damaged. The *Heureux* and *Mercure*, which had run ashore, were alone in good condition.

An amusing anecdote is related of Nelson, who received on board the *Vanguard* Rear-Admiral Blanquet and the seven surviving captains of the captured French ships, and entertained them with characteristic hospitality. A few days after they had embarked on board the admiral's ship, these officers, who were all wounded, were as usual dining with him, when Nelson, half-blind from the injury to his eyes, not thinking what he was about, offered to one captain, who had lost most of his teeth by a musket-ball, a case of tooth-picks. On discovering his error, the gallant admiral became excessively confused, and in his trepidation, handed his snuff-box to the captain on his right, who had lost his nose.

The results of Nelson's victory of the Nile were great and far-reaching. As a French writer says:—

"Aboukir ruined all our hopes; it prevented us from receiving the remainder of the forces that were destined for us; it left the field free for the English to persuade the Porte to declare war against us; it rekindled that which was hardly extinguished with the Emperor of Germany; it opened the Mediterranean to the Russians, and planted them on our frontiers; it occasioned the loss of Italy and the invaluable possessions in the Adriatic, which we owed to the successful campaigns of Buonaparte; and, finally, it at once rendered abortive all our projects, since it was no longer possible for us to dream of giving the English any uneasiness in India. Add to this that the people of Egypt, whom we wished to consider as friends and allies, instantaneously became our enemies, and, entirely surrounded as we were by the Turks, we found ourselves engaged in a most difficult defensive war, without a glimpse of the slightest future advantage to be derived from it."

Nelson despatched the *Leander*, Captain Thompson, with his flag-captain, Berry, to Lord St. Vincent, off Cadiz, with his despatches, but the gallant officers and men were not destined to fulfil the mission. On the 18th August, being within six miles of the west end of Candia, Captain Thompson sighted a strange sail standing towards him, which proved to be the *Généreux*, one of the ships that had escaped from Aboukir Bay. The *Leander* being of greatly inferior force, and having 80 men short of her complement, her captain deemed it his duty to avoid so unequal a conflict, and made every endeavour to escape. But the enemy rapidly overhauled the *Leander*, and at 9 A.M. ranged up within half gun-shot of her port or weather quarter, and an action being inevitable, Captain Thompson shortened sail and replied to a shot ahead by a broadside. The two ships gradually neared each other, keeping up a constant and heavy fire, until 10.30, when the *Généreux* ran aboard her opponent on the port bow, and dropped alongside. But so effective was the fire of the *Leander's* small-arm men that every effort of the enemy to board was frustrated, and a breeze springing up, the *Généreux* disengaged herself from her opponent and forged ahead. The heavy fire of the French seventy-four had brought down the frigate's mizen-mast on the starboard quarter, her fore-topmast over the port bow, and her fore and main-yards on the booms, but there was no thought of surrender, and Captain Thompson, having succeeded in wearing his ship with the aid of his spritsail, luffed under the stern of the *Généreux*, and poured a broadside into her from all those of her starboard guns not covered by the wreck of her mizen-mast.

The action raged with unabated fury until 3.30 P.M. when the *Généreux* stood athwart-hawse of the *Leander*, and had her at her mercy, the greater number of her foremost guns being disabled. Unwilling to inflict needless slaughter on a brave adversary, Captain Lejoille hailed to know if she surrendered, to which Captain Thompson was fain to reply in the affirmative as his ship was totally unmanageable, having only the bowsprit and shattered stumps of the fore and main-masts standing, and her guns being disabled. The surrender was signified by displaying a French flag at the end of a pike, but as none of the *Généreux's* boats could float, one of her midshipmen and the boatswain swam on board and took over charge.

The defence made by the *Leander* was highly honourable to her officers and men, and a defeat against such odds was not less deserving of admiration than many a victory. For six hours, a ship carrying 51 guns, with a broadside weight of metal of 432 pounds, and having a crew of 282 men and boys, including the 14 wounded in the recent battle, sustained the attack of a ship-of-the-line mounting 80 guns, throwing a broadside of 1,024 pounds, having on board 936 men, including a portion of the crew of the *Timoléon*. In thus worthily upholding the honour of the British flag, the *Leander* lost three midshipmen, and 32 seamen and marines killed, and 57 wounded, including Captain Thompson (severely in three places), Captain Berry, two lieutenants, her master, one master's mate, one midshipman and the boatswain, her casualties being thus one-third of her crew.

The *Généreux*, though successful, suffered even more severely, if we are to credit the account given by some of her officers to those of her prize, the number of casualties being 100 killed, including her first lieutenant, and 180 wounded.

To the disgrace of Captain Lejoille* he treated his prisoners with a harshness against which Captain Thompson in vain remonstrated, and robbed that officer of his pistols and shirts, except three, and gave him an old coat in exchange from his stock of clothes, and even deprived him of his cot, though he was severely wounded. Not until the *Généreux* had arrived at Corfu, a fortnight after the action, was the musket-ball extracted from Captain Thompson's arm by the surgeon of his ship, and then the operation was performed by stealth. The same barbarous treatment was accorded to the seamen of the prize, but it is only just to observe that the conduct of the captain of the *Généreux* was exceptional.

Captains Thompson and Berry and most of the officers were at length permitted to return to England on *parole*, and were, according to usage, tried by court-martial for the loss of the *Leander*,† when the verdict of the court acquitting Captain Thompson, was to the effect, " that the gallant and almost unprecedented defence of Captain Thompson, of his Majesty's late ship *Leander*, against so superior a force as that of the *Généreux*, is deserving of every praise his country and this court can give, and that his conduct, with that of the officers and men under his command, reflects not only the highest honour on himself and them, but on their country at large." Captain Thompson, upon his return to the shore from the *America*, 64, was saluted by three cheers from all the ships at Sheerness, and he and Captain Berry, who also received the thanks of the court, were knighted.

After his victory Nelson used all despatch to refit his prizes and send them to England. With great forethought, in order to give the Indian Government early intimation of Buonaparte's design on their possessions in the East and of his victory on the 1st August, the admiral despatched Lieutenant Duval of the *Zealous*, to Bombay, where that officer, travelling by Aleppo, Bagdad, and Bussorah, arrived on the 21st October, in the Indian Navy cruiser *Fly*. Nelson also took the precaution to send to England the *Mutine*, now commanded by Commander Hon. Thomas Bladen Capel (Captain Hardy having been appointed his flag-captain in the *Vanguard*), with duplicate despatches for the Admiralty, and the brig actually passed the *Généreux*, having in tow the *Leander*.

* This officer was killed in March of the following year, while attacking the port of Brindisi, which surrendered.

† It is a singular circumstance that during the former war with France on the 18th July, 1783, while cruising in the West Indies, the *Leander*, then commanded by Captain Payne (who commanded the *Russell* in Lord Howe's action on the 1st June, 1794), engaged the *Pluton*, 74, which was partially disabled, but sheered off with the loss of one lieutenant and four men killed and eleven wounded.

By the morning of the 14th, seven ships of the British fleet and the prizes*—*Franklin, Tonnant, Aquilon, Conquérant, Peuple Souverain,* and *Spartiate*—were refitted and sailed under command of Sir James Saumarez, and the admiral left Aboukir Bay for Naples, on the 19th, with the *Vanguard, Culloden,* and *Alexander,* while Captain Hood was directed to cruise off the port of Alexandria with the *Zealous, Goliath,* and *Swiftsure,* and the frigates *Emerald* and *Artemise, Bonne Citoyenne* sloop, and *Seahorse,* which had joined him two days before. It is reported that Buonaparte on receiving the despatch from Rear-Admiral Ganteaume, conveying the loss of his fleet, betrayed no emotion, only observing, " We have no longer a fleet. Well, we must either remain in this country, or quit it as great as the ancients."

For his victory Sir Horatio Nelson was created Baron Nelson of the Nile and of Burnham Thorpe in Norfolk, and received a pension of £2,000 a year for himself and his two next heirs, and of £1,000 from the Irish Parliament. Pitt was desirous of creating Nelson a Viscount, but, as he said in a letter to Lord Hood, " it was objected to in a certain quarter, because he was not commander-in-chief," a pretext which Lord Hood denounced, as well he might, as " a flimsy reason," " for," said the gallant admiral in a letter to Nelson, " your lordship stood in the situation of commander-in-chief at the mouth of the Nile. You could not possibly receive advice or assistance at the distance of near 1,000 leagues from Earl St. Vincent."

The East India Company showed their appreciation of the great services he had rendered in thwarting Napoleon's designs on their Indian possessions, by a grant of £10,000. The Resolution of thanks of the Directors is dated the 24th April, 1799, and is addressed to " The Right Hon. Rear-Admiral Lord Nelson," for his " ever-memorable victory over the French, near the mouth of the Nile, on the 1st, 2nd, and 3rd August, 1798." Nelson, in his reply, dated " *Foudroyant,* Bay of Naples, 3rd July, 1799," states that, " having in my younger days served in the East Indies, I am no stranger to the munificence of the Honourable Company." This refers to his lordship's service in the *Seahorse,* between the years 1773—1776, and it is a curious fact that the great admiral was a candidate for the post of Superintendent of the Bombay Marine, or Indian Navy, as it afterwards became.

---

* The *Heureux, Mercure,* and *Guerrier,* being in too bad a state to be refitted, were burnt. On arriving at Gibraltar, the *Peuple Souverain* was converted into a guard ship under the name of *Guerrier,* and the five remaining prizes arrived in safety at Plymouth. The only ships that were fit to go to sea were the *Spartiate, Tonnant,* and *Franklin,* and the last, renamed the *Canopus* (the classical name of the town of Aboukir), was considered the finest two-decker afloat, and served as a model for nine others of her class built in British dockyards.

Foreign sovereigns, as the Sultan, the King of Sardinia, and the Emperor of Russia, conferred valuable gifts upon Nelson, while the King of Naples created him Duke of Bronté, in Sicily, with domains worth £3,000 a year. Gold medals were presented to his lordship and to each of his captains, and the first-lieutenants were promoted to the rank of commander. The amount paid for the purchase of the prizes into the Navy, including the three ships burnt at Aboukir, was distributed among the seamen of the fleet, a further sum of 2,000 sequins being given by the Sultan to the wounded of Nelson's own ship, the *Vanguard*. Both the Legislatures of Great Britain and Ireland voted him their thanks, and when Parliament met on the 20th November, the victory was referred to in the following terms in the speech from the throne:—
"The unexampled series of our Naval triumphs have received fresh splendour from the memorable and decisive action in which a detachment of my fleet, under the command of Rear-Admiral Lord Nelson, attacked, and almost totally destroyed, a superior force of the enemy, strengthened by every advantage of situation. By this great and brilliant victory, an enterprise, of which the injustice, perfidy, and extravagance had fixed the attention of the world, and which was peculiarly directed against some of the most valuable interests of the British empire, has, in the first instance, been turned to the confusion of its authors; and the blow thus given to the power and influence of France has afforded an opening which, if improved by suitable exertions on the part of other powers, may lead to the general deliverance of Europe."

CHAPTER X.

Events in the Mediterranean—Capture of Minorca—Actions between Single Ships in 1798—The *St. George* and Spanish Privateers—*Melampus* and *Volage*—*Speedy* and *Papillon*—*Coburg* and *Revanche*—*Seahorse* and *Sensible*—The *Sibylle* and *Fox* at Manilla—Loss of the *Resistance*—Capture of the *Seine*—*Lion* and four Spanish Frigates—Boats of the *Melpomene*—*Espoir* and *Liguria*—Capture of the *Flore* and *Furie*—Loss of the *Ambuscade*—Lord Nelson at Naples—The British Navy at Capua, Gaeta and Rome—Defence of Acre by Sir Sydney Smith—Operations on the Coast of Egypt and in Holland—Loss of the *Proserpine* Frigate, and Boat Actions in 1799—The *Sibylle* and *Forte*—The *Dædalus* and *Prudente*—Destruction of the *Preneuse*—The *Espoir* and *Africa*—*Clyde* and *Vestale*—Capture of Spanish Frigates with Specie—Cutting-out of the *Hermione*—Actions in the Channel and at Gibraltar—Acquisition of Surinam—Loss of the *Queen Charlotte* by Fire—Wreck of the *Repulse* and *Marlborough*—Siege of Genoa—Cutting-out of the *Prima*, Galley—Capture of the *Généreux* and *Guillaume Tell*—Surrender of Malta and Curaçoa—Capture of the *Pallas* and *Heureux*—Boat Expeditions on the French and Spanish Coasts—Cutting-out of the *Désirée* and *Cerbère*—Capture of the *Concorde* and *Médée*—The *Seine* and *Vengeance*—The *Milbrook* and *Bellone*.

LORD NELSON detached from Naples the 74-gun ships *Alexander*, Captain Ball, *Culloden*, Captain Troubridge, and *Colossus*, Captain Murray, to co-operate with a Portuguese squadron in the blockade of Malta, which was held by 3,000 French soldiers, who had retired to Valetta, in the harbour of which lay the *Guillaume Tell*, the frigates *Diane* and *Justice*, and three Maltese ships, under the command of Rear-Admiral Villeneuve. On the 24th October Nelson joined Captain Ball with the *Vanguard* and *Minotaur*, and on the following day the garrison of the neighbouring island, 217 men, capitulated, and some British marines took possession. Soon afterwards the French armies overran the whole of Piedmont, and the dethroned King Charles Emanuel retired to the Island of Sardinia, and King Ferdinand of Naples, having driven the French out of Rome on the 29th November, was dispossessed of the "Eternal City" on the 15th December, and five days later embarked with his family and attendants on board the *Vanguard*, which landed him at Palermo in Sicily.

Meantime a combined Turkish and Russian army drove the French out of the Ionian Islands, except Corfu, and Captain Hood, with three 74-gun ships and three frigates, blockaded the French squadron left at Alexandria by Admiral Brueys, consisting of the 64-gun ships *Causse* and *Dubois*, eight frigates, four brigs and nine gun-boats, having on board 4,948 officers and men, the whole under the command of Rear-

Admiral Ganteaume. Captain Hood and the commanders of the *Goliath* and *Swiftsure* were not officers to remain idle, and on the 25th August, Captain Foley despatched the boats of the *Goliath*, under the orders of Lieutenant Debusk, to cut out a French ketch, mounting three 18-pounders and four swivels, with a crew of 70 men, which that officer accomplished with success, himself receiving a wound in a personal encounter with the commander of the ketch.

Two seamen of the *Alcmene* performed a gallant action. The frigate chased a gun-boat, bringing despatches from Buonaparte, which were thrown overboard by the commander, whereupon these men sprang into the sea, though the ship was going over five knots through the water, and brought them on board, for which they each received a pension of £20 from the City of London. Mr. Fane, midshipman of the *Emerald*, also performed an act of humanity, deserving of record. The French cutter, *Anemone*, of 4 guns and 60 men, from Toulon, having on board Adjutant-General Camin and an aide-de-camp of Buonaparte's, with despatches, being closely chased off Alexandria, ran ashore on the beach, where the crew were soon surrounded by armed Arabs. The cutter was dashed to pieces in the surf, when the boats of the *Swiftsure* and *Emerald* pulled for the shore in order to save the crew from being slaughtered by the infuriated natives, and Mr. Fane swam through the breakers, pushing before him a keg with a rope attached to it. By these means he saved an officer and four seamen, but the general and aide-de-camp and many men were ruthlessly murdered, and the remainder carried away into the desert.

Earl St. Vincent was not idle, though he could not induce the Spanish commander-in-chief at Cadiz, Don Joseph Massaredo, to venture out. Early in November his lordship despatched Commodore Duckworth to effect the reduction of Minorca, with the *Leviathan*, 74, Captain Digby; *Centaur*, 74, Captain Markham; 44-gun frigates *Argo*, Captain Bowen, and *Dolphin*, Captain Nisbet; *Aurora*, 28, Captain Caulfield; *Cormorant*, 20, Lord Mark Kerr, and *Peterel*, 16, Captain Long, together with several transports, having on board some troops, under General Hon. Charles Stuart. The expedition appeared off Fournella on the 7th November, and the same evening the troops were landed as well as the stores and supplies, and the whole island surrendered without the loss of a man. On the 13th three Spanish ships were sighted, accompanied by the British sloop *Peterel*, which they had taken, and the squadron gave chase, when the *Argo* recaptured the *Peterel*.

During the year 1798 some actions took place between light squadrons and single ships which merit brief mention. Lieutenant Mackey and crew of the *George*, of 6 guns and 40 men, deserve signal honour for their gallant defence against the combined attack of two Spanish privateers, respectively of 12 guns and 109 men and 6 guns and 68 men. The action took place on the 3rd January, while the *George* was on passage from Demerara to Martinique. The crew repulsed two attempts to board, but at the third attempt they were overpowered with the loss of one officer and seven men killed, and Lieutenant Mackey and 16 seamen wounded, though the victors paid heavily for their triumph, their loss being 32 killed and many more wounded. Seldom has a more gallant defence been recorded, even in the annals of the Navy.

A French privateer, the *Cheri*, of 26 guns and 230 men, offered a stout resistance to the *Pomone*, 40, Captain Reynolds, off Ushant, on the 5th January, but she was forced to haul down her flag with the loss of her gallant captain and 14 men killed and 19 wounded, and the stubbornness of her defence was attested by her sinking immediately afterwards. The *Kingfisher*, 16-gun brig, with a crew of 120 men, Captain Pierrepoint, brought to action the French privateer *Betsey*, of 16 guns and 118 men, which, however, shot away the jibboom of her adversary, and made sail to escape, but another spar being rigged out, the British brig again gave chase, and overhauled the *Betsey*, which was compelled at length to haul down her flag, having lost seven killed and many wounded, including the two senior officers. Lieutenant Pym, first lieutenant of the *Babet*, of 20 guns, captured with the ship's boats, after a strenuous resistance, the *Désirée*, of 6 guns and 46 men, of whom 11 were killed and drowned and 15 wounded. As the launch did not come up till the enemy had struck her colours, Lieutenant Pym actually effected this brilliant service with the pinnace only, which had a crew of 12 men, of whom two were killed and the remainder wounded.

The French 22-gun corvette *Volage* showed fight against the *Melampus*, 36, Captain Graham Moore, and after a spirited resistance, which reflected credit on her crew, numbering 195 men, was compelled to haul down her colours. The *Volage* was added to the Navy, under her own name, and did good service under her new masters. Another notable little ship in the Navy, and one that recalls reminiscences of the great Lord Cochrane, was the *Speedy*, 14-gun brig, Captain Downman, which sighted, off Vigo, and engaged, the French privateer, *Papillon*, of 14 guns (all 12- and 8-pounders, those of the *Speedy* being but 4-pounders), and 160 men. A running fight took place on the 3rd February, and was renewed on the following day, but the *Papillon* succeeded in escaping, though the *Speedy* recaptured a prize brig which the privateer had taken. The *Speedy* lost a lieutenant, the boatswain and three men killed, and four wounded, and was much cut up aloft, necessitating her return to port to refit. The British cutter, *Marquis Coburg*, carrying 12 guns and 66 men, fought and captured, after a severe action, the French lugger privateer *Revanche*, of 16 guns and 62 men. The latter had two of her masts and fore-yard shot away, and lost seven killed and eight wounded, and sunk soon after she surrendered, when the prize crew and prisoners were saved with difficulty. A French privateer schooner, of the same name, was captured in the West Indies by the *Recovery*, after a smart action. The combatants were well-matched, the advantage both as regards men and weight of broadside being slightly on the side of the Frenchman. The 14-gun brig *Victorieuse*, Captain Dickson, a prize from the French, also repulsed the attack of two French privateers, having respectively 12 guns and 80 men and 6 guns and 50 men, which tried to board the British brig, and she succeeded in capturing the smaller of her assailants. Before the close of the year the *Victorieuse* and 14-gun brig *Zephyr*, Commander Champain, cannonaded two forts, mounting 6 guns, in the Island of Margarita, in the West Indies, and they were carried by assault by a detachment of troops and seamen from the ships.

Captain Digby, commanding the *Aurora*, 32, on the north-west coast of Spain, performed good service in destroying some vessels and engaging batteries; and Captain Skinner, commanding the packet *Princess Royal*, having six guns and 32 men, while on his way to New York from Falmouth, defended his little ship for two hours against every effort to capture her by the French privateer brig *Aventurier*, of 16 guns and 85 men, and eventually drove her off so greatly damaged that she had to return to Bordeaux to refit. An instance of a gallant resistance on the part of the enemy is afforded by the action off the coast of Sicily between the *Seahorse*, 46, Captain Foote, having a crew of 292 men, and the French frigate, *Sensible*, carrying 36 guns and 300 men, including General Baraguay d'Hilliers and his suite, on their way from Malta to Toulon. After a running fight, the *Seahorse* brought her antagonist to close action, and compelled her to surrender in eight minutes, with the loss of 18 killed and 37 wounded, or according to French accounts, of 52 and 53 respectively.

An exploit worthy special mention was performed in the East Indies. On the 5th January, the *Sibylle*, 38, Captain Cooke, an officer second to none in the Navy for gallantry and devotion, and the *Fox*, 32, Captain Pulteney Malcolm, sailed from the Portuguese settlement of Macao for Manilla, capital of the Spanish colony of the Phillipines, with the object of capturing two richly-laden vessels about to sail thence.

They sighted the island of Luconia on the 11th, and disguising themselves so as to pass as two frigates of Admiral Sercey's squadron, entered the bay of Manilla. On the following day the ships arrived off Cavita, the port of the capital, where the *Fox* was boarded by a Spanish guard-boat, and soon after a barge and felucca came off, with Admiral Alaba and other officers of standing, offering the hospitality of the port. Captain Cooke, who had come on board the *Fox*, introduced himself as Commodore Lautour, and having gained all the information he required, made himself known to his astonished visitors. Meantime the crews of the Spanish boats were brought on board, and a party of British seamen, having exchanged clothes with them, proceeded in their boats with others of the two frigates towards three Spanish gun-boats, which were boarded and seized without resistance, and 118 officers and men were removed as prisoners. Having learned that there were three 74-gun ships and a frigate in the port, and acquired other important information, all the officers and men, numbering some 200, were feasted and sent ashore, and the frigates quitted the bay, taking with them the three Spanish gunboats. Unhappily one of the gun-boats foundered in a heavy squall a few nights later, and the prize crew, consisting of a lieutenant, midshipman, and 10 seamen, were drowned. The *Sibylle* and *Fox* also engaged two strong batteries in the neighbouring island of Mindanao, but were unable to make any impression on them, and had to cut their cables and make sail, the *Fox* having had four killed and 15 wounded, besides being much cut up aloft, and the *Sibylle* lost her master, besides a few casualties. A few days later, while the boats' crews were engaged in replenishing their stock of water, they were attacked by the natives, and two men were killed, one mortally wounded, and nine carried away into the woods, but eventually the men were recovered by the Sultan of Mindanao.

But a much greater disaster befell the British Navy in the East, in the destruction of the 44-gun frigate *Resistance*, Captain Hon. Edward Pakenham, when, from some inexplicable cause, at one o'clock in the morning of the 24th July, she suddenly blew up; and out of 332 souls on board, only 13 escaped. These survivors, more or less burnt, were rescued for even a worse fate than their shipmates. Having constructed a raft, they tried to make the island of Sumatra, distant about nine miles, but a gale springing up, the raft was dashed to pieces, and four only succeeded in reaching the shore, when they became prisoners to the Malays. Finally, only one, named Thomas Scott, was released from captivity, and survived to tell the tale.

One of Admiral Sercey's frigates, the *Seine*, of 40 guns, while on her way home from Mauritius, had sighted the Penmarcks on the French coast, when three British frigates appeared in sight, and the *Pique*, 36, Captain David Milne, overhauling her, engaged the Frenchman in a running fight for two hours and a half, the ships exchanging broadsides abreast of each other. The *Seine* ran aground, as did also the *Pique* and the 38-gun frigate, *Jason*, Captain Stirling, which had come up and participated in the action, and after maintaining a gallant resistance, the French frigate struck her colours, having sustained a loss, out of 610 men on board including 280 soldiers, of 170 killed and about 100 wounded. The *Pique*, which bore the brunt of the action, lost her fore-topmast and was much cut up aloft, and became a total wreck, notwithstanding strenuous efforts to heave her off. The *Jason* suffered little in her masts and rigging, and was got off the sand-bank. The total loss of the two ships was 9 killed and 18 wounded, including the second lieutenant of the *Jason* killed, and her captain and two midshipmen wounded. The *Seine* was got off, and the crew of the *Pique*, which was destroyed, were turned over to her, and on the arrival of the prize in port, she was commissioned by Captain Milne under her own name. Lieutenant Bigot, the gallant commander of the *Seine*, was soon exchanged, and on his return to France, the Directory promoted him to the rank of captain.

The boats of the *Flora*, 36, Captain Middleton, which chased into the port of Cerigo, in the Levant, the French 18-gun brig *Mondovi*, cut her out from under the protection of the batteries with trifling loss. Off Leghorn the privateer brig *Eagle*, of 14 guns and 57 men, successfully defended herself, after a protracted action, with the brig *Lodi*, of 18 guns and 130 men, conveying despatches to General Buonaparte in Egypt. The loss of the *Eagle* is not given, but it was very heavy, and she came out of the action with only the stump of her mainmast standing. The *Lion*, 64, Captain Manley Dixon, being off Carthagena, sighted four 34-gun Spanish frigates, and notwithstanding the disparity of force, cleared for action. The *Lion* tackled one of them, the *Santa Dorotea*, and engaging her closely, forced her to haul down her colours, when her consorts, who had made feeble efforts to cover her, hauled their wind and escaped. The *Santa Dorotea*, out of a complement of 371, lost 20 killed and 32 wounded, and had her fore-topmast and mizen-mast shot away.

A gallant exploit was that effected by the boats of the *Melpomene*, 38, Captain Sir

Charles Hamilton, and 14-gun brig *Childers*, Commander O'Bryen, while cruising off the coast of France. At 10 P.M. five boats, manned with 70 men, under the orders of Lieutenant Shortland, of the *Melpomene*, pulled for the harbour of Corigion, where lay at anchor an armed brig and several merchant vessels, and at 3 A.M., being alongside the brig, carrying 14 guns and 79 men, they boarded and captured her, killing and wounding 16 of the enemy. The brig was brought out under fire of some batteries, and in the teeth of an adverse gale that sprang up. For his gallantry Lieutenant Shortland received promotion.

The British brig *Espoir*, Commander Bland, of 14 guns and 80 men, while convoying some vessels near Gibraltar, was attacked by a square-rigged ship, the *Liguria*, of 26 guns and 120 men, which hailed her to surrender, and fired a broadside into her. Captain Bland returned the compliment, and a spirited action ensued, lasting from 7 to 11 P.M., when the *Liguria* hauled down her colours, having lost her boatswain and six men killed and her commander and 13 wounded. The only loss the *Espoir* sustained was her master killed and six men wounded, but the action was nevertheless very creditable to her officers and crew, and her commander was made a captain.

The *Indefatigable*, 44, Sir Edward Pellew, captured off the Gironde river, after a twenty-four hours' chase, the French corvette *Vaillante*, of 20 guns and 175 men, which, being a fine new ship, was added to the Navy under the name of the *Danae*. The 18-gun brig *Hazard*, Commander Butterfield, also compelled the surrender of the French armed ship *Neptune*, mounting 10 guns, and having a crew of 53 men, with 270 troops, who maintained a heavy musketry fire on the British brig and made repeated attempts to board her. Another capture was made in the same month of August by the British frigates, *Naiad*, 38, Captain Pierrepoint, and *Magnanime*, 44, Captain Hon. Michael de Courcy, which chased off Cape Finisterre and forced to surrender, the French 36-gun frigate *Décade*, which was added to the Navy. Early in September the privateer *Flore*, 32, was captured off the Gironde by the British frigates *Phaeton* and *Anson*. The prize, when the French frigate *Vestale*, had been captured off the Penmarcks, in 1761, by the *Unicorn*, 28, and was added to the British Navy, under the name of *Flora*, but was sunk in 1778, at the evacuation of Rhode Island, to prevent her falling into the hands of the insurgent Americans, who, however, weighed her, and sold her to the French Government, by whom she was disposed of at the conclusion of peace in 1783.

The *Sirius*, Captain King, a powerful frigate, carrying 44 guns, captured two Dutch ships in succession, off the Texel, one the *Furie*, of 36 guns and 328 men, including 165 soldiers, and the second, the *Waakzaamheid*, of 26 guns and 222 men, of whom 122 were French troops. The ships being about two miles apart, the *Sirius* first overhauled the smaller one, which surrendered without firing a shot, and then made sail after the *Furie*, which hauled down her colours after a brisk engagement, having experienced a loss of eight killed and 14 wounded. On board the two prizes were found 6,000 stand of arms, besides ordnance stores, which, with the troops, were intended for service in Ireland. Both ships were bought into the Navy, the *Furie* being named the *Wilhelmina*, as there was one *Fury* already in the service.

We will only make brief mention of the gallant repulse of French privateers off Naples, by the privateer schooner *Herald*, carrying 28 men, the former having, as is stated, 30 casualties; and the capture in the West Indies of a French privateer of 18 guns and 117 men, by the *Perdrix*, 22, Captain Fahie, when the former had six killed and five wounded. An event that demands a more detailed record, but for a reason the reverse of satisfactory, is the action off Bordeaux, on the 14th December, between the *Ambuscade*, Captain Jenkins, carrying 40 guns and 190 men, a portion of her crew being absent in prizes, and the French corvette *Baionnaise*, of 32 guns and 250 men, including 30 soldiers. The *Ambuscade* chased the stranger, which shortened sail on seeing escape was impossible, and an engagement ensued. The British frigate was getting the best of it when a gun burst, committing much havoc and injuring 11 men. Taking advantage of the confusion the *Baionnaise* made sail, but was again overhauled by the *Ambuscade*, when the former, suddenly putting her helm up, ran foul of the frigate, and the French troops commenced a fusilade with deadly effect. Soon Captain Jenkins was dangerously wounded, the first lieutenant and master were killed, the second lieutenant and marine officer were wounded, and the command devolved on the purser. The gunner now reported that the ship was on fire abaft, on which some of the guns' crews quitted their quarters, and the enemy, taking advantage of the confusion, boarded the *Ambuscade* by the bowsprit, and obtained possession of the frigate. The British loss was ten killed and 36 wounded, and the corvette, according to French accounts, had no less than 30 killed, including the military officer in command of the troops, and 30 badly wounded, among whom were Captain Richer and his first lieutenant, the number of slightly wounded not being given. Captain Jenkins and his officers and ship's company were subsequently brought before a court-martial, but were acquitted of blame for the loss of their ship, which, however, was generally attributed to the unseamanlike manner in which she was handled, and the lax discipline of her crew.

It being found expedient to evacuate the points in San Domingo occupied in the early part of the war, a convention was entered into with Toussaint L'Ouverture, and in May, 1798, the troops were removed by the *Thunderer*, 74, and other ships. Early in September the Spaniards made an attack on the British settlement in Honduras with a flotilla, having on board 500 seamen and 2,000 soldiers, but they were repulsed by the sloop-of-war *Merlin*, 16, Captain Moss, and five colonial gunboats, having crews of the aggregate of 254 officers and men, and a detachment of troops. The Spaniards retreated from Belize to Campeachy, and made no further attempt to attack the British settlements.

During the early months of 1799, Lord Bridport continued to watch the French fleet in Brest, but, nevertheless, Vice-Admiral Bruix managed, on the 25th April, to elude the British commander-in-chief, who was off the port with sixteen sail-of-the-line. Admiral Bruix had under his command one 120-gun ship, the *Ocean*, three of 110 guns, the *Invincible, Terrible*, and *Républicain*, the 80-gun ships *Formidable* and *Indomptable*, and nineteen seventy-fours, besides five frigates, and had five rear-admirals under his orders. The aggregate strength of the crews manning this powerful fleet was 22,761, exclusive of 1,000 soldiers, the three-deckers averaging 1,160 men, the 80-gun ships, 874, and the seventy-four's, 780.

The *Nymphe*, 36, Captain Fraser, discovered the fleet on the following morning, and communicated the intelligence to Lord Bridport, who sent a despatch vessel to Lord Keith, blockading off Cadiz nineteen Spanish sail-of-the-line, and to the commander-in-chief of the Mediterranean fleet, Earl St. Vincent, at Gibraltar, and himself made sail for Cape Clear, where he ordered his fleet to concentrate. But though he soon found himself at the head of twenty-six sail-of-the-line, Admiral Bruix had steered a course for Cadiz, where his fleet, consisting of twenty-five battle-ships, was sighted on the 4th May by Lord Keith, who got his fleet of fifteen sail under weigh and prepared for action. But the French commander-in-chief passed into the Mediterranean, whither he was followed on the 12th by Lord St. Vincent, with sixteen sail, which, off Minorca, were joined by Rear-Admiral Duckworth, with four ships. The departure of Lord Keith from before Cadiz on the 6th enabled the Spanish fleet of seventeen battle-ships, including six three-deckers, to get out to sea, and they passed the Straits of Gibraltar on the 17th, and reached Carthagena in safety, beyond eleven of the number losing one or more masts in a heavy gale, in which the superior seamanship and efficiency of the British fleet was attested by their escaping without mishap, though equally exposed to the fury of the tempest. Admiral Bruix made good his entry into Toulon, whence he again issued to effect a junction with the Spanish fleet, and Lord St. Vincent, owing to failure of health, surrendered the command to Lord Keith, detaching Admiral Duckworth with four ships to reinforce Lord Nelson at Palermo, and leaving twenty-one sail under his successor's orders, including a reinforcement of five ships brought by Rear-Admiral Whitshed. This fleet, reduced to nineteen sail by the despatch of the *Bellerophon* and *Powerful* to Palermo, succeeded in capturing, off Cape Sicie, a squadron of three French frigates and two brigs, which were all added to the Navy.

Lord Keith cruised about unsuccessfully in the hope of encountering the French fleet, which anchored at Carthagena, where Admiral Massaredo lay with his ships, when the combined fleets, numbering forty sail of the line, besides frigates and corvettes, again put to sea, and repassing the Straits, arrived at Brest, where they remained inactive throughout the remainder of the year. Meantime Lord Keith continued his game of hide and seek, and being reinforced by sixteen ships from the Channel fleet, under Admirals Cotton and Collingwood, also quitted the Mediterranean at the head of thirty-one sail, but arrived off Brest on the 14th August, a day too late to intercept the enemy.

Shortly before the fleet appeared off Cadiz, on its way to Toulon, five Spanish ships escaped and succeeded in reaching Rochefort, whither Lord Bridport detached five ships-of-the-line, four frigates, and three bomb-vessels under Rear-Admiral Pole. But the fire of the French batteries was so superior to that of the British bomb-vessels and frigates which could participate in the attack, that the attempt failed, and in the middle of September the Spanish ships made their escape to Ferrol.

Lord Nelson was not idle at Palermo. On being joined by Captain Troubridge with a squadron from Alexandria on the 31st March, he detached that officer with four seventy-four's and two bomb vessels to blockade the port of Naples, which the French had captured on the 24th January, and seize the neighbouring islands of Ischia, Procida, and Capri, and made preparations for the defence of Sicily. On hearing of the probable arrival in the Mediterranean of the Brest fleet, Lord Nelson concentrated the ships under his command, and in May and June cruised in the adjacent waters with sixteen sail-of-the-line, having shifted his flag from the *Vanguard* to the *Foudroyant*, 80, whither he was accompanied by Captain Hardy. Meantime Captain Foote, commanding the 38-gun frigate *Seahorse*, remained off Naples, with a small force on the departure of Captain Troubridge to join Nelson, and in conjunction with Cardinal Ruffo, acting for the King of the Two Sicilies, and a Russian force, part of the great Austro-Russian army that had entered Italy under General Suvaroff, compelled the Republican insurgents to surrender the forts defending Naples.

Nelson arrived after terms had been agreed upon between the contending parties, but refused to be bound by the agreement, though Captain Foote had signed the document. An unfortunate circumstance now took place. Prince Caraccioli, captain of the Neapolitan Navy, who had thrown in his lot with the Republican cause—forced, as he stated, to obey the French—having escaped from one of the forts, was captured on the 29th June, disguised as a peasant, and taken on board the *Foudroyant*. Clarke and McArthur, in their "Life of Lord Nelson," describe the scene that now took place :—

"Captain Hardy, who was on deck at the time, had his attention suddenly attracted to a clamour that prevailed, and it was some time before he could gain information from the Italians who were on board, that the 'traitor Caraccioli was taken.' It was with the utmost difficulty that this humane officer could restrain the assaults and violence of the Neapolitan royalists towards this unhappy victim of French perfidy, who, with his hands bound behind him, and wretchedly attired, displayed a painful instance of all human grandeur. When last on board, this prince had been received with all the respect and deference that were then due to his rank and character. Captain Hardy immediately ordered his noble prisoner to be unbound, and to be treated with every attention that was in his power. Some refreshments were immediately offered, which he declined, and he was then given in charge as a prisoner to the first-lieutenant, Mr. W. S. Parkinson, and shown into his cabin. Two additional sentinels were then placed at the outside of the wardroom."

An hour after his arrival, Caraccioli was arraigned on board the *Foudroyant*, before a court-martial of Neapolitan naval officers, with his bitterest enemy, Commodore Count Thurn, as President, and notwithstanding his age of three score and ten, forty of which had been passed in his country's service, he was sentenced to death, and Lord Nelson issued an order for his immediate execution on board the Neapolitan frigate *Minerva*.

"During the awful interval that ensued," says the biographer already quoted, "from the close of his trial to the execution of his sentence, Caraccioli twice requested

Lieutenant Parkinson to go and intercede with Lord Nelson, at first for a second trial, and afterwards that he might be shot.

"'I am an old man, sir,' said Caraccioli; 'I have no family to lament my death. I therefore cannot be supposed to be very anxious about prolonging my life; but the disgrace of being hanged is dreadful to me.'

"Lord Nelson replied, 'Caraccioli has been fairly tried by the officers of his own country; I cannot interfere.' On being urged a second time by Lieutenant Parkinson, he exclaimed with much agitation, 'Go, sir, and attend to your duty.'"

At 5 P.M. Caraccioli was removed from the *Foudroyant*, and hanged at the fore-yardarm of the *Minerva*, and his body was afterwards sunk in the Bay of Naples. The incident is one of the few in the life of the great national hero that is regrettable.

On the 8th July King Ferdinand IV. returned to Naples in one of his frigates, escorted by the *Seahorse*. As a detachment of 800 French troops continued to garrison the fort of St. Elmo, Captain Troubridge, having landed with some British and Portuguese marines, co-operated with the Russian and Neapolitan forces in reducing the fort, which capitulated, the allied loss being five officers and 32 men killed and five officers and 79 wounded. Captain Troubridge also commanded 1,000 seamen and marines from the British fleet at the siege of Capua, about fifteen miles from Naples, which was surrendered by its garrison of 2,817 men. A few days later the fort of Gaeta surrendered, and its garrison of 1,500 troops was conveyed to Toulon, and by the end of September Captain Troubridge received the capitulation of Civita Vecchia, and Rome itself was surrendered to General Bouchard, commanding the Neapolitan troops, aided by a detachment of seamen, under Captain Louis, of the *Minotaur*, who rowed up the Tiber in his barge, and hoisted the British flag on the Capitol of the Eternal City.

Meantime Buonaparte was not idle in Egypt. Early in January, 1799, he marched from Cairo with 13,000 men, 27 field pieces, and 11 siege howitzers, to effect the conquest of Syria, Achmet Djezzar, Pasha of the province, having defied him from Acre. He took with him some of his most famous generals, Regnier, Kleber, Lannes, and Murat, and left the remainder of his army, some 17,000 men, to hold the country. On the 3rd March Sir Sydney Smith arrived off Alexandria in the *Tigre*, 74, and superseded Captain Troubridge, who sailed to join Lord Nelson. Sir Sydney had arranged a plan of co-operation with the Turks against Buonaparte, and now despatched his fellow prisoner in the Temple, Lieutenant Wright, to the Pasha at Acre with the same object.

On the 7th an express was received from Achmet Djezzar, announcing that Buonaparte had captured Jaffa, and on the following day the commodore despatched the *Theseus*, 74, Captain Miller, to Acre, with Colonel Phelipeaux, of the Engineers, to assist him with his advice in preparing for the defence of that place. Commodore Smith himself sailed a few days later, and anchored in the Bay of Acre, where he found the *Theseus*. This energetic officer landed on the following day, and with the assistance of Colonel Phelipeaux, Captain Miller and other officers, commenced putting the town, with its crumbling walls, in a condition to stand a siege. In this he was actively assisted by the Pasha, but the time at their disposal was short. During the night of the 17th he discovered the French advanced guard marching by the seaside, upon which he sent the launch of the *Tigre*, with a 32-pounder carronade and 16 men, under the orders of Lieutenant Bushby, to the mouth of the river Kerdannah to guard the ford. At daybreak that officer opened fire upon the French troops, who fell back to the base of the promontory of Mount Carmel, when the main body marched by another road and invested the town on the north-east side, where the defences were much stronger. The non-employment of guns convinced the commodore that the French expected their guns by sea, and the same morning a flotilla, consisting of one corvette and nine sailing gun-boats, hove in sight, when, after a three hours' chase, seven of the latter were captured—including one taken that morning from the British—mounting 32 guns and laden with a siege train and ammunition. These guns were at once landed for the defence of Acre, and the prizes were employed in harassing the enemy's boats and cutting off his supplies brought by coasters from Alexandria. In one of these attempts to cut out some craft in the port of Caiffa, the boats of the *Theseus* and the *Tigre*, covered by the gun-boats, suffered considerably, losing four midshipmen and eight seamen killed, and one midshipman and 26 wounded.

The French, meantime, pushed their approaches, and were employed in mining the tower against which batteries were playing. To destroy this mine a sortie was made on the 7th April by a detachment of seamen and marines, while the Turkish troops attacked the trenches on either hand, and Lieutenant Wright, of the *Tigre*, commanding the seamen pioneers, succeeded in demolishing the mine, but received two musket-balls in his right arm while thus engaged. In this service the British loss was Major Oldfield, of the marines, and two privates killed, Lieutenants Wright

BOATSWAIN

(About 1829).

and Beatty (of the marines), two midshipmen, seven marines, and 12 seamen wounded. The Turkish troops were also successful, and returned bringing the heads of sixty French soldiers.

On the 27th April arrived overland from Jaffa, nine battering guns, brought by Rear-Admiral Perrée's squadron from Alexandria, and on the 1st May, after many hours' cannonade from 23 pieces of ordnance, Buonaparte ordered an assault on the breach. The French troops advanced to the attack with great gallantry, but the flanking fire brought to bear on the enemy's trenches by the *Theseus* and *Tigre*, moored on either side, and by the gun-boats and launches, was so heavy and effective, that the French troops were repulsed with slaughter. The British loss was Captain David Wilmot, commanding the frigate *Alliance*, one midshipman and four seamen killed, and one lieutenant and eight men wounded. The besieged also experienced a great loss at this time in the death by fever of Colonel Phelipeaux, who had so ably directed the engineering operations. Nothing daunted by his failure, Buonaparte continued to batter the works, and made more than one attempt to storm, but met with continued ill-success. At length, on the 7th May, the fifty-first day of the siege, a considerable reinforcement of troops was signalled for the allies from Rhodes, and Buonaparte resolved to make a final desperate attempt on the town before they were landed. After maintaining a very heavy fire, the storming columns advanced to the attack under better conditions, as they had thrown up traverses and epaulments, but the flanking fire from the British afloat, and especially heavy discharges of grape from a 15-pounder in the lighthouse, and a 24-pounder in the north ravelin, caused fearful havoc in their ranks, but yet, notwithstanding every effort, the enemy made a lodgment in the northeast tower, which they strengthened by two traverses across the ditch.

It was an anxious moment, as the Turkish troops were not yet landed, but Sir Sydney Smith was equal to the crisis. The commodore landed with the ship's boats at the mole head, and led the crews, armed with pikes, to the breach, where he was joined by the Pasha, and soon a portion of the troops from the transports arrived on the scene, and made a sortie, but were repulsed with loss. So the conflict raged all day; and a little before sunset Buonaparte, who, surrounded by a group of generals, had taken his station on an eminence known as Richard Cœur de Lion's Mount, ordered a final attempt to carry the place by assault. The French columns advanced unmolested over the breach, but on descending from the ramparts, they were met by the Turkish soldiers sword in hand, and were driven back, General Rambeaud being among the dead and General Lannes among the wounded. This closed the incidents of an eventful day.

The neighbouring tribesmen now rallied to the cause of their co-religionists, and commenced to cut off the French supplies.

The British squadron experienced a serious loss by an accident that took place on the 14th May, on board the *Theseus*. As the seventy-four was engaged chasing Admiral Perrée's squadron, some seventy shells that had been got up from the magazine, exploded in some inexplicable way on the deck, killing 40 men, including Captain Miller and three other officers, and nine men who jumped overboard were drowned. In addition, 47 were injured from severe burns, among the number being two lieutenants, the master, surgeon, chaplain, one midshipman, and the carpenter. The poop and afterpart of the quarter-deck were blown to pieces, the booms were destroyed, eight of the main-deck beams were broken, and the ship was set on fire in several places and aloft. By great exertions the flames were subdued, but the ship was reduced to the condition of a wreck. The *Theseus* also lost in action 4 killed, 15 wounded, and 5 prisoners. The *Tigre's* casualties in action with the enemy ashore and afloat, numbered 17 killed, 48 wounded, 4 drowned, and 77 prisoners, and the *Alliance* had one killed and three drowned.

On the night of the 20th May, Buonaparte abandoned the siege, and leaving 23 guns in the hands of the besieged, made a precipitate retreat. Thus his great schemes for ascendency in the East and the conquest of British India, of which the acquisition of Acre was to be the first step, were baffled, and he afterwards declared with bitterness that "his destiny was foiled by an English post-captain." Retreating by Jaffa and El Arish, where he had left a garrison, Buonaparte entered Cairo on the 14th June, a discomfited general, whose claims to invincibility were rudely dispelled in the breach at Acre. Berthier places the loss of the French army during the expedition at 500 killed and 1,800 wounded, and 700 died of disease, but it is said to have been much greater.

Sir Sydney Smith sailed from Acre on the 12th June, and having refitted his squadron at Larnica, in Cyprus, proceeded to Constantinople to concert measures with the Porte for the expulsion of the French from Egypt. Accordingly the Sultan despatched a powerful fleet of thirteen seventy-fours, nine frigates, and seventeen gun-boats, with a large number of transports, having on board some 18,000 troops, who effected a landing at Aboukir and captured the fort, having a French garrison of 300 men. But Buonaparte arrived from Cairo at Alexandria, and marching thence on Aboukir, inflicted a crushing defeat on the Turkish army, whose loss, according to their account, was 10,000 killed and driven into the sea, and 2,000 prisoners, and that of their conquerors, 200 slain, including three generals, and 750 wounded, among the number being Murat.

On the 5th August, Buonaparte quitted Aboukir for Cairo, where he remained eleven days, making arrangements for leaving the country, and transferring the command to General Kléber; and on the 21st arrived at Alexandria. The required opportunity to quit the country was afforded by Sir Sydney Smith, who had appeared off the coast with the *Tigre* and *Theseus*, sailing for Cyprus; and at 10 P.M. on the 22nd August, Buonaparte, accompanied by General Berthier, embarked on board the frigate *Murion*, flagship of Rear-Admiral Ganteaume, and in company with the frigate *Carrère*, having on board Generals Lannes, Murat, and Marmont, and two small vessels, sailed from Egypt on the following morning. The squadron bearing the great soldier, who was to be Emperor of France and Dictator of Europe, with some of his most famous marshals, avoided the British cruisers by hugging the African coast, and touching, on the 1st October, at his native island of Corsica, where he heard of the loss of Italy and the invasion of Holland by a British army under the Duke of York, he sailed thence on the 7th, taking in tow a felucca, manned with an expert crew of oarsmen, in which to escape in case the frigates were attacked, and on the 9th landed at Frejus, having thus eluded all the British cruisers with which the Mediterranean was swarming.

Towards the end of October, Sir Sydney Smith returned to the Egyptian coast with a Turkish fleet and a considerable body of troops from Constantinople, which were disembarked near Damietta; but the French, who had collected in some force, attacked the division that first landed, of whom over 2,000 were killed and 800 made prisoners.

Reference was made above to a British attack on Holland. This was a purely military expedition, and the Navy had no share in the discredit that attaches to the ill-success with which it was conducted. The fleet, consisting of one hundred and fifty ships-of-war and transports, was under the command of Lord Duncan; but beyond landing the troops and taking possession of thirteen Dutch ships-of-war at the Helder, and a second squadron of eight two-deckers and frigates in the Texel, which surrendered to Admiral Mitchell, the Navy had few opportunities of distinguishing itself. On the whole, twenty-five ships, out of the fifty-five constituting the Dutch Marine, were surrendered, as the crews, who held contrary political opinions to the officers, refused to fight, and of the number, eighteen were purchased into the British Navy, of which ten only went to sea. The Dutch Navy received at Camperdown and on this occasion a blow from which it never recovered. The expedition terminated by the evacuation of Holland by the combined British and Russian forces under the Duke of York, the British loss alone being 556 killed and 2,800 wounded. During the campaign the Navy experienced the loss, by shipwreck on the coast, of the *Nassau*, 64, and the *Blanche* and *Lutine* frigates, when the first lost one-fourth of her crew, and the *Lutine* the whole, except two men, besides £140,000 in specie, which she was conveying from Yarmouth to the Texel for the payment of the troops.

The country also sustained a loss in the wreck, on the 1st February, 1799, of the 28-gun frigate *Proserpine*, Captain Wallis, which sailed from Yarmouth for Cuxhaven, with the Hon. Thomas Grenville, on a mission to Berlin. The *Proserpine* got on some sands, six miles off Newark Island, at the mouth of the Elbe, and after suffering great hardships, as the ship showed signs of breaking up under the pressure of the ice, the officers and men left her and made their way on the ice to the island. During the journey 12 seamen and marines and a woman and child were frozen to death, but the remainder, numbering 173, reached Cuxhaven, and ultimately returned to England, when the discipline and good conduct of all concerned received the commendation of the court-martial convened to try Captain Wallis and his officers and ship's company.

During the year 1799 there were some frigate actions deserving a brief record. The most striking of these duels was that between the British 48-gun frigate *Sibylle*, Captain Cooke—an officer whose name has already received honourable mention in these pages—and the *Forte*, of 52 guns, commanded by Captain Beaulieu de Long, one of the ships of Rear-Admiral Sercey's squadron, in the East Indies, which at the time consisted, besides the *Forte*, of the *Preneuse* and *Prudente*. The *Forte* was an especially fine frigate, well officered and manned, and had committed such great depredations on British commerce that Captain Cooke sailed from Madras on the 19th February, for the special purpose of cutting short her career of mischief. This promised to be a task of no common difficulty, as the *Sibylle*, originally a French 40-gun frigate, captured by the *Romney*, 50, in June, 1794, was a ship of 1,091 tons, and the enemy she was in quest of measured 1,400 tons, and her broadside weight of metal was 100 pounds more, being respectively 503 and 604 pounds. As regards the strength of the crews, the two frigates were of equal force.

The *Sibylle* steered for the Sandheads, off the Hooghly, and on the evening of the 28th February, attracted by the flash of her guns, came up with her adversary, which had just captured two rich prizes, the *Endeavour* and *Lord Mornington*, from China. After some manœuvring, the wind being light and the weather fine, about midnight the *Sibylle* approached within a mile of the *Forte*, which presented a formidable appearance with her two rows of ports lit up by her battle lanterns.

Tacking under the bows of the British frigate, she commenced the action by firing some of her port guns as they began to bear, and drew "first blood" by bringing down the *Sibylle's* jib. Captain Cooke, however, reserved his fire until the enemy had passed abaft his beam, when at 12.45 he put his helm up, and passing her within pistol-shot range, poured the whole of his port broadside into her stern, raking her fore and aft. Then luffing up, the gallant and skilful captain of the *Sibylle* brought his ship alongside his antagonist to leeward and let him have a second broadside as close and deadly. Now ensued a furious action between these frigates, which might well be regarded as the champions of the rival nations. The darkness of night was lit up by the lightning flashes of the guns, and the neighbouring shores of the Sunderbunds resounded with the roar. Thus, as they lay broadside to broadside, the battle raged at a distance that never exceeded point-blank musket-range, when, about 1.30, Captain Cooke received a mortal wound from a grape-shot. The first lieutenant, Mr. Lucius Hardyman, succeeded to the command, but already it was noticeable that the fire of the French frigate had become slacker, and an hour after Captain Cooke was carried below, it entirely ceased.

The *Forte* was hailed if she had surrendered, but the crew of the *Sibylle*, receiving no reply, re-commenced their fire. Still the enemy's guns were silent, and a second time the firing ceased, and a demand was made for her surrender. At this time the rigging of the *Forte* was filled with men as though with the object of making sail, when the *Sibylle* recommenced her fire and set her fore-sail and top-gallant sails. A few minutes later all three of the *Forte's* masts and her bowsprit came down, an event received with three cheers by the British seamen at their quarters, who ceased firing. Thus at 3.30 in the morning of the 1st March, after an action extending over two hours and three quarters, the French frigate *Forte* became a prize to the superior gunnery and prowess of the British frigate *Sibylle*. The latter, out of a crew of 371 men and boys, including some soldiers from a Scotch regiment, had one officer and four men killed, and Captain Cooke (mortally) and 16 men wounded. Her rigging and sails were cut to pieces and all her spars, especially the main and mizen-masts and their yards, were badly wounded.

Far greater was the loss sustained by her adversary, which, out of 370 men on board, the remainder of her complement having been sent away in prizes, had no less than 65 killed, including her captain, first lieutenant and some other officers. When taken possession of by Mr. Manger, third lieutenant of the *Sibylle*, the scene of carnage presented on her decks was indescribable. The ship was also a wreck. The bowsprit had been shot off close to the figure head, the fore-mast one foot above the forecastle, the mainmast 18 feet above the quarter-deck, and the mizen-mast 10 feet above the poop. All the boats, booms, wheel, capstan, binnacle, and everything else on the decks were cut to pieces, and the forecastle bell was pierced by a grape-shot and was long kept at Fort William, in Calcutta, as a trophy of this memorable action. Her upper works were partially beaten in, and the quarter-deck and forecastle barricades were destroyed, and upwards of 300 round shot were counted in her hull, while several of her guns were dismounted and even her cables, stowed in the tiers, did not escape the well-directed broadsides of the *Sibylle*. The victory was due to the splendid gunnery of the crew of the British frigate, who took advantage of Captain Cooke's skilful handling at the beginning of the action, by pouring in two broadsides which caused heavy loss to the enemy, and the early fall of the two superior officers must also have greatly discouraged the men.

The two French prizes, on seeing the result of the action, made sail and managed to escape, as the *Sibylle*, which followed in pursuit, could carry but little sail on her main-mast. The two frigates were jury-rigged at their anchorage at the Sandheads, whence they proceeded to Calcutta. The *Forte* was added to the Navy, under her own name, but was lost by shipwreck before arriving in England.

The gallant Captain Cooke, after lingering in much suffering until the 28th May, died at Calcutta, universally lamented, and a monument was erected to his memory by the East India Company. His first lieutenant received promotion to the rank of commander.

The *Prudente*, of 30 guns, also one of Admiral Sercey's squadron in the East Indies, was captured by the 38-gun frigate *Dædalus*, Captain Ball, on the 9th February. The *Prudente* was in company with a prize when sighted, and the *Dædalus* gave chase. The first shot was fired about noon, from the stern-chasers of the French frigate, which then shortened sail, and the action commenced, the *Dædalus* bearing up across the stern of the *Prudente*, into which she poured a raking broadside at half pistol-shot range, and, luffing up under her lee, engaged the enemy broadside to broadside, thus adopting the tactics of the *Sibylle* in her action with the *Forte*, three weeks later. The *Prudente* lost her mizen-mast in a quarter of an hour, and at 1.20 hauled down her colours, being much cut up aloft and in her hull. Out of a crew of 301 men she had lost 27 officers and men killed, and 22 wounded, while the *Dædalus*, which commenced the action with 212 hands, had only two killed and 12 wounded. The victory was a very creditable one to the officers and men of the British frigate, whose broadside weight of metal was only 32 pounds in excess of that of her adversary.

The last of the three frigates of Admiral Sercey's squadron, the *Preneuse*, of 40 guns and 300 men, shared the fate of her consorts, and was not suffered to return to La Belle France. While passing off Algoa Bay, near Cape Town, on the 20th September, she was sighted by the armed storeship, *Camel*, Captain Lee, and the 16-gun sloop, *Rattlesnake*, Commander Gooch, both much undermanned, as their captains and a portion of their crews were serving on shore with the army. The *Preneuse* stood in for the bay after dark on the 20th September, and engaged both ships, which had their top-masts and yards on deck. The action continued all night, but at daybreak the frigate ceased firing and stood out of the bay. The *Camel* suffered a good deal in her rigging, and a shot in her hull caused a leak from which she made six feet of water. Both ships had only a slight loss in killed and wounded. A few days later the *Preneuse* encountered a foeman more worthy her fighting strength.

The *Jupiter*, 50, Captain Grainger, joined her consorts from Table Bay, and sailing again on the 9th October, on the following day overhauled the French frigate, after a running fight kept up all night. But owing to the heavy sea, the *Jupiter*, being a two-decker, could not open her lower-deck ports, and was only able to employ her light 12-pounders. The *Preneuse* meanwhile shot away her opponent's rigging, and the *Jupiter* had to abandon the pursuit, and returned to Table Bay. On nearing Mauritius on the 11th December, the *Preneuse* was chased by the *Tremendous*, 74, Captain Osborn, and *Adamant*, 52, Captain Hotham, and finding escape impossible, Captain L'Hermite ran his ship ashore under some batteries about three miles from Port Louis, where she was destroyed by some boats from the British ships, under Lieutenant Grey, first of the *Adamant*.

A catastrophe took place in the East Indies which caused great loss of life. The 16-gun sloop, *Trincomalee*, Captain Rowe, when cruising in the Straits of Babel Mandeb, at the entrance to the Red Sea, engaged a French privateer of 22 guns, but from some unexplained cause, blew up while alongside her opponent, which also went down by the force of the concussion. Only two men were saved of the British ship, and about 115 of her opponent's crew were drowned.

The *Wolverine*, of 13 guns and 70 men, Commander Mortlock, engaged two French luggers, having respectively 8 guns and about 70 men and 14 guns and 80 men. The crews of the luggers made desperate attempts to board the *Wolverine*, but were beaten back, though at the termination of the conflict her gallant commander, who had received three wounds in the action, was mortally wounded. This same ship, *Wolverine*, in conjunction with the *Arrow*, 28, Captain Portlock, standing into shoal water on the Dutch coast, attacked a ship and brig at anchor in the narrow passage leading from the land to Harlingen, and both were captured after a spirited resistance, when the ship *Draak*, of 24 guns and 180 men, was destroyed, but the brig *Gier*, carrying 14 guns and 80 men, was taken to England and fitted out as a cruiser. In the Mediterranean, the *Leviathan*, 74, and *Argo*, 44, chased two Spanish frigates off Majorca, and the latter, commanded by Captain James Bowen, overhauled and captured one of them, the *Santa Teresa*, 42, having a crew of 280 men and 250 soldiers, which surrendered after receiving a broadside. The prize was a new ship, just out of dock, and was purchased into the service.

Off the Spanish coast the British brig, *Espoir*, Commander Sanders, of 14 guns and 80 men, boarded and captured, after a spirited action, the xebec (a three-masted vessel) *Africa*, mounting 18 guns, with a crew of 75 seamen and 38 soldiers. The latter lost one officer and eight men killed, and her commander, two officers, and 25 men wounded, while the *Espoir* had only four casualties.

Lieutenant Worth, commanding the 16-gun brig *Telegraph*, having a crew of 60 men, engaged off the French coast, and took, after an engagement lasting three and a half hours, the privateer brig *Hirondelle*, of 16 guns and 72 men. The latter lost five killed and 14 wounded, and the *Telegraph*, whose commander received promotion, had only five men wounded. Off the port of Lorient, the *San Fiorenzo*, 36, Sir Harry Neale, and *Amelia*, 38, Captain Hon. Charles Herbert (formerly the French ships *Minerve* and *Proserpine*), engaged a squadron of three French frigates and a gunboat, and drove them off, though the *Amelia* was partially crippled by the loss of her main-topmast and fore and mizen-topgallant-masts. Both ships suffered considerably aloft in repelling the enemy, and had a midshipman and two men killed and 35 wounded. The French ships were reported to have lost heavily, and the official *Moniteur* acknowledged that the captain of one was mortally wounded, and a second had 15 killed.

The French 36-gun frigate, *Vestale*, the old opponent of the *Terpsichore*, was forced to haul down her colours, after an engagement lasting nearly two hours, by the *Clyde*, 38, Captain Cunningham. In the action, which took place off Rochefort on the 20th August, the British frigate had only two killed and three wounded, while the *Vestale*, out of 230 men actually on board, lost 10 killed and 22 wounded, and was much cut up in her hull and rigging. A sister ship of the *Clyde*, the *Tamar*, Captain Western, captured, off Surinam, after a brief action of ten minutes, the French 28-gun frigate *Republicaine*, which was reduced to the condition of a wreck, and lost nine killed and 12 wounded out of a crew numbering 175 men. Thus the disparity of force was even greater in this instance than the last.

A gallant exploit was performed by the boats of the 32-gun frigate *Success*, under Lieutenant Facey, who had 41 officers and men under his command. This small force cut out a Spanish polacre, of 10 guns and 113 men, from the harbour of La Selva, but not without some loss, four being killed, and a lieutenant and eight seamen badly wounded. Lieutenant Facey was made a commander for his daring deed. The *Alcmene*, 32, Captain Digby, captured the French privateer *Courageux*, of 28 guns and 253 men, on the Spanish coast, and a few weeks later cut out two Spanish vessels from the port of Vivero without loss. The 14-gun brig *Speedy*, Commander Jahleel Brenton, and *Defender*, the latter a privateer of Gibraltar, also brought out three Spanish armed vessels after a spirited action. Later in the year Commander Brenton gave chase to four coasting vessels, which took shelter under some old forts, and compelled them by his fire to cut their cables and drift ashore. On the 6th November, he attacked in the most gallant manner twelve Spanish gunboats, and covered the escape of a merchant brig, but the *Speedy* suffered considerably aloft in the encounter, and had to run to Tetuan Bay in order to plug up the shot-holes.

Good service was likewise performed on the coast of Holland by the 16-gun brigs *Pylades* and *Espiegle*, and 10-gun cutter *Courier*, in cutting out the late British gun-brig *Crash*, having 12 guns and 60 men. These ships' boats cut out from under a battery the Dutch schooner *Vengeance*, which subsequently blew up, and the crews landing, spiked the guns of the battery.

The intrepidity of our sailors, when confronted with greatly superior forces, received an illustration in the attack made by the *Cerberus*, 32, Captain Macnamara, off Cape Ortugal, on no less than five Spanish frigates, convoying 80 sail of merchantmen. The *Cerberus* engaged in succession three of the enemy's frigates, and managed to escape with difficulty from her foes who had surrounded her. The 38-gun frigate *Revolutionnaire*, captured off the coast of Ireland the French privateer *Bordelais*, of 24 guns and 202 men, which was added to the Navy under her own name; and the *Naiad*, 38, Captain Pierrepoint, chased two Spanish 32-gun frigates, bound for Vera Cruz from a Spanish port with specie to the value of £340,000. The *Ethalion*, *Triton*, and *Alcmene*, joined in the pursuit, when the *Thetis*, containing the greater portion of the specie, was captured, after a running fight of an hour with the *Ethalion*, and the *Santa Brigida* surrendered, after making skilful efforts to escape off the rockbound coast near Cape Finisterre. The treasure captured in the ships was conveyed from Plymouth to London, and was divided among the fortunate captors, the captains each having £40,730, the lieutenants £5,091, and other ranks in proportion, the share of the seamen and marines being £182 4s. 9d.

In the West Indies also, those waters so fertile in deeds of British daring since the days of Drake, our Navy increased its reputation by acts of gallantry. In March the 36-gun frigate *Trent*, Captain Otway, was cruising in company with the 12-gun cutter *Sparrow*, Lieutenant Wiley, off the island of Porto Rico, when she sighted a merchant ship and three schooners, at anchor under the protection of a 5-gun battery. Captain Otway despatched his boats, covered by the *Sparrow*, when the battery was stormed, and the ship and one of the schooners were boarded and brought off, the other two having been scuttled by their crews. In the following month the *Amaranthe*, Commander Vesey, of 14 guns and 86 men, captured off Jamaica a privateer of 6 guns and 26 men, which made a noble defence, losing no less than 14 killed and five wounded.

When detailing the mutinies in the British Navy in 1797, we recorded the circumstances under which the crew of the 32-gun frigate *Hermione*, after murdering their officers, carried the ship into the Spanish port of La Guayra, and gave her up to the enemies of their country. The Spaniards fitted the *Hermione* with 44 guns, and sent her to sea, with a crew of 321 men, exclusive of 72 marines. Learning that she was about to sail from Porto Cabello to Havannah, Sir Hyde Parker, commanding on the Jamaica station, detached the *Surprise*, Captain Hamilton, carrying 34 guns and 197 men, to see what he could do to regain possession of her. On arriving off Porto Cabello, Captain Hamilton found the *Hermione* moored head and stern between two strong batteries, at the entrance of the harbour, but nothing daunted, he resolved to undertake what appeared the foolhardy task of cutting her out. Mustering his crew, he made known to them his intention, which was greeted with three cheers, and at 8 P.M. on the evening of the 24th October the gallant captain of the *Surprise* pushed off from his ship with all the boats, manned with 100 officers and men. About midnight they encountered the *Hermione's* launch, having a 24-pounder and 20 men, rowing guard some 1,200 yards from the ship, but pushing past her, Captain Hamilton, undeterred by a fire directed towards him by the main-deck and forecastle guns, made for the ship, and soon was alongside her. Scrambling up, with the gunner, Mr. Maxwell, and eight or ten of his men, he made good his footing on the enemy's forecastle, and was immediately joined by the gig's crew, who had boarded on the port bow, led by the surgeon, Mr. McMullen. Meanwhile the two cutters, attacking at the gangways, had not fared so well. Both had been beaten off, but on the other hand, the launch, under the second lieutenant, and the jolly boat, commanded by the carpenter, had cut the bower and stern cables, and being reinforced by some of their crews, Captain Hamilton, leaving the gunner with about a dozen men to make his way along the starboard gangway, hastened along the port side to the quarter-deck, which was the rendezvous.

A desperate struggle took place on the quarter-deck, where the Spanish officers had taken up their station, and Captain Hamilton and the gunner were severely wounded, but at the critical moment the crews of the cutters, under the first lieutenant and lieutenant of marines, joined their comrades, and the enemy were driven below. While the men detailed for the duty ran aloft to loose the fore and mizen-topsails, and the boats, under the second lieutenant, took the ship in tow, the rest of the men, led by the surgeon and marine officer, so closely followed the Spaniards down the after companion ladder to the main-deck, that they had no time to recover from their confusion. After a brief resistance the gallant British tars compelled the enemy to call for quarter, and so the British frigate *Hermione* once more changed hands, and returned to her old allegiance. The prize, by the use of sails and oars, was taken from under the fire of the batteries, which had now opened on her, inflicting considerable damage aloft and in the hull, so that they had to rig pumps to keep her afloat, and ultimately she was taken out of gun-shot, and on the 1st November anchored at Port Royal, in Jamaica.

Without doubt this achievement stands, perhaps, unparalleled in naval history for its audacity and success, and no feat of arms can be regarded as beyond the capacity of seamen who could achieve such a conquest. The victors had only 12 wounded, whereas the enemy lost no fewer than 119 killed and 97 wounded; and the survivors were sent back to Porto Cabello in a captured schooner.

Captain Hamilton was knighted for this achievement, which, though it enhanced his reputation as a daring officer, cost him much suffering. His wounds were many and severe. He first received a tremendous blow from the butt-end of a musket, which broke over his head, and knocked him senseless on the deck; then he had a severe sabre-wound on the left thigh, another wound by a pike in the right thigh, and a contusion on the right shin-bone by a grape-shot; one of his fingers was much cut, and his loins and kidneys were so much bruised, that ever after he was under medical treatment. Sir Edward Hamilton, says his biographer, Mr. Marshall, while returning home in April of the following year, to be treated for his injuries, was so unfortunate as to be captured by a privateer and carried into a French port; from whence he was sent to Paris, where he was taken particular notice of by Buonaparte, who at length agreed to his being exchanged for six midshipmen. Previously to his departure from Jamaica, the Legislature presented him with a sword of the value of 300 guineas; and on his arrival in England after his exchange, the Common Council of London voted him the freedom of the City.

Considerable credit was gained by the *Crescent*, 36, Captain Lobb, and *Calypso*, 16, Commander Baker, having a convoy in charge from England for Jamaica, for the seamanlike way in which they out-manœuvred a Spanish squadron, consisting of a 64-gun ship, a frigate of 40 guns, and a 16-gun corvette, and not only saved their charge from capture, but took the smallest of the three ships-of-war. Not less remarkable was the smartness and gallantry displayed by the *Solebay*, 32, Captain Poyntz, cruising off St. Domingo, in capturing the armed store-ship *Egyptien*, of 20 guns and 137 men, and 12-gun brig *Levrier*, forming part of a squadron of four ships, and then, after a chase, compelling the others to surrender, one of which, carrying 16 guns and 107 men, was purchased into the service under the name of *Nimrod*.

So numerous were the deeds of gallantry performed by the Navy, that they can only receive a bare mention. Among such was the capture, off Flushing, of the French privateer *Guerrier*, of 14 guns and 44 men, by the cutter *Courier*, of 12 guns and 40 men, commanded by Lieutenant Searle, who had before distinguished himself during the war, and now received promotion. Also the action off Dover between the 28-gun brig *Racoon*, Commander Lloyd, and the *Intrépide*, 16-gun lugger, of Calais, which was captured after a brave resistance, her casualties being 13. In this case the British vessel was of superior force as regards crew and size. The cutter *Viper*, Lieutenant Pengelly, of 14 guns and 48 men, also captured, after a close action lasting three-quarters of an hour, the French privateer lugger *Ferret*, of the same force, but having 57 men, of whom four were killed, and her commander, chief officer, and six severely wounded. Last, and even more brilliant, was the recapture of the 10-gun cutter *Lady Nelson*, which had been surrounded and taken by some Spanish privateers and gun-boats off Cabrita Point, in sight of the *Queen Charlotte*, Lord Keith's flagship, and the *Emerald*, lying at Gibraltar. The boats of these ships had been sent to the assistance of the cutter, but were too late, whereupon Lieutenant Bainbridge, in the flagship's launch, having a crew of 16 men, boarded the *Lady Nelson*, which was in tow of two of the privateers, and carried her, after a struggle in which six or seven of the enemy were killed or knocked overboard, and seven French officers and 27 men were captured.

During the year 1799, the only naval expedition was one despatched from Martinique against the Dutch possession of Surinam, consisting of the *Prince of Wales*, 98, flagship of Lord Hugh Seymour, *Invincible*, 74, four frigates, a 20-gun ship and one gun-boat, having on board a detachment of troops under General Trigge. After some negotiations the settlement was surrendered on the 20th August, together with two French and Dutch corvettes, which were added to the Navy.

Buonaparte, now First Consul of France, addressed a communication, dated Christmas Day, 1799, to King George, proposing terms of peace, but they were deemed inadmissible. At the end of April, Lord Bridport resigned the command of the Channel fleet, consisting of 38 sail-of-the-line, to Earl St. Vincent, who arrived off Brest in the *Namur*, 90, and continued the blockade of the combined French and Spanish fleets of forty-five sail. Sir Edward Pellew was detached, in June, with seven seventy-four's and five frigates, with some troop-ships having on board 5,000 soldiers, under General Maitland, to make a descent on the Morbihan, but the enterprise was abandoned.

The British Navy sustained serious loss in the destruction of three fine ships-of-the-line, though not at the hands of the enemy. On the 9th March the *Repulse*, 64, struck on a sunken rock about seventy-five miles south-west of Ushant, and becoming a total wreck, had to be abandoned, when the crew were made prisoners, with the exception of four officers and eight seamen, who succeeded in reaching Guernsey in a boat. On the 17th March, while the *Queen Charlotte*, 100, flagship of Lord Keith in the Mediterranean, was proceeding from Leghorn (where the admiral and ten others of the crew had landed) to the southward, under command of Captain Todd, she was discovered to be on fire, and notwithstanding every effort to save her, was totally destroyed. Of her crew on board at the time of the catastrophe, ten being on shore at Leghorn, 156 were saved by boats, and no less than 673 perished, including the captain, three lieutenants, the captain of marines, purser, surgeon and three of his mates, 18 midshipmen, four master's mates, and some warrant officers.* The third ship lost was the *Marlborough*, 74, Captain Sotheby, which, while cruising off the French coast, struck on a shoal near Belleisle, and though she was got off, made so much water that she had to be abandoned, and sank at her anchors. The *Captain*, 74, cruising with her, took off the ship's company, who were acquitted of all blame by a court-martial.

In the siege of Genoa, where General Massena had retired with the remnant of

---

* The following account of the loss of the *Queen Charlotte* is by the carpenter :—"At about twenty minutes to six o'clock in the morning, as I was dressing myself, I heard throughout the ship a general cry of fire. I immediately ran to the fore-ladder to get on deck, and found the whole half deck, the front bulk-head of the admiral's cabin, the coat of the mainmast, and the boats' covering on the booms all in flames ; which, from every report and probability, I apprehended was occasioned by some hay, that was lying under the half-deck, having been set on fire by a match in a tub, which was usually kept there for signal guns. The main-sail at this time was set, and almost immediately caught fire, the people not being able, on account of the flames, to come to the clue garnets.

"I immediately went to the forecastle and found Lieutenant Hon. H. Dundas and the boatswain encouraging the people to get water to extinguish the fire. I applied to Mr. Dundas, seeing no other officer in the forepart of the ship (and being unable to see any on the quarter-deck from the flames and smoke between them), to give me assistance to drown the lower decks, and secure the hatches to prevent the fire falling down. Lieutenant Dundas accordingly went down himself, with as many people as he could prevail upon to follow him ; and the lower-deck ports were opened, the scuppers plugged, the fore and main hatches secured, the cocks turned, water drawn in at the ports, and the pumps kept going by the people who came down, as long as they could stand at them. Owing to these exertions I think the lower-deck was kept free from fire, and the magazines preserved from danger for a long time ; nor did Lieutenant Dundas or myself quit this station until several of the middle-deck guns came through the deck. At about nine o'clock, finding it impossible to remain any longer below, Lieutenant Dundas and myself went out at the foremost lower-deck port, and got upon the forecastle ; on which, I apprehend, there were then about 150 of the people drawing water, and throwing it as far aft as possible upon the fire. I continued about an hour on the forecastle, till finding all efforts to extinguish the flames unavailing I jumped from the jib-boom and swam to an American boat approaching the ship, by which boat I was picked up and put into a tartan then in charge of Lieutenant Stewart, who had come off to the assistance of the ship. Captain Todd, with Mr. Bainbridge, the first lieutenant, remained upon deck to the last moment, giving orders for saving the crew without thought for their own safety."

the French army, a British squadron, under Lord Keith, assisted the Austrian general Melas, by blockading the port, and on several occasions co-operated with the troops in attacks on the outworks. At the same time Captain Downman, in the *Santa Dorotea*, 36, with the *Chameleon*, 18, Lieutenant Jackson, blockaded the neighbouring fortress of Savona, and their boats rowed guard off the harbour's mouth for forty-one nights, until the 15th May, when the place surrendered. During the early part of the month, the town of Genoa was bombarded by the gunboats, mortar vessels, and armed boats of Lord Keith's squadron, under Captain Beaver, of the *Aurora*, 28. A gallant service was performed by this officer in cutting out the *Prima*, a large galley, having a crew of 257 men, besides 300 galley slaves, chained to her 52 oars, and mounting two long 36-pounders, which, with some gunboats, attempted to reduce the fire of the bombarding flotilla. Notwithstanding that the galley was moored in the harbour, the entrance to which was guarded by batteries, Captain Beaver, at the head of 10 boats, manned with about 100 officers and men, soon after midnight on the 21st May, made a dash for the *Prima*, which was first boarded amidships by a boat from the *Haarlem*, under Midshipman Caldwell, and the other boats attacking at other points, the galley was carried after a severe struggle. The chains mooring her to the mole were then cast adrift, and she was towed out under a heavy but ineffectual fire, the British loss being only five wounded, and that of the enemy 16. Lord Keith sent back the galley slaves to General Massena, who is said to have caused them to be shot, as a punishment for having, in their anxiety to regain their freedom, used every endeavour to pull the galley away from the mole clear of the enemy's batteries.

On the 4th June Genoa was surrendered, and Massena retired with the garrison of 8,000 men to Nice. But on this very day, Buonaparte entered Milan with a large army, and having defeated the Austrians, who had evacuated Genoa after three days' possession, on the 14th June the victorious First Consul overthrew Melas at the great battle of Marengo, with the loss of 4,500 slain, 8,000 wounded, 7,000 prisoners, and 30 guns, his own loss being 2,000 killed and 3,000 wounded. On the following day a convention was signed at Alexandria, by the terms of which France became possessed of twelve fortresses, including Genoa and Savona, besides Milan and Turin. A few days later, Massena returned to Genoa, and so sudden was his entry, that the *Minotaur* had some difficulty in warping clear of the mole.

An important capture during the year 1800 was that of the island of Malta, where, since its acquisition by the French two years before, General Vaubois had remained shut up in the fort of Valetta, with 3,000 men, blockaded by a squadron of British and Russian ships, and confined on the land side by a mixed force of British, Neapolitans, and Maltese. Some supplies were thrown into the place in January and February, 1799, by a schooner from Ancona, and the French 36-gun frigate *Bondense*, from Toulon, which eluded the blockading squadron, but after these were exhausted, the garrison began to suffer from the pangs of hunger. In February, 1800, Buonaparte despatched a squadron with supplies, consisting of the *Généreux*, 74 —the ship which had escaped from the Nile and captured the *Leander*—bearing the flag of Admiral Perrée (captured in the preceding June, but soon after exchanged), the *Badine*, 28, two corvettes, and several transports, with 3,000 troops, and to intercept these reinforcements and supplies, Lord Keith, the commander-in-chief, and Lord Nelson, second in command of the Mediterranean fleet, cruised off the island with six sail-of-the-line, which established a close blockade of the Port of Valetta.

On the 18th February, the *Alexander*, 74, temporarily commanded by Lieutenant Harrington, Captain Ball being on shore at Malta with the allied troops, signalled Admiral Perrée's squadron, and the *Success*, 32, Captain Peard, gallantly threw herself across the path of the *Généreux*, which she raked, receiving in return the fire of the seventy-four. Later in the afternoon, Lord Nelson in the *Foudroyant*, with the *Northumberland*, 74, Captain Martin, closed up with the *Généreux*, when, seeing escape hopeless, she hauled down her colours, having lost, during her brief resistance, Admiral Perrée, who was wounded by a splinter in the left eye, and soon after by a round shot, which carried off his right leg at the thigh. The gallant officer died in a few minutes, and in him the French Navy lost one of its best and most chivalrous officers.

Driven to desperation, General Vaubois despatched the *Guillaume Tell*, 80, bearing the flag of Rear-Admiral Decrès, on the 30th March, with advices to Buonaparte that, if not succoured by the month of June, he must surrender his trust. Taking advantage of a dark night and a strong southerly gale, the *Guillaume Tell* put to sea, but at midnight was discovered by the *Penelope*, 36, Captain Henry Blackwood, who despatched the *Minorca*, brig, to give notice to the *Lion*, 64, Captain Manley Dixon—who, in the absence of Lord Nelson, returned to England, and Commodore Troubridge, was senior officer—of the escape of the French 80-gun ship, and made sail in pursuit. Arriving up with the chase at 12.30 A.M., Captain Blackwood first luffed up under her stern and gave her his port broadside, and then bearing up under her port quarter, let her have his other broadside, receiving in return only the enemy's stern-chasers. The *Guillaume Tell* continued her flight, but the teazing fire of her little adversary inflicted considerable damage, and by daylight she had lost her main and mizen-topmasts and main-yard. Soon after the *Lion*, a small sixty-four, carrying 300 men, overhauled her and ranging up close to the great French eighty, poured in a broadside from her treble-shotted guns, and luffing up, took up a position close across the bows of the *Guillaume Tell*, whose jib-boom she soon shot away. But the heavy metal of the French ship so damaged the *Lion* that, being unmanageable, she fell astern, still firing, as did also the *Penelope*.

At six o'clock, the *Foudroyant*, 80, Captain Sir Edward Berry, came up under a crowd of sail, and running close alongside, poured in a broadside, and hailed her to surrender. To this demand the gallant French admiral replied with every gun he could bring to bear, and so effectually that his second broadside brought down his opponent's fore-topmast, main-topsail-yard, and jib-boom. The *Foudroyant* dropped astern, and having repaired damages, again ranged up alongside the *Guillaume Tell*, whose main and mizen-masts had been shot away, and resumed the action, the *Lion* and *Penelope* occasionally firing at her on the port side. At 8 o'clock the enemy's foremast went over the side, and twenty minutes later the dismasted ship—having the *Foudroyant* on her starboard, and the *Lion* on her port quarter, and the *Penelope* close ahead—with most of her guns disabled by the wreck, and rolling a sheer hulk on the water, hauled down the flag which her officers and men had defended with great courage. Her loss in this action was upwards of 200 killed and wounded out of 919 men, as deposed by her officers, though Captain Dixon places her crew at 1,000.

Though the laurels were decidedly with the defeated party, the victors had just cause for pride. Captain Blackwood displayed equal seamanlike skill and gallantry in tackling his powerful adversary, one broadside of which would have sunk him, and so did Captain Dixon, with his inferior weight of metal and diminished crew. The *Foudroyant*, a ship of slightly inferior force to the *Guillaume Tell*, turned the scale, and Sir Edward Berry, one of Nelson's favourite captains, who had been present on board the *Leander* in her even more heroic defence against the *Généreux*, disclaimed equal credit with those officers. The total British loss in the action was 17 killed and 101 wounded, of whom the *Foudroyant* had eight killed, and her commander, one lieutenant, three midshipmen, boatswain, and 58 men wounded, exclusive of five injured by the fall of the mizen-mast; and the *Lion*, seven killed, and a midshipman and 37 men wounded. After repairing damages, the *Penelope*, taking the prize in tow, steered for Syracuse, and thence the *Guillaume Tell* sailed for Portsmouth, and under the name of *Malta* became, next to the *Tonnant*, the largest two-decker in the British Navy. By her capture and that of the *Généreux*, the whole of the ships-of-the-line of Admiral Brueys' fleet at the battle of the Nile were accounted for by the victorious navy of England.

Though all hope of succour had passed away, General Vaubois refused to surrender. Towards the end of August he sent away the 40-gun frigates *Diane* and *Justice*, which were, however, espied and chased by the vigilant Captain Peard, of the *Success*, and the former, having only a reduced crew of 114 men, was captured after a brief resistance, though the *Justice* managed to reach Toulon. The *Diane* was added to the Navy under the name of *Niobe*. At length, recognising the futility of further holding out, and reduced to the utmost extremity of famine, the French garrison agreed to negotiate, and on the 5th September, the fortress of Valetta and island of Malta passed into British possession. In the port were found two sixty-fours, only one of which was seaworthy, and a frigate not worth removing. Captain Ball, of the *Alexander*, 74, who had served on shore with the troops, and was beloved and trusted by the islanders, was appointed first governor of Malta.

In August a combined military and naval expedition proceeded to Ferrol, on the coast of Spain, where about 8,000 troops, under Sir James Pulteney, were landed, but though they took possession of the heights that overlook the town, the commander considered the place too strong to be reduced, and the troops were re-embarked. No part of the discredit attaching to this *fiasco* is attributable to the squadron under the command of Sir John Borlase Warren, which co-operated with the land forces. The admiral proceeded to Gibraltar with the ships, consisting of the *London*, 98, and the 74's *Renown*, *Impétueux*, *Courageux*, and *Captain*, and the fleet of transports, and thence Lord Keith sailed for Cadiz, with 22 sail-of-the-line, 37 frigates and sloops, and 80 transports, having on board 10,000 men, under the command of Sir Ralph Abercromby. To a summons to surrender, the governor of Cadiz replied that the plague was raging in the town, on which the expedition returned to Gibraltar. The gallantry displayed by the army in the memorable expedition to Egypt, in the following year, under its heroic commander, showed that the cause of the failure at Ferrol lay not in the British soldier, but in his leader.

The only colonial acquisition during the year was the surrender, without resistance, of the Dutch island of Curaçoa, in the West Indies, and indeed the respectable inhabitants, alarmed at the depredations of some 1,500 desperadoes who were in possession of the west end of the island, claimed the protection of Captain Watkins, commanding the British frigate *Nereide*, who on the 13th September received the surrender of the island.

Some noteworthy actions between single ships occurred during the year 1800. On the 5th February the sloops-of-war *Fairy*, 16, Commander Horton, and *Harpy*, 18, Commander Bazeley, stood over from Jersey towards St. Malo, and the same afternoon brought to action the French 38-gun frigate *Pallas*, bound thence to Brest. The engagement took place within pistol-shot range, but the *Pallas* made sail at the end of two hours, and was chased by the sloops, which were joined by the 38-gun frigate *Loire*, Captain Newman, *Danae*, 20, Lord Digby, and *Railleur*, 16, Commander Turquand. The pursuit continued all day, and soon after 11 P.M. the *Loire*, having overhauled the *Pallas*, commenced a close action, in which a battery on the nearest of the Seven Islands, distant about 750 yards, joined by opening fire on the approaching ships *Railleur*, *Harpy*, and *Fairy*. The firing continued until about 1.30 on the following morning, when the French frigate surrendered to overwhelming force, but not until her masts were in such a tottering state that all three went over the side. The total British loss was nine killed and 36 wounded, but that of the enemy was not specified, though it must have been considerable. The prize was a fine new ship, and had never before been to sea. She did good service in the British Navy, under the name of the *Pique*, and the officers who had been instrumental in her capture, Commanders Bazeley and Horton, received promotion to the rank of captain. Another valuable addition to the Navy was that of the ship-rigged privateer *Heureux*, of 22 guns and 220 men. Mistaking the British 36-gun frigate *Phoebe*, Captain Barlow, for an Indiaman, she bore down upon her, but too late found that she had caught a tartar, and after a brief resistance, struck her colours with the loss of 18 killed and 25 wounded.

Captain Watkins, of the *Nereide*, the same officer who received the surrender of the island of Curaçoa, captured the *Vengeance*, of 18 guns and 174 men, which he chased when in company with four other privateers, which made their escape; but, on the other hand the Navy lost the *Danae*, 20, Lord Digby, through the treachery of a portion of her crew. On the 15th March, these men mutinied and took possession of the ship, wounding the captain and master, and took her into Cameret Bay, where they gave her up to the French 16-gun brig *Colombe*. The officers of the *Danae* were landed at Brest, and soon afterwards returned to England on parole, but the crew, including the mutineers, were thrown into prison at Dinan.

The *Peterel*, Commander Austen, of 16 guns and 89 men, 30 of her crew being absent in a prize, engaged between Toulon and Marseilles, and captured, after a running fight of ninety minutes, the *Ligurienne*, of 16 guns and 104 men. The capture was effected within six miles of the latter city, under fire of a shore battery, and though the *Peterel* had touched a rock. Commander Austen had before, when serving under the orders of Sir Sydney Smith, off the coast of Egypt and Syria, given evidence of activity and skill.

It would be impossible to give an account of a tithe of the acts of gallantry performed by British sailors, and we can only briefly mention a few of the most noteworthy incidents. The Spanish 36-gun frigates *Carmen* and *Florentina* were captured off Cadiz, after exerting every effort to escape from the British seventy-four's *Leviathan*, Captain Carpenter, and *Swiftsure*, Captain Hallowell, and 36-gun frigate *Emerald*. The *Carmen*, out of 340 men, had 11 killed and 16 wounded, and her consort, having a crew of 314, lost 12 killed and her captain, first lieutenant, and 10 seamen wounded. Both ships were added to the Navy.

Successful boat attacks were made off Cape Tiberon, by the *Calypso*, 16, Commander Baker, when the French privateer schooner *Diligente*, 6 guns and 39 men, was carried, and by Lieutenant Wilson, commanding the lugger *Lark*, of 14 guns and 50 men, who engaged and forced on shore in the Texel the French privateer cutter *Impregnable*, and then pushing off in his boats, boarded and brought off the cutter, which he took to Yarmouth. The boats of Sir John Warren's squadron—the seventy-four's *Renown* and *Defence*, and frigates *Fisgard* (late *Résistance*) and *Unicorn*—eight in number, under the command of Lieutenant Burke, cut out from under a battery in the small harbour of St. Croix, within the Penmarck rocks, a gun-boat, two chasse-marées, and eight merchant vessels. In the same month of June the boats' crews of the seventy-fours and *Fisgard*, under Captain Byam Martin, of the frigate, landed and stormed a battery in Quimper River, and on the 1st July the boats of the squadron attacked, at the island of Noirmoutier, the armed ship *Thérése*, of 20 guns, a lugger of 12, and a cutter and three schooners, all moored within the sands at the bottom of the bay, under the protection of some batteries. The expedition, numbering 192 officers and men, boarded and carried all these armed vessels, together with fifteen sail of merchantmen having stores for Brest, all of which Lieutenant Burke, the officer in command, caused to be destroyed. On their way back, the boats grounded and became exposed to the fire of several batteries on Noirmoutier island, and of 400 soldiers, and though Lieutenant Burke succeeded in embarking 100 of his men in a French vessel, which they dragged for two miles over the sand until they floated her, and thus the party effected their escape, the remainder of the detachment were compelled to surrender. The gallant officer who commanded on this occasion was leader of a division of twenty boats from Admiral Warren's squadron, which successfully attacked the *Guépe*, privateer, of 18 guns and 161 men, which had taken shelter close to some batteries near Vigo. The boats got alongside the privateer at twenty minutes to 1 A.M. on the 29th August, and in a quarter of an hour, after a desperate hand-to-hand struggle, carried the *Guépe*, which had 25 killed and 40 wounded, including her commander (mortally). The boarding party lost four killed, one drowned, and three lieutenants and 17 men wounded, among the latter being Lieutenant Burke, who received the rank of commander for an act of gallantry which was only the last of a series.

Another brilliant cutting-out affair was that conducted on the evening of the 3rd September by Captain Hillyar, of the *Niger* frigate, with eight boats from his ship and the *Minotaur*, 74. The objects of the attack were two Spanish armed corvettes, *Esmeralda* and *Paz*, each mounting 30 guns, at anchor in the Roads of Barcelona. A dash was first made at 9 P.M. for the *Esmeralda*, which fired her broadside at the advancing boats, but without effect, and was carried after a short struggle. The cheers with which the British seamen greeted this success was the signal for the crew of the *Paz* to cut their cable and seek protection under the battery at the mole-head, but the time was too short, and the British attack too fierce, and she also was soon a prize, and by 11 P.M. both the corvettes were brought off in safety, with the loss of only three killed, and the master of the *Minotaur* and four wounded, the casualties of the enemy being 24 in all.

A very daring attack was made on the 7th July by a flotilla, consisting of the *Dart*, two gun-boats and four fire-ships, with boats from the frigates *Nemesis* and *Andromeda*, on four French frigates in the Roads of Dunkirk. Soon after midnight, Commander Campbell, commanding the *Dart*, after firing a broadside into one French frigate, laid his ship alongside the *Désirée*, 38, when Lieutenants McDermott and Pearce boarded her on the forecastle and quarter, and speedily obtaining possession, the ship's sails were set and she was taken out. In achieving this dashing service the British had only 12 casualties, while the French frigate is said to have lost 100 men. The three other frigates escaped, and eluded the attack of the fire-ships. Commander Campbell and his first lieutenant, Mr. McDermott, were promoted for their conduct on this occasion, and the prize was added to the Navy.

No event more gallant is recorded in these pages than the cutting-out of the *Cerbère*, a brig mounting 7 guns and having a crew of 87 men, by Lieutenant Coghlan, commanding the 14-gun cutter *Viper*. This officer undertook the task with a ten-oared cutter from one of Sir Edward Pellew's squadron, having with himself 20 men, a boat from the *Viper*, and another from the *Amethyst*. He found the crew of the *Cerbère* at their quarters, ready to give him a warm welcome, but nothing daunted, and though without the aid of his two other boats, which he had left far behind, the gallant officer boarded the enemy on the quarter. Twice were he and his band of heroes driven back into the boat, but it was only to try their fortune a third time, and at length, having killed six and wounded 20 of the enemy, they stood victorious on the deck of the brig. The British loss on this memorable occasion was one killed and eight wounded, including the commander (in two places) and another officer. The other boats had now arrived, and the prize was towed out from under the fire of the batteries. Sir Edward Pellew only did justice to Lieutenant Coghlan when he spoke in the following terms of his conduct in an official letter to Lord St. Vincent, who himself presented him with a sword:—"I trust I shall stand excused by your lordship for so minute a description, produced by my admiration of such courage, which, hand to hand, gave victory to a handful of brave fellows over four times their number, and of that skill which formed, conducted, and effected so daring an enterprise."

The officers and men of the privateer brig *Rover*, of Nova Scotia, defeated every attempt to capture their little ship, made by a superior Spanish force off the Venezuelan coast. The *Rover* had fourteen 4-pounders and 54 men, all told; the enemy consisted of a schooner, mounting 12 guns (6 and 12-pounders), with a crew of 85 men, and three gun-boats, which sought to carry the brig by boarding. The latter, however, was so skilfully manœuvred that she was able to pour raking broadsides into her adversaries, and finished by carrying the schooner by boarding, when the gun-boats sheered off. The loss of the Spaniards in the captured vessel alone was 14 killed and 17 wounded. Not less worthy of commendation was the capture off Guadaloupe of a French armed sloop, of 8 guns and 98 men, by the 10-gun schooner *Gypsy*, tender of the

Leviathan, having a crew of 42 men, and commanded by Lieutenant Boger. The action lasted for about two hours, when the sloop hauled down her colours, with the loss of her commander and four men killed and 11 wounded, that of the *Gypsy* being three in the former category, and nine, including Lieutenant Boger, in the latter.

A boat action took place near Malaga, in which an officer afterwards well known as Sir Francis Beaufort, Hydrographer to the Navy, bore a distinguished part. Late in the evening of the 27th October, the boats of the *Phæton*, under the orders of her first lieutenant, Mr. Francis Beaufort, proceeded to cut out the Spanish polacre* ship *San Josef*, of 8 guns and a crew of 34 seamen, besides 22 soldiers, which lay moored under the protection of a 5-gun battery. The barge and two cutters boarded the polacre, which was carried after an obstinate resistance, in which 19 of the enemy were wounded, and one British seaman killed, and three officers, including Lieutenant Beaufort (severely) and one seaman wounded. The polacre was added to the Navy as a sloop-of-war, and received the name of *Calpe*, the ancient designation of Gibraltar.

The capture of two French frigates by a British 64-gun ship and some East-Indiamen, was a sufficiently noteworthy event to merit record. The *Belliqueux*, Captain Bulteel, was escorting some outward-bound China ships, when, on the 4th August, being off the coast of Brazil, she sighted a French squadron, consisting of the *Concorde*, 40, Commodore Landolphe, and the 36-gun frigates *Médée* and *Franchise*, with a prize used as a tender, which had sailed from Rochefort in the preceding March, and after committing serious depredations on British commerce on the coast of Africa, had refitted in the Rio Plata. Commodore Landolphe, considering this a favourable opportunity to pick up a prize or two, at 7 A.M. stood towards the convoy, which, nothing loth to try conclusions, accepted the challenge and bore down. The *Belliqueux* directed her course towards the *Concorde*, as the largest ship, and compelled her to strike, after a conflict of ten minutes' duration, while the Indiamen, *Exeter*, Captain Meriton, and *Bombay-Castle*, Captain Hamilton, stood for the *Médée*, and two others, the *Coutts*, Captain Torin, and *Neptune*, Captain Spens, gave chase to the *Franchise*. The former French frigate, having 315 men on board, hauled down her flag, according to Captain Bulteel's account, at 7 P.M., but Captain Brenton states in his "History of

---

* A polacre is a vessel whose masts are formed of one spar only from truck to heel.

the Navy," that she surrendered after midnight to the *Exeter* alone.* The *Franchise* made good her escape by the expedient of throwing overboard her anchors, boats, booms, and some of her guns, and the tender also got away.

The career of the French frigate *Vengeance*, which had engaged the American frigate *Constellation*, was brought to a close off the coast of St. Domingo. The British frigate *Seine* (a prize to the *Jason* and *Pique*, in June, 1798), carrying 48 guns and a crew of 281 men, commanded by Captain Milne, brought the *Vengeance*, of 52 guns and 326 men, to close action at 8 A.M., on the 21st August, after a long chase begun twenty-four hours before, during which the *Seine* suffered greatly in her rigging and sails from the enemy's stern-chasers. The action raged with fury for two hours and a half, when the French frigate hailed to say she surrendered, having had her fore and mizen-masts and main-topmasts shot away, and being much damaged in her hull. Her loss was 35 killed, but the wounded was not stated; that of her victorious opponent was her second lieutenant (bearing the same well-known naval name as her commander), and 12 seamen killed, and her master, captain's clerk, and 26 men wounded. The victory was, in every way, creditable to the officers and crew of the *Seine*, as the enemy's ship was of superior strength as regards crew, size, and weight of metal, the relative broadsides being 434 and 498 pounds. The prize was taken in tow and carried to Jamaica, where she arrived with nine feet of water in her hold and dismasted, her wounded main-mast having gone over the side. She was purchased into the Navy, but was in too damaged a condition to go to sea, and the first lieutenant of the *Seine*, Mr. Chetham, according to custom in such cases, received promotion.

The gun known as the carronade, which, during the great war, had warm advocates and equally earnest opponents, was worked in some few instances on the non-recoil system which, to most naval officers, would appear to be a system that must carry away breechings, injure the upper works, capsize the guns themselves, and expose

---

* Brenton says:—"The chase was long, and at midnight, Captain Meriton of the *Exeter* found himself coming very fast up with the enemy, while the *Bombay-Castle*, another Indiaman, commanded by Captain Hamilton, was still very far astern. The position was critical, and the British officer, with great presence of mind, formed his determination. Running alongside the Frenchman with all his ports up, he commanded him to surrender to a superior force; with this order, supposing himself under the guns of a ship-of-the-line, the French captain instantly complied. Meriton gave him no time for deliberation, but sent an officer and brought him on board, and he delivered his sword to the English captain, in due form, on the quarter-deck. The *Bombay-Castle* was still at a great distance, but on coming up the prisoners were quickly taken out and divided. By this time the French captain began to recover from his surprise, and looking very attentively at the little guns on the quarter-deck, asked Captain Meriton, what ship it was to which he had surrendered? Meriton drily answered, 'To a merchant-ship.' The indignant Frenchman begged to be allowed to return with his people to the frigate, and fight the battle again."

the gun's crew outside the bulwarks to musketry fire, as they necessarily were not run in to load. But the principle had its adherents, and we will give an undoubted instance when it was employed with advantage. The *Milbrook*, a schooner of only 148 tons, was mounted with sixteen 18-pounders, fitted on the non-recoil system, in which her commander, Lieutenant Matthew Smith, had unbounded confidence. On the 13th November, when lying becalmed off Oporto, and having under his protection a small convoy, he descried the French privateer *Bellone*, of Bordeaux, mounting 30 guns, and an action ensued. While the privateer fired three broadsides he had discharged eleven, owing to the saving of time in not having to run out the guns, and in a couple of hours the *Bellone* hauled down her colours. But unfortunately Lieutenant Smith had not a boat that could swim, all having been pierced with shot, and the *Bellone* made sail and escaped, her loss in the action, out of a crew of 250 men being, it was stated, 20 killed and 47 wounded, including her captain and chief officer. The *Milbrook* had also suffered severely, her masts, yards and sails being cut to pieces, and ten of her guns dismounted, while of her crew of 47 men, she had 12 wounded, including two officers. To have saved his convoy and put to flight a ship having a broadside weight of metal nearly four-fold greater than that of his little schooner, was a brilliant feat, and Lieutenant Smith received promotion, and the English merchants at Oporto presented him with a piece of plate.

The cutting-out feats performed by the Navy on the French and Spanish coasts in this year, as throughout the war, are too numerous to record in detail; a matter of regret that is lessened by the knowledge that they may be found fully detailed in the pages of Brenton, Marshall, and James, that most painstaking and reliable of all the Naval Historians of the Great War.

CHAPTER XI.

The Battle of Copenhagen—Results of Lord Nelson's Victory—Submission of Sweden and Russia—The Boulogne Flotilla of Invasion—Repulse of the British Boat Attacks—Admiral Ganteaume's attempts to reach Egypt—Loss of the *Swiftsure*—Capture of the *Success* and *Bravoure*—The Defence of Porto Ferrajo—Services of the Navy in the Expedition to Egypt—Sir James Saumarez at Algeciras—His Second Action in the Straits of Gibraltar—Cutting out of the *Sénégal*—Lieutenant Fitton's Exploit—Capture of the *Chiffonne*—The *Phœbe* and *Africaine*—Lord Cochrane's Early Career—Naval Officers and their Ratings—The *Speedy* and *Gamo*—Cutting-out of the *Chevrette*—Other Boat Actions—Services of the *Sylph*—The Peace of Amiens.

THE Northern powers, Sweden, Denmark and Russia, in 1801, made common cause with France to compel England to abandon the right of search for contraband of war in neutral ships, and the country had to put forward even greater exertions than in the past to meet the hostile combination ranged against her. During the year the supplies voted for the Navy rose to upwards of $16\frac{1}{2}$ millions sterling, and the number of seamen was increased to 105,000, and of marines to 30,000.

The bombardment of Copenhagen, the chief purely naval operation undertaken during the year, arose out of this pretension of England to enforce the right of search. On the 25th July in the preceding year, three British frigates and a sloop fell in with some Danish merchantmen under the protection of the 40-gun frigate *Freya*, whose commander resisted the demand of Captain Baker, of the *Nemesis*, 28, that he should be permitted to examine his convoy. A brief action ensued, when the *Freya* hauled down her colours and was taken to the Downs. Russia having placed an embargo on all British shipping in her ports, and the northern powers having concluded a convention, having for its object an armed neutrality menacing England, a fleet sailed from Yarmouth Roads on the 12th March, consisting of fifteen sail-of-the-line, soon reinforced by three more with a large number of frigates, bomb-vessels and fire-ships, making in all 53 sail.

The Commander-in-Chief of this vast armada was Sir Hyde Parker, who had his flag in the *London*, 98, but as the second-in-command was Lord Nelson, in the *St. George*, 98, we need hardly add that the country and the service looked to the subordinate officer as practically the leader of the enterprise. The fleet encountered heavy gales, but by the 21st, most of the ships were collected under the admiral, who

H.M.S. VICTORIA, 121 guns.
(THE LAST THREE-DECKER--LAUNCHED IN 1859.)

anchored at the entrance of the Sound. Two days later the British Minister, who had been sent to the Danish capital to negotiate, returned, having failed in his efforts, and it was not until the morning of the 30th March, that the fleet, favoured with a fair wind, got under weigh and stood into the Sound, headed by Lord Nelson, who had shifted his flag into the *Elephant*, 74, Captain Thomas Foley, she being a lighter and more handy ship. The batteries at Elsinore and the castle of Cronenburg opened a distant and ineffective fire, to which a reply was made by a few broadsides from the van ships, and by the seven bomb-vessels, which threw shells.

Soon after noon the fleet anchored about 15 miles from the city of Copenhagen, which was reconnoitred by the three Admirals, Sir Hyde Parker, Lord Nelson, and Rear-Admiral Graves, accompanied by Captain Domett of the flagship, and Colonel Stewart, commanding a small body of troops taking part in the expedition. A council of war was held that evening to determine upon the course of action, and though some proposed to abandon the attack, urging the formidable strength of the defences, and others suggested delay, Lord Nelson strenuously advised prompt action, and offered, with ten sail-of-the-line and all the smaller craft, to effect the reduction of the fortifications. The Commander-in-Chief accepted the proposal, and in addition to what his enterprising vice-admiral demanded, gave him two 50-gun ships. The following was the composition of the squadron placed at the disposal of Lord Nelson, who was accompanied in the *Elephant* by his flag-captain, Thomas Masterman Hardy, who served in the action as a volunteer :—

	Elephant	Vice-Admiral Lord Nelson, K.B.		Frigates.	
		Captain Thomas Foley	38	*Amazon*	Captain Henry Riou
	Defiance	Rear-Admiral Thomas Graves	36	*Désirée*	,, Henry Inman
		Captain Richard Retalick		*Blanche*	,, Graham E. Hammond
74	*Edgar*	,, George Murray	32	*Alcmene*	,, Samuel Sutton
	Monarch	,, James Robert Mosse	24	*Jamaica*	,, Jonas Rose
	Bellona	,, Sir Thomas Thompson	28	*Arrow*	,, William Bolton
	Ganges	,, Thomas F. Fremantle		*Dart*	Commander John F. Devonshire
	Russell	,, William Cuming		Brigs.	
	Agamemnon	,, Robert D. Fancourt		*Cruiser*	,, James Brisbane
64	*Ardent*	,, Thomas Bertie		*Harpy*	,, William Birchall
	Polyphemus	,, John Lawford			
54	*Glatton*	,, William Bligh			
	Isis	,, James Walker			

Bomb-vessels—*Discovery, Explosion, Hecla, Sulphur, Terror, Volcano* and *Zebra*; fire-ships—*Otter* and *Zephyr*, besides gun-brigs and cutters.

The task undertaken by the victor of the Nile was an onerous one, and was rendered more difficult from the circumstance that the Danes had removed or misplaced the buoys that marked the very intricate channel that gave approach to the capital, but Lord Nelson, the same night in which he had been entrusted with the task of bringing the Danish Government to submission, proceeded in a boat, accompanied by some officers, including Commander Brisbane of the *Cruiser*, to ascertain and re-buoy the water channel, a narrow passage lying between the island of Saltholm and the Middle Ground, a shoal which extends along the entire sea front of the city. This accomplished, Nelson made a second examination of the Danish defences, and resolved to attack from the southward.

Accordingly on the following day, the 1st April, the whole British fleet weighed in the morning, and about six miles from the city, re-anchored off the north-western extremity of the Middle Ground shoal, between which and the town was a deep-water channel, about 1,200 yards in width, in which the Danish block-ships and gun-boats lay moored close to the defences. Lord Nelson made a final examination of the position in the *Amazon* at 1 P.M., and soon after his return to the *Elephant*, hoisted the signal to get under weigh, which was received by the seamen of the fleet with a cheer, and soon afterwards the only ships that remained at the anchorage were the eight line-of-battle ships, retained by Sir Hyde Parker. Preceded by the *Amazon*, commanded by "the good and gallant Riou"—as Lord Nelson described him in his despatch announcing his death in the great victory about to be achieved—the ships of Nelson's division, numbering thirty-six sail in all, entered the Upper Channel and coasted along the edge of the great shoal until they had reached its southern extremity, where, about 8 P.M., the fleet anchored.

Under Nelson's instructions, Captain Hardy, of the *St. George*, examined in a small boat the channel leading to the Danish fleet, and actually sounded with a pole, to prevent noise, round the nearest of the enemy's ships. About 11 P.M. he returned to the *Elephant*, with the gratifying intelligence that the depth of water rendered an advance practicable, an assurance so gratifying to the Vice-Admiral that it banished all sleep during the night.

The Danish fleet, the defeat of which forms one of the greatest achievements of our national hero, consisted of eighteen vessels, some two-decked ships, cut down and converted into floating batteries, frigates, and smaller craft, mounting in all 628 guns, of which 48 were 36-pounders, 360 were 24-pounders, and 70 were 18-pounders, manned by 4,849 seamen, exclusive of artillerymen and soldiers. These ships were moored in a line over 2,000 yards in length, flanked at the north or town end by the Tekroner (or Crown) batteries, one of thirty 24-pounders, and the other of thirty-eight 36-pounders, having furnaces for heating shot, which again were commanded by two two-decked block-ships. The entrance into the harbour and dock was protected by a chain, and by some batteries on the north shore, as well as by the Tekroner forts, and by two seventy-four's, a 40-gun frigate, and two 18-gun brigs. Along the shore of the island of Amak, to the southward of the ships, were more batteries, and the line of defence covered an extent of between three and four miles.

The 2nd April, a day big with the fate and honour of an ancient monarchy, broke, bringing with it a fair wind from the south-east, and by eight o'clock all the captains assembled on board the flagship, and received from the illustrious admiral their instructions, and the stations they were respectively to occupy. The ships-of-the-line were to anchor by the stern abreast of the Danish vessels, while the *Amazon*, *Alcmene*, *Arrow*, and *Dart*, with the fireships, acting under Captain Riou's orders, were to co-operate in the attack on the ships at the entrance to the harbour, the bomb-vessels were to take up an outside position, and cast their shells over the British ships, and the *Jamaica* and *Désirée*, with the smaller vessels, were to rake the Danish line. At 9.30 the British fleet weighed in succession, the *Edgar* leading. The *Agamemnon* next in succession, says Lord Nelson in his despatch, " could not weather the shoal of the Middle, and was obliged to anchor," whereupon the *Polyphemus* followed the leading ship, and was succeeded by the *Bellona* which grounded 450 yards from, and almost abreast of, the rear of the Danish line. The *Russell* also grounded with her jib-boom almost over the *Bellona's* taffrail, on perceiving which Lord Nelson ordered the helm of the *Elephant*, which was next in the line, to be starboarded, and she passed along the port beam of those ships, as did all the ships astern of the Admiral. Meantime the Commander-in-Chief took up a new position with his eight ships, but at too great a distance to take part in the engagement.

The "lofty British line," as Campbell calls Nelson's ships in his noble lyric, "The Battle of the Baltic," having taken up their appointed stations, with about 100 yards between each ship, opened fire at ten o'clock, but it was not till an hour and a half later, that the whole of the following ships were engaged:—*Edgar*, *Polyphemus*, *Isis*, *Ardent*, *Monarch*, *Glatton*, *Elephant*, *Ganges*, and *Defiance*. The absence of the *Russell*, *Bellona*, and *Agamemnon* were severely felt. Most of the frigates and small vessels played their parts well, especially the *Amazon*, and four other ships with which

Captain Riou fearlessly engaged the heavy Tekroner batteries, and the *Désirée*, which raked the *Provesteen*, and drew off some of her fire, but on the other hand, owing to the strength of the current, the *Jamaica* and the gun-boats could take no part in the action, and the bomb-vessels were of little use.

The battle raged with fury for three hours, but the enemy appeared resolute as ever. At length Sir Hyde Parker, urged by his flag-captain, and observing that the *Bellona*, *Russell*, and *Agamemnon* were unable to participate, while the three ships he detailed to assist his second-in-command, the *Defence*, *Ramillies*, and *Veteran*, were making but slow progress, hoisted the signal for discontinuing the action, though in justice to the veteran Admiral it should be stated that he did this rather from the generous motive of authorising Nelson's retirement, should he deem his force insufficient for the duty he had undertaken.

The manner in which Nelson received this unwelcome signal was eminently characteristic, and the incident cannot be better told than in the words of his biographer, Southey:—"About this time the signal-lieutenant called out that No. 39 (the signal for discontinuing the action), was thrown out by the Commander-in-Chief. He continued to walk the deck, and appeared to take no notice of it. The signal-officer met him at the next turn, and asked him if he should repeat it. 'No!' he replied, 'acknowledge it.' Presently he called after him to know if the signal for close action was still hoisted, and being answered in the affirmative, said, 'Mind you keep it so!' He now paced the deck, moving the stump of his lost arm in a manner which always indicated great emotion. 'Do you know,' said he to Mr. Ferguson, 'what is shown on board the Commander-in-Chief? Number 39!' Mr. Ferguson asked him what that meant. 'Why, to leave off action.' Then, shrugging up his shoulders, he repeated the words, 'Leave off action? Now d——n me if I do!' 'You know, Foley,' turning to the captain, 'I have only one eye, I have a right to be blind sometimes!' and then putting the glass to his blind eye, in that mood of mind which sports with bitterness, he exclaimed, 'I really do not see the signal.' Presently he exclaimed, 'D——n the signal! Keep mine for closer battle flying! That's the way I answer such signals. Nail mine to the mast.'"

Nelson only acknowledged the distasteful signal, but would not repeat it, and his second-in-command, Rear-Admiral Graves, only displayed it at the lee main-topsail yard-arm, where it could not be distinguished, and still kept the signal for close action flying at the main-topgallantmast-head. The *Amazon* and other frigates were, however, compelled about this time to cease engaging the Tekroner batteries, the fire from whose heavy guns was too much for them. Captain Riou, who had received a wound in the head, observed bitterly, as he gave the orders to haul off, "What will Nelson think of us?" He was not destined to know that his commander did justice to his gallantry, for as the *Amazon* exposed her stern to the raking fire of the batteries, when retiring, a round-shot cut him in two. Thus ended the career of one of the most promising officers of the navy.

The determination of Nelson, and the resolute manner in which his seamen stood to their guns, at length began to have a visible effect. About 1.30 the Danish fire slackened, and half an hour later, it ceased along nearly the whole of the line astern of the *Zealand*, and some of the prames, or gun-rafts, and lighter vessels had gone adrift. Nevertheless, the block-ships fired on the boats sent to take possession of them, and the batteries in Amak island did so likewise.

"This," says Southey, "arose from the nature of the action; the crews were constantly reinforced from the shore, and fresh men coming on board did not inquire whether the flag had been struck, or, perhaps, did not heed it; many, or most of them, never having been engaged in war before, knowing nothing, therefore, of its laws, and thinking only of defending their country to the last extremity." Lord Nelson was naturally offended at this conduct, and before sending in the fire-ships to burn the surrendered vessels, wrote the celebrated letter to the Crown Prince of Denmark, wherein he says:—"Vice-Admiral Lord Nelson has been commanded to spare Denmark when she no longer resists. The line of defence which covered her shores has struck to the British flag; but, if the firing is continued on the part of Denmark, he must set on fire all the prizes that have been taken, without having the power to save the men who have so nobly defended them. The brave Danes are the brothers, and should never be the enemies of the English." A wafer was then given him with which to close the document, but he ordered a candle to be brought from the cockpit, and sealed the letter with wax, affixing a larger seal than he ordinarily used. "This," said his lordship, "is no time to appear hurried and informal."

In the meantime the destructive cannonade still kept up by the *Defiance*, *Monarch*, and *Ganges*, and the near approach of the *Defence* and *Ramillies* (the *Veteran* being far astern) silenced the fire of the ships, but the great Tekroner fort, having been engaged with only frigates and sloops, and being comparatively uninjured, continued its fire, and, as about 1,500 men had been thrown into it from the shore, was considered too strong to be stormed. Nelson was making preparations to withdraw the fleet out of the intricate channel while the wind continued fair, when the Danish Adjutant-General Lindholm came off, bearing a flag of truce, and the Tekroner ceased firing. The Crown Prince sent to enquire the particular object of Nelson's note, to which his lordship replied by letter that humanity was the object; that he consented to stay hostilities in order that the wounded Danes should be taken on shore; and that he should take his prisoners out of the vessels, and burn and carry off his prizes as he should think fit. The admiral concluded with a hope that the victory he had gained would lead to a reconciliation between the two countries. The bearer of the missive was referred to the Commander-in-Chief for a final adjustment of the terms, and Nelson took the opportunity afforded by this delay to order the leading British ships, all of which were much crippled in their rigging and sails, to weigh or slip in succession.

The *Monarch* led the way, and touched upon the shoal, but the *Ganges*, taking her amidships, pushed her over it. The *Glatton*, drawing less water, passed clear, but the *Defiance* and *Elephant* grounded about a mile from the Tekroner, and in spite of the exertions of their crews, remained there for many hours. The *Désirée*, also, at the opposite end of the line, having gone to assist the *Bellona*, became fast on the same shoal as the latter, which, however, soon got afloat. Soon after the *Elephant* had grounded, Lord Nelson quitted her, and followed the Danish Adjutant-General to the *London*, flagship to Sir Hyde Parker, where the negotiations were completed.

Without reckoning the two "prames," which sank in shoal water, the British fleet captured or destroyed thirteen out of the eighteen floating batteries to the southward of the Tekroner batteries; so that the engagement may be claimed as a victory; but the Danes, from the circumstance that Nelson, from motives of humanity, made a first overture by writing to the Crown Prince, pretended to regard their discomfiture, which concluded with an act of submission to the British demands, as at most a drawn battle. There can be but one opinion that to thread an intricate and unknown channel, whence return by a change of wind might have been impossible to ships shattered after a close engagement with formidable batteries and a long line of block-ships, armed with guns of a superior calibre, was a bold and hazardous venture, and probably only a Blake or Nelson would have attempted such a task or carried it to a successful conclusion. For these reasons "The Battle of the Baltic" evoked enthusiastic plaudits in England, and is regarded by professional critics as an operation denoting superlative daring and genius on the part of the great seaman who carried it through.

According to the Danish accounts, the guns mounted on their floating-batteries were 628, as opposed to 700 in the British ships-of-the-line, a calculation which excludes the Tekroner batteries and the frigates and sloops opposed to them. The enemy displayed great steadiness and resolution, and Nelson, with characteristic generosity, was foremost in acknowledging it, as the following anecdote, taken from the *Naval Chronicle*, shows :—" During the repast (at the palace) Lord Nelson spoke in raptures of the bravery of the Danes, and particularly requested the Prince to introduce him to a very young officer, whom he described as having performed wonders during the battle by attacking his own ship immediately under her lower guns. It proved to be the gallant young Welmoes, a stripling of seventeen. The British hero embraced him with the enthusiasm of a brother, and delicately intimated to the Prince that he ought to make him an admiral, to which the Prince very happily replied, ' If, my lord, I were to make all my brave officers admirals, I should have no captains or lieutenants in my service.' This heroic youth had volunteered to take the command of a prame, which is a sort of raft, carrying six small cannon, and manned with 24 men, who pushed off from the shore, and in the fury of the battle placed themselves under the stern of Lord Nelson's ship, which they most successfully attacked, in such a manner that, although they were below the reach of the stern-chasers, the British marines made terrible slaughter among them; twenty of the gallant men fell by their bullets, but their young commander continued knee-deep in dead at his post until the truce was announced."

The British loss was heavy, being 255 killed and 688 wounded,* according to the official returns, though more than half of the latter are stated to have died of their wounds. Including those slightly wounded, not given in the returns, the total casualties were not short of 1,200. That of the Danes was, according to the estimate of the

---

* The casualties were distributed as follows :—The *Elephant*, the captain of marines and one master's mate, and eight seamen and marines killed, and two officers and eleven wounded ; the *Ganges*, her master and six killed, and the pilot wounded ; the *Monarch*, her captain and 55 killed, and one lieutenant, five midshipmen, the boatswain, and 157 wounded; the *Defiance*, a lieutenant, the pilot, and 22 killed, and three officers and 48 wounded ; the *Amazon*, her captain, one midshipman, the captain's clerk, and 11 killed, and two officers and 21 wounded ; the *Bellona* had 11 killed, and her captain (who lost his leg), two lieutenants, four midshipmen, one master's mate, and 64 wounded ; the *Polyphemus* had one midshipman and five men killed, and her boatswain and 24 wounded ; the *Isis*, her master, two midshipmen, a marine officer, and 29 men killed, and a lieutenant, 3 midshipmen, and 84 wounded ; the *Edgar* had her first lieutenant, a marine officer, and 30 men killed, and two lieutenants, five midshipmen, and 104 wounded ; the *Ardent* had one midshipman and 29 men killed, and 64 wounded ; and the *Glatton*, 18 killed, and three officers and 34 men wounded. The frigates *Blanche*, *Alcmene*, *Dart*, and *Désirée* had between them 15 killed, including the first lieutenant of the *Dart*, and 33 wounded. The *Russell*, which got aground, had only six wounded.

commandant, Commodore Fischer, between 1,600 and 1,800, including 270 lost in the *Dannebrog* alone, which caught fire and blew up; but this was the lowest estimate, and the British accounts place it much higher, giving the total loss, including prisoners, as about 6,000.

The thanks of both Houses of Parliament were voted to the British fleet, but Lord Nelson was awarded no special mark of Royal favour. Rear-Admiral Graves, however, received the Bath, and the first lieutenants of all the ships were promoted, as were also Commanders Devonshire, Brisbane, and Birchall, to the rank of captain.

During the night of the 2nd April, the British ships aground, except the *Désirée*, were floated off, and those of the shattered prizes that were not burnt, were brought out by the crews of the British fleet; and during the next few days, all, except the *Holstein*, 60, were destroyed, not being fit for service. An armistice was concluded for fourteen weeks, Denmark engaging to take no part in the hostilities threatened by Sweden and Russia, while the prisoners were released, and the British fleet was furnished with provisions.

On the 12th April Sir Hyde Parker sent home the *Monarch* and *Isis* with the wounded men, together with the *Holstein*, and leaving the *St. George*, flying Nelson's flag, and a few frigates, in the Roads, sailed with the rest of the fleet, which threaded its tedious way through the dangerous navigation of the "Grounds," between the island of Amak and Saltholm; and to the amazement of the people on both shores of the Baltic, the heavy ships-of-the-line made their appearance in those waters by this difficult route. The fleet now reached Kioge Bay, and Admiral Parker opened negotiations at Carlscrona, where a Swedish squadron had taken shelter, and a convention was concluded with the court of Stockholm, by which the Swedish Government agreed to treat for terms of accommodation.

Lord Nelson, anticipating fighting, rejoined the Commander-in-Chief at Kioge Bay, and re-hoisted his flag on board the *Elephant*, having quitted the *St. George*, which was detained by contrary winds, and pulled a distance of 24 miles in a six-oared cutter in the teeth of a strong wind and adverse current. Mr. Briarly, master of the *Bellona*, whose local experience was great, had succeeded in passing the *St. George* over the "Grounds," and accompanied the vice-admiral. He says:—"The moment he received the account he ordered a boat to be manned, and, without waiting for a boat-cloak (though you must suppose the weather pretty sharp here at this season of the year), and having to row about twenty-four miles with the wind and current against him, jumped into her, and ordered me to go with him, I having been on board that ship (the *St. George*), to remain till she got over the 'Grounds.' All I had ever seen or heard of him could not half so clearly prove to me the singular and unbounded zeal of this truly great man. His anxiety in the boat for nearly six hours lest the fleet should have sailed before he got on board one of them, and lest we should not catch the Swedish squadron, is beyond all conception. I will quote some expressions in his own words. It was extremely cold, and I wished him to put on a great-coat of mine which was in the boat. 'No, I am not cold; my anxiety for my country will keep me warm. Do you think the fleet has sailed?' 'I should suppose not, my lord.' 'If they have we will follow them to Carlscrona in the boat'"—the distance to which place, Mr. Briarly goes on to state, was about fifty leagues. At midnight on the 19th April, Lord Nelson reached the *Elephant*. On the day succeeding that on which the King of Sweden had come to terms, despatches were received by Sir Hyde Parker, then not far from Carlscrona, on his way to the Gulf of Finland, containing overtures from the Czar, Alexander I., who had just ascended the throne on the death of Paul. The British admiral returned to Kioge Bay, where he received letters of recall, and left for England, making over the command to Lord Nelson.

Almost the first signal of the new Commander-in-Chief was to weigh, and on the 7th May, the fleet, consisting of seventeen sail-of-the-line, two ships of 54 and 50 guns, and a few frigates, set sail from its anchorage. Lord Nelson sent word to the Swedish Admiral at Carlscrona, that if he found him at sea he would attack him, and leaving seven sail-of-the-line and a frigate to cruise off that port, steered with the remainder for the Gulf of Finland, and, on the 14th, anchored in Revel roads to overawe the Russian fleet. But they had quitted the port, on the 3rd, for Cronstadt, while Sir Hyde Parker was lying inactive in Kioge Bay. The Czar repeated his friendly intentions, and on the 17th, Nelson sailed from Revel, and two days later, the Russians and Swedes raised the embargo on British shipping, and amicable relations were restored. Lord Nelson returned to England on the 19th June to recruit his health, and towards the end of July, the British fleet left the Baltic, having successfully accomplished its mission.

Buonaparte concluded peace, on the 9th February, with Germany, turned his attention once more to his favourite project of the invasion of England, and prepared a grand flotilla at Boulogne, the command of which he conferred on Admiral La Touche-Treville. Nine divisions of gunboats were assembled, and also a considerable body of troops, who were exercised in artillery practice. To counteract these efforts Lord Nelson was appointed to the defence of the coast between Beachy Head and Orfordness, and on the 30th July, hoisted his flag on board the *Medusa*, 32, Captain John Gore.

His lordship stood across the Channel towards Boulogne, on the 3rd August, with about thirty vessels, and on the following day, some bomb-vessels threw shells among the French flotilla moored in front of the town. Nelson undertook the more difficult task of bringing off the flotilla with four divisions of boats, accompanied by a division of mortar-boats. Shortly before midnight on the 15th August, the boats pushed off from the *Medusa*, but owing to the darkness and the tide, the divisions got separated. Some boats of the first division, under Captain Somerville, shortly before daylight attacked and captured a brig* lying close to the pier-head, but were unable to bring her off, as she was secured with a chain. They were compelled to abandon their prize under a heavy musketry and grape fire from the shore and from three luggers and another brig, and lost one officer and 17 men killed, and seven officers and 48 wounded.

The second division was not more successful and suffered even greater loss. A portion, led by Captain Parker, got quickly alongside the *Etna*, brig, carrying the French commodore's pennant, moored off the mole-head, but every effort of the boarding party to gain her deck was baffled by a strong netting triced up to the brig's lower yards, and ultimately they had to retire under a heavy fire of guns and small arms from about 200 soldiers on board the brig. The other sub-division, under Lieutenant Williams, carried a lugger, but was repulsed in an attack on the brig *Vulcan*. This division sustained a loss of two midshipmen and 19 seamen and marines killed, and Captain Parker (mortally), two lieutenants, a master, one midshipman, the commander of the *Greyhound*, revenue cutter, and 36 men, wounded. The third division, under Captain Cotgrave, was also unsuccessful, and experienced a loss of one midshipman and four men killed, and one officer and 29 men wounded. The fourth division, owing to the strong tide, was unable to attack in the assigned quarter, and returned without attempting anything. Nothing could exceed the

* These brigs were vessels of from 200 to 250 tons, armed with from four to eight heavy long guns, generally 24 and 18-pounders, and in some instances, 36-pounders. The flat, or raft, which formed the description of vessel of which the invasion flotilla was composed, drew but three-and-a-half feet of water, had very stout bulwarks, and carried 30 men in crew, besides 150 soldiers; she was armed with one 13-inch mortar, one long 24-pounder, and four swivels, and had also an abundance of small arms.

gallantry of the crews of the attacking boats, but the enemy were too numerous and well prepared, and success was impracticable.

The French claim to have captured four English boats with a loss of only 10 killed and 30 wounded, but as a partial set off, a few days later, the boats of the *Jamaica*, 24, sloops *Gannet* and *Hound*, and the gun-boats *Tigress* and *Mallard*, under the orders of Lieutenants Agassiz and Le Vescounte, attacked and brought off three flat-boats, which, with three others (scuttled by the enemy), came out from St. Valery to attack the British squadron, but were driven ashore. These flats were forty-eight feet in length by twenty in breadth, and mounted one brass 8-inch howitzer.

Owing to the vigilance of the British cruisers, Buonaparte had been wholly unable to send supplies and reinforcements to the army he had left in Egypt under General Kléber, but the case was urgent, and at length, after one unsuccessful attempt, Rear-Admiral Ganteaume, undoubtedly one of the best officers of the French Navy, was enabled to take advantage of a northerly gale, which drove off the British blockading squadron, to quit Brest with seven sail-of-the-line and two frigates, having on board 5,000 troops. A few days later the British frigate *Concorde*, of 40 guns and 224 men, Captain Barton, sighted the French squadron, and being chased by the *Bravoure*, of 42 guns and 320 men, hove to when she had lost sight of the enemy, and a close engagement ensued. The *Bravoure*, finding her adversary more than a match for her, made sail and rejoined her consorts, having lost in the action 10 killed and 24 wounded, including her captain, the casualties of the *Concorde* being four and 19 respectively.

The French squadron passed through the Straits of Gibraltar on the 9th February, and was closely followed by Captain Peard, commanding the 32-gun frigate *Success*, the only ship at Gibraltar, who was desirous of apprizing Lord Keith, the British Commander-in-Chief in the Mediterranean, of the direction taken by the French fleet. Admiral Ganteaume, however, captured the *Success*, and hearing of the approach of a superior force, altered his course, and steered for Toulon, where he arrived unmolested. Meantime the *Concorde* reached Plymouth on the 3rd February, whereupon Lord St. Vincent, commanding the Channel fleet, despatched Sir Robert Calder with seven sail-of-the-line and two frigates to the West Indies, as Admiral Ganteaume's most probable destination.

Buonaparte, on hearing of the arrival at Toulon of the squadron he had destined for the relief of his army in Egypt, sent peremptory orders to Ganteaume to proceed immediately to Alexandria, and on the 19th March, that officer sailed with seven line-of-battle-ships, three frigates, and three transports. The same night he encountered a severe gale of wind, in which one of his ships carried away her main-mast and had to return, and a transport, having parted company, was captured by the frigate *Minerva*, Captain George Cockburn. Again the ubiquitous British fleet, which marred all the plans of the First Consul, appeared on the scene. Sir John Borlase Warren, who had entered the Mediterranean in search of the French admiral on the 13th of the preceding month, having under his command seven sail-of-the-line, sighted the enemy on the 25th, and Ganteaume again put back to Toulon.

A third time, on the 27th April, the admiral, under orders from Buonaparte, put to sea with the object of attempting to reach Egypt, and on the 7th June, had arrived about 70 leagues to the westward of Alexandria, with four two-deckers, one frigate, one corvette, and four store-ships. He now detached the corvette to reconnoitre the coast, but being chased by the seventy-fours *Kent* and *Hector*, she took refuge in the port. Acting on the opinion that she had been captured by the British squadron, Ganteaume entered the port of Bengazi, in Tripoli, with the object, conformably to his instructions, of landing his troops, but Lord Keith's squadron hove in sight, and he cut his cables and made sail to escape, leaving behind two of his store-ships. The enemy, however, gained an unexpected prize.

On the 24th June, the *Swiftsure*, 74, Captain Hallowell, sighted the fleeing French squadron, which surrounded him, and the superior sailing qualities of the enemy's ships rendered abortive every effort to escape. Captain Hallowell now bore down under all sail, in the hope of effecting his escape to leeward, but the three rearmost French ships tacked and closed on him, and after maintaining a running action for an hour and a half, he was compelled to haul down his colours. The *Swiftsure* lost, out of 450 men at their quarters, two killed and eight wounded, but her spars, rigging, and sails were cut to pieces, and to prolong the action with four ships-of-the-line would only have caused unavailing bloodshed. Admiral Ganteaume succeeded in reaching Toulon with his prize on the 22nd July.

A French force of 5,500 men landed on the island of Elba, and laid siege to Porto Ferrajo, but Sir John Warren drove away the blockading squadron, consisting of the *Bravoure* and *Succés* (late *Success*), and the 40-gun frigate *Pomone*, Captain Gower, and after a short chase, brought to action and captured the frigate *Carrère*, of 40 guns and 352 men, which was purchased into the Navy. The *Bravoure* and *Succés* now made an attempt to capture the *Phœnix*, 36, Captain Halsted, which lay at anchor off Piombino, on the coast, about seven miles from Elba, but on the 2nd September the two frigates were sighted by Captain Cockburn, in the *Minerve*, who chased them in company with the *Pomone* and *Phœnix*. The Frenchmen now sought to regain Leghorn, but they were overhauled by the *Minerve*, and ran ashore, when the *Succès* was got off and restored to the Navy, but the *Bravoure* lost her three masts and became a total wreck. Admiral Warren now took an active part in the defence of the fortress, landing 450 marines and 240 seamen, under the command of Captain Long, who attacked and destroyed some of the French batteries, but the force was compelled to retire with the loss of 15 killed—including Captain Long, while gallantly leading on his men to carry a narrow bridge—33 wounded, and 77 made prisoners. The French general, however, failed to gain possession of Porto Ferrajo.

The next important expedition conducted by this country during the year 1801 was that for the expulsion of the French from Egypt, in which the Navy bore a subordinate, but essential, part. By the 31st January, an army, with a powerful fleet of over sixty sail, including seven ships-of-the-line, had assembled at Marmorice Bay, on the coast of Asia Minor, and after a considerable delay, due chiefly to the tardiness of our allies, the Turks, the whole expedition of British and Turkish ships-of-war and transports, having on board 16,000 troops, arrived at Aboukir on the 1st March. At this time the French army of occupation in Egypt numbered 21,000 men of all arms, under the command of General Menou, who had succeeded General Kleber, on the assassination of that able officer by a fanatical Syrian, on the 14th June preceding. On the 3rd February two French frigates had succeeded in landing some reinforcements and munitions of war at Alexandria, and on the same day that Lord Keith cast anchor at Aboukir, a French frigate and corvette, with troops and stores, arrived at the same port, having eluded the vigilance of the British cruisers.

Owing to a succession of heavy weather it was not until the 8th March that the disembarkation of General Abercombie's army could be commenced, and this was successfully accomplished by the boats of the fleet, under the superintendence of Captain Hon. Alexander Cochrane, of the *Ajax*. The flanks of the flotilla of boats were guarded by British gun-vessels, while two bomb-vessels were told off to shell the enemy, and three sloops-of-war were moored broadside on to the beach as close as was practicable. To co-operate with the army, a naval brigade of 1,000 seamen, under the command of Sir Sidney Smith and five captains of frigates, embarked in the launches, in which also the field-artillery was stowed. As the boats neared the shore they were saluted with a heavy fire of grapeshot and musketry from behind the sandhills, and a cannonade from the castle of Aboukir, but the landing was effected in good order. In the action that ensued the naval brigade performed valuable service in dragging the guns up the heights, and during the day they experienced a loss of 22 killed, and seven officers and 63 seamen wounded. Major-General Moore, the hero of Corunna, drove the enemy from their positions, and, on the 12th, the army moved towards Alexandria. On the following day an action was fought in which the seamen and marines participated, while the gun-boats on the lake, commanded by Captains Frederick Maitland and James Hillyar, maintained a fire on the right flank of the army. The Navy lost on this occasion two lieutenants of marines, one midshipman, and 27 seamen and marines killed, and four officers and 50 men wounded.

On the 18th March the castle of Aboukir surrendered, and a Turkish squadron of two seventy-fours, and four frigates and corvettes, anchored in the bay. Three days later took place the battle of Alexandria between the British and French armies, each numbering about 10,000 men, though the French had 1,380 cavalry against only 300 opposed to them, and 46 guns to 35. The victory was complete, but it was dimmed by the loss of the veteran commander, Sir Ralph Abercrombie, who was removed on board the *Foudroyant*, Lord Keith's flagship, where he expired a week later. The British loss in this decisive action was 247 killed, including a master's mate and three seamen—the Marines being now in garrison at Aboukir—and 1,243 wounded, among whom were Sir Sidney Smith, one lieutenant and 48 men of the Navy.

Some more Turkish ships arrived at Aboukir, with 5,000 men, who were landed on the 3rd April and, in company with a detachment of 800 troops, gained possession of the town and castle of Rosetta, which commanded the western branch of the Nile. The castle of Jullien, on the banks of the Nile, was also reduced, a division of British and Turkish gunboats, under the orders of Captain Curry, of the *Fury*, acting in conjunction with Colonel Spencer's brigade. On the 15th April the canal of Alexandria was cut by the British, and thus the waters were admitted into Lake Mareotis, whose bed had been dry for centuries. By this means General Menou, who had retreated into the city with 6,000 men, was isolated from the detachments of 4,000, under General Lagrange, entrenched in the vicinity, and of 5,000 at Cairo, under General Belliard. General Hutchinson, who now commanded the British army, on the 5th May commenced his march with 8,000 allied troops to attack Lagrange, accompanied by a division of gunboats, under the orders of Captain Stevenson, but the French retreated towards Cairo, and the fort of Rahmanieh surrendered, after an attack in which Captain Curry assisted with four flats and three armed launches. The British army advanced slowly, and on the 20th June arrived before Cairo, which was surrendered by General Belliard.

Meantime a body of British and native troops, from Bombay, under General Baird, acted in conjunction. On the 21st April the *Leopard*, 50, Captain Surridge, bearing the flag of Rear-Admiral Blankett, with some frigates, sloops, and transports, having on board a party of the 86th Regiment, anchored at Suez, which was occupied on the following day. Landing the detachment of 320 men, the squadron sailed for Kosseir, where were lying the *Romney*, 50, Sir Home Popham, the *Sensible*, 36, Captain Sauer, with several transports, which had landed two divisions of the Indian contingent under Generals Baird and Murray. Between the 10th and 15th June they started from Kosseir across the desert to Kenneh, on the Nile, but, owing to the difficulty of procuring boats to descend the river, General Baird did not arrive at Cairo until several days after the surrender of the Egyptian capital. The British squadron now sailed from Kosseir on their return to Bombay, but Admiral Blankett died at Mocha, where the *Leopard* and *Romney* cast anchor.

By the 10th August the whole of the French prisoners taken at Cairo and other ports, numbering 13,500 men, had sailed from Aboukir, and preparations were made by General Hutchinson for the reduction of Alexandria. Escorted by the flotilla of gunboats, under Captain Stevenson, General Coote's division of 5,000 men proceeded with the boats of the fleet across Lake Mareotis, and occupied a position to the westward of the town. On the night of the 18th August a combined military and naval attack was made on the fortified island of Marabou, which protects the entrance to the western, or great, harbour of Alexandria. The naval force, consisting of the launches of the squadron, under Captain Cochrane, with four sloops and brigs, and three Turkish corvettes, entered the harbour. The British batteries opened fire on the town on the 26th, and on the following day, General Menou sent an officer to treat for terms, which were agreed to. On the 2nd of September Alexandria capitulated, and the garrison of 8,000 men, with 1,300 sailors, were sent to France, while the ships-of-war, consisting of a 64-gun ship, three frigates, and some smaller vessels, fell into the hands of the victors. These were divided between the British and Turkish navies, and the *Régénérée* and *Egyptienne* were decided acquisitions, the former receiving the name of *Alexandria*.

It would be impossible to over-estimate the importance of the services rendered by the navy in this successful and admirably conducted expedition, and Lord Hutchinson heartily acknowledged them in the following order:—"The labour and fatigue of the Navy have been continued and excessive; it has not been of one day or one week, but for months together. In the Bay of Aboukir, on the new inundation, and on the Nile for 160 miles, they have been employed without intermission, and have submitted to many privations with a cheerfulness and patience highly creditable to them and advantageous to the public service."

In March, 1801, Buonaparte induced King Charles of Spain to cede to France, either by sale or hire, six sail-of-the-line lying at Cadiz, and in order to man them with French crews, and co-operate with another Spanish squadron in entering the Tagus and attacking the capital of Portugal, against which Spain had declared war on the 27th February, Buonaparte despatched Admiral Linois from Toulon with the 80-gun ships *Indomptable* and *Formidable*, *Desaix*, 74, and the 36-gun frigate *Muiron*. Accordingly, on the 13th June, the French admiral sailed from Toulon, bound for Cadiz, with directions to effect a junction with the six ships newly manned by French crews, under Admiral Dumanoir le Pelley, and a Spanish squadron of six sail, under Admiral Moreno. Owing to head-winds it was not until the 4th July that Admiral Linois, learning that Cadiz was blockaded by a British squadron, bore up for Algeciras, where he anchored the same day in full view of Gibraltar. At this time Sir James Saumarez was stationed off Cadiz with the following ships:—

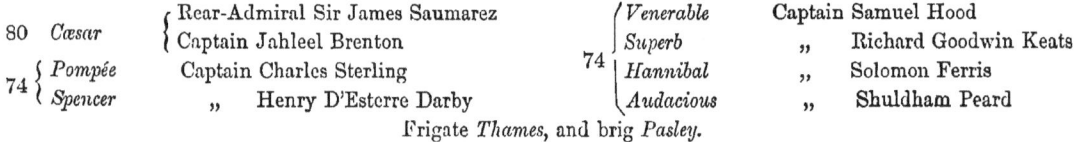

Early on the 5th July the admiral received a notice from Commander Hon. George Dundas, commanding the 14-gun polacre sloop *Calpe*, the only British vessel then at the Rock, of the arrival of the French squadron at Algeciras, and weighed to engage the enemy. The ships, however, were becalmed, and it was not until the following morning that, a breeze having sprung up, they were enabled to round Cabrita Point, and carry out the admiral's instructions to attack the enemy as they came up in succession. Meanwhile, Admiral Linois had made arrangements to give his assailants a warm welcome by warping his ships close in shore, under protection of the batteries that defended the roads, and of 14 heavy gunboats. His flagship, the *Formidable*, was moored abreast of the San Iago battery, mounting five 18-pounders, which gave a flanking fire; the *Desaix* about 500 yards astern, and to the southward of the flagship, and the *Indomptable* about the same distance astern of the *Desaix*. The frigate *Muiron* took her station a little within and to the northward of Isla Verda, on which was a battery of seven 24-pounders. Three of the gunboats were anchored about a quarter of a mile to the south-west of the last-named island, four others between Fort San Iago and the *Formidable*, and the remaining seven off a point of land about half a mile to the northward of the tower of Almirante.

The *Cæsar*, flagship of the British admiral, and two other ships, were over three miles astern, when, at 8.30, the *Pompée* received the fire of the *Muiron*, and successively, of the *Indomptable*, *Desaix*, and *Formidable*, to which she replied by a broadside at each of the two latter ships, and, the wind dying away, she dropped her anchor close to the *Formidable's* starboard bow, upon which the British seventy-four opened a heavy fire. A few minutes later the *Audacious* and *Venerable* dropped their anchors, the one abreast of the *Indomptable*, and the other at a greater distance from the quarter of the *Formidable*. A furious cannonade now ensued between these three British ships and the five French ships, gunboats, and batteries; but soon the *Pompée*, owing to the strength of the current, swung with her head towards the broadside of the *Formidable*, which had suspended her fire, and could only ply her starboard guns on the batteries of San Iago and Almirante, and at the gunboats moored in front of them. At about 9.15 A.M. the *Cæsar* got up and, dropping her anchor ahead of the *Audacious*, sent a spring on board the *Venerable*, which ship was on her starboard quarter, and opened her heavy broadside upon the *Desaix*. The *Hannibal*, a few minutes afterwards, also came into action on the starboard bow of the *Cæsar*, and the *Spencer*, lying to leeward of the line, was exposed to the heavy fire of the Spanish batteries.

The *Hannibal*, under orders from Sir James Saumarez "to go and rake the French admiral," which was pouring a heavy fire into the *Pompée*, as she lay exposed to it head on, cut her cable and, making sail, tacked for the *Formidable*, but unfortunately, when almost within hail of her, she grounded. Notwithstanding, the *Hannibal* kept up a fire on the French flagship with her foremost guns, and directed the others on the gunboats and the batteries of Almirante and San Iago. A light breeze from the north-east now sprang up, whereupon the French ships obeyed their admiral's signal to cut their cables and run ashore. Sir James Saumarez directed his captains to cut their cables, and the *Cæsar*, wearing round the *Audacious* and *Venerable*, soon brought her guns to bear upon the *Indomptable*, into whose bows, with her foresail to the mast, she poured several destructive broadsides, which brought down her fore-topmast. The *Venerable* and *Spencer* also cut their cables, but were unable, owing to lack of wind, to co-operate in the attack upon the southernmost French ships and the island battery, and the *Venerable* had her mizen-topmast shot away as she was in the act of wearing. The *Pompée*, after remaining nearly an hour without being able to bring a gun to bear, was towed out of action by the boats of the squadron. The flagship and *Audacious* lay exposed to the heavy guns of the island battery, without the power of returning a shot, and at length, at 1.35, the British admiral discontinued the action, and in company with the *Audacious*, *Venerable*, and *Spencer*, a light breeze having sprung up, made sail, leaving the dismasted and shattered *Hannibal* to contend alone with the enemy. So great was her loss that Captain Ferris was compelled, after a time, to order his men to cease firing, and take shelter below, and soon afterwards he hauled down his colours.

In this unfortunate action the loss of the British squadron was very severe, being 121 killed, 240 wounded, and 14 missing, supposed to be drowned.* The ships were much shattered, especially the *Cæsar* and *Pompée*, which had their masts, yards, sails and rigging cut to pieces, and all their boats sunk or injured so that they could not float. The enemy lost even more heavily, the French owning to 306 killed, including two captains, and 280 wounded, and the Spaniards to a loss of 11, exclusive of those wounded. The ships and forts suffered considerable damage, and five Spanish gunboats were sunk, so that the enemy, though they boasted loudly of what they called a victory, had little real cause for self-gratulation.†

The French contention that the *Pompée* struck was not borne out by facts, for

---

* The casualties were thus distributed:—*Cæsar*, her master, and eight men killed, an officer and 24 wounded, and one officer and seven missing. *Pompée*, her master, one midshipman and 13 men killed, and three lieutenants, three other officers and 63 wounded. *Venerable*, one midshipman and two men killed, and two midshipmen and 23 wounded. The *Hannibal* had two officers and 73 men killed, and four officers and 58 men wounded, and six missing. *Audacious*, eight killed, and one officer and 31 wounded. *Spencer*, one midshipman and five men killed, and one midshipman and 26 wounded.

† According to the French account "three French sail-of-the-line and a frigate were attacked by six English sail-of-the-line and a frigate; the English were completely beaten, and took refuge at Gibraltar, leaving in the possession of the French the *Hannibal*, 74 guns; and another ship-of-the-line struck, but was afterwards towed off by a great number of English gunboats." "The action," says the Madrid *Gazette Extraordinary*, "was very obstinate, and bloody on both sides; and likewise on the part of our batteries, which decided the fate of the day." And it adds: "The fire of our batteries was so hot and well supported that the enemy suffered most from them; and particularly it is to that of San Iago we owe the capture of the English ship, for her bold manœuvre of attempting to pass between the French rear-admiral's ship, the *Formidable*, and the shore, made her take the ground, and, notwithstanding the utmost exertion to get her afloat, it was found impossible to move her; then the fire from the battery very soon dismasted her, and compelled her to strike."

though her colours were shot away, they were quickly replaced. But, nevertheless, it was a defeat for us, as our ships retired from the conflict, and considering the rarity of such an event in naval warfare, it was not astonishing that the success was publicly announced in the theatres of Paris.

Yielding to the urgent representations of Admiral Linois, and to those of Rear-Admiral Dumanoir le Pelley, who, on the 13th June, had arrived at Cadiz from Brest with the two 40-gun frigates, *Libre* and *Indienne*, with a detachment of officers and seamen for the six ships-of-the-line equipped in that port, Admiral Massaredo, the Spanish Commander-in-Chief, on the 9th July, detached Vice-Admiral de Moreno, with five French and one Franco-Spanish sail-of-the-line and three frigates, to Algeciras to the assistance of the French squadron, which apprehended a fresh attack from the discomfited British ships. With the alacrity and resource that so prominently distinguishes British seamen, the crews had repaired them, with the exception of the *Pompée*, which was too much shattered to proceed to sea on so short a notice; and at noon of the 12th, when the enemy began to move and took up their stations in line of battle off Cabrita Point, the British squadron weighed anchor and stood out to engage the allied fleet. The flagship *Cæsar*,* which had suffered greatly, had been refitted with a smartness never surpassed in the history of naval war, the seamen working all day, and in alternate watches each night between the 6th and 12th July, and she gallantly led the van, followed by the following ships:—*Venerable*, *Superb*, which had not participated in the recent action, *Spencer* and *Audacious*, the 32-gun frigate *Thames*,

---

* "The *Cæsar*," says Captain Edward Brenton in his history, "lay in the mole, in so shattered a state that the admiral gave her up also, and, hoisting his flag on board the *Audacious*, expressed his intention of distributing her men to the effective ships. Captain (Jahleel) Brenton requested that his people might remain on board as long as possible, and, addressing them, stated the admiral's intentions in case the ship could not be got ready. They answered, with three cheers, 'All hands to work day and night, till she is ready.' The captain ordered them to work all day and watch and watch all night. By these means they accomplished what has, probably, never been exceeded. On the 8th they warped her into the mole and shipped the lower mast; on the 9th they got their new mainmast in. On the 11th the enemy showed symptoms of sailing, which only increased, if possible, the energies of the seamen. On Sunday, the 12th, at dawn of day, the enemy loosed sails, the *Cæsar* still refitting in the mole, raising powder, shot, and other stores, and preparing to haul out. At noon the enemy began to move, the wind fresh from the eastward, and as they cleared the bay, they took up stations off Cabrita Point, which appeared to be the rendezvous on which they were to form their line-of-battle. At one o'clock the enemy's squadron was nearly all under way; the Spanish ships *Real Carlos* and *Hermenegildo*, of 112 guns each, off Cabrita Point; the *Cæsar* was warping out of the mole. The day was clear; the whole population of the Rock came out to witness the scene; the wall, mole-head and batteries were crowded from the dockyard to the ragged-staff; the *Cæsar's* band playing, 'Come, cheer up, my lads, 'tis to glory we steer,' the military band of the garrison answering with, 'Britons, strike home.' The effect of this scene it is difficult to describe; Englishmen were proud of their country, and foreigners who beheld the scene wished to be Englishmen. So general was the enthusiasm among our gallant countrymen that even the wounded men begged to be taken on board, to share in the honour of the approaching conflict."

the *Calpe*, brig *Louisa,* and Portuguese frigate *Carlotta*. The following were the ships of the combined squadron, under the command of Vice-Admiral Moreno and Rear-Admiral Linois, who, quitting their respective flagships, repaired on board the Spanish frigate *Sabina*.

Spanish.		French.	
112	{ *Real Carlos* / *Hermenegildo*	80	{ *Formidable* / *Indomptable*
96	*San Fernando*	74	{ *St. Antoine* / *Desaix*
80	*Argonauta*		
74	*San Augustin*	Frigates *Libre* and *Muiron*	
	Frigate *Sabina*		

The British squadron bore away in chase, led by Captain Keats in the *Superb*, which, shortly before midnight, lost sight of her consorts, except the *Cæsar*, quite three miles astern, and opened fire on the *Real Carlos*, then about 350 yards on her port beam. At the third broadside the three-decker, which had lost her fore-topmast, was observed to be on fire, and dropped astern in evident confusion. The *Superb*, leaving her adversary to her fate, made sail and engaged the *St. Antoine*, bearing the broad pennant of the French Commodore Le Ray, which surrendered after an action lasting only half an hour. About the same time a terrible catastrophe happened to the Spanish squadron. The *San Hermenegildo*, mistaking the *Real Carlos* for an enemy, notwithstanding that she was on fire and incapable of resistance, had been firing into her, and presently fell on board of her, when she also caught fire. Soon after, the *Real Carlos* blew up, and fifteen minutes later, the second three-decker shared her fate, when, out of 2,000 men on board the two ships, all perished, except 38 taken on board the *Superb*, and 262 who reached the *St. Antoine*.

The British two-decker, who had only one lieutenant and 14 men wounded, remained by the *St. Antoine*, together with the *Calpe*, *Louisa*, and *Carlotta*, while the rest of the squadron continued in chase. At five o'clock on the morning of the 13th, the *Venerable* came up with the *Formidable*, which carried "jury" topmasts, and commenced an action, assisted by the frigate *Thames*. Soon after the British seventy-four had her mizen-mast shot away, and shortly before seven, when the combatants had been for some time engaged within pistol-shot range, her main-mast carried away by the board, when the French 80-gun ship took advantage of the chance of escape, and made sail towards Cadiz. Soon afterwards the *Venerable's* fore-mast went over the side, and, the wind being light and the ship without steerage way, she struck upon the rocky shoals of San Pedro, about 12 miles distant from Cadiz.

In this action the *Venerable* lost her master and 17 seamen and marines killed, and one lieutenant, two midshipmen, the boatswain, and 83 wounded. The enemy's ships appeared inclined to attack the British seventy-four in her shattered condition, but the sight of the *Superb* and *Audacious* coming up in the distance, caused them to haul off for Cadiz, where they arrived in safety. With the assistance of the *Thames* and of the boats of the *Cæsar* and *Spencer*, Captain Hood and his gallant ship's company hove the *Venerable* into deep water, and she was then taken in tow, and, by the following morning, had completed her jury rig.

For his successful action with a greatly superior squadron, which he drove back into Cadiz, Sir James Saumarez was created a Knight of the Bath, with a pension of £1,200 a year, and the first lieutenants of the *Cæsar*, *Superb*, and *Venerable* were promoted, while the officers and men received the thanks of Parliament.

The year 1801, like all those of this long and memorable war, was distinguished by some picturesque and gallant feats performed, in single action, by British ships and boats. The first of the series was an exploit achieved, on the 3rd January, by the boats of the *Melpomene*, 38, commanded by Sir William Hamilton, who, determining to make an attempt to cut out the French brig *Sénégal*, of 18 guns and 60 men, and an armed schooner, lying within the bar of the Senegal river, sent five boats, with 60 seamen, and 35 volunteers from the African corps, under the orders of Lieutenant Dick. The party pushed off at 9.30 in the evening, and passing through the heavy surf on the bar, and eluding discovery from the battery at the point, arrived close to the brig. But when within a few yards of her they were met by a discharge of her bow guns, which sank two boats and killed Lieutenant Palmer, of the *Melpomene*, and seven men. Nothing daunted, the remaining boats boarded the brig, and after a severe struggle, lasting twenty minutes, carried her. The schooner having, meanwhile, taken refuge under the guns of the battery, Lieutenant Dick made sail down the river with his prize, which, however, grounded on a shoal, where she sank. Leaving the brig, that officer pulled back to the *Melpomene*, receiving on the way a heavy fire from the battery at the point. The British loss in this affair was Lieutenants Palmer and Vyvian, of the Marines, one midshipman, and eight men killed, and three officers and 15 men wounded.

In the West Indies, the *Garland*, schooner, commanded by Lieutenant MacKenzie, boarded and carried the French schooner *Eclair*, of four guns and 45 men, after a smart conflict, with slight loss, and the prize, a fine new vessel, from Rochefort, was added to the Navy, and fitted with 12 guns. The services rendered by Acting-Lieutenant Fitton, in a Spanish prize, the tender of the *Abergavenny*, were of a very remarkable character. This officer was gifted, to an extraordinary degree, with the activity and resource which so distinguished his profession. He had captured and destroyed a large number of merchantmen on the Spanish main, and, on the 23rd January, engaged and drove ashore near Carthagena, the Spanish Guarda Costa *Santa Maria*, of six guns and 60 men. As the enemy kept up a hot fire of musketry, Lieutenant Fitton leaped into the water with his sword in his mouth, followed by his crew, carrying their cutlasses in a similar position, and swimming to the schooner, boarded, and after a stout resistance succeeded in capturing her. In this brilliant affair, says James—"the tender lost two seamen killed and five wounded, and of her small crew, numbering originally but 45, many were too sick to attend quarters, but four or five, also, who were on the sick list, heedless alike of the doctor's injunctions and their own feeble state, had, when the call for boarders was made, sprung over the side with their comrades. The loss on board the *Santa Maria* amounted to five men killed and nine wounded, including her commander, who had both his hands carried away by a grapeshot." Lieutenant Fitton, being unable to carry off the prize, set her on fire, after freeing her crew.

A gallant, but only partially successful, attempt to bring off some merchant vessels was made by Captains Israel Pellew and Lawrie, commanding the frigates *Andromache* and *Cleopatra*. While cruising off the coast of Cuba these gallant officers descried 25 sail, lying at anchor in the Bay of Levita, under the protection of three armed galleys. Under the command of Captain Lawrie the boats of the frigates pushed off about 9.30 on the night of the 22nd March, and about midnight arrived within gunshot of the galleys, when they were received with rounds of grape and musketry. Pushing on, the British seamen boarded several of the vessels, but were only able to bring off one of the galleys. In effecting this service some of the boats were sunk, and the first lieutenant of the *Andromache*, a midshipman, and a master's mate of the *Cleopatra*, and six seamen were killed, and 12 wounded. The Spaniards had nine killed, and several wounded in the captured galley alone.

In the East Indies, also, the honour of the flag was upheld by the capture of the French 36-gun frigate *Chiffonne* by the *Sibylle*, 38, Captain Adam, off the Seychelles Islands, in the Indian Ocean. The *Chiffonne* was lying in Mahé Roads when discovered on the 19th April by the British frigate. Captain Adam, threading the winding and intricate channel, anchored 200 yards off the enemy, and at 10.42, within seventeen minutes of opening fire, the *Chiffonne* hauled down her colours and, cutting her cable, drifted on a reef, when the crew escaped ashore in the boats. A party of the *Sibylle's* men landed to attack a battery which had assisted the enemy by its fire, when the people manning the guns fled. The *Chiffonne*, which was purchased into the Navy, and did good service under her own name, lost in this action 23 killed and three wounded, while her successful antagonist had only three casualties.

That French seamen could fight a losing battle with gallantry was proved by the way in which the *Curieux*, of 18 guns and 168 men, sustained for half an hour the fire of the *Bordelais*, Captain Manby, carrying 24 guns, and with a crew of 195 men. The brig was surrendered after her hull had been so riddled with shot that she foundered, carrying with her the greater number of the wounded, who, with the killed, amounted to about 50, including her captain, who had both legs shot off and survived only a few hours.

Other captains of the French service were not equally anxious for the honour of their flag, and the 18-gun brig *Penguin*, Commander Mansel, in vain used every endeavour to bring to action a French corvette of 20 guns, with two consorts, apparently armed merchantmen. The *Penguin* forced one of the latter to haul down her flag, and had a spirited engagement with the corvette, which, however, took advantage of the brig losing her fore-topmast to make sail and escape to Teneriffe.

A remarkable victory, after a well-contested action, was gained by the frigate *Phœbe*, Captain Barlow, carrying 44 guns and 239 men, over the *Africaine*, Commodore Saulnier, having on board 400 troops, in addition to her crew of 315, together with a great quantity of arms and ammunition for the French army in Egypt. The ships, being on the African shore, near Ceuta, engaged at pistol-shot range for two hours, when, at 9.30 in the evening, the French frigate, having five feet of water in the hold, her masts so injured that they were tottering to their fall, her guns mostly dismounted, and her decks covered with the dead and dying, hauled down her colours. The gallant French soldiers and seamen had done all and more than all that the most rigorous rules of honour demanded of gallant men. Of the soldiers and sailors on board her, the *Africaine* lost Commodore Saulnier, one general, 13 officers, and no less than 185 men killed, and 3 generals, 14 officers, including her second-in-command, and 125 men wounded, the greater part mortally. These were the numbers actually given by the officer in command to Captain Barlow, who, however, stated that the real loss was considerably greater, especially in killed. Such courage is beyond praise, and speaks more than words for the deadly accuracy of the fire of the seamen gunners of the British frigate, which had only one seaman killed, and her first lieutenant, master, and 10 wounded. Captain Barlow did his best to refit his prize and his own ship, which had suffered almost equally aloft, but after vainly endeavouring to work to windward, bore up for Minorca. The captain of the *Phœbe* was knighted, and his first lieutenant received promotion, while the prize was added to the Navy under the name of the *Amelia*.

The reader will remember the brilliant service rendered by Captain (now Sir Edward) Hamilton, in cutting out the *Hermione*, an exploit which stands unsurpassed amid the numberless similar deeds of daring of the British Navy. This officer, while commanding the 36-gun frigate *Trent*, discovered a French ship lying at anchor off the isles of Bréhat, under the protection of an armed cutter and lugger, and sent his boats to cut her out. The service was effected with the usual dash, and some shore boats and the lugger were driven off and chased on the rocks.

The 14-gun brig *Speedy* has been more than once mentioned in these pages as having done good service under the command of Lieutenant Jahleel Brenton. She surpassed her previous achievements when that enterprising officer was succeeded by a still more famous seaman, Lord Cochrane, one of the best specimens of the type of Drake and Grenville.

Lord Cochrane had entered the service eight years before with the rating of ship's-boy, so that his rise was rapid. And here we may take the opportunity of mentioning that this and other apparently menial or plebeian ratings, under which so many officers of distinction entered the service, do not bear the interpretation that might naturally be placed on them. It merely denoted that, in his lordship's case, as in that of others, there was no vacancy among the midshipmen, or "volunteers," as young gentlemen were also called. Thus many of the officers of whom we have given brief biographical notices, entered the Navy with the rating of captain's servant, first, second or third class boys, able seaman (A.B.), ordinary seaman (O.S.), and the like. Macaulay, by his references to those gallant seamen, Sir Christopher Mings, Sir John Harborough, and Sir Cloudesley Shovel, gave rise to the idea that because these officers entered the Navy under such ratings, they were of plebeian origin. Of the family and antecedents of Mings before he became captain of the *Centurion*, in 1662, we know nothing; but Sir John Harborough was of ancient descent, and even Sir Cloudesley Shovel, who, according to Campbell, began life as a shoemaker, is said by some to have been a scion of an ancient but decayed family, and the Heralds acknowledged this when granting him his arms, on the 6th January, 1692, in commemoration of his services.

Many similar instances occur in the later annals of the Navy. Thus the great Earl St. Vincent was borne on the books of two ships in which he first served as A.B., as was Admiral J. W. Maurice; and Sir William Parker (see his "Life" by Admiral Phillimore) was rated as a foremast hand. Lord Nelson, who went to sea at the age of twelve with his maternal uncle, Captain Suckling, was another distinguished example; and in 1773, when fifteen, his name was borne on the books of the *Carcase*, bomb-vessel, as coxwain to Captain Lutwidge. Among other admirals, Charles Ogle, in 1788, when thirteen years of age, was "captain's servant" in the *Adventure*, 44, and Sir George Cockburn filled that rating in the books of two ships before he actually went to sea in 1786. Sir William Hotham, while a scholar at Westminster, between 1779 and 1785, was rated as captain's servant, and Sir Willoughby Lake actually went afloat with that rating when a child of seven, on board the *Roebuck*, 24. Other notable instances are Sir James Byam Martin, in the *Pegasus*, the Hon. Sir John Talbot, who was rated as Nelson's "servant" in the *Boreas*, and Lord Waldegrave, who entered the Navy as a "first-class boy."

But there is alive at the present time (August, 1891), in his hundred and first year, a gallant officer, who is a living example of this strange practice, which had its counterpart, we may observe, in the Army, where officers held commissions in regiments while in the nursery. Admiral-of-the-fleet Sir Provo Wallis, the sole survivor of the memorable action between the *Shannon* and *Chesapeake*, in 1813, was borne on the books of the 36-gun frigate *Oiseau* as an A.B., though he was just four years of age. To return to Lord Cochrane's services.

Lord Cochrane first embarked in the *Hind*, 28, commanded by his uncle, the Hon. Alexander Cochrane, who had served with distinction in command of the *Vesuvius*, bomb-vessel, under Sir George Rodney. His lordship sailed in June, 1793, when seventeen and a half years of age, and was rated in the ship's books as boy, his pay being £7 yearly. In 1800 he was lieutenant on board the *Queen Charlotte*, bearing the flag of Lord Keith in the Mediterranean, when he was ordered to take charge of the *Généreux* after her capture, and proceeded to Port Mahon. Here he expected to receive command of the *Bonne Citoyenne*, but was appointed to the *Speedy*. The *Speedy* is described by his lordship in his interesting "Autobiography of a Seaman," as a little craft of 158 tons, carrying fourteen 4-pounders and having a complement of six officers and 84 men.

The cabin was so low that it was not possible to stand upright in it,* and when he shaved he had to thrust his head through the skylight. But his lordship made light of discomforts, and his services in convoying merchant ships and capturing those of the enemy, made his name a terror on the Spanish littoral, and the Madrid Government despatched ships with the express object of capturing the little brig.

Early in April Lord Cochrane sighted and gave chase to a large merchantman, which turned out to be the 32-gun xebec† frigate, *Gamo*, disguised to lure his lordship, and so ensure his capture. But Lord Cochrane was equal to the occasion, and as escape was impossible he resolved on a ruse. Hoisting the Danish flag, and placing a man dressed in the uniform of the Danish Navy, he gave out that the *Speedy* was the Danish brig-of-war, *Clomer*. Not quite satisfied, the Captain of the *Gamo* sent a boat to board the brig, when the officer in command was politely informed that she was two days from Algiers, and at the same time was reminded that a visit would involve a long quarantine on return to port. But the crew of the *Speedy* were not at all pleased at being robbed of their anticipated trial of strength with the Spanish frigate, and their commander, who was not the man to baulk them, promised that if they ever again encountered the *Gamo* on the high seas, they should have their wish realized.

On the 6th May their desire was gratified, and an action took place, as honourable to the British Navy as almost anything in its long and glorious annals. Two days before, the *Speedy*, when off Barcelona, had captured a 4-gun tartan, and a privateer of seven guns, and beat off a swarm of gunboats which had been sent out to decoy the little brig within reach of the *Gamo*. On the previous day Lord Cochrane stood off shore repairing damages, and at daylight, on the following morning, the frigate was seen bearing down in chase. Prize crews had reduced the crew of the *Speedy* to 54 men and boys, but his lordship was determined that this time there should be no complaint of not having a fair fight, so he mustered the crew to their quarters, and cleared for action. Chase was given, but owing to light winds, it was nearly

---

* The author of this work served for two years in the Indian Ocean in the Hon. Company's schooner *Mahé*, of the same dimensions and tonnage as the *Speedy*, and carrying one swivel 32-pounder, and four 12-pounder howitzers, with a crew of 54 men, and has a lively recollection of the discomforts of service in this class of vessel. As in the *Speedy*, the cabin was five feet high, and there was a skylight which gave the only light and air, but the men's quarters were without either. Language fails to convey an idea of the condition of the atmosphere when the hatches were battened down during the monsoons in that climate, and few of the officers and men long retained their health.

† A xebec is a three-masted vessel, peculiar to the Mediterranean, having a projecting bow and overhanging stern. The xebec is built with a narrow floor, for speed, and of great beam to enable her to carry a press of sail.

9 A.M. before the *Speedy* came up with the enemy, which she then discovered to be the *Gamo*. Her crew, therefore, had their wish gratified sooner than they expected, but they were prepared to take advantage of it. The brig was the first to open fire, to which a prompt response was made, when the *Gamo's* crew twice attempted to finish the conflict by throwing an overwhelming number of boarders on the decks of their diminutive opponent. This, however, was frustrated, until at the end of three-quarters of an hour, Lord Cochrane resolved on the desperate expedient of himself boarding at the head of his men. Suddenly running his little craft alongside his opponent, which towered above her, the gallant officer, followed by his crew, scrambled up the sides of the *Gamo*, and after a struggle lasting about ten minutes, succeeded in carrying the frigate, whose colours were lowered in submission.

Of 54 men and boys on board the *Speedy*, four were killed, and the first lieutenant, Mr. Parker (severely), boatswain, and six seamen were wounded, while the loss of the *Gamo* actually exceeded the whole number of the brig's crew. Of 319 seamen and marines on board, she had her commander, boatswain, and 13 men killed, and 41 wounded. That a boarding party of 40, all told, including Lord Cochrane, his brother, Mr. Midshipman the Hon. Archibald Cochrane, and Lieutenant Parker, should have overcome a crew sevenfold their strength, is one of the most astonishing instances of the reckless hardihood that characterises British seamen of which we have record. It is said that Lord Cochrane practised a ruse at a critical period of the struggle on the xebec's decks. Finding his handful of men overmatched, with the utmost coolness he hailed the *Speedy*, which was then manned by three individuals, including the surgeon, who was at the helm, to send him fifty more men.

The prize was carried to Port Mahon, and Lord Cochrane received promotion to the rank of captain, and his first lieutenant to that of commander.

In the following June the *Speedy*, in conjunction with the 18-gun brig, *Kangaroo*, Captain Pulteney, attacked a battery at Oropeso, and a xebec of 20 guns, and three gunboats, under the protection of which some Spanish merchantmen had taken shelter. The fire of the brigs sunk the xebec and all the gun-vessels, and silenced the battery, when their boats, under the orders of Lieutenant Foulerton, first of the *Kangaroo*, succeeded in bringing out three brigs laden with wine and bread, and the remainder were sunk to prevent their sharing the same fate. In the boat attack, a midshipman was killed, and two lieutenants and eight seamen and marines were wounded.

A feat not less daring than the cutting out of the *Hermione* or the *Cerbère*, and higher praise cannot be given, was the cutting out of the French corvette *Chevrette*, 20, from under some batteries in Camarat Bay, near Brest, by the British frigates *Doris*, *Uranie*, and *Beaulieu*. On the night of the 21st of June, the attempt was made by the boats of these frigates under the orders of Lieutenant Losack of the *Ville-de-Paris*, flagship of Admiral Cornwallis, who, early in the year, had succeeded to the command of the Channel fleet, Earl St. Vincent having been appointed First Lord of the Admiralty. The difficulty of the feat had been increased by the circumstance that, on the previous night, an attempt had been made on the corvette, but owing to the boats becoming scattered, the enterprise had to be abandoned. But nothing daunted by their failure, Captain Charles Brisbane, and the other commanders, resolved to persevere, and this, though the *Chevrette*, on discovering the boats, had run a mile and a half higher up the Bay, and taken shelter under some heavy batteries, while to prevent a successful issue to a repetition of the enterprise, her crew was increased to 339 men, by the addition of a detachment of soldiers, and a gunboat, mounting two long 36-pounders, was moored at the entrance of the Bay.

About 9.30 P.M., Lieutenant Losack again pushed off with the boats of the three frigates, and one from the *Robust*, 74, making fifteen in all, with about 280 officers and men. But on the way Lieutenant Losack proceeded with six boats to capture a look-out boat, and as he did not quickly return, and the night was far advanced, and they had still six miles to pull, the officer next in command, Lieutenant Keith Maxwell, of the *Beaulieu*, resolved to make the hazardous attempt with the remaining nine boats, containing only 180 men. Accordingly he issued his orders, detailing men to proceed aloft to cut loose the *Chevrette's* sails with their cutlasses, and others to cut the cables with which she was moored.

On arriving within sight of the corvette, at about 1 A.M., on the 22nd, they were received with a fire of grape and musketry, but disregarding this the boats gave way for the ship, the *Beaulieu's* boats, under Lieutenants Maxwell, Pasley, and Sinclair (of the marines) boarding on the starboard bow and quarter, and those of the *Uranie*, under Lieutenant Neville, one from the *Robust*, under Midshipman Warren, and one from the *Doris*, under Lieutenant Barker, on the port bow. A desperate conflict now ensued, and the result was for some time doubtful. The French actually boarded the boats in turn, but the British seamen, though they had lost their firearms, in the attempt to clamber on board, made such effective use of the cutlass, that they gained a footing on the enemy's deck, and the gallant tars who had been told off to loose the sails, fought their way aloft, and notwithstanding that the foot-ropes had been triced up, they succeeded in fulfilling their trust, and the topsails and courses were let fall and the cable cut. On perceiving the sails loosed and the ship commencing to drift out of the bay under the influence of a gentle breeze that had opportunely sprung up, the French despaired of success. Some jumped overboard and others down the hatchways, and within five minutes of the commencement of the struggle, all was over, and the British sailors were masters of the ship. As the corvette, with her sails sheeted home, slowly made her way out of the Bay, under the fire of the batteries, Lieutenant Losack joined with his boats and assumed the command.

During the brief, but desperate, struggle, the British had lost Lieutenant Sinclair,* Mr. Midshipman Warren, and nine seamen and marines killed, and Lieutenants Neville and Burke (the latter mortally) three midshipmen, one master's mate, and 49 men wounded. In addition, a marine had been drowned when the *Beaulieu's* barge was sunk by a shot, the total loss being thus 69 out of 180 engaged.

But the *Chevrette* suffered even more. She had her captain, two lieutenants, three midshipmen, one military officer, and 85 soldiers and sailors killed, and one lieutenant, four midshipmen and 57 men wounded. Altogether it will be conceded that no more brilliant feat of arms has been performed, even by the British Navy, than the cutting out of the *Chevrette*, and Lieutenant Maxwell, no less than his senior, Lieutenant Losack, who did not actually participate in the enterprise, received well earned promotion to the rank of commander.

We will only chronicle the gallant manner in which the boats of the British frigates *Fisgard*, *Diamond*, and *Boadicea*, cruising off Corunna, cut out of that port, on the night of the 20th August, a new ship pierced for 20 guns, a gunboat, and a

* "Lieutenant Sinclair, of the Marines, was killed in the act of defending Mr Crofton, midshipman of the *Doris*, who, in his efforts to get on board the corvette, was wounded in two places. Mr. John Brown, boatswain of the *Beaulieu*, after forcing his way into the *Chevrette's* quarter-gallery, found the door planked up, and so securely barricaded, that all his efforts to force it were ineffectual. Through the crevices in the planks he discovered a number of men sitting on the cabin deck, armed with pikes and pistols; and with the fire of the latter was frequently assailed while attempting to burst in. He next tried the quarter, and after an obstinate engagement, gained the taffrail. The officer who commanded the party was at this time fighting his way up a little farther forward. For an instant, while looking round to see where he should make his push, Brown stood exposed, a mark to the enemy's fire; when, waving his cutlass, he cried, "Make a lane there," and gallantly dashed among them, and fought his way forward till he reached his proper station, the forecastle, which the men, animated by his example, soon cleared of the enemy. Here Mr. Brown remained during the rest of the contest, not only repulsing the French in their frequent attempts to retake his post, but attending to the orders from the quarter-deck, and assisting in casting the ship and making sail, with as much coolness as if he had been on board the *Beaulieu*. Henry Wallis, who had been appointed to take charge of the corvette's helm, fought his way to the wheel; and although severely wounded, steadily remained at his post, steering the *Chevrette* until beyond the reach of the batteries.

merchantman, all moored under the protection of some batteries. Under the command of Lieutenant Pipon, who received promotion, the boats' crews boarded and brought out all these vessels without sustaining loss.

Not less gallant was the conduct of two boats' crews, 18 officers and men in all, of the 18-gun sloop *Lark*, which, under the orders of Lieutenant Pasley, cut out a Spanish privateer schooner, carrying three guns and 45 men, which had taken shelter within some reefs on the coast of Cuba. In this affair one seaman was killed, and an officer and 12 men were wounded, within two of the entire party engaged, while the privateer had 21 killed, including her commander, and six wounded.

Equally exemplary was the conduct of the officers and men of the *Pasley*, of 16 guns and 54 men, which engaged off the coast of Spain, and captured, by boarding, after a sharp action, a Spanish privateer carrying 10 guns and 94 men. In this affair the *Pasley* lost her gunner and two seamen killed, and her commander, Lieutenant Woodbridge, two officers and five men wounded, while the prize had no less than 21 killed, including her captain and two senior officers, and 13 wounded. It was a brilliant achievement against greatly superior force, and Lieutenant Woodbridge by his promotion only received the reward due to distinguished merit.

There is a certain mystery attaching to the success on the Spanish coast of the brig *Sylph*, Commander Dashwood. While chasing a Spanish schooner off Santander, on the 31st July, the *Sylph* sighted a 28-gun frigate, when she hove to and engaged her for an hour and twenty minutes, during which her rigging and sails were cut to pieces. The *Sylph* ceased firing, and when out of gun-shot, repaired damages. On the following morning she again descried her antagonist, and stood towards her, but the latter declined to renew the action and made sail for the land. The *Sylph*, under orders from Admiral Cornwallis, returned to Plymouth to refit, and again resumed her station on the Spanish coast. On the 28th September Captain Dashwood again sighted a French frigate, and notwithstanding the disparity of force, made sail, and gaining the weather-gage, brought her to action at pistol-shot range. At the end of two hours the frigate wore and stood away under all sail, the *Sylph* being unable to chase, owing to the damaged condition of her rigging. In the former action the loss was only one killed, and a midshipman and 8 seamen wounded, and in the second encounter only the same young officer was wounded. For his gallantry in engaging a ship of such superior force—which he claimed to be the French frigate

Artemise, of 44 guns and 350 men, though the point has been disputed—Commander Dashwood received promotion to the rank of captain.

During the year 1801, a combined military and naval force took possession, without resistance, of the West India Islands possessed by Denmark and Sweden; and as a punishment for the action of Portugal in excluding British shipping from her ports, the town and forts of Funchal, in the Madeiras, were occupied by a British squadron and military force. In the East Indies, also, the island of Ternate, belonging to Holland, was surrendered, after a prolonged resistance of some weeks, to a combined force, under Colonel Barr and Commodore Hayes of the Indian Navy.

But the treaty of peace, signed at Amiens,* between France and England, put an end to the state of hostilities that had existed uninterruptedly for nine years, but the peace thus patched up was a hollow one, and scarcely were the bonfires extinguished by which its conclusion was celebrated, than the torch of war was lit again, and its lurid light burnt over Europe and half the world, until a more stable peace was assured by the exhaustion of France and the imprisonment in St. Helena of the firebrand who had sacrificed countless millions of treasure and hundreds of thousands of lives to his insensate ambition.

* The preliminaries of peace were signed in London on the 1st October, and on the 12th of the same month hostilities were suspended between France and England. By the provisions of the treaty of Amiens, we restored to France Pondicherry, Chandernagore, and her other settlements in India, the islands we had conquered in the West Indies, and Foul Point in Madagascar. We also agreed to cede Malta and the adjacent islands to the Order of St. John of Jerusalem, to whom they belonged before the war, and evacuated Porto Ferrajo, in Elba, the French, on their part, quitting Roman and Neapolitan territory. To Holland we restored the Cape of Good Hope and all our conquests in the West Indies, and Dutch Guiana, Malacca, and the islands of Banda, Amboyna and Ternate, but we retained Trincomalee and her other settlements in Ceylon. We also retained the Spanish island of Trinidad, but restored to Sweden and Denmark their possessions in the West Indies. From this brief abstract it will appear that England sacrificed nearly every foreign colonial possession won by her arms in both hemispheres. Fortunately, Malta, Pondicherry, and some other conquests were not surrendered before war was again declared between this country and France. The Navy list of 1802 consisted of 180 ships-of-the-line, and 665 other vessels, the total thus being 845. The number of line-of-battle ships added to the Navy during the war from the Navies of foreign powers, was:—French 27, Dutch 17, Spaniards 5, and Danish 1; total, 50.

CHAPTER XII.

Rupture with France—Attacks on the French Flotilla and Towns in the Channel—Lord Nelson in the Mediterranean—Boat and Frigate actions—Loss of the *Minerve*—Services of the *Racoon*—Loss and Recapture of the *Lord Nelson*—Boats of the *Blanche* at St. Domingo—Recapture of the French and Dutch colonies in the West Indies—Events in the East Indies—Commodore Dance and Admiral Linois—The *Marengo* and consorts with the *Centurion*—French Preparations for the Invasion of England—Actions with the Invasion Flotilla—Lord Nelson's pursuit of the French Fleet, under Admiral Villeneuve, to the West Indies—Defence of the Diamond Rock—Return of Nelson to England—Cutting out of the *Curieux*—Exploits in the West Indies—Cutting out of the *Atalante*—The *Wilhelmina* and *Psyche*—Loss of the *Lily* and Repulse of the boats of the *Galatea*—Repulse at Curaçoa and Capture of Surinam.

THE Peace of Amiens was in reality little more than a suspension of hostilities, and both France and England employed the brief breathing space before war again broke out, in marshalling and adding to their forces by land and sea. War was formally declared by England on the 16th May, 1803, and an order was issued for detaining the ships of Holland, then known as the Batavian Republic, which was no more than an appanage to the country ruled by Buonaparte, who, in the following year, exchanged his title of First Consul for that of Emperor.

On the day succeeding the declaration of war, Admiral the Hon. William Cornwallis, the gallant and skilful officer still commanding the Channel fleet, sailed with a squadron of ten ships-of-the-line and frigates for a cruise off Ushant to watch the French fleet in Brest. The blockade was maintained until Christmas day, when Admiral Cornwallis, who carried his flag in the *Ville-de-Paris*, 112, named after the ship captured by Sir George Rodney, in his memorable action of the 12th April, 1782, was compelled by stress of weather to retire to the Channel ports.

Meantime Buonaparte continued fitting out in all the ports in the Channel a flotilla of gunboats for the invasion of England, which were watched by British cruisers, and as occasion offered, were attacked by them. On the 24th June the boats of the 18-gun brigs *Cruiser* and *Jalouse* boarded and captured a French brig and schooner, which they had chased ashore near Cape Blanc Nez; and on the 1st August, the boats of the *Hydra*, 32, brought off, under a heavy musketry fire from the shore, a lugger near Havre. The towns of Dieppe, Granville, and Calais, were bombarded in September, but not with any great effect or loss on either side.

H.M.S. VICTORIA.
1ST CLASS BATTLE-SHIP.

Lord Nelson was appointed to the command in the Mediterranean, and sailed on the 20th May from Spithead, with his flag in the world-renowned *Victory*, in company with the 32-gun frigate *Amphion*, Captain Thomas Masterman Hardy, who is so closely associated with the hero in his last great victory and death. In accordance with his orders, he left the *Victory* with Admiral Cornwallis off Ushant, and shifting his flag into the *Amphion*, sailed for the Mediterranean. After visiting Malta and Naples, Nelson joined the fleet, consisting of eight sail-of-the-line and two frigates, off Toulon, and assumed command, superseding Sir Richard Bickerton. Admiral Cornwallis dispensed with the services of the *Victory*, which continued her course to the Mediterranean, and on the way captured the French 32-gun frigate *Embuscade* (formerly the British frigate *Ambuscade*). The *Victory* fell in with the Mediterranean fleet on the 30th July, when Lord Nelson rehoisted his flag on board her, taking with him Captains Murray and Hardy, the latter being succeeded in the command of the *Amphion* by Captain Sutton, late of the *Victory*. After cruising off the French and Spanish coasts, Lord Nelson anchored on the 31st October in Agincourt Sound, among the Maddelena islands, on the north coast of Sardinia, a noble harbour, recently discovered and surveyed by Captain Ryves, of the *Agincourt*, from which it received its name. Having obtained a supply of beef and water, Nelson sailed on the 9th November for Toulon, but the severity of the weather and the inefficient* state of his squadron induced him to return to Agincourt Sound, after detaching his frigates to watch the port of Toulon, in which eight French sail-of-the-line lay ready for sea.

Some frigate actions, worthy of being chronicled, took place during the year 1803. Soon after the declaration of war, the 36-gun frigate *Doris* captured the *Affronteur*, of 14 guns and 92 men, which made a gallant resistance to a ship of superior force; the *Franchise*, 36, surrendered to three seventy-fours of the Channel fleet, and was added to the Navy under the same name; the *Endymion* captured the *Bacchante*, of 18 guns and 200 men, which was also purchased into the service; and the French 16-gun corvette *Mignonne*, was captured off St. Domingo by the *Goliath*, 74. Finally, off the same island, the 40-gun frigate *Creole*, having on board 530 soldiers in addition to her crew, hauled down her colours to the *Vanguard*, 74, after receiving a few shots.

* Lord Nelson says, in a letter to the Admiralty, "The *Superb* is in a very weak state, but Keats is so superior to any difficulties, that I hear but little from her. The *Kent* is gone to Malta, fit only for a summer passage. Every bit of twice-laid stuff belonging to the *Canopus* is condemned, and all the running rigging of the fleet, except the *Victory*. We have fitted the *Excellent* with new main and mizen rigging; it was shameful for the dockyard (Portsmouth) to send a ship to sea with such rigging."

On the other hand we sustained a loss by the capture of the *Minerve* (a French prize) commanded by Captain J. Brenton, brother of the naval historian, which, on the 2nd July, grounded at the entrance of Cherbourg Harbour, and surrendered after sustaining the fire of the enemy's batteries and gunboats, and losing 11 men killed and 16 wounded. The commander of the *Minerve* remained in captivity in France for two-and-a-half years, and the greater part of her crew were not released until the peace in 1814. Captain Brenton was tried by court martial at Portsmouth for the loss of his ship, but was acquitted, and he and his officers and ship's company, many of whom had died while in confinement in France, received the encomiums of the court. The capture of this fine ship which, though classed as a 38-gun frigate, mounted 48 guns, was a subject of congratulation in France, and was announced in the theatre at Brussels by Buonaparte, who falsely informed the audience, that she had surrendered to two *Chaloupes Canonnières* (gun-vessels) and hence she received the name of *Canonnière*.

A noteworthy exploit was that by two boats of the *Loire*, 38-gun frigate, which, under the orders of Lieutenant Temple and Midshipman Bridges, cut out from under some batteries in the Isle of Bas, the 10-gun brig *Venteux*, a gallant exploit which gained promotion for both the officers.

The French seventy-fours, *Duquesne* and *Duguay-Trouin*, and 40-gun frigate *Guerrière*, attempted to return from Cape François, in St. Domingo, to Europe, but were chased by some British ships, and the *Duquesne*, after a running fight of some hours' duration, surrendered to the *Vanguard*, 74, Captain Walker, and 32-gun frigate *Tartar*, Captain Perkins. The other ships made good their escape, after encountering, off Cape Ferrol, and receiving the fire of the *Boadicea*, 38, Captain John Maitland, and a few days later, of the *Culloden*, 74, from which they, with difficulty, managed to get away into Corunna.

The seas, indeed, so swarmed with British cruisers that it was a difficult matter for the French to carry a prize, when they made one, into port. This was shown in the case of the *Lord Nelson*, belonging to the East India Company. The Indiaman, which mounted 26 guns and carried a crew of 102 men, besides passengers, on the 14th August, encountered the French ship-rigged privateer *Bellone*, of 34 guns and 260 men, and an action of a determined character ensued, but at the end of an hour and a half, the privateer boarded and carried the Indiaman, which sustained a loss of five killed and 31 wounded. While making her way up to Corunna, the *Lord Nelson*, which had a prize crew of an officer and 41 men, was attacked by a 14-gun privateer cutter, but beat her off. On the 25th August, however, the prize was sighted and chased by the 18-gun brig *Seagull*, Commander Burke, which brought her to action at 7 o'clock in the evening. A running engagement continued all night, and in the morning, the brig, having suffered much aloft, hauled off to repair damages. This completed, the *Seagull* was about to renew the action, when a British squadron of four sail-of-the-line, under Sir Edward Pellew, hove in sight, and the *Colossus* overhauled and recaptured the *Lord Nelson*.

The 18-gun brig *Racoon*, Commander Bissell, engaged on the 11th July, off the coast of St. Domingo, and captured, after a close action, the *Lodi*, of 10 guns and 61 men, which had fifteen casualties, and was disabled aloft by the accurate fire of the British brig. A few weeks later, the enterprising captain of the *Racoon* sighted off the island of Cuba, a vessel which proved to be the French 18-gun brig *Mutine*, full of soldiers she was transporting. The latter, after firing a broadside, attempted to cross the hawse of the *Racoon*, which, porting her helm, gave her a return broadside, which brought down some of her spars. The *Mutine* then ran on shore, a fate the British brig narrowly escaped, and landed the troops, but the *Racoon* continued to fire on her and shot away her mainmast. When morning dawned, the French brig was discovered on her beam ends and half full of water, with both her masts over the side. In the following October Commander Bissell performed further excellent service. While cruising off Cuba, he discovered in-shore a French brig, schooner and cutter, all full of men, and engaged them in succession. The first to strike, upon receiving the *Racoon's* fire, was the brig, *Petite Fille*, having on board 180 troops, including about 50 officers. The schooner and cutter now bore down and attempted to board the brig, when the detachment of troops they were carrying would give them the superiority. With seamanlike smartness, Commander Bissell so manœuvred that he was enabled to pour alternate broadsides into his two assailants at pistol-shot range, and after thus carrying on a running fight for over an hour, the cutter surrendered. She proved to be the *Amélie*, of four guns, having upwards of 70 troops on board. The *Racoon* now gave chase to the *Jeune Adéle*, schooner, of six guns and carrying over 80 soldiers, which also surrendered. Meantime, the crew of the brig overpowered the prize crew, and ran her on shore, but Commander Bissell rescued his men.

Among acts of gallantry should be mentioned the chase and capture, by the two small boats of the British cutter *Sheerness*, of eight guns and 30 men, of two French chasse-marées off Brest Harbour, when Lieutenant Rowed in command, with four men, beat off a French boat, with an officer and nine men, who attempted to recapture one of the chasse-marées. Equally praiseworthy was the conduct of Lieutenant Scott and the 26 men who formed the crew of the cutter *Princess Augusta*. Two schooners, which carried respectively 12 guns and 70 men, and eight guns and 50 men, attacked the little cutter on both sides, but the latter repulsed every attempt to board, and ultimately beat them off, though with the loss of her brave young commander and two men killed and two wounded.

A boat of the 16-gun brig *Atalante*, with an officer and six men, boarded and cut out a brig on the French coast, killing six of her crew and driving the remainder below; and Lieutenant Henderson and 17 men in the cutter of the brig *Osprey*, 18, boarded and captured, under a heavy fire, a privateer schooner, of four guns and 43 men, the lieutenant and four seamen being wounded.

A very gallant exploit was performed by Lieutenant Nicholls, of the Marines, at the head of 13 men in a small boat of the 36-gun frigate *Blanche*. An attempt at daybreak, to cut out from off the coast of St. Domingo, the French cutter *Albion*, of eight small guns and swivels, and 43 men, had failed, but Lieutenant Nicholls made good his offer to carry the cutter before daybreak. The boat received two volleys of musketry as she approached, but the gallant officer sprang on board at the head of his men. The French captain fired his pistol at the British officer, who was severely wounded, but he retaliated on his assailant who fell dead. Soon the enemy were overpowered and driven below, and the cable being cut, sail was made on the cutter, on which the battery opened fire. At this moment the barge, with 22 men under Lieutenant Hon. W. Lake, came alongside, when that officer took command, and the prize, under the influence of a fair breeze, and towed by the two boats, soon reached the frigate in the offing. In this gallantly conducted affair, the credit of which was wholly due to Lieutenant Nicholls, who received pistol balls in the side and thigh and through the arm, the British loss was two killed and four wounded.

On the previous day the launch of the *Blanche*, carrying a 12-pounder carronade, with a crew of 28 men, under Mr. John Smith, master's mate, was equally successful in an attack on a fine French schooner, having one pivot-gun and 30 men. The schooner was only carried after a severe conflict, in which she had six casualties, the launch losing one seaman killed and two wounded. Still a third act of gallantry was performed by a cutter of the *Blanche's*, under the command of Midshipman

A'Court. This young officer had been sent ashore with eight men to bring off some sand, but descrying a schooner becalmed, he pulled up astern, and notwithstanding a musketry fire which severely wounded two of his party, boarded the vessel, which he and his brave fellows carried, though the schooner had on board a detachment of over 30 soldiers. The French colonel in command, a veteran who had served under Buonaparte in Italy, pleaded as an excuse of his pusillanimity in surrendering to an officer and six men, that he and his soldiers were suffering from sea sickness.

Captain Graves, of the *Blenheim*, 74, while lying off Martinique, having received intelligence of a French schooner-rigged privateer, of 18 guns and 66 men, which had committed great depredations in neighbouring waters, determined to make an attempt to cut her out from under the protection of a strong battery, mounting six 24-pounders. With this object he despatched 64 seamen, under the command of Commander Ferris, of the *Drake*, 14-gun brig, to attack the schooner, and 60 marines, under Lieutenant Beatty, to storm the battery. The combined operation was judiciously carried out, both parties arriving simultaneously at their respective destinations. The battery was surprised and the schooner was boarded and captured with the loss of only one man killed and five wounded.

On the other hand the Navy experienced a loss in the stranding, near Cape Barfleur, on the night of the 10th December, of the *Shannon*, 36, a fine new frigate, though to prevent her falling into the hands of the enemy, Commander Edward Brenton, of the 16-gun sloop-of-war *Merlin*, which was in company, sent his boats and burnt the ship under a heavy fire from some batteries. Captain Gower, commanding the *Shannon*, and his officers and crew, were made prisoners, and the former languished in captivity for three years, before they were released.

During 1803 and the three following years, the Navy was engaged, in conjunction with the Army, in reconquering some of the colonial possessions of the Powers with which we were again at war, that had been surrendered by the Treaty of Amiens. Commodore Samuel Hood co-operated with his squadron in the capture of the islands of St. Lucia and Tobago, and the Dutch possessions of Demerara, Essequibo, and Berbice. Commodore Loring, from Jamaica, also blockaded the French ports of Cape François and St. Nicholas Mole, in the Island of St. Domingo, which were invested by the negro insurgents, and by the end of November, General Rochambeau, the French commander at the former port, despairing of success, signed a capitulation, by which the French ships were to surrender.

The 40-gun frigate *Surveillante* came out and was taken possession of, but the *Clorinde*, of the same force, grounded on some rocks under the Haytian Fort St. Joseph, and her crew, with 700 soldiers, besides women and children, were exposed to imminent peril from the sea, or the tender mercies of the cruel negroes. In this dilemma Acting-Lieutenant Nisbet Willoughby boarded the frigate, and receiving her submission from the general commanding the French troops, obtained the consent of the Haytian General Dessalines, to consider the prisoners as under the protection of the British flag. Moreover, with his barge and some other boats, he succeeded in heaving off the *Clorinde*, and thus, to the uncommon exertion and professional abilities of this young officer, as Admiral Duckworth said, was due the preservation of more than 900 lives, and the acquisition of a fine frigate, which, with her sister ship, the *Surveillante*, was long borne on the Navy list. The French garrison at St. Nicholas Mole, taking advantage of the absence of the British squadron, embarked in some small vessels and succeeded in landing in Cuba in safety. The French during this expedition to St. Domingo, which was now freed from their presence, acknowledge to a loss of 20 generals and upwards of 40,000 men, an estimate which doubtless includes colonial troops.

On the 6th March Admiral Linois had sailed from Brest for the East Indies—with a squadron consisting of the *Marengo*, 80, *Belle Poule*, 40, and 36-gun frigates *Atalante* and *Sémillante*, and two transports, having on board General Decaen and 1,350 troops—in order to take possession of Pondicherry in terms of the Treaty of Amiens, but on the arrival of the *Belle Poule* on the 16th June, the commandant refused to restore the settlement. On the 5th July, Vice-Admiral Rainier arrived from Bombay at Cuddalore roads, about twenty miles to the southward of Pondicherry, with the *Centurion*, 50, Captain Rainier (flagship), *Tremendous*, 74, Captain Osborn, 64 gun-ships *Trident*, Captain Surridge, and *Lancaster*, Captain Fothergill, *Sheerness*, 44, the frigates, *Concorde*, *Dédaigneuse* and *Fox*, and sloop-of-war *Victor*.

A few days later Admiral Linois joined the *Belle Poule* at Pondicherry, but finding himself outnumbered, and being aware that hostilities were impending, he hurriedly slipped his cables, and leaving behind his anchors and even his long boat, set sail for Mauritius, where he arrived on the 16th August. A few days later intelligence was received at Bombay of the declaration of war, and on the 13th September, the Government at Calcutta was apprised of the actual outbreak of hostilities. Admiral Linois, having detached the *Atalante* to Muscat, quitted

Mauritius, on the 8th October, with the *Marengo, Belle Poule, Sémillante,* and 20-gun corvette *Berceau,* having troops on board, and taking some prizes on the way, visited the British settlement of Bencoolen, on the Island of Sumatra, where they committed more depredations, and on the 10th December, anchored at Batavia, capital of the Dutch possessions in Java.

Admiral Linois, having received information, proceeded in search of the East India Company's China fleet, and on the 14th February, in the following year, sighted off Pulo Auro a fleet of thirty-nine sail, including sixteen ships belonging to the East India Company, on their passage from Canton to England, with rich cargoes. But Commodore Dance, who carried his broad pennant in the *Earl Camden*, was not the man to tamely surrender his valuable charges, and on hearing from the *Ganges*, armed brig, which he sent to reconnoitre, that the strangers were French ships-of-war, he prepared for action, continuing his course under easy sail. Night came on, the British fleet lying to, with the crews at their quarters, and on the morning of the 15th, Admiral Linois, who had acted with caution, under the impression, occasioned by the bold front shown by Commodore Dance, that three of the ships were vessels-of-war, now edged away to attack the rear with his squadron, which at this time consisted of the *Marengo, Belle Poule, Sémillante, Berceau* and the Batavian 16-gun brig *Aventurier*.

The British commander, thereupon, signalled his ships to tack in succession, bear down in line, and engage on arriving abreast of the enemy, which was gallantly done, in close order, by the *Royal George, Ganges, Earl Camden, Warley, Alfred,* and other Indiamen. The French admiral opened fire at 1.15 P.M., which was replied to by the ships as they came up, and after the cannonade had lasted 43 minutes, the *Marengo* and her consorts ceased firing, and stood away under all sail to the eastward, leaving the Indiamen masters of the field.* Commodore Dance now hoisted the signal for a general chase, which was discontinued at 4 o'clock. Enough had been done for honour by these sixteen armed merchantmen, which, though they carried

* Admiral Linois acknowledges a defeat in the following passage of his despatch :—"The headmost enemy's ship, having sustained some damage, bore away, but, supported by those astern, again brought her broadside to bear, and, as well as the others, kept up a very spirited fire. The ships which had tacked rejoined those which were engaging us, and three of the fresh engaged ships manœuvred to double our rear, while the remainder of the fleet, crowding sail and bearing up, evinced an intention of surrounding us. By this manœuvre the enemy would have rendered my situation dangerous. The superiority of his force was ascertained, and I had no longer to deliberate upon the part I should take to avoid the consequences of an unequal engagement; profiting by the smoke, I hauled up, and steering east-north-east, I increased my distance from the enemy, who continued the pursuit of the squadron for three hours, discharging at it several ineffective broadsides."

from 30 to 36 guns each, with crews of 140 men, including natives, could scarcely be considered a match for a powerful line-of-battle ship, two large frigates, and a brig-of-war. Commodore Dance was awarded the honour of knighthood, and he and his officers and men received pecuniary rewards, and votes of thanks from the East India Company, the Patriotic Fund,* and other public bodies.

Admiral Linois, unlike many officers of the French Navy, was undoubtedly a man deficient in enterprise, as we find by his conduct in the following September. The *Centurion*, 50, temporarily under the command of Lieutenant Phillips, was lying in Vizagapatam Roads, waiting to escort two Indiamen to Madras, when Admiral Linois made his appearance in the *Marengo*, accompanied by the *Atalante* and *Sémillante*, all from Mauritius, the coast of Ceylon, and Bay of Bengal, where they had made several prizes. Lieutenant Phillips cleared for action, and cut his cables, signalling to the two Indiamen to quit their anchorage, but the *Princess Charlotte* remained at her station in shore of the *Centurion*, and the *Bombay*, in obeying orders, ran on shore, where she became a total wreck. When the *Atalante* was within two hundred yards of the *Centurion*, which was now crowding all plain sail, the latter poured a broadside into her, and a few minutes later, the *Marengo* and *Sémillante* opened fire, which was returned by the British ship, assisted by a shore battery of three guns. After the unequal action had lasted about three quarters of an hour, the enemy hauled their wind, and stood out of the anchorage.

The *Centurion*, of which Captain Lind now assumed the command, stood along the shore, but soon brought up about a mile and a half from the town, being unable to get out to sea, owing to her damaged condition aloft. The *Marengo* now stood in again, and anchoring about a mile distant, renewed the action, supported by the *Atalante*, while their consort took possession of the Indiaman *Princess Charlotte*. The *Centurion* had suffered severely in her hull, spars, and rigging by the enemy's fire, but about 1.15, nearly two hours after renewing the engagement, the *Marengo* weighed, and, accompanied by the two frigates, stood out to sea, leaving to the *Centurion* the

* The Patriotic Fund was originated at a meeting of the subscribers to Lloyd's Coffee House, held on the 20th July, 1803, Mr. Brook Watson in the chair. The object is explained in the third resolution:—"That to animate the efforts of our defenders by sea and land, it is expedient to raise by the patriotism of the community at large, a suitable fund for their comfort and relief, for the purpose of assuaging the anguish of their wounds, or palliating in some degree the more weighty misfortune of the loss of limbs, of alleviating the distresses of the widow and orphan; of soothing the brow of sorrow for the fall of dearest relatives, the props of unhappy indigence or helpless age; and of granting pecuniary rewards, or honourable badges of distinction, for successful exertions of valour or merit."

honours of the day. The casualties on either side were trifling. Admiral Linois, in his official account, pleaded as excuse for his pusillanimity, shortness of water, and the assistance afforded to the *Centurion* by a battery on shore, and spoke of her "extraordinary" armament, which had no existence.

On the outbreak of war, Buonaparte devoted his energies to the chief object of his ambition, the subjection of England. With this object the French Ministry of Marine was directed to assemble in seven Channel ports, a flotilla of 1,339 armed vessels and 954 others, under the command of Admiral Bruix, for the transport of a vast army, while every department in France voted sums for the construction of a ship-of-the-line, and the dockyards of Brest, Toulon, Lorient, and Rochefort resounded with preparations for the humiliation of "perfidious Albion." The ships thus collected were intended to cover the disembarkation of the army of invasion. The Brest fleet of twenty-three sail, under Admiral Ganteaume, having on board between 30,000 and 40,000 troops, was to combine with seven Dutch sail-of-the-line from the Texel, and, reinforced by Admiral Villeneuve's fleet of twenty sail from Lorient, the grand *coup* was to be put in execution. But the safety and honour of this country were safe in the keeping of officers like Lord Keith, commanding in the Downs, Admiral Cornwallis, who, in January, resumed his old station off Ushant, Commodore Sir Sidney Smith, who watched the ports of Flushing and Ostend, and other officers who were stationed off Dunkirk, Calais, Havre, Boulogne, and the remaining Channel ports, where the flotilla of invasion was assembled.

Many exploits were achieved by the enterprising British officers engaged in watching the ports, among the most daring of whom was Commander John Wright, Sir Sidney Smith's companion in his imprisonment in Paris, and one of his officers in the *Tigre*, on the Syrian and Egyptian coasts. Captain Wright commanded the 18-gun brig *Vincejo*, with a crew of 75, all told, of whom 24 were boys, which, being becalmed off the Morbihan River, was attacked by a flotilla of seventeen armed vessels, having a total of 35 guns and over 700 men. The brig maintained the unequal conflict for over two hours, when, her hull and rigging being greatly damaged, three of her guns disabled, and 14 of the crew killed and wounded, Commander Wright, who had received a wound in the groin, struck her colours. The gallant officer subsequently died in the Temple prison, in Paris, under circumstances that were never cleared up, though Buonaparte denied having had any hand in this sad termination to a promising career.

In May two brigs of Sir Sidney Smith's squadron, the *Cruiser*, 18, Commander Hancock, and *Rattler*, 16, Commander Mason, performed excellent service in attacking a flotilla of 68 French and Dutch vessels, mounting upwards of 100 guns, and carrying over 4,000 troops, with a loss to the enemy of 18 killed and 60 wounded. The two brigs were assisted late in the action by the frigates *Antelope*, *Penelope*, and *Aimable*, and the squadron experienced a loss of 13 killed and 32 wounded.

In July Havre was bombarded by a squadron under Captain Robert Oliver, of the *Melpomene*, 38, and the flotilla in Boulogne Roads was attacked by the squadron under the command of Rear-Admiral Louis, Commodore Owen, of the *Immortalité*, doing excellent service. Many gun-vessels were driven ashore by a severe gale, and foundered with over 400 sailors and soldiers, under the eyes of Napoleon, who, having now assumed the Imperial dignity, came down to the port as the headquarters of the invasion flotilla, to inspect the preparations.

In August there were lying in the roads of Boulogne, off which Commodore Owen cruised with a division of five or six ships, a hundred and forty-six gun-vessels, sixty-two of which were brigs, the remainder being luggers, and, on the 16th, upwards of 80,000 troops were assembled at the port to do honour to the great Dictator of France, who distributed decorations and animated his Army and Navy by his presence and encouraging speeches. In order to gratify the Imperial visitor, Admiral Bruix, the Naval Commander-in-Chief, organized an attack on the British brig *Bruiser*, by a division of gunboats, which brought the *Immortalité* on the scene. Two days later the Emperor went afloat in his barge, accompanied by Marshals Soult and Mortier, and Admiral Bruix, when sixty gunboats and upwards of thirty luggers stood out from the shore, and were attacked by the British sloop *Harpy*, gun-brig *Adder*, and armed cutter *Constitution*, which also engaged the batteries when the French flotilla retired to their protection. Other vessels participated in the firing, but towards evening the British squadron retired out of range, with the exception of the cutter, which was sunk by a shot. Before leaving for Paris the Emperor had doubtless become convinced of the impracticability of his scheme for the invasion of England, with the ubiquitous and active British Navy watching every port and the entire French coast line of the Channel, but the preparations were too elaborate, and the promises of success too pronounced for the attempt to be abandoned.

With the spring of 1805, however, a concentration of the French and Dutch divisions of the flotilla stationed at Ostend, Dunkirk, and Calais, was made at the port of Ambleteuse, and Marshal Davoust's corps, proceeded from Ostend to Calais to join the Grand Army of Invasion. Sir Sidney Smith was as indefatigable as ever, and many encounters took place while the gun-vessels and transports, laden with stores, were proceeding from one port to another. In these the frigates *Leda, Chiffonne, Renommée, Ariadne, Hebe,* and *Immortalité,* sloops *Harpy, Railleur, Falcon, Arab, Calypso,* and *Champion,* and the squadron of gun-brigs did good service, though occasionally they suffered heavy loss owing to their being becalmed off the coast, when the enemy would sally out and attempt their capture, while they were exposed in action to the fire of the shore batteries. The squadron of observation in the Downs assisted in these operations, but the chief credit was due to the *Immortalité,* whose captain, the writer of the French work, *Précis des Evénements,* describes as having displayed "an audacity and perseverance that elicited admiration."

By the end of July, 1805, there were assembled at Boulogne alone, one of the seven ports of departure, 578 armed vessels and 526 transports, while the grand total in the ports was 2,293 sail, which were intended to convey to England 163,000 men, including 16,000 sailors, and 9,000 horses. The flotilla was divided into six divisions, the first stationed at Etaples, which was to carry Marshal Ney's corps; the 2nd and 3rd at Boulogne, to embark Marshal Soult's command; the 4th, stationed at Vimereux, to carry Marshal Lannes' corps; the 5th, consisting of the mixed Franco-Dutch flotilla, assembled at Ambleteuse, to embark Marshal Davoust's corps; and the 6th, or reserve, division, was concentrated at Calais, with some divisions of dragoons and one of Italian infantry.

Napoleon again visited Boulogne on the 3rd August, to witness a trial embarkation, and expressed himself as greatly surprised and pleased at the celerity and success of the manœuvre. But there lay before him in the Channel the tireless Navy of England, watching every movement, and until they could be beguiled away, he knew well all these preparations never could be put to the issue. To gain temporary command of the Channel, for however short a time, was absolutely essential to carry out his plans, and Napoleon ordered a naval combination of his and the Spanish fleets, under Villeneuve, with a view of concentrating an overwhelming armament in the Channel.

On the 11th August, soon after Villeneuve's action with Sir Robert Calder, the Emperor learned that the combined fleet had put into Ferrol, and on the 31st he heard that they had sailed. His hopes were raised, only, however, to be dashed to the ground a few days later, by the receipt of intelligence that Villeneuve, instead of steering for the Channel, with the twenty-nine sail under his command, was on his way for Cadiz. Marshal Berthier had written, on the 22nd August, by direction of the Emperor, to Marmont, Commander-in-Chief of the Army in Holland, that in the event of the non-arrival of the fleet, "owing to contrary winds, or the lack of enterprise on the part of our Admirals," the expedition to England would be delayed for another year, and on the 4th September, the Emperor left Boulogne for Paris, and the troops, encamped at Ostend, Ambleteuse and Boulogne, making forced marches to the Rhine, effected a junction with others from Hanover and France, at Munich, and early in 1806, the crushing victory of Austerlitz, attested the brilliant genius of this extraordinary man, who, had he possessed an admiral like Nelson, supreme at sea as he was on land, might have enslaved the island which formed the barrier to the realization of his far-reaching plans.

The gunboats at all the ports, except Boulogne, were now dismantled and laid up, but the annihilation of the French and Spanish fleets at Trafalgar, less than two months after his departure from Boulogne, put an end to the possibility of a resumption of his plans for the invasion of England. Thus to her Navy was due the safety of the country from the shame and ruin of foreign conquest, and the vast army of volunteers and the long line of "towers along her steep" were never called on to prove their efficacy to beat back the invaders.

During the year 1804, Lord Nelson continued to watch the Toulon fleet from his headquarters at the anchorage in Agincourt Sound, whence he would proceed on a cruise along the shores of the Italian, French, and Barbary coasts. Admiral La Touche-Tréville lay in the roads of Toulon with eight sail-of-the-line, besides frigates, but though he came out on the 14th June with his whole force, on Lord Nelson standing towards him with only five ships, he returned to port. Nelson wrote on the 18th June, "We chased him into Toulon the morning of the 15th, and I am confident he meant nothing beyond a gasconade." But the French admiral reported that Nelson had fled before him with ten sail-of-the-line, and Napoleon thereupon promoted him to a higher grade of the Legion of Honour, and conferred on him a lucrative appointment.

Admiral La Touche-Tréville died at Toulon on the 18th August, without having carried into effect the Emperor's orders to join the invasion flotilla off Boulogne, and was succeeded in the command by Admiral Villeneuve, who was ordered to detach some ships to retake Goree and ravage the British settlements on the West African coast, and himself to proceed with the main body, now reinforced to ten sail-of-the-line, besides frigates, to the West Indies with troops. Having first captured Dominica and St. Lucia, and effected a junction with Admiral Missiessy's squadron of five sail, Villeneuve was to possess himself of Surinam and the other Dutch colonies in this quarter, and returning to Europe, was to raise the blockade of Ferrol, taking with him the five sail there, appear off Rochefort, and join Admiral Ganteaume's Brest fleet of thirty sail-of-the-line in the descent on England. But all these grand plans hatched in the brain of Napoleon, ended, as we have said, in failure, though his fleet was augmented by the addition of 20 Spanish ships-of-the-line, ready for sea at Cadiz, Ferrol, and Carthagena, on the declaration of war by that Power, through the inferiority of the French and Spanish admirals, officers, and ships' companies to those of the British Navy.

Nelson quitted his station off Toulon for the Maddelena Islands, on the 3rd January, 1805, leaving the 38-gun frigates, *Active* and *Seahorse*, to watch the port, and on the 17th, Villeneuve put to sea with eleven sail-of-the-line, seven frigates and two brigs, having on board 3,500 troops, under General Lauriston. The French fleet was sighted and followed by the British frigates until 2 A.M. on the 19th, when they bore up for Agincourt Sound, and about 2 P.M. of the same day the frigates signalled to Lord Nelson the departure of the enemy from Toulon. The same afternoon his lordship weighed with eleven line-of-battle-ships and the frigates, *Seahorse* and *Active*, the only ones he possessed, notwithstanding repeated protests to the Admiralty. The British Commander-in-Chief sent the latter to gain information of the destination of the enemy's fleet, but without success, and being of opinion that they had gone to Egypt, steered for Alexandria. Here, however, he could learn nothing, and stood back towards Malta, and when near the island, received information from Naples that Villeneuve had encountered bad weather when crossing the gulf of Lyons, and put back to Toulon.

The British fleet anchored off Cagliari on the 27th February, but only for a few days, though owing to the strong headwinds it could make little way, and repeatedly put back, but at length, on the 15th March, the indomitable admiral gained his old station off Cape San Sebastian, to westward of Toulon. Here he cruised about until the end of the month, when he anchored in the gulf of Palma to revictual. Taking advantage of the absence of the British fleet, Villeneuve sailed once more, on the

29th March, and on the 6th April, anchored at Carthagena, whence he passed the Straits of Gibraltar, and on the 8th April, cast anchor in Cadiz Bay, where he was joined by one French and five Spanish ships-of-the-line and one frigate, having 1,600 troops on board. On the following day the combined fleet of seventeen sail-of-the-line and seven frigates sailed for Martinique. Meanwhile, Nelson had received intelligence from the frigate *Phœbe*, of the departure of Villeneuve, and took up a station about midway between the coasts of Africa and Sardinia, but failing to sight him, bore up for Palermo, and then stood to the westward, but owing to adverse winds* only succeeded, on the 4th May, in fetching Mazari Bay, on the African shore, near the Straits of Gibraltar.

It was the 13th May before Villeneuve anchored in Fort Royal Harbour, in the island of Martinique, whither he was pursued by Lord Nelson, acting on some information he received at Gibraltar from Rear-Admiral Campbell, of the Portuguese Navy, who had formerly served under his command. By extraordinary exertions his lordship filled up with water and provisions for five months in a single night, and at 9 in the morning of the 9th May, sailed out of Lago Bay, and detaching the *Royal Sovereign*, off Cape St. Vincent, to assist the *Queen*, 98, Rear-Admiral Knight, and *Dragon*, 74, Captain Griffiths, in convoying through the Straits the fleet of transports having on board 5,000 troops, under General Craig, he crowded all sail for the West Indies with his remaining ships-of-the-line and three frigates,† in chase of a hostile fleet which he knew outnumbered him by eight sail-of-the-line and six frigates. But his lordship, who has been accused of rashness, expected to be joined by six ships-of-the-line on reaching Barbados, whither he sent ahead one of his frigates to direct Admiral Cochrane to prepare to meet him.

It was not until the 3rd June that the British Commander-in-Chief gained certain

---

* Lord Nelson felt keen disappointment at not meeting the enemy's fleet, as is shown by his letters at this time. He writes to Captain Ball, commandant at Malta, under date the 19th April:—"My good fortune, my dear Ball, seems flown away, I cannot get a fair wind, or even a side wind—dead foul! dead foul!—but my mind is fully made up what to do when I leave the Straits, supposing there is no certain information of the enemy's destination. I believe this ill-luck will go near to kill me, but, as these are times for exertion, I must not be cast down, whatever I may feel."

To Lord Melville, at the Admiralty, he writes :—" I am not made to despair ; what man can do shall be done. I have marked out for myself a decided line of conduct, and I shall follow it well up, although I have now before me a request from the physician of the fleet, enforcing my return to England before the hot months. Therefore, notwithstanding, I shall pursue the enemy to the East or West Indies, if I know that to be their destination, yet, if the Mediterranean fleet joins the Channel, I shall request, with that order, permission to go on shore."

† The following were the ships of Lord Nelsons fleet:—*Victory, Canopus, Superb, Spencer, Swiftsure, Belleisle, Conqueror, Tigre* and *Leviathan*, and the frigates *Amazon, Amphion*, and *Decade*.

information of the presence of the combined fleet in the West Indies, and on the following day his lordship anchored in Carlisle Bay, where he found Cochrane with only two of his seventy-fours, the *Northumberland* and *Spartiate*, his remaining four ships being at Jamaica with Admiral Dacres. Nelson went in search of the enemy towards Tobago and Trinidad, and arrived off Grenada on the 9th June, and at Antigua four days later. Leaving the *Northumberland*, Admiral Cochrane's flagship, on the station, his lordship, still without certain information regarding the movements of the French fleet, stood to the northward on his return to Europe, and on the 19th July, anchored in the Bay of Gibraltar.*

Meantime, from some unexplained cause, Villeneuve remained in Fort Royal Harbour, in Martinique, until the latter part of May, when he undertook the reduction of the Diamond Rock,† about six miles off the entrance to the harbour, which was garrisoned by a party of 107 officers and men, under Commander Maurice, who commissioned the post as the British sloop-of-war *Diamond Rock*. The French ships detached to reduce the rock consisted of two seventy-fours, a 36-gun frigate, a brig of 16 guns, and eleven gun-boats, with between 300 and 400 troops. Commander Maurice abandoned the lower works, mounted with three guns, and concentrated his efforts of defence on the batteries midway up the rock and on its summit, mounting respectively one 24-pounder and two 18-pounders. The enemy bombarded the rock between the 31st May and 2nd June, when, having expended his powder, Commander Maurice capitulated. The British loss in this singular conflict was only two killed and one wounded, and the French owned to having had about fifty casualties, though Captain Maurice was of opinion that, exclusive of the loss in the ships and gunboats, three of which were lost, the detachment landed on the rock had thirty killed and forty wounded.

* Nelson notes in his diary that, "Our whole run from Cape St. Vincent to Barbados was 3,227 miles; so that our run back was only 232 miles more than our run out, allowance being made for the difference of the latitudes and longitudes of Barbados and Barbuda; average per day 34 leagues wanting nine miles."

† The Diamond Rock was occupied in January, 1804, by Commodore Samuel Hood, commanding the *Centaur*, 74, and with incredible difficulty, five of the *Centaur's* guns, three long 24, and two 18-pounders, were mounted in different parts of this stupenduous rock. The mode of getting them from the ship to an eminence so much higher than her mast-heads was characteristic and ingenious; a cable was made fast by one end to the ship and the other end to the rock, along which passed a traveller, or running loop; to this was suspended the cannon, or whatever else it was desirable to remove, and which by means of suitable tackles, was dragged up the acclivity of the cable to the summit of the rock. "Were you to see," says a writer in the *Naval Chronicle*, who was on the spot, "how along a dire, and I had almost said, a perpendicular acclivity, the men are hanging in clusters, hauling up a four-and-twenty pounder by hawsers, you would wonder; they appear like mice hauling a little sausage; scarcely can we hear the governor on the top of the rock, directing them with his trumpet, the *Centaur* lying close under it, like a cocoa-shell, to which the hawsers are affixed."

Villeneuve, who was reinforced by two new 74-gun ships, bringing up his fleet to a strength of twenty sail-of-the-line, besides seven frigates, and two brigs, sailed on the 4th June, and doubled Antigua, where he heard from an American schooner, that, on the previous day, a homeward-bound convoy had sailed from that island. Before night, these ships, numbering fifteen sail, were overhauled and captured, the merchandise being of the value of £200,000. Now, for the first time, the French admiral learnt of the presence of Nelson in the West Indies, and resolved to return to Europe. Precipitately sending back the troops he had embarked from Martinique and Guadaloupe, in four of his frigates, he ordered the commanders to join him at the Azores. Having executed their mission the French frigates were returning to the fleet when they fell in with this captured convoy, under the escort of a frigate, but being misled by the *ruse* practised by the British 18-gun sloop, which, making sail to escape, fired guns as though a fleet was ahead, the French Commodore set fire to all the merchantmen to prevent their being recaptured. This done they set sail for the rendezvous and rejoined Villeneuve on the 30th June.

Continuing his course for France, on the 3rd July, Villeneuve overtook a British privateer, having as prize a Spanish galleon with treasure on board of the value of nearly £600,000, which was recaptured, and the privateer burnt off Cape Finisterre, where the combined fleet arrived on the 9th July. Baffling winds were met, which continued until the 22nd, when they encountered an unexpected foe in Vice-Admiral Calder's squadron of eight sail.

Villeneuve had executed Napoleon's instructions, which were to mislead Nelson, and draw him away from Europe, thus leaving the coast clear for his ambitious project for the invasion of England, in which Villeneuve was to take part. But his great scheme was frustrated, when, apparently on the point of its realization, by a combination of adverse circumstances.

On arriving at Gibraltar on the 19th July, Lord Nelson went on shore on the following day, "for the first time," as he says, "since the 16th June, 1803, and from having my foot out of the *Victory*, two years, wanting sixteen days." Two days later the fleet stood across to Tetuan to water, thence proceeding to Ceuta, and on the 25th, Lord Nelson received intelligence from England that the brig *Curieux*, which he had sent home with despatches, had fallen in with Villeneuve's fleet, on the 19th June. Passing the Straits his lordship arrived off Cape St. Vincent, where he gleaned some information from the log-book of an American merchantman, which induced him to stand to the northward in pursuit of his enemy; but he saw nothing of Villeneuve, and on the 15th August, joined the Channel squadron, under Admiral Cornwallis, when he heard of the action off Cape Finisterre, between the former and Sir Robert Calder, who had effected a junction with him on the previous day with eight sail-of-the-line. The same evening Nelson continued on his course for Portsmouth, with the *Victory* and *Superb*, leaving the remainder of his ships, except the *Belleisle*, which steered for Plymouth, with Cornwallis, who had now under his command thirty-four battle ships. Three days later his lordship anchored at Spithead, and striking his flag, proceeded to his estate at Merton, for a short period of much-needed rest.

Some boat and frigate actions worthy of notice took place during the year 1804. One of the best conducted and most successful of these was the cutting out of the *Curieux*, brig of 16 guns and 70 men (other accounts place the number at 100), by four boats of the *Centaur*, 74, under the orders of Lieutenant Reynolds. The *Curieux* was lying at anchor and ready for sea, under a fort close to the entrance of the careening station in Fort Royal Harbour, Martinique, when about forty-five minutes after midnight, the *Centaur's* boats, having pulled a distance of no less than twenty miles, suddenly appeared to the astonished gaze of the watch on deck. The barge, under Lieutenant Reynolds' personal command, made for the stern where hung a rope ladder, to which two boats were fastened. As the officer mounted the ladder, followed by his men, he cut one of the lines fastening the boarding nettings, and was soon joined by his other boats' crews.

A short, but desperate, hand to hand struggle ensued, but the enemy were driven below or to the forecastle, and the seamen, cutting her cable, and loosing the sails, soon got the *Curieux* under weigh, and succeeded, under a heavy fire from three batteries, in bringing her alongside the *Centaur*. In affecting this gallant exploit the British loss was only nine wounded, including Lieutenants Reynolds and Bettesworth, and Midshipman Tracy; sad to say the first named officer, who received five serious wounds, succumbed to his injuries, and one of the wounded seamen also died. The *Curieux* had an officer and nine men killed, and thirty wounded, including her captain and all his officers except one, many of whom died. The prize was added to the British Navy, under her own name, and carried Lord Nelson's despatches on his return from the West Indies, as already stated.

Two days after this affair, the schooner *Eclair*, Lieutenant Carr, of 12 guns and

60 men, engaged and beat off a French privateer from Guadaloupe, carrying 22 guns and 220 men, including 80 soldiers, after a spirited action lasting three-quarters of an hour. A few weeks later, a cutter of the *Eclair*, under the orders of Mr. Salmon, master, with 10 men and the surgeon (serving as a volunteer), boarded and cut out in the most gallant manner, from the harbour of Guadaloupe, the French privateer schooner *Rose*, of one gun and 49 men, of whom five were killed and ten wounded, including the commander.

Lieutenant King, of the *Centaur*, temporarily commanding the 14-gun brig *Drake*, performed good service in the West Indies. He cut out a schooner from Martinique, and landed and spiked the guns of a fort, and recaptured from a privateer a large ship, mounting 18 guns, but in taking possession she blew up, when two officers and four men were killed and many others were wounded. The barge and pinnace of the *Blenheim*, 74, under the orders of Lieutenant Furber, gallantly cut out the French schooner *Curieuse*, but she was moored by a chain, and in endeavouring unsuccessfully, to bring her off, three men were killed, three missing, and 19, including 5 officers, were wounded. Lieutenant Forrest, of the armed sloop, *Fort Diamond*, was more successful in breaking the chain by which a privateer of 10 guns and 60 men, was moored off Martinique, and brought her off.

The privateer, *Egyptienne*, of 36 guns and 248 men, formerly a frigate in the French Navy, was captured in the West Indies, after a running fight of three hours and twenty minutes, by Commander Shipley, of the 14-gun sloop-of-war *Hippomanes*— a Dutch corvette captured at Demerara in the preceding year, when that colony was occupied by the English. The *Egyptienne*, two days before, had been engaged by the 18-gun brig *Osprey*, Commander Younghusband, and after a close action, lasting one hour and twenty minutes, sheered off and made her escape. The *Osprey* was much cut-up aloft, and had 17 casualties, while her opponent, twice her tonnage, and with double her crew and guns, lost 8 killed and 19 wounded.

Not long after, the *Hippomanes*, now commanded by Commander Kenneth Mackenzie, encountered off the island of Antigua, the French privateer, *Buonaparte*, of 18 guns and 146 men, which, mistaking her from her build, for a trader, bore down towards her. An action ensued, fought with great spirit on both sides, and soon the two ships fell on board of each other. Commander Mackenzie lashed her bowsprit to his ship's mainmast, and boarded, but only about 17 officers and men followed him, and the Frenchmen rallied, and in a few minutes five of the party were killed and eight wounded, including the captain, in 14 places. He, however, succeeded in regaining his ship with eight others, the remainder being taken prisoners, and thus the action ended.

The *Wolverine*, Commander Henry Gordon, of 13 guns and 76 men, was not equally successful in defending herself against the privateer *Blonde*, having a complement of 240 hands, but her officers and crew fought their little ship to the last extremity, as she foundered directly after hauling down her colours, having lost in the action of thirty minutes' duration, an officer and four men killed, and 10 wounded. About five months later the *Blonde* fell in with the 38-gun frigate *Loire*, Captain Frederick Maitland, and after a chase of twenty hours' duration, and a running fight of fifteen minutes, she struck her colours.

The Navy, during the year, sustained a loss in the shipwreck of the 36-gun frigate *Apollo*, Captain Dixon, when 61 officers and men, including the commander, were drowned. The *Apollo*, in company with the *Carysfort*, 28, Commander Fanshawe, was convoying 69 sail from Cork to the West Indies, of which 40, besides the frigate, went ashore on the coast of Portugal, near Cape Mondego, and were lost.

One of the most brilliant exploits of the war was the cutting out, in Texel Roads, of the Dutch brig *Atalante*, of 16 guns and 76 men. Five boats, containing 60 officers and men, from the 18-gun brig *Scorpion*, Commander Hardinge, and 14-gun brig *Beaver*, Commander Pelly, proceeded, under the personal command of those officers, to effect the service, which they executed, after a severe hand-to-hand struggle. A strong gale coming on, it was two days before the victors could sail with their prize, but so difficult was the navigation that a further three days elapsed before they succeeded in their object.

For their meritorious conduct, Commanders Hardinge and Pelly were promoted to post rank, and Lieutenant Bluett, who was wounded, also received a step in rank. The Dutch captain, as brave a sailor as ever trod a deck, was killed, sword in hand, after refusing quarter, offered to him by Commander Hardinge, who had killed an officer in personal combat, but was disarmed by the captain, and on the point of being slain, when he was rescued by the master of the *Scorpion*. The last honours were paid to the hero by his chivalrous opponent, who, during the ceremony, hoisted the Dutch colours and fired three volleys as the body descended into the deep. Such an incident tends to assuage the horrors of war and it is gratifying to place it on record.

In the East Indies the *Wilhelmina*, Commander Lambert, an old Dutch prize, of 21 guns and 134 men, engaged a ship of greatly superior force, and beat her off, after a hard-fought action that reflected credit on her officers and men. The French privateer *Psyche*, mounting 36 guns, and having a crew of 250 men, mistook the *Wilhelmina* for an Indiaman and stood towards her, and on the morning of the 11th April, the ships engaged at short range. At first they tried broadsides at each other, tacking and wearing as they did so, but soon they engaged with their yard-arms nearly locked, until the French privateer, finding that she had made a mistake in the quality of her opponent, ceased firing and crowded all sail to escape.

The *Wilhelmina* was so much damaged aloft—her main-topmast being over the side and most of her spars wounded, and her rigging and sails cut to pieces—that she was unable to give chase, and her casualties were confined to 10 men wounded. On the other hand, the *Psyche*, according to the captain of an Indiaman on board her, had seven feet of water in her hold at the conclusion of the action, and lost her second captain and 10 men killed, and her commander (dangerously) and 32 men wounded, 13 of them mortally. Considering the disparity of force, the result was, therefore, highly creditable to the officers and ship's company of the *Wilhelmina*, and Commander Lambert had clearly earned the promotion he received.

It was not without a desperate fight that ten boats from the frigates *Seahorse*, *Narcissus*, and *Maidstone*, brought out from the Bay of Hyères a settee, one of twelve, lying under the protection of the batteries. The boats were under the command of Lieutenant Thompson, first of the *Narcissus*, and the attack, which was made about midnight on the 11th July, was executed in the face of a heavy fire of grape and musketry, by which a midshipman and three men were killed, and five officers and 18 seamen and marines were wounded.

Even more sanguinary and with less good fortune was the fight maintained for two hours and ten minutes, by the *Lily*, sloop-of-war, of only 200 tons, carrying 16 guns and a crew of 80 men and boys, with the French ship-rigged privateer, *Dame Ambert*, formerly the British packet, *Marlborough*, armed with 16 guns, and having a complement of 140 men. The action took place off Cape Roman, on the American coast, and the privateer, having cut up her antagonist aloft by the superior range of her guns, lashed the *Lily's* bowsprit to her taffrail. Eight times did the crew of the *Dame Ambert* attempt to board the sloop, only to be repulsed, but on the ninth occasion they made good their footing and carried the British ship, which had slain, in the desperate conflict, her captain, first lieutenant, and the greater portion of her crew, 15 or 16, including the remainder of the officers, being among the wounded. The privateer had five men killed and eleven wounded, and if we are to trust the British account of the relative numbers of the crews of the combatants (though the French place that of the *Dame Ambert* at only 75 men), the officers and ship's company of the *Lily* displayed heroism of no common order, and deserve as much honour as if they had scored a victory.

Great as the carnage in this encounter was, it was excelled by that which took place within a month, when a gallant, but—under the circumstances—rash attempt was made to cut the *Lily* out by the boats of the 32-gun frigate *Galatea*. The prize, now preparing for sea as the privateer, *General Ernouf*, was lying at the Saintes, off Guadeloupe, when Captain Heathcote resolved to make an attempt to bring her out. The *Galatea* was discovered, and 30 soldiers were added to the privateer's crew, and an armed schooner was moored athwart her hawse to give an enfilading fire, and every preparation made to repulse an attack.

Nevertheless, four boats from the frigate, having in them about 90 officers and men, under the orders of Lieutenant Hardyman, first of the *Galatea*, pulled towards the harbour under cover of the night on the 13th August. They were discovered, but the gallant Hardyman, nothing daunted, eager to be the first to board, pulled ahead in the barge, and at a few minutes past one in the morning, clambering up the side of the ship, gave an example of heroism to his men which they were emulous to follow. A terrible struggle ensued. Lieutenant Hardyman fell mortally wounded, and out of 27 officers and men in the barge, only three escaped scatheless. The other boats, which backed up the barge, suffered to an almost equal extent, and after for nearly an hour making most gallant, but unavailing, efforts to carry the privateer, the remainder of the brave fellows returned to their ship under the fire of the batteries. Of the whole number engaged, 65 were killed and wounded, among the former, besides the commanding officer, being the master of the *Galatea* and a midshipman.

More successful were three boats of the 32-gun frigate *Tartar*, which, under the orders of Lieutenant Mullah, boarded and carried, after a spirited resistance, the French privateer schooner *Hirondelle*, of 10 guns and 50 men, lying at anchor on the coast of St. Domingo. The British loss was slight, but the privateer had nine killed, three drowned, and six wounded.

An attempt, having an unsuccessful result, was made on the Dutch Colony of Curaçoa. This island had surrendered without resistance to the frigate *Nereide*, Captain Watkins, in September, 1800, but having been returned to Holland at the peace, Sir Thomas Duckworth determined to effect its recapture. With this object, in January, 1804, he sent the seventy-fours, *Theseus*, Captain Bligh, and *Hercule*, Captain Dunn, the 36-gun frigates, *Blanche*, Captain Mudge, and *Pique*, Captain Ross, and the 10-gun schooner, *Gipsy*, acting-lieutenant Michael Fitton, the same officer who had done such good service in these seas and had been present at the capitulation of the island. While the frigates blockaded the Port of St. Ann, Captain Bligh, on the last day of January, landed a force of 605 men, of whom 200 were marines, under the orders of Captain Dunn, and after some skirmishing, batteries were erected, commanding the town and fortifications, which mounted no less than 100 guns. These were armed with four 18-pounders and three small field-pieces, and opened fire, but no progress was made. Disease also broke out, necessitating the re-embarkation of 63 men, and 30 of the *Hercule's* marines, who were Polish prisoners taken at St. Domingo, evinced a disposition to desert. At length, on the 25th February, Captain Bligh gave up the attempt, and the force was re-embarked, having sustained a loss during the operations of one midshipman, and 17 seamen and marines killed, and three marine officers and 39 men wounded. During this arduous service the officers who displayed special gallantry were Lieutenant Nesbit Willoughby, who commanded the battery, and appeared to lead a charmed life, Lieutenant Nicolls, commanding the marines, and Mr. Fitton, who received his commission as Lieutenant.

More successful was the attempt on Surinam, which had fallen to British arms in 1799, but was returned to the Dutch at the peace. In this instance a body of 2,000 troops, under Sir Charles Green, co-operated with the Navy, under Commodore Samuel Hood, who had under his command the *Centaur*, 74, the frigates, *Pandour*, *Serapis*, and *Alligator*, sloop-of-war *Hippomanes*, and the *Drake*, brig. The frigates, pushing over the bar, engaged the batteries, and the troops were landed, and captured a fort, whereupon the Commandant surrendered the Colony, together with a 32-gun frigate, a corvette of 18 guns, a 10-gun schooner, and seven gunboats. In achieving this important success, the British loss was only eight killed and 21 wounded.

During the year 1804, the former French settlement of Goree, garrisoned by only 54 soldiers, was captured on the 17th January by an expedition from France, having on board 565 men, but it was retaken on the 8th March, by the *Inconstant*, 36, Captain Dickson, and a detachment of troops.

Great as was the admiration excited among all classes of their countrymen, by the daring and intrepidity displayed by our seamen in the numberless encounters with the enemy, the public interest was earnestly fixed on the tremendous drama unfolding under their eyes, as the vast French and Spanish armaments, prepared with such ostentatious display, for the long-threatened invasion of these shores, were concentrated in the Channel ports and at Brest and Ferrol. It was recognised that the time had come when a decisive blow must be struck against the Naval Coalition, if England was to be relieved from the burden of anxiety that weighed upon her like a nightmare, and all eyes from William Pitt, the Prime Minister, downwards, instinctively turned to the seaman, who, by his services, character, and unrivalled genius for war, commanded the confidence alike of landsmen, and of all ranks in his own profession, as the hope of England, and the terror of our enemies. Lord Nelson was at this time enjoying a brief and unwonted interval of rest at Merton, but now, as throughout his career, he responded with alacrity to the call of duty, and in his last and greatest fight, rendered up his life for his beloved country, a bright example to her sons for all time.

CHAPTER XIII.

Capture of four Spanish Frigates, and Declaration of War by Spain—Movements of Admirals Cornwallis and Ganteaume—Sir Robert Calder's Action off Cape Finisterre—Admiral Cornwallis' Partial Action off Brest—Nelson proceeds to sea to encounter the combined French and Spanish Fleets.

TOWARDS the close of the year 1804 England found herself involved in war with Spain, which arose out of a misunderstanding. Rear-Admiral the Hon. Alexander Cochrane, commanding off Ferrol, sent home a report, which was afterwards disproved, that an armament was fitting out at that port, where, he declared, a Spanish and French military force was assembling for embarkation. Acting on this information, the Admiralty dispatched a squadron off Cadiz to intercept four frigates bound thither with specie from Monte Video. On the 5th October, the British squadron—consisting of the 44-gun frigate *Indefatigable*, Captain Graham Moore, the *Lively*, 38, Captain Graham Hammond, and the 32-gun frigates *Medusa*, Captain Gore, and *Amphion*, Captain Sutton—sighted the four Spanish frigates, *Medea*, 40, and *Fama*, *Clara*, and *Mercedes*, each of 34 guns, off Cape Santa Maria, and Captain Moore sent an officer to the Spanish Admiral with an intimation that he proposed to execute his orders to detain the squadron. Meanwhile the British ships took up their positions alongside the enemy, and when the Lieutenant returned with an unsatisfactory reply, the *Indefatigable* fired a shot across the bows of the *Medea*, and an action ensued. The result did not long remain doubtful. Within nine minutes the *Mercedes* blew up alongside the *Amphion*, when out of 280 men and passengers, only one officer and 40 men were rescued. Ten minutes later the *Medea* struck her colours, having lost two killed and 10 wounded out of a complement of 300 men. Within five minutes the *Clara* surrendered to the *Lively*, of her crew of 300 losing seven killed and 20 wounded, and the *Fama*, which had struck to the *Medusa*, but attempted to escape, was overhauled by the *Lively*, and compelled to strike, her loss, out of a complement similar to the *Mercedes*, being 11 killed and 50 wounded.

The cargoes of the three captured frigates were of the value of nearly one million sterling, but the circumstances of the capture were regrettable, if they did not form a flagrant breach of the comity of nations, for at this time the two countries were at peace. Naturally the utmost indignation prevailed in Spain, and on the 12th December, war was formally declared by the King, who engaged to supply Napoleon with between twenty-five to twenty-nine sail-of-the-line, and placed at his disposal a fleet of seventy ships for his favourite invasion scheme. To meet these preparations one hundred and five line-of-battle-ships were borne on the British Navy List, but of these only eighty-three were fit for sea.

Admiral Cornwallis, who had been blockading Brest for twenty months, still lay off Ushant with eleven sail-of-the-line, while the French fleet, ready for sea, which he was watching, numbered no less than twenty-one ships. By the 3rd February, the blockading fleet was increased to sixteen sail, but it again fell to its original number by the departure of Vice-Admiral Calder for Ferrol with five ships-of-the-line. Towards the end of March, 1805, Admiral Cornwallis, whose health had suffered by his exertions, temporarily resigned the command of the Channel Fleet to Lord Gardner, who, by the first week in April, had under his orders twenty-one sail-of-the-line. Admiral Ganteaume sailed from Brest on the 14th April with forty ships, of which twenty-one were of the line, and the British Admiral did his utmost to bring the enemy to action, but the latter returned on the following day to port. Villeneuve had left Toulon, Napoleon having planned that the two fleets should effect a junction in the West Indies, and after ravaging the British colonies, and decoying Nelson thither, should steer for the Channel, where his fleet would be augmented to sixty sail by the Rochefort squadron. When Ganteaume was unable to sail for the West Indies, owing to the watchfulness of the British Commanders, Napoleon directed Villeneuve to hasten back to Ferrol, and joining the ships there, proceed to Brest, and thence sail for Boulogne, when four or five days' command of the Channel would enable the grand invasion *coup* to be effected.

Admiral Cornwallis resumed command of the Channel Fleet, now consisting of eighteen sail, on the 6th July, and two days later he received intelligence of the departure of the French and Spanish fleets from the West Indies, and orders from the Admiralty to detach Rear-Admiral Stirling with five sail to join Vice-Admiral Sir Robert Calder, who, on the 16th February, had proceeded to assume command of the squadron blockading Ferrol—where lay ready for sea ten French and Spanish ships-of-the-line—in place of Admiral Hon. Alexander Cochrane, who sailed with five ships and a frigate for the West Indies, in pursuit of the Rochefort squadron. Thus reinforced, Admiral Calder, an officer of some distinction, who had served as Sir John Jervis's flag captain at St. Vincent, fought an action which, though indecisive, had important results. By the arrival of Admiral Stirling his fleet was raised to the following fifteen ships-of-the-line:—

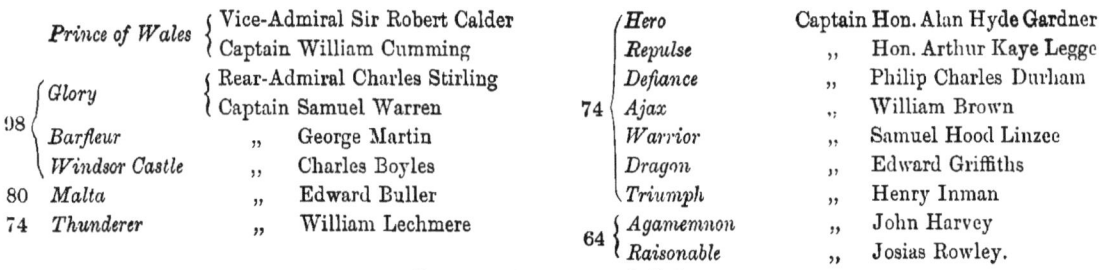

Admiral Calder's instructions were to intercept Villeneuve's French and Spanish fleet, reported to be on its way to Europe. On the 22nd July the hostile ships made their appearance, Cape Finisterre being then 39 leagues distant, and Ferrol 49. The British line of battle was formed, and at 3.20 in the afternoon, the Admiral made the signal to engage the enemy, whose strength, twenty sail-of-the-line and seven frigates, could with difficulty be ascertained in the foggy weather then prevailing. The action was commenced, about 5.15, by the *Argonauta* firing at the *Hero*, the British van ship, and the *Espana* at the *Sirius*, which had made an attempt to capture a Spanish galleon in tow of the *Sirène* frigate. Soon the cannonade became general, and, by 6, the British ships, except the *Dragon*, which was coming up astern under a press of sail, were engaged, but owing to the fog and smoke the line became disordered, and some of the ships had more than one opponent. The *Windsor Castle*, which lost her fore-topmast, was the principal sufferer, and was taken in tow by the *Dragon*, and the *Ajax*, *Prince of Wales*, *Thunderer* and *Malta*, were also a good deal damaged; while of the enemy's ships, the *San Rafaël*, *Firme*, and *Espana*, having dropped to leeward, suffered greatly from the British fire.

Soon after 8 the *Firme*, which was most severely handled and had lost her masts, hauled down her colours, and not many minutes afterwards, the *San Rafaël*, also dismasted, followed her example. The *Espana* was rescued from a like fate by the assistance gallantly afforded her by the *Pluton*, *Mont Blanc*, and *Atlas*, which latter was only saved from capture by the *Neptune* and other ships.

Sir Robert Calder threw out the signal to discontinue the action at 8.25, but owing to the fog and darkness it was not until an hour later that the firing ceased, and the British ships lay to for the night, which was passed in repairing damages and preparing to renew the battle on the morrow. The British loss was only 39 officers and men killed and 159 wounded. The *Windsor Castle* and *Agamemnon* alone lost a topmast and the *Ajax* a yard. The casualties in the allied fleet were 476, but with the exception of the two prizes, the ships had not suffered much aloft.

At daybreak on the 23rd July, the fleets were about seventeen miles apart, but the wind was light, and at noon the allied fleet bore up towards the British squadron, which awaited the attack, but at 4, when about nine miles distant, they hauled to the wind, thus declining to renew the action. Admiral Calder resumed his course, and on the following morning, the 24th July, had gained a position ahead and to windward of the enemy, when it lay in his power to force an engagement, which, however, he declined to do, so that both commanders were equally to blame for not bringing matters to a final issue. By the evening the rival fleets were out of sight of each other, and Sir Robert Calder continued his course for a British port with his two prizes in tow of the frigates, actuated by the orders of the Admiralty to be on his guard against a junction of Villeneuve's fleet, with the combined squadron of ten sail blockaded in Ferrol, and with the squadron of five ships escaped from Rochefort.

Nevertheless, much discontent was aroused in England at a caution, which though perhaps judicious, would not have characterised the actions of Lord Nelson, and Sir Robert Calder demanded a court martial to enquire into his conduct. This was held at Portsmouth in December, on board his flagship, the *Prince of Wales*, and the admiral was "severely reprimanded" for not having done his utmost to renew the action on the 23rd and 24th July, though he was acquitted of cowardice. When we remember the verdict of naval courts on Admiral Herbert (Lord Torrington) for his indecisive action at Beachy Head, with a superior fleet, and on Admiral Keppel for his battle under similar conditions, for which they were acquitted, we must consider that hard measure was meted out to Admiral Calder, who captured two ships from a superior fleet, with a second hostile squadron close at hand, and having regard to the warnings of the Commander-in-chief of the Channel and Mediterranean fleets, as well as of the Admiralty. Doubtless this harsh view of his conduct was arrived at under the national feelings excited by the glories and decisive victory of Lord Nelson at Trafalgar, in the preceding October, over a superior combined fleet under the same admiral.

The two prizes proceeded to Plymouth, where they anchored on the 31st July, and Sir Robert Calder returned with fourteen sail-of-the-line to the rendezvous off Cape Finisterre, where he expected to meet Lord Nelson's squadron, and then steered for Ferrol, the blockade of which he resumed. A reconnoissance of that port and Corunna, by the *Dragon*, revealed the fact that Villeneuve's fleet in the latter place, and the ships in Ferrol, numbered together twenty-nine sail-of-the-line, and the Vice-Admiral—as his squadron had been reduced to nine ships, by the return of the *Malta* to England to refit, and of Rear-Admiral Stirling's four sail to resume the blockade of the now empty port of Rochefort—abandoned the blockade of Ferrol, and on the 24th August rejoined the Channel fleet off Ushant.

Meanwhile, Admiral Villeneuve had sailed three days before with the combined French and Spanish fleet of twenty-nine ships, besides frigates, intending to join Admiral Allemand at Rochefort, but receiving information, which proved incorrect, that twenty-five British sail-of-the-line were at hand, Villeneuve altered his determination and steered for Cadiz, where he cast anchor on the 20th August, after chasing away Vice-Admiral Collingwood's squadron of four ships, which, however, on the following day, resumed their station off the port, where now lay, including the six Spanish ships already there, thirty-five French and Spanish sail-of-the-line. The Emperor Napoleon heard with the greatest indignation of Villeneuve's arrival at Cadiz, instead of at Brest, where he expected him to effect a junction with Admiral Ganteaume, with the object of carrying out the long projected descent on England, and despatched Vice-Admiral Rosily to supersede the unfortunate commander who had excited his wrath.

Admiral Ganteaume, expecting the arrival of Villeneuve off Brest, sailed out of port on the 31st August, with his whole fleet of twenty-one ships-of-the-line, five frigates and three smaller vessels, and anchored between Camarat and Bertheaume Bays. Admiral Cornwallis received the same day the intelligence of the departure of the enemy, whom he reconnoitred in his flagship, the *Ville de Paris*, and, early on the following day, steered in to attack the French fleet at their anchorage. Admiral Ganteaume got under weigh at 8 A.M., and an hour and half later, the *Alexandre*, 80, leading the enemy's line, fired a broadside, but without effect, at the 44-gun frigate *Indefatigable*, Captain Ross. A desultory engagement now ensued, in which the

Ville de Paris, *Cæsar* and *Montagu*, were engaged at long range with the three rearmost French ships, and some shore batteries. Shortly before noon the British fleet stood out in order of battle, the enemy being evidently unwilling to engage. During the firing a shell from the batteries burst on board the flagship, and a fragment struck Admiral Cornwallis, but being spent only caused a contusion. The three ships engaged suffered in their rigging and sails, but not to any great extent.

Admiral Ganteaume, doubtless acting under orders, made no effort to get out to sea, and it was not until the 13th December that, taking advantage of a brisk gale of wind, and the absence of the blockading fleet, which had returned to port to refit and revictual, eleven sail-of-the-line, four frigates, and a corvette, succeeded in escaping to sea.

Admiral Collingwood was strengthened, on the 22nd August, by four sail-of-the-line, and a week later, Sir Robert Calder joined him with eighteen ships. Collingwood continued to cruise off Cadiz until the 28th September, when Vice-Admiral Lord Nelson arrived and assumed command of the fleet.

Nelson had not been long permitted to enjoy his well-earned rest on his small estate at Merton, before he was called upon to resume his command and crown his unique career by the greatest victory even he had achieved, and yield up his life in the service of his country. Captain Hon. Henry Blackwood, of the *Euryalus* frigate, who had been despatched by Collingwood with the news of the arrival of Villeneuve at Cadiz, reached Portsmouth on the evening of the 1st September, and posting up to the Admiralty, stopped on his way at Merton. It was four o'clock in the morning, but the admiral was already up and dressed. On seeing his friend he exclaimed, "I am sure you bring me news of the French and Spanish fleets. I shall yet have to beat them." His lordship followed the captain of the *Euryalus* to town, and proposed to the Government to return at once to Cadiz. Both Mr. Pitt and Lord Barham, the First Lord of the Admiralty, eagerly closed with his proposal, the Prime Minister asking him to state what amount of force he required to ensure victory; while the latter, handing him the Navy List, desired him to choose his own ships and his own officers. In reply to Pitt, Nelson explained that his object was not limited to defeating the enemy, but, like the Roman orator of old, when reiterating that *Carthago delenda est*, he desired to annihilate the naval power of France and Spain. To Lord Barham, the great admiral, who knew and did justice to his brother seamen, replied, "Choose yourself, my lord; the same spirit animates the whole profession; you cannot go wrong."

On the night of the 13th September, after little more than three weeks' rest on shore, Nelson quitted his house, and travelling all night, reached Portsmouth the next morning. Though eager to undertake the duty, for his only thought was of his country's weal, Nelson embarked with a presentiment that he was going to his death. A month before he had told his brother that had he, instead of Calder, met the French, they might have been parted for ever, since he knew that the enemy "had meant to make a dead set at the *Victory*," and in his diary, meant for no eye but his own, he expresses his humble and entire "submission, should it be God's good providence to cut short my days upon earth." The scene that took place at Portsmouth, when, at noon on the 14th September, Nelson embarked on board the *Victory*, was a most moving one. The townspeople collected in the streets through which he was expected to pass, and old seamen, relics of victories achieved under Hawke and Rodney, reverently stood hat in hand as they recognised, in the shattered form of the hero of the Nile and Copenhagen, a greater warrior than any under whom they had served. Women pressed close to him, that they might gaze their full on one whose proverbial gentleness had won their hearts, as much as the victories, which had more impressed the sterner sex. All classes broke into a cheer as they recognised the slight figure, rendered familiar by the engraver's art, of the man who had already secured the safety of their country, and whose name appeared in their eyes synonymous with victory. Many of the spectators were even moved to tears, and some invoked on his head the protection of Heaven. It was in vain that a guard of soldiers strove to keep the crowd from pressing too closely upon him, and Nelson himself could not restrain tears of gratitude, as he marked the personal affection with which he was regarded. Turning to his companion, Captain Hardy, he said, "I had their hurrahs before, I have their hearts now." The next morning, Sunday, the 15th September, at 8 o'clock, the *Victory*, accompanied by the *Euryalus*, sailed for Cadiz, and off Plymouth was joined by the *Ajax* and *Thunderer*. As he approached the fleet, Nelson sent ahead the frigate with instructions to Collingwood not to salute or hoist the colours, by which the enemy might be apprized of the arrival of a reinforcement; and he wrote also to the Governor of Gibraltar to prevent any notice being given in the *Gazette* of his arrival before Cadiz.

On the 28th September he joined Collingwood off Cadiz, and assumed command of the fleet, now consisting of twenty-seven sail-of-the-line. He was received by the officers and seamen of the fleet with enthusiasm, and every heart now burned for the hour of battle, confident it would be also the hour of victory. In order to keep the enemy in ignorance of his strength, so that they might be induced to put to sea, Nelson withdrew to a distance of sixteen or eighteen leagues west of Cadiz, keeping close in shore two frigates, the *Euryalus* and *Hydra*, to signal to four line-of-battle-ships, which, under Captain Duff, of the *Mars*, were distributed inside the line. On the 1st October the *Euryalus* reconnoitred the port of Cadiz, when a fleet of eighteen French and sixteen Spanish ships-of-the-line, with four frigates and two brigs, were made out at anchor in the outer harbour. A few days after his arrival Nelson detached Rear-Admiral Louis, with five sail, to Gibraltar for provisions and water, and his strength was still further diminished by the despatch to England of the *Prince of Wales*, bearing Sir Robert Calder's flag, as the Admiral's presence was required in England for his trial, and of the *Donegal* to Gibraltar. The fleet, however, was brought up to a strength of twenty-seven sail-of-the-line, by the arrival, between the 9th and 13th October, of the *Royal Sovereign*, into which Collingwood shifted his flag, *Belleisle*, *Africa*, and *Agamemnon*, under his old friend, Sir Edward Berry.

Nelson's great *desideratum* was frigates, of a deficiency in which he had frequently complained in the Mediterranean, but Captain Blackwood did much to supply the want by his activity, and he was joined by four from England. On the 10th October, Nelson issued to the admirals and captains of the fleet a plan of attack he had devised, which for its novelty and completeness has been universally regarded as a masterpiece. In this plan occurs the celebrated order that "In case signals cannot be seen or clearly understood, no captain can do very wrong if he places his ship alongside that of an enemy." The following were the ships that took part in the great battle impending:—

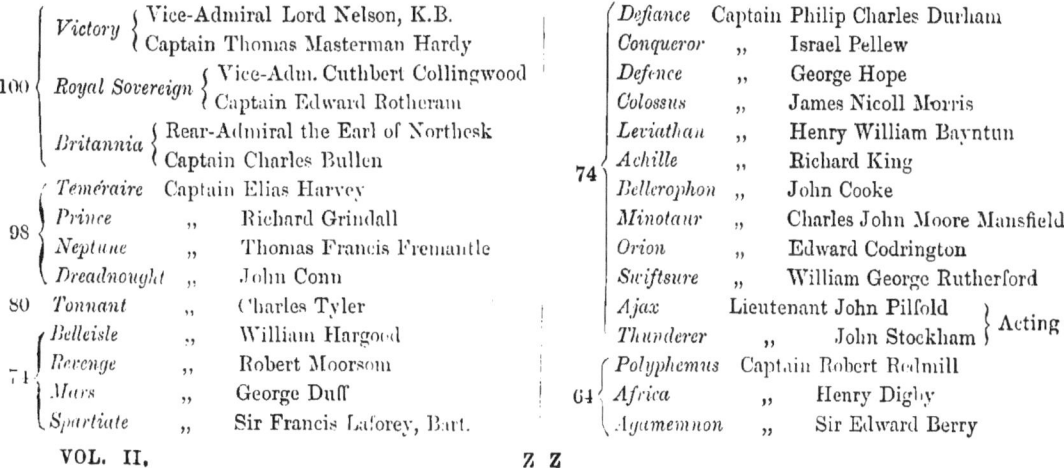

Frigates, *Euryalus*, Captain the Hon. Henry Blackwood, *Naïad*, Captain Thomas Dundas, *Phœbe*, Captain the Hon. Thomas Bladen Capel, and *Sirius*, Captain William Penose.

Schooner *Pickle*, Lieutenant Lapenotiere, and cutter *Entreprenante*, Lieutenant Purver.

On the very day on which Lord Nelson arrived to take command of the Mediterranean fleet, Villeneuve received peremptory orders from the French Emperor to put to sea, and passing the Straits, land the French troops on the Neapolitan coast, sweep the Mediterranean of all British commerce and cruisers, and enter the port of Toulon to refit and revictual.

At midnight of the 17th the wind shifted to the eastward, and on Saturday, the 19th October, the combined fleet weighed, having on board the French troops which had been re-embarked. Only twelve ships got out this day, and these lay becalmed until the afternoon, when a breeze sprang up, but at daylight of the 20th the remainder of the fleet, consisting of twenty-one ships-of-the-line, with five frigates and two brigs, got out to sea. The weather at first was thick, but about 2 P.M. it cleared up.

Villeneuve, stung by Napoleon's reproaches at his uniform want of success and enterprise, and determined to strike a blow before his supercession by Admiral Rosilly, had spent his time while at Cadiz in carefully reorganising his fleet, and that of his Spanish coadjutor, Admiral Gravina. So confident was he now of victory, that he wrote to Admiral Decres, the French Minister of Marine, that, "Napoleon should soon be satisfied, and that he might reckon on the most splendid success." *
The allied fleet consisted of the following ships:—

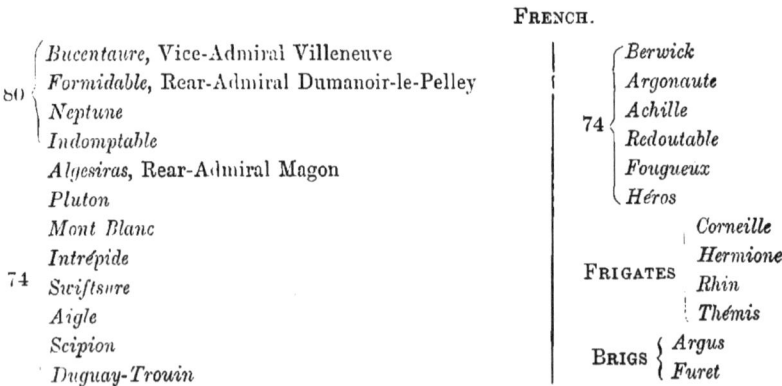

* In his orders to his officers Villeneuve says :—"There is nothing to alarm us in the sight of the English fleet; their 74-gun ships have not 500 men on board; the seamen are harassed by a two years cruise" (alluding to the state of Lord Nelson's ships in January, 1805) "they are not more brave than we are, they have infinitely fewer

SPANISH.

130	*Santissima-Trinidada*, Rear-Admiral Cisneros		
112	{ *Principe de Asturias*, Admiral Gravina		*San Augustin*
	Santa Anna, Vice-Admiral Alava		*San Ildefonso*
100	*Rayo*	74	*San Juan Nepomucino*
80	{ *Neptuno*		*Monarca*
	Argonauta		*San Francisco de Asis*
74	{ *Bahama*		*San Justo*
	Montanez	64	*San Leandro*

Villeneuve took the immediate command of the main division of the fleet, consisting of twenty-one sail-of-the-line, with Vice-Admiral Alava and Rear-Admiral Dumanoir under his orders, while the remainder, or reserve, was divided into two squadrons of six ships each, under Gravina and Rear-Admiral Magon. One of the French advanced frigates having made the signal for eighteen sail of British ships, the combined fleet cleared for action, and at 5 P.M. tacked and stood towards the Straits, but about eight wore and stood to the north-west. During the night every movement of the hostile fleet was reported to Nelson by Captain Blackwood, whose invaluable services were fully appreciated by his lordship. Thus in expectation and preparation passed the eve of the memorable battle of Trafalgar. At daybreak on the 21st October, the two fleets were in sight of each other, about twelve miles apart, and at 6, the combined fleet, then on the starboard tack, was seen from the decks of the British ships, the *Victory* being at this time distant from Cape Trafalgar about twenty-one miles. A little before 7, Lord Nelson made the signal to form the order of sailing in two columns and prepare for battle, and a few minutes later, in obedience to a signal, the two columns of the British fleet bore up to the eastward under all sail. The near approach of the British fleet rendering an action unavoidable, Villeneuve, at 8.30 A.M., ordered his fleet to wear and form a line in close order on the port tack; but, owing to the westerly wind and heavy ground swell, it was not until 10 that the manœuvre was accomplished, and even then the line was in the shape of a crescent, and instead of the ships being in line ahead, some were at a considerable distance to leeward, and others to windward of their proper stations. For the most part, says James, to whose admirable and exhaustive account of the battle we are indebted, the ships were two, and in some cases, three deep.

Some interesting details are given by Captain Blackwood of Nelson during the

motives to fight well, and possess less love of country. They are skilful at manœuvring. In a month we shall be as much as they are. In fine, everything unites to inspire us with hopes of the most glorious success, and of a new era for the imperial marine."

forenoon of this his last day upon earth. More than once the Admiral asked Blackwood what he should consider a great victory, and when his friend replied that fourteen or fifteen prizes would be a glorious result, he said, "I shall not, Blackwood, be satisfied with less than twenty." It is a pleasing trait of Nelson's character that no man was less vainglorious, or more ready to attribute his successes to a Divine Power, in dependence upon whose will he relied with a simple piety. After the battle of Trafalgar the following beautiful prayer, breathing the sublimest spirit of patriotism, which he had penned in the retirement of his cabin, was found among his papers. "May the great God whom I worship grant to my country, and for the benefit of Europe in general, a great and glorious victory, and may no misconduct in any one tarnish it, and may humanity after victory be the predominant feature in the British fleet. For myself, individually, I commit my life to Him who made me; and may His blessing light upon my endeavours for serving my country faithfully. To Him I resign myself and the just cause which is entrusted to me to defend. Amen—Amen—Amen!"

With these noble sentiments animating his breast, did the great Seaman enter upon the conflict, which was to be the last in which he was to participate.

END OF VOL. II.

www.ingramcontent.com/pod-product-compliance
Lightning Source LLC
Chambersburg PA
CBHW061934290426
44113CB00025B/2907